The
SOAP OPERA
Encyclopedia

The SOAP OPERA Encyclopedia

Newly updated and expanded edition

Christopher Schemering

Ballantine Books · New York

For Ann

Library of Congress Catalog Card Number: 85-90565

ISBN: 345-35344-7

Cover design by James R. Harris
Cover photo of Martha Byrne and Brian Bloom (Lily and Dusty on
As the World Turns): Mike Fuller/CBS.
Text Design by Holly Johnson
Manufactured in the United States of America

First Edition: November 1985
Revised Edition: January 1988
10 9 8 7 6 5 4 3 2 1

CONTENTS

NOTES AND ACKNOWLEDGMENTS

This book tells the story of the television soap opera—a history of the phenomenon for the student, a reference guide for the librarian, a fact-filled binge for the fan.

The A to Z program entries include background information on every daytime and prime-time television soap opera broadcast on the three major networks, as well as a selection of syndicated, cable, and foreign efforts. A biographical section features profiles of more than two dozen stars and writers who have contributed most to the soap opera explosion. Rounding out the book are a number of special appendixes which mix technical information and trivia.

The longer program entries—from *As the World Turns* to *Dallas*, from *Peyton Place* to *The Young and the Restless*—include premiere and cancellation dates, background information, a synopsis of the major storylines, a critical review, and cast lists of who played who and when, starting with the most recent performer who played the role and working backwards. (This way the reader can immediately identify the actor currently playing a specific part.) For current and long-running soaps, dates of performers' tenure are included wherever they could be verified by network records or other primary sources. Although characters are listed more or less in the order they first appeared in the drama, characters whose storylines crossed often and families of characters are linked so the reader's memories of stories may more easily be awakened.

There are shorter entries for little-known network serials, such as *These Are My Children*, the TV version of *Painted Dreams*, radio's first soap; or *Miss Susan*, a bizarre 1951 NBC effort that starred Susan Peters, an actress confined to a wheelchair. Although this book studies mostly traditional American soap opera—continuing dramas that focus on family conflict and romance—other TV serials of interest have been included: cable efforts, such as the religious *Another Life* and the sexy *A New Day in Eden*; imported serials, including *The Forsyte Saga* and *Upstairs, Downstairs*; syndicated efforts, such as *Mary Hartman, Mary Hartman*; and the soaps of the old DuMont network, including television's first true dramatic serial, *Faraway Hill*.

The biographical section profiles such performers as Mary Stuart, whose role on *Search for Tomorrow* is the longest running in the history of television; Joan Collins, who created one of soap opera's all-time favorite villainesses on prime time; and Anthony Geary, the first media star created exclusively by exposure on daytime soap opera. The biographies also include the most famous writers of dramatic serials, including Irna Phillips, who opened Pandora's soap box with her radio creations a half century ago. These profiles describe both the onscreen and offscreen personas of the stars and include birth dates as well as theater, film, and TV credits.

The appendixes include a complete listing of the nominees and winners of the Daytime Emmy Awards, a chronology of television serials, and listings of the most famous graduates of daytime drama (Warren Beatty, Jill Clayburgh). Throughout the program entries there are often references to the importance of television ratings to a show's survival. The appendix on the Nielsen ratings explains in detail what the ratings system is and what a rating point and a "share" of the audience represent. This appendix also ranks the most popular daytime dramas by season.

Sources for a definitive history of soap opera are in a shambles. Magazine articles, books, and network records contradict one another; few sources agree on dates, spellings, or even simple plot developments. The process of researching and writing this book over the past few years has been its own soap opera, a continuous drama of sorting out and checking information from trunks of memorabilia I've collected since the late '60s.

Since so many sources proved contradictory, primary sources of information were personal journals written while watching serial drama over the years; the network files of ABC, NBC, CBS; press releases; listings in *TV Guide* from 1953, checked against editions from various regions, and cross-checked against various newspapers across the country; trade periodicals; and interviews with serial performers and technical personnel. Such sources are not infallible, however, and verifying dates for performers' tenure was a recurring problem. Therefore, I would appreciate corrections, comments, and suggestions from readers for future editions of this book:

> Christopher Schemering
> ℅ Ballantine Books
> 201 East 50th Street
> New York, NY 10022

Assisting me in this sometimes Herculean task of preserving soap opera history were the staffs of the Broadcasting Division of the Library of Congress; the Television Information Office; Allen Rosenberg, Creative Director of Sterling Magazines; Joseph Lilley of the International Dark Shadows Society; and Jeanne Irwin, Ann Marie Irwin, Jean Wiggins, Marilyn Thrall and soap expert Clayton Logan. Last minute assistance was provided by the Broadcast Pioneers Library, Sally Ann Morris, Denise Clifton, Polly Hazen, and Margaret H. Schemering. Especially helpful were the program information departments of the three networks, who made their files available for my research: Betty Jane Reed of NBC, Barbara Cronin of ABC, and John Behrens of CBS. These sources were invaluable in drawing up comprehensive cast lists and providing program content and accurate dates.

I also wish to express my gratitude to the many gracious stars of daytime television who assisted me in this project, among them, Denise Alexander and John Beradino of *General Hospital*; Larry Bryggman of *As the World Turns*; Jacquie Courtney and Doug Watson of *Another World*; Judith Light and Robin Strasser of *One Life to Live*; Ron Tomme and Tudi Wiggins of *Love of Life*; Mary Stuart of *Search for Tomorrow*; and Ruth Warrick of *All My Children*.

Additional courtesies were extended by the most respected writers of serial drama, including Bill Bell of *The Young and the Restless*; Harding Lemay, who wrote *Another World* during its Golden Age; Henry Slesar, whose stint as headwriter on *The Edge of Night* was one of daytime TV's longest; Agnes Nixon, the creator of *All My Children*, *One Life to Live*, and three other soaps; and Roy Winsor, the father of the television serial, who created *Search for Tomorrow* and a half dozen other shows.

Finally, thanks to Ann La Farge of Ballantine Books, whose enthusiasm for the project reactivated mine, and to Anthony Jackubosky, whose assistance over the past five years went beyond the call of duty.

NOTES AND ACKNOWLEDGMENTS TO THE SECOND EDITION

Since the original publication of this book in November 1985, the soap opera scene has changed tremendously. While the prime-time serials have declined in popularity, perhaps because of emphasis on storylines that feature international intrigue and intentionally "camp" character portrayals, the daytime dramas have begun to downplay espionage stories and have returned to the basics: romance and family drama. The upshot has been a real dog fight among the three networks with such shows as NBC's *Days of Our Lives*, ABC's *General Hospital*, and CBS's *The Young and the Restless* all jockeying for the top position. Anything goes, and usually does! What has *not* changed is the growing interest in soap operas—their dramatic quality, their history, and the hold they've had on TV audiences for almost five decades.

I'm grateful for the letters I've received from fans and for their suggestions, many of which have been incorporated into this edition. As well as updating the storylines of current soap operas, I've included more anecdotes and "trivia" about ongoing soaps, updated and added still more biographies to the "Who's Who" section, revised the appendixes and brought them up to date, and refined the dating of *all* the cast lists (a particular favorite among readers). Also, I've included some rare new photos in the two picture sections.

For the second edition, I am especially indebted to serial expert John Kelly Genovese, who insisted on total accuracy and kept me continually on my toes. Also, thanks to Martha Byrne and Brian Bloom of *As the World Turns* who agreed to grace the cover of the book; Douglas Marland and Helen Wagner, also of *As the World Turns*; Erika Slezak of *One Life to Live*; Beverlee McKinsey of *Guiding Light*; and Deidre Hall of *Days of Our Lives*.

Additional courtesies were extended by Mary C. Ternes of The Martin Luther King Memorial Library; Janet Storm and Wendy Savodnik of CBS; Mary Ann Sack of Procter and Gamble; Audrey Wolf, David White, and Robert Gillis. And thanks to the staff at Ballantine Books: Jenny Mandel, Jimmy Harris, Holly Johnson, and Laurie Rovtar.

Finally, a heartfelt embrace of gratitude for my friend and mentor Ann La Farge.

INTRODUCTION— A Short History
of Television Soap Opera

Twenty million Americans watch daytime TV dramas every day; 60 million watch at least once a week. The figures for prime-time serials go even higher; almost 90 million people watched the "Who Shot J.R.?" segment on *Dallas* on November 21, 1980. Yet very little is known about the early stirrings of serials—commonly called soap operas—on television.

Serials can be traced all the way back to the ancient folk tales told by Persian storytellers in the bazaars and collected in the fifteenth century as *The Arabian Nights' Entertainments* or *A Thousand and One Nights.* The tales are framed by the narrator Scheherazade, who avoids death by weaving stories for the executioner-king, leaving him hanging with the question, "What happens next?" and putting off her execution day by day until the king eventually falls in love with her. Medieval storytellers in Europe often relied on a similar framing device, adding to the technique a juxtaposition of several storylines.

Serials became popular again with Dickens and other nineteenth-century novelists who published their stories in magazines by installment. Radio adapted many of these novelistic techniques in the 1930s with its daytime dramas called "soap operas"—"soap" because they were sponsored by soap companies, "operas" because they showcased larger-than-life emotions and melodramatic, librettolike plots.

Radio soaps had been thriving for almost two decades when the old DuMont TV network began to experiment with television soap operas. Shortly after DuMont's WABD in New York began broadcasting in May 1944, Lever Brothers sponsored three weeks of daily TV versions of the radio soaps, *Big Sister* and *Aunt Jenny's True Life Stories.* According to the trade journal *Sponsor*, the "results were good to excellent, but [the TV productions] were primarily the result of an advertiser's desire to 'feel the way' into TV, and to give his staff a workout with visual technique." Although there had been other dramatic serials produced for local broadcast as early as 1946—such as the one-day airing of *Big Sister* on a local station in Chicago and the thirteen-part serial *War Bride* in Schenectady—the first network soap was the DuMont effort *Faraway Hill*, which premiered October 2, 1946, and was broadcast simultaneously in New York and Washington, D.C. By the time DuMont had produced *A Woman to Remember* (a television soap about a radio soap) and the highly successful *Captain Video* (TV's first space opera) in 1949, the network had expanded to include most of the major cities on the East Coast.

NBC entered the soap opera derby early in 1949 with Irna Phillips' *These Are My Children*, based on her very first radio serials, *Painted Dreams* and *Today's Children*. CBS jumped into the race in 1950 with *The First Hundred Years*, a highly publicized serial about marriage. Although both shows were failures, the network sensed the great commercial potential of dramatic programming during the daytime. In September 1951, CBS launched two powerhouse soaps, *Search for Tomorrow* and *Love of Life*, both created by Roy Winsor. The network quickly added other successful programs to its daytime lineup, including a radical departure from the radio-styled soaps: the visually oriented character drama, *As the World Turns*. An Irna Phillips' creation, the show was the first major half-hour serial and was packed with dramatic ambiguity, close-ups, and in-depth conversations. By 1956, CBS had a half dozen certified hits.

NBC inaugurated one flop after another in an industrious but ineffective attempt to make a dent in the CBS monopoly, but CBS totally dominated the soap scene through the '50s and most of the '60s. What NBC failed to understand was that their early serials, *Three Steps to Heaven*, *Concerning Miss Marlowe*, and others, focused invariably on career women caught up in a myriad of fantasy romances. This was fine for radio where women used their imagination to wile away part of the evening, but television had an immediacy and a reality which fairly cried out for heroines whom the '50s women, at home with the baby boomers, could identify with. Having learned their lesson, NBC finally began to rock the boat in the mid '60s with the introduction of three hit soaps, *The Doctors*, *Another World*, and *Days of Our Lives*, while ABC entered the race with the future gold mine *General Hospital*.

CBS and Procter & Gamble, the soap company that supplied CBS with most of its daytime programming, ruled daytime TV with an iron hand. Run much like the movie studios of the '30s and '40s, employing a stable of writers working at the peak of their powers and the most talented performers of the New York theater, Procter & Gamble's soap operas were conservative in content, strongly conceived and plotted, and immensely popular.

Agnes Nixon, an Irna Phillips' protégée, began to inject a bit of social controversy during the '60s, starting with a cancer storyline on Procter & Gamble's *The Guiding Light*. Nixon was such a formidable writer that after establishing P & G's *Another World* as a hit, she was offered the opportunity to create two new serials for ABC. These shows, *One Life to Live* in 1968 and *All My Children* in 1970, presented an altogether new concept in soap operas, built around potent social issues and including ethnic characters, strong male types, and comic situations. It was an era of experimentation and upheaval in daytime television. ABC introduced the gothic serial *Dark Shadows* in 1966. The show starred film actress Joan Bennett, but became wildly successful only when a charming vampire named Barnabas appeared on the scene. *Dark Shadows* became a cult hit. *New York Times* film critic Renata Adler and Jacqueline Kennedy both admitted to being fans of the serial.

In 1971, *As the World Turns* was temporarily deposed from the top spot by NBC's melodrama *Days of Our Lives* and ABC's *General Hospital*. In the same year, Harding Lemay took over as headwriter of *Another World*. Agnes Nixon had created a love story on this show in which passively sweet Alice Matthews and the socially deprived Rachel Davis vied for the affection of Steve Frame. The romantic triangle brought *Another World* its initial popularity, but Lemay developed it into a sophisticated drawing-room drama and the show skyrocketed to the top of the ratings in the mid '70s.

Perhaps in response to the highly publicized "relevance" campaign and more youthful storylines on ABC, conservative CBS gave the go-ahead to *The Young and the Restless* in 1973. This innovative serial featured flaw-lessly beautiful young performers, semi-nudity, lush productions, tear-stained drama, social awareness, and musical interludes, all wrapped up in a fairy-tale atmosphere of dramatic lighting and sweeping camera tech-niques. Many of these features were immediately borrowed by other soaps.

The mid '70s brought a renaissance in daytime drama, while movies went into a temporary decline. It was a bizarre time in film history, with women making only occasional appearances, usually as somebody's girl-friend in the buddy films or as the inevitable bimbo in the popular violent cop films and comedies of the era. And while movies were not connecting with the female audience and the theater was growing progressively ab-stract, prime-time TV dramas for the most part ignored women and love relationships.

Daytime television capitalized on the void left by other entertainment mediums and began to dramatize an even broader range of female char-acters and women's issues. Although a wave of young women novelists were making their mark in contemporary fiction, their point of view was a limited one. Heroines of the novels of Erica Jong, Lois Gould, Anne Roiphe, and a dozen others tended to be urban, upper middle class, Jewish, career oriented, angst-ridden, and sex-obsessed. On the soaps the scope was much broader and the women more resilient—spunky rather than philosophical. Either out of choice or economic necessity, the women on the soaps checked out of the boudoir and the kitchen and into the offices.

Every adult female on *Ryan's Hope*, set in New York City, held down a job—from barmaid to doctor—to support herself or her family. On *The Edge of Night*, a detective serial, Assistant D.A. Brandy Henderson battled with defense lawyer Adam Drake in witty dialogue reminiscent of Bacall and Bogart. On *The Young and the Restless*, the aftermath of Chris Brooks's rape was carefully scrutinized. Cathy Craig on *One Life to Live* was raising a child out of wedlock and struggling to make it as a writer. *All My Children*'s Erica Kane had the first legal abortion dramatized on television and Fran Bachman, in *How to Survive a Marriage*, was attempting to deal not only with her husband's death, but with funeral parlors, bills, and lack of credit, illustrating that while movies and novels end, life—on and off the soaps—moves on.

With the creation of stronger women characters came the presentation of less "serviceable" male characters—those dreamboats and charming cads who once had nothing better to do than invite a vacuum-pushing heroine to lunch. The new male characters adjust to those changes in society that the males in other mediums seemed able to ignore. This adjustment brought a new sharpness to the dramatic conflicts, an across-the-board improve-ment in dialogue and story variety, and a strong injection of humor into the serials. With more realistic male characters presented, daytime drama began to attract a substantial male audience. *The Edge of Night* had always claimed a large male viewership, but by the late '70s the audience for *All My Children* and the action-oriented *General Hospital* was one-third men.

While not all the daytime serials were consistently sympathetic to the women's movement, the variety of opinions expressed was wide and well articulated. The one medium that had always been committed to women had kept up with the times, dramatizing issues of interest to women and presenting them in a realistic and entertaining way. The very first radio soap, Irna Phillips' Chicago effort *Painted Dreams* in 1930, had laid the groundwork with kindly, homey Mother Moynihan (called Mother Moran on the network revision, *Today's Children*), who dispensed advice to her "feminist" friend with the words, "In your plan, women wouldn't be havin' time to be havin' children and keepin' a home. I'm thinkin' that a country is only as strong as its weakest home. When you're after destroyin' those things which make up a home, you're destroyin' people."

A little more than forty years later, on *Search for Tomorrow*, Kathy Phillips pursued a law career, had an abortion, and demanded that she and her husband split the household responsibilities. However, on the conservative, top-rated *As the World Turns*, a wounded Dr. Bob Hughes barked at his wife, Jennifer, who was going back to school after years as a housewife: "I'm the father and you're the mother. The bulk of responsibility in raising Frannie falls on your shoulders." The "truth-tellers" of the show—Nancy Hughes and Ellen Stewart—concurred and the back-to-school storyline was dropped as Jennifer was killed in an automobile accident. But the soaps can usually be counted on to chart personal growth and realistic character change. It was a sign of the times when that same Dr. Bob Hughes—played in the '80s by the same actor—chewed out the male interns for their sexist treatment of Dr. Annie Stewart. It was also a sign of the times when *Search for Tomorrow*'s optimistic heroine Jo, after thirty years of inspiring those around her, divorced her troublesome husband.

Still, millions found *As the World Turns* and other soaps without a social conscience more attractive than the contemporary-minded ABC soaps. *Another World* in its heyday was the liveliest theatrical showcase in New York, while *As the World Turns* remained a smash hit because it continued to tell powerful stories slowly and surely. The show was old-fashioned in the best sense of the word, with strong characterizations, domestic drama, and romance, all swept up in a tantalizing production-code atmosphere fraught with subtext, intrigue, and irony. The soap most resembled the movies of the '30s, with Kim Reynolds, reminiscent of Garbo, nobly rising above adversity, and the Bette Davis–like Susan Stewart steamrolling over anything in her path. The situations were often outrageous, but the commitment to the inner lives of the heroines was dramatic dynamite, touching on emotions on a subliminal, almost atavistic level.

Although the conservative *As the World Turns* had a five-year comeback, CBS began housecleaning in the '70s, cancelling *The Secret Storm* after twenty years and *Love of Life* after thirty years on the air. The network decided to throw out traditional themes and techniques and old-fashioned values on their other serials, renovating the old chestnuts *Guiding Light* and *As the World Turns* by the turn of the decade in an attempt to keep up with the fast-moving ABC soaps.

In 1978, Gloria Monty took over as producer of ABC's *General Hospital*, revolutionizing daytime TV with shorter scenes, new editing techniques, cross-cutting, splashy sets, regular location shooting, and fast-paced, action-oriented storylines. The devices proved so popular that other shows began to experiment with changes. With the Luke-and-Laura storyline, *General Hospital* zoomed to the top of the ratings and stayed there for the next five years. The wedding of Luke and Laura in 1981 (with Elizabeth Taylor in attendance) brought daytime TV its highest ratings, reams of publicity, and respect by the news media and within the TV industry. By the end of 1984, CBS and NBC had made strong comebacks with witty and romantic storylines, and the daytime crown was up for grabs.

Soap operas were finally being noticed. One reason was money. Advertisers currently shell out over $1.7 billion a year to promote their products during daytime television. With the low production costs and 60 million loyal fans who watch daytime dramas every week, the daytime soaps take in over $700 million in profit a year. The shows also attract more than one-quarter of American women between the ages of eighteen and forty-nine, the prime target group for advertisers. If you include the game shows, daytime TV accounts for up to 75 percent of the networks' profits.

While a weekly episode of *Magnum, P.I.* or *Dallas* costs $900,000 to produce, five sixty-minute episodes—an entire week—of daytime soaps can be produced for far less. *General Hospital* alone accounted for one-quarter of ABC's profits for several years.

The eruption of dramatic serials on prime-time has also affected the way people think about soap operas. In 1978, CBS launched *Dallas*, the most popular prime-time soap since *Peyton Place*. Focusing on a rich Texas family, it spawned the spin-off *Knots Landing* and propelled Larry Hagman, who played the dastardly J.R., to superstar status. The success of *Dallas* brought a slew of imitators, including the hits *Falcon Crest* and *Dynasty* and failures such as *Flamingo Road* and *Emerald Point*. In the 1983–84 and 1984–85 seasons, *Dallas, Dynasty, Falcon Crest*, and *Knots Landing* were all among the top-ten-rated prime-time shows.

Although dyed-in-the-wool fans of daytime drama considered the prime-time soaps as preposterous (yet wickedly entertaining) versions of the real thing, the prime-time shows have created an enormous interest in soap opera in general. These shows, in which a tragedy seems to precede every commercial, are totally escapist entertainment, where a Pam or a Krystle finds herself in a world of Beautiful People, teeters vicariously on its perimeter, and falls off occasionally in moods of high-fashion despair and extravagant sorrow. Fanciful conceits with no discernible roots in reality, these shows provide harmless escape hatches to gasp and giggle over after a long workday in the real world.

Today, daytime drama at its best still dramatizes family conflict and the rampant unresolved emotions that love relationships invariably produce. With movies and prime-time series now offering almost a complete diet of "glamorous" escapism, it is only on daytime television that there is a real sense of ordinary lives being lived, decisions being made, relationships being savored and skewered. It seems at this time to be the last hold-out among the dramatic media to employ the family unit as part of its structure. In Ruth Martin's backyard on *All My Children* neighbors are laughing over iced tea; at one of Ed Bauer's barbeques on *Guiding Light* friends are gathering to share another's good fortune; in Ada Hobson's kitchen on *Another World* "just folks" are enjoying family camaraderie over a beer. The Bauers, the Hughes, the Woleks, and the Martins are much like one's own family; their strengths and frailties are our own.

Daytime drama is a speeded-up, stylized version of real life, with its own set of rules and conventions. A bastard art—like the movies—the soaps are essentially a fusion of theatrical conventions and novelistic devices, perfectly suited for television. Problems are not solved in an hour or two but in days or months. Kay Chancellor's alcoholism on *The Young and the Restless* has been a day-to-day, year-to-year problem since the mid '70s, for example.

As an audience gets to know a cast of characters and watches the situations that shape them, the emotional investment becomes intense, volatile, dramatically satisfying. As characterizations grow and the narrative stretches out over months and years and becomes more complex and ambiguous, one's involvement deepens, forcing one to come to terms with the quirks of human nature, the darker sides of fundamentally good people. And thus there is the possibility of the viewer experiencing something new or complex or feeling some way he has never felt before. And that is the point of all good drama: to illuminate the human condition.

When the wrong-side-of-the-tracks Willis Frame on *Another World* finally admitted to the exquisite Alice that he really didn't love her but only the *idea* of loving her, the revelation was so poignant and inevitable that the loyal viewer was almost embarrassed to watch. One saw the tactless honesty and felt the cruelty of the situation and knew the pain of both.

Similarly, on *One Life to Live* the long, rocky marital relationship between Dorian Lord and Herb Callison produced decidedly ambivalent responses among viewers. Herb was aware of, and even enjoyed, Dorian's machinations and game-playing, but when she overstepped herself, violating Herb's code of honor though not her own, Herb left her, only to be curiously drawn back to her. Whom was one to root for? As Dorian rocked back and forth on the balls of her feet, a jangle of raw, erotic nerve, baiting the strong-minded Herb, it was a continual test whether Herb loved-hated-couldn't-live-without the complex Dorian or whether he merely wanted to have her on *his* terms.

Soaps can make for a good, casual time or can be embarrassingly bad, in the same manner as some terrible novels or films. However, those special moments of resonance on serials touch people's lives with an impact that other popular arts rarely achieve. What could be more painful than watching Dr. Susan Stewart, who struggled with alcoholism for months on *As the World Turns*, show up drunk at a hearing on her staff reinstatement? Or more hilarious than feisty Opal Gardner on *All My Children* trying to snag a husband? Or more touching than the prom dance on *Guiding Light* when the destructive Phillip Spaulding fell irretrievably, hopelessly in love with Beth Raines?

In 1961, playwright William Inge said, "I feel that soap opera is a [peculiarly] American form. People sneer at it, but it has the basis for a truer, more meaningful drama. Italian opera and drama grew out of the *commedia dell'arte*, and I feel that in soap opera we have the roots for a native American drama." Perhaps Inge was right. Soaps have always celebrated the American themes of familial affections, hope, and the need for growth and change. So, too, have the serials themselves changed, taking root in a new sophistication, blossoming into a fascinating dramatic form. And in the spring of 1979, on the serial appropriately titled *One Life to Live*, soap opera spilled over into art—on its own terms and by any of the critical rigors brought to bear on any dramatic medium.

Years of storylines and characters' lives came together on this drama when the tormented figure of Karen Wolek, who had fought desperately to climb out of her self-hatred and the hell she had created for others, was finally forced to reveal her past in a public forum. Karen's confessions were riffs built upon riffs that exploded into arias of shame. When Karen cried out in horror at the culmination of her confession, "He was the first of so many men," it was as powerful and haunting and operatic a lament as "I have always depended on the kindness of strangers," Blanche DuBois' exit line in *A Streetcar Named Desire*, or "I fell in love with James Tyrone and was so happy for a time," Mary Tyrone's tragic line from *Long Day's Journey Into Night*. Judith Light's performance as Karen Wolek was a theatrical tour de force that will burn in the memory of the millions who were lucky enough to experience it.

If one compares the occasional sequence in soap opera to the greatest in American drama, it is the surprising truth. What else is *Long Day's Journey Into Night*, with its round-robin of family accusations and layers of open-ended, thwarted catharsis, except the stuff of great American soap opera?

Some of the more appealing daytime dramas have outgrown the term "soap opera," as food products replaced detergent as the major advertiser. But the name "soap operas" will stick, and for good reason. Soaps often do have operatic power. Just as motion pictures are still known as "movies," so in the same spirit I use the term "soap opera" as a synonym for "serial," as a term of affection and in the cause of historic preservation.

And now—drumroll, please—a panorama of over forty years of televised serial drama: what the soaps have been, what they've become, what they are.

PART ONE

Daytime and Prime-Time Soap Operas: A to Z

ALL MY CHILDREN
January 5, 1970–   ABC

The brainchild of Agnes Nixon, *All My Children* has been a winning, often dazzling blend of social realism, romantic fantasy, and high satire. Among the issues tackled have been child and wife abuse, Vietnam, rape, prostitution, homosexuality as an alternative lifestyle, and mental health. Television's first legalized abortion was dramatized here. These subjects have not been discussed in a vacuum but have been fully integrated into the drama, and have never gotten in the way of the more entertaining aspects of the show, such as the popular young-love story of Jenny and Greg or the broad, drawing-room antics of Phoebe and Langley. *All My Children* has been a consistent hit with a mass audience as well as with such specialized audiences as college students, men, blacks, and office workers. It has also become, with the arrival of the popular videocassette recorder, the most taped program on the air, according to a front-page story in *USA Today*.

Agnes Nixon had originally offered *All My Children* to Procter & Gamble, who declined the offer during the mid '60s. A couple of years later, Nixon brought *Another World* from the bottom of the ratings to near the top, using the destructive character of Rachel (modeled after *Children*'s Erica) as the catalyst for explosive drama. ABC, seeing NBC's ratings erupt, immediately negotiated with Nixon to create a serial for them. The upshot in 1968 was *One Life to Live*, which featured social issues and ethnic characters in a traditional two-family soap structure.

When ABC asked Nixon for still another show, she dusted off the *All My Children* script that had lain in a drawer for years. The show placed the emphasis on young love—a definite departure from tradition. Within four years of its premiere, *All My Children* was number one in the ratings. It has stayed close to the top ever since.

The serial originally focused on two families, the established, well-to-do Tyler clan and the upwardly mobile Martins. The Tylers—Charles and Phoebe, their children Ann and Lincoln, and grandson Chuck—were the classic rich soap family: unstable, slightly spoiled, emotionally insecure. The Martins, headed by Grandma Kate, her sons Paul and Joe, and Joe's children Jeff, Tara, and Bobby, provided the Pine Valley community with a backbone of morality and common sense. (Joe's son Bobby is *All My Children*'s biggest mystery: early in the serial's run he went upstairs to polish his skis, and hasn't been heard from since.)

From the beginning, the main storylines have revolved around a series of romantic triangles. The first and most famous was the Tara-Chuck-Phillip story: young love complicated by outside interference, by the men's long friendship, and by the sensitive woman caught between them. For many years the Ann-Paul-Nick triangle was given a full-scale treatment, and at the turn of the last decade, Cliff and Nina's love affair, another young-love story complicated by family meddling, enjoyed great popularity. That plot, which included bravura performances by James Mitchell and Gillian Spencer as Nina's parents, Palmer and Daisy Cortlandt, was highlighted by the marriage of Nina and Cliff on September 3, 1980, the most sumptuous wedding seen on daytime television up to that date.

At the beginning of *All My Children*'s second decade, with Tara and Phillip written out and Cliff and Nina's marriage on the rocks as Nina became attracted to Steve Jacobi, the show introduced its third popular youth romance. The love story of Jenny and Greg was beset with unhappy complications (Greg's grasping mother, the devious young Liza, Greg's paralysis) but it served as the taking-off point for the hilarious performance of Dorothy Lyman, who played Jenny's gum-chewing mama, Opal Gardner. Lyman, who had previously delighted audiences on *The Edge of Night* (playing a similar character) and *Another World*, created a comic sensation and won two Emmies for the role before moving on to prime-time television.

Opal was in a long line of *All My Children*'s larger-than-life, love-to-hate caricatures (Billy Clyde Tuggle, Edna Thorton, etc.) designed to offset the often saccharine love stories. Lyman, with her amazing energy and inventiveness, was able to transcend caricature, but critics complained that these unbelievable characters knocked realistic domestic drama right out the window. The most famous and long-running of these characters were, of course, the luscious bitch-brat Erica Kane and the grand matriarch Phoebe Tyler. Erica, headstrong and impetuous, steamrollered over men in search of fulfillment but never found it. Before she had reached her thirties, Erica had married and divorced three times and had left many others biting the dust. In 1984, she married the rich, brooding Adam Chandler, thus setting off a season of gothic storytelling. Phoebe was equally uncompromising in her neverending obsession with social propriety and her family's happiness. (When Phoebe was confined to a wheelchair, actress Ruth Warrick dubbed herself "a bitch on wheels.") These flamboyantly unsympathetic characters have somewhat mellowed after a decade of troublemaking but still manage to have a finger in every storyline pie.

With the exit of Dorothy Lyman's Opal in 1983 and the onscreen death of Jenny Gardner the following year, *All My Children* began still another star-crossed youth romance, zeroing in on Jenny's brother Tad, the show's young anti-hero, and Hillary Wilson, Phoebe's new step-daughter. Tad (played by Michael Knight, perhaps the best young actor in daytime drama) wonderfully combined the romantic longing of sister Jenny with the outrageous, comic ambitiousness of mother Opal. *All My Children* again sparkled with poignance and wit. On a sad note, Kay Campbell, the actress who played Grandma Kate for fifteen years (and the only character who never gave up on Tad), died in May 1985. In tribute to Campbell's memory, the part of Kate was not recast.

Probably television's most consistently entertaining and intelligent serial, *All My Children* has a blend of styles that may, for some, be emotionally unsatisfying. In a single segment there are snippets of *Sixty Minutes*, *Love Story*, and *The Carol Burnett Show*. No tone is sustained. As witty as Phoebe and some of the far-out Pine Valley residents are, they're more caricature than character, and easy targets for satire. For its first decade *All My Children* was plagued by cheap-looking sets, one-dimensional male characters, and insecure direction and camera work, a situation corrected when Jacqueline Babbin took over as producer. But life is often just as messy as this show, and the individual segments are engaging, the actors likable, the writing witty, the emphasis on family laudable, and the presentation of social issues outstanding. Mary Fickett, who was the first daytime performer to win an Emmy, took that honor for an anti-war speech she made as Ruth Martin, mother of a G.I. who was missing in action.

All My Children has also been blessed by that precious soap opera commodity, continuity, both in its cast and its writing, having only two headwriters in its history, Agnes Nixon and Wisner Washam. (Washam's wife, Judith Barcroft, played Ann Tyler longer than any other actress; his son, Ian, played Little Phillip.) The show has been nominated for Outstanding Daytime Drama every year from 1976 to 1987, and has been the subject of two books: *All Her Children* (Doubleday, 1976), written by novelist Dan Wakefield, and *The Confessions of Phoebe Tyler* (Prentice Hall, 1980) by Ruth Warrick.

All My Children continues to employ the savvy formula which has served it so well in the past: puppy love (Charlie Brent–Julie Chandler) juxtaposed with powerful social issues (Mark's cocaine intervention) and the indefatigable shenanigans of Erica Kane, who recently found herself caught between three men—Jeremy Hunter, Matt Connolly, and Travis Montgomery.

For the record, Erica's husbands have been 1) Jeff Martin, 2) Phil Brent, 3) Tom Cudahy, and 4) Adam Chandler. Mike Roy, Kent Bogard, and Jason Maxwell have also bitten the dust (literally) attempting to get the little lady down the aisle. Nick Davis, Brandon Kingsley, and Bonkers escaped by a whisker. Raising Kane, indeed!

CAST

Erica Kane	Susan Lucci 1970–
Phoebe Tyler	Ruth Warrick 1970–
Ruth Brent Martin, R.N.	Mary Fickett 1970–
Dr. Joseph Martin	Ray MacDonnell 1970–
Paul Martin	William Mooney 1972–82; 1984–85
	Ken Rabat 1970–72
Kate Martin	Kay Campbell 1970–85
	Christine Thomas 1970
	Kate Harrington 1970
Tara Martin Brent	Nancy Frangione 1977–79; 1985
	Mary Lynn Blanks 1979–80
	Stephanie Braxton 1974–76
	Karen Lynn Gorney 1970–74; 1976–77
Dr. Jeff Martin	Jeffrey Byron 1986–87
	James O'Sullivan 1977–79
	Robert Perault 1976–77
	Charles Frank 1970–75
	Christopher Wines 1970

Dr. Charles Tyler	Hugh Franklin 1970–83; 1985
Mona Kane	Frances Heflin 1970–
Phillip Brent	Nicholas Benedict 1973–79
	Richard Hatch 1970–72
Amy Tyler	Rosemary Prinz 1970
Nick Davis	Lawrence Keith 1970–78; 1983
Ann Tyler Martin	Gwyn Gilliss 1979–81
	Judith Barcroft 1971–77
	Joanna Miles 1970–71
	Diana De Vegh 1970
Lincoln Tyler	Peter White 1974–81; 1984; 1986
	Nicholas Pryor 1971
	Paul Dumont 1970–71
	James Karen 1970
Dr. Chuck Tyler	Richard Van Vleet 1975–84; 1986
	Chris Hubbell 1973–75
	Gregory Chase 1972–73
	Jack Stauffer 1970–72
Mary Kennicott Martin	Susan Blanchard 1971–75
	Jacqueline Boslow 1971
Dan Kennicott	Daren Kelly 1976–79
Eddie Dorrance	Warren Burton 1978–79
	Ross Petty 1978
Peg English	Patricia Barry 1980–81
Brooke English	Julia Barr 1976–
	Harriet Hall 1981
	Elissa Leeds 1976
Billy Clyde Tuggle	Matthew Cowles 1977–80; 1984
Marestella LaTour	Kathleen Denzina 1977–82
Dr. Frank Grant	John Danelle 1972–82
	Don Blakely 1972
Nancy Grant	Lisa Wilkinson 1973–84
Donna Beck Tyler	Candice Earley 1976–
	Francesca Poston 1976
Benny Sago	Vasili Bogazianos 1980–
	Larry Fleischman 1976–79
Edna Thornton	Sandy Gabriel 1977–80; 1983–86
Kitty Shea	Francesca James 1972–77
Kelly Cole	Francesca James 1978–80; 1981;
	1983; 1984; 1986
Myrtle Lum Fargate	Eileen Herlie 1976–
Mark Dalton	Mark LaMura 1977–
Ellen Shepherd	Kathleen Noone 1977–
Devon Shepherd	Tricia Pursley 1977–81; 1983–84
Harlan Tucker	William Griffis 1977–81; 1983
Wally McFadden	Patrick Skelton 1980–81
	Nigel Reed 1980
	Jack Magee 1978–80

Claudette Montgomery	Susan Plantt-Winston 1977–80
	Paulette Breen 1975
Margo Flax	Eileen Letchworth 1972–76
Dr. David Thornton	Paul Gleason 1976–78
Dr. Christina Karras	Robin Strasser 1976–79
Edie Hoffman	Marilyn Chris 1972
Bill Hoffman	Michael Shannon 1972
Jason Maxwell	John Devlin 1972–73
	Tom Rosqui 1972
Hal Short	Dan Hamilton 1975
Stacey Coles	Maureen Mooney 1975
Wyatt Coles	Bruce Gray 1975
Jamie Coles	Jason Lauve 1975
Caroline Murray	Patricia Dixon 1975–79
Tyrone	Roscoe Orman 1976
Carl Blair	Steven James 1979–84
	John K. Carroll 1977–79
Dr. Russ Anderson	Charles Brown 1979–80
	David Pendleton 1978–79
Nigel Fargate	Alexander Scourby 1976–77
	Sidney Armus 1976
Charlie (Phillip) Brent	Robert Duncan McNeill 1985–
	Josh Hamilton 1985
	Brian Lima 1976–80
	Ian Washam 1972–76
Tad (Gardner) Martin	Michael Knight 1982–86
	John E. Dunn 1978–81
	Matthew Anton 1973–77
Daisy Cortlandt	Gillian Spencer 1980–87
Palmer Cortlandt	James Mitchell 1979–
Nina Cortlandt	Taylor Miller 1979–84; 1986–
	Barbara Kearns 1985–86
	Heather Stanford 1984–85
Dr. Cliff Warner	Peter Bergman 1979–87
Myra Murdoch	Elizabeth Lawrence 1979–
Tom Cudahy	Richard Shoberg 1977–
Sean Cudahy	Alan Dysert 1979–81
Langley Wallingford	Louis Edmonds 1979–
Sybil Thorne	Linda Gibboney 1979–81
Betsy Kennicott	Carla Dragoni 1979–82
Kurt Sanders	William Ferriter 1980–81
Leora Sanders	Lizbeth MacKay 1980–81
Mrs. Johnson	Carol Burnett 1976
Verla Grubbs	Carol Burnett 1983
Charwoman	Elizabeth Taylor 1983
Brandon Kingsley	Michael Minor 1980–82
Sara Kingsley	Tudi Wiggins 1980–82
Pamela Kingsley	Kathleen Kamhi 1980–82

Rick Kincaid	Stephen Parr 1981–82
Melanie Sawyer	Carol McCluer 1981–82
Carrie Sanders Tyler	Andrea Moar 1980–83
Jesse Hubbard	Darnell Williams 1981–
Ray Gardner	Gil Rogers 1977–79; 1982
Opal Gardner	Dorothy Lyman 1981–83
Jenny Gardner	Kim Delaney 1981–84
Greg Nelson	Jack Armstrong 1986
	Laurence Lau 1981–85
Enid Nelson	Natalie Ross 1981–
Liza Colby	Alice Haining 1984
	Marcy Walker 1981–84
Marian Colby	Jennifer Bassey 1983–
Larry Colby	Joseph Warren 1983–84
Lars Bogard	Jack Betts 1983
	Robert Milli 1982–83
	William Blankenship 1982
Kent Bogard	Lee Godart 1982
	Michael Woods 1982
Olga Svenson	Peg Murray 1982–
Simone	Viveca Lindfors 1983
Judith Sawyer	Gwen Verdon 1982
Silver Kane	
(Connie Wilkes)	Deborah Goodrich 1982–83
Angie Baxter	Debbi Morgan 1982–
Les Baxter	Antonio Fargas 1982–83; 1987
Pat Baxter	Lee Chamberlain 1982–
Sam Brady	Jason Kincaid 1982–84
Dottie Thornton	Tasia Valenza 1983–86
	Dawn Marie Boyle 1977–80
Amanda Cousins	Amanda Bearse 1982–84
Alfred Vanderpoole	Bill Timoney 1983–86
Steve Jacobi	Dack Rambo 1982–83
Lynn Carson	Donna Pescow 1983
Mike Roy	Hugo Napier 1984–85
	Nicolas Surovy 1983–84
Adam Chandler	David Canary 1983–
Stuart Chandler	David Canary 1983–
Ross Chandler	Robert Gentry 1983–
Joanna Yaeger	Meg Myles 1983–84; 1987
Gil Barrett	Stephen McNaughton 1983
Linda Warner	Melissa Leo 1984–85
Peggy Warner	Amy Steel 1980
Jasper Sloane	Ronald Drake 1982–
Zack Grayson	Robert LuPone 1984–85
Tony Barclay	Brent Barrett 1983–84
Judy Barclay	Maia Danziger 1983–84
Father Tierney	Mel Boudrot 1977–
Candy Brown	Elizabeth Forsyth 1981–

Bonkers	Himself 1982–84
Cynthia Preston	Jane Elliot 1984–86
Andrew Preston	Steve Caffrey 1984–86
Bob Georgia	Peter Strong 1984–85
Yvonne Caldwell	Vanessa Bell 1984–85; 1987
Eugene Hubbard	Tom Wright 1984–85
Bryan Sanders	Curt May 1985–
June Hagen	Carole Shelley 1984–86
Shelia Thomas	Cynthia Sullivan 1984
Hillary Wilson	Carmen Thomas 1984–
Mickey Barlowe	Marie Reynolds 1985
Mary Georgia	Geraldine Court 1985
Jeremy Hunter	Jean LeClerc 1985–
Alex Hunter	Mitchell Ryan 1985
Natalie Hunter	Kate Collins 1985–
Giles St. Clair	Giles Kohler 1985
Julie Chandler	Lauren Holly 1986–
	Stephanie Winters 1985–86
Robin McCall	Deborah Morehart 1985–87
Wade Matthews	Christopher Holder 1986
Skye Patterson	Robin Christopher 1987–
	Antoinette Byron 1986–87
Matt Connolly	Michael Tylo 1986–
Victor Borelli	Antony Ponzini 1986–87
Travis Montgomery	Larkin Malloy 1987–
Barbara Elliot	Susan Pratt 1987–
Cecily Davidson	Rosa Langschwadt 1987–
Noelle Keaton	Claire Beckman 1987–
	Rosalind Ingledew 1987
Mitch Beck	Brian Fitzpatrick 1987–
Elizabeth Carlyle	Lisa Eichhorn 1987–

ANOTHER LIFE

June 1, 1981–October 5, 1984   CBN

When the announcement of a religious soap opera—a "soap with hope"—was made in 1979, the Christian Broadcasting Network promised that the serial would deal with the everyday staples of commercial soaps, including murder, adultery, greed, homosexuality, and rape. What emerged two years later was considerably tamer. Although Roy Winsor, creator of *Search for Tomorrow* and *The Secret Storm*, had a hand in its development, *Another Life* (the working title was *The Light Inside*) suffered from a critical case of indecision. The material never really touched on the controversial, the characters and issues were seen in black-and-white terms, and the show often spun off into mini-sermonettes. The question of how much of a religious slant to apply to the material was never quite resolved. And the theme—how positive, optimistic answers can be found to life's dilemmas if one puts oneself into the hands of a higher authority—was alternately heralded and soft-pedaled.

Available to 22 million households via the CBN cable network and carried over twenty-five broadcast stations in the U.S. and in a number of foreign countries, *Another Life* focused on nurse Terry Davidson and her family: sensitive daughter Lori, wisecracking son Peter, and villainous sister Nancy. (Terry's husband and mother were killed six months after the premiere in an automobile accident.) Its opening story concerned Lori's fight against nasty gossip maliciously spread by the evil Miriam, who claimed Lori had slept with Miriam's husband. Lori and her family spent weeks trying desperately to clear her name, though it never occurred to anyone that Lori should take a polygraph test. She was later involved in an auto accident and married the handsome doctor who cured her of paralysis. (An attempted rape and catatonic state followed.) *Another Life*'s second major story saw the hard-drinking, heavy-smoking, adulterous Jeff Cummings, one of the Davidsons' neighbors, develop cancer and turn his life around, becoming a born-again Christian. In the soap's most heavy-handed moment, Jeff was miraculously cured when a beam of spiritual light entered his hospital room. Bob Aaron, the former chief of daytime drama at NBC and one of the soap's creators, left the show, declaring such writing "deplorable."

In the shake-up that followed, *Another Life*'s strange duality continued, seesawing between secular and evangelized themes. Its characters continued to fall into the established saint/sinner patterns. Miriam, who was the soap's female J.R., was kidnapped and held hostage, and upon her release embraced Christianity with a vengeance. Playboy Russ Weaver was shot, had an out-of-body experience in hell, was revived, and vowed to turn his life around. Again the changes and conversions were highly melodramatic, operating unfortunately in an atmosphere of fear of pain or death rather than one of hope. Instead of a slow evolution of self-examination and positive change that soap operas often document so well, *Another Life* opted for the theatrical no-atheists-in-the-foxhole route.

In 1984, the low-rated *Another Life* was cancelled just as the drama had become more sophisticated and attractive, featuring a mystery story about a Bible and a plot about a quasi-religious organization called Domi. John Cardoza was the first executive producer, followed by David M. Hummel, who brought a number of New York soap veterans to join the cast in Virginia Beach, where the show was taped. The producers included Lynwood King, and the writers included Steve Sylvester, Cheryl Chisholm, Chris Auer, Linda Culpepper, Susan McBridge, Bro Herrod, and Edna Brown.

CAST

Terry Davidson	Mary Jean Feton
Scott Davidson	John Corsault
Peter Davidson	Darrel Campbell
Lori Davidson Martin	Debbie McLeod
	Jeanette Larson
Dr. Ben Martin	Matt Williams

Nora Lindsay	Naomi Riseman
Nancy Lawson	Nancy Mulvey
Jeff Cummings	Tom McGowan
Liz Cummings	Carolyn Lenz
Charles Carpenter	Randy Kraft, Jr.
Helen Carpenter	Suzanne Granfield
Courtney Carpenter	Susan C. Carey
Miriam Carpenter Mason	Ginger Burgett
Paul Mason	Robert Bendall
Erick Mason	Matt McGowan
Gene Redlon	Eddie Hailey
Ione Redlon	Edye Byrde
Carla Redlon	Elain Graham
Samantha Marshall	Dee Dee Bridgewater
Becky Hewitt	Susan Scannell
Russ Weaver	Christopher Roland
Carrie Weaver	Marty McGaw
Vince Gardello	Michael Ryan
Dr. Dave Phillips	Tom Urich
Amber Phillips	Peggy Woody
Stacey Phillips	Karen Chapman
Kate Phillips Carothers	Dorothy Stinnette
Lee Carothers	Jim Williams
	Paul Gleason
Dan Myers	Kim Strong
Gil Prescott	J. Michael Hunter
Babs Farley	Julie Jenny
Harold Webster	Alan Sader
Dr. Alex Greeley	Bob Burchette
Ron Washington	Nicholas Benedict
Hugo/Jeremy Lancelot	Kelly Gwin
Blue Nobles	Chandler Hill Harben
Vicki Lang	Annamarie Smith
Lucille Figgins	Frankie Cardoza
Sgt. John Brubaker	Rick Warner
Vanessa Fazan	Diane Seely
Dr. Brian Graham	Paul Tinder
Barbara	Lori March

ANOTHER WORLD

May 4, 1964–   NBC

"We do not live in this world alone, but in a thousand other worlds." With this epigraph, read at the opening of each episode and serving as its guide, *Another World* has evolved over the years from strict melodrama to love story to sophisticated drawing-room drama to a soap opera in transition.

With the domestically oriented *As the Word Turns*, which premiered in

1956, firmly entrenched in the American consciousness, writer Irna Phillips turned her attention to creating a new serial, a melodrama similar to Roy Winsor's *The Secret Storm*. But instead of emphasizing inner passions, Phillips concentrated on external events that affected a middle-class family in Bay City, a university town in the northern part of the Midwest. *Another World* began with the death of William Matthews and its effect on his immediate family—his wife Liz and children Susan and Bill (who was later killed in a boating accident)—and his brother's family—Jim and Mary Matthews and their children Pat, Russ, and Alice.

In its first year the show dramatized an illegitimate pregnancy, an illegal abortion, and a murder and subsequent trial, all revolving around a single character Pat Matthews. (Fifteen years later, when Pat killed Greg Barnard in self-defense, the program ingeniously flashed back to the Tom Baxter murder.) Phillips tried her hand at describing a youthful romance between Bill Matthews and the orphaned Missy Palmer ("adopted" by the Matthews), and in an unusual move, the character of Mike Bauer was recruited from another Procter & Gamble soap, *The Guiding Light*. Mike became involved with Pat, and then with John's daughter, Lee Randolph, before returning to Springfield.

Phillips, more at home with the domestic drama and homey philosophy of *As the World Turns*, was clearly out of her element in the exotic melodrama she had created. Amid rumors of early cancellation, James Lipton became the new headwriter. Lipton introduced his own set of characters, putting the Matthews family on a back burner. Subsequently, the ratings floundered even more. Agnes Nixon took over and *Another World* soon took off.

Nixon killed off Lipton's characters in a plane crash and brought the Matthews family back into the story. The show began to broadcast in color just as the characters became less black and white: Nixon introduced the ambitious, complex Steve Frame and paired him with the passively sweet Alice Matthews, then created Rachel Davis, a girl from the wrong side of the tracks, who became obsessed with Steve and soon insinuated herself into the Matthews' lives by marrying Alice's brother Russ. The ingeniously written romantic triangle and the exciting chemistry among George Reinholt as Steve, Jacqueline Courtney as Alice, and Robin Strasser as Rachel had audiences flocking to the show. In just a short time *Another World* rose to the number-two position in the ratings, an unprecedented jump. Nixon, who had created what was to become soap opera's most famous and longest-running love triangle, was grabbed by ABC to create some winners for them, which she promptly agreed to, producing *One Life to Live* in 1968 and *All My Children* two years later.

Robert Cenedella served as *Another World*'s next headwriter, developing Nixon's strong storylines and throwing in some of his own melodrama. In 1970 the show was the first to spin off another daytime soap opera. (Years before, *As The World Turns* had spun off *Our Private World*, a prime-time serial.) Titled *Another World-Somerset* at first, then *Somerset*, the spin-off had a respectable six-year run. Initially, Cenedella served as headwriter for both shows, but with the ratings falling on the mother show, P & G assigned Cenedella to work exclusively on the spin-off. (See SOMERSET.)

Looking for someone who could bring freshness and vitality to the show, P & G took a chance in hiring Harding Lemay, whose only previous soap experience was writing dialogue for the spooky Candian serial *Strange Paradise*. But Lemay's memoir *Inside, Looking Out*, a powerful examination of self and family which was nominated for a National Book Award, contained the ingredients of emotionally charged drama. Thus in 1971 began *Another World*'s golden age.

Lemay developed the Steve-Alice-Rachel triangle so intriguingly that it remained *Another World*'s major story for four years. The popular Robin Strasser left the role of Rachel to pursue other acting opportunities, but when her replacement did not work out she returned for six months. Finally, Victoria Wyndham was cast in the part. Lemay, fascinated with the character and the actress now playing her, slowly began to change the character of Rachel from villainess to vindicated heroine. Rachel soon became the focus of the serial and Wyndham its new star. Lemay introduced a new villainess, Iris Carrington, and her doting, playboy father, Mac Cory, whom the new Rachel became involved with, to Iris's great chagrin.

As the show shifted its emphasis away from Courtney and Reinholt, who had brought *Another World* its initial popularity, trouble brewed backstage. Reinholt was reported to be "difficult" to work with, but the actor insisted he merely wanted to change some ludicrous inconsistencies in the script and his "perfectionism" could only help the show. On January 6, 1975, *Another World* became the first daytime soap to expand to an hour, causing more tension on the already troubled set. George Reinholt, whose performances had recently become unappealingly mannered, was fired, as Steve was reported killed in a helicopter crash in Australia. Jacqueline Courtney, whose acting Lemay deemed too "soap operaish," was also let go and the role of Alice was recast. For the first time the fan magazines refused to whitewash the firings and the subsequent brouhaha. Their honest treatment of the backstage shenanigans was instrumental in raising the journalistic standards of the soap opera press. Courtney and Reinholt joined the cast of *One Life to Live* and became nearly as popular in their new roles.

With *Another World* enjoying huge ratings and sweeping the Emmies, Lemay and producer Paul Rauch endeavored to change the show into something even more distinctive. Rauch brought in the most elegant sets and costuming daytime television had ever known. Rauch and Lemay, both from theater backgrounds, hired dozens of the best actors and directors from the New York stage, including Douglass Watson (Emmy winner 1980 and 1981), Irene Dailey (Emmy winner 1979), Beverlee McKinsey (Emmy nominee 1977, 1978, 1979, 1980), and Anne Meacham (the star of several Tennessee Williams plays; Williams was one of *Another World*'s biggest fans). These performers joined theater legend Constance Ford and several talented young actors to form the finest cast ever assembled for a television serial.

Ringing a variation on the "another world" theme, Lemay introduced one member after another of the poor Frame family—Emma, Willis, Sharlene, Vince, Janice, and cousin Molly—who ambitiously yearned for the "other world" that Bay City and the Matthews family represented. These characters, based on Lemay's own large family, were juxtaposed against the rich Corys and the established, well-loved Matthews family. The show soon evolved into a drawing-room drama—theater derived from domestic battling, class distinction (though sidestepping relevant social issues), and, most emphatically, doomed romances. At times *Another World* resembled an American *Smiles of a Summer Night* with its insistence on romantic mismatches and a roundelay of love.

Another World's popularity continued for years but the inflated ratings due to several melodramatic storylines (inevitably ending in murder and a subsequent trial) went against the show's own theatrical grain and violated its long-standing avoidance of soap opera clichés such as amnesia, blindness, and courtroom drama. The serial also had continuity problems, beginning with the dismissal of Jacquie Courtney and Virginia Dwyer, who as Alice and Mary Matthews were the show's cornerstones. Restless stage actors came and went, to the displeasure of an audience who became loyal to a performer only to see the role recast or written out. Lemay also had problems writing for the young; and inexperienced but talented actors—such as Eric Roberts, who played Ted Bancroft—were cavalierly dismissed.

Another World had a final blast of popularity in 1978 when housekeeper Sven wreaked havoc in the Cory home and terrorized the hapless Rachel for weeks. In a matter of months the ratings rose to take the show to number one, and then fell to number nine, as *Another World* lost about three million viewers to *General Hospital*, which was making a strong comeback.

On March 5, 1979, P & G and Paul Rauch, undaunted by *Another World*'s erratic ratings, boldly lengthened the show to an unprecedented ninety minutes. Later that year they replaced Harding Lemay as headwriter with associate writer Tom King and Robert Soderberg, who had been with *As the World Turns* for five years. The last of the Frames were written out and the rich, troubled Halloway family were written in, then quickly written out again. More action stories were developed, including cultism, kidnapping, and gambling, and many other soap staples were reinstated such as car crashes and long, drawn-out hospital operations. Only one story was successful: the introduction of Mitch Blake, his seduction of Rachel, and the romantic intrigue that followed the Caribbean melodrama. (*Another World* had been desperately trying to find someone who could realistically break up Rachel's intransigent devotion to Mac. They found an excellent, if short-lived, antihero in William Grey Espy's moody Mitch Blake.)

The show was cut back to an hour on August 4, 1980, to make room for *Another World*'s second spin-off, *Texas*. (The show also had two "unofficial" spin-offs, produced by Paul Rauch and created by Harding Lemay. See LOVERS AND FRIENDS and FOR RICHER, FOR POORER; also see TEXAS.) Later, the show went through a series of writing changes. L. Virginia Browne emphasized the younger characters, focusing on Jamie, the baby who had caused all that trouble between Steve, Rachel, and Alice years before. The hard-working Richard Bekins (at one point he appeared in

267 straight episodes) gave a striking performance as the drug-addicted Jamie, who became involved with the two-timing Cecile, a dead ringer for the old Rachel.

Headwriter Corinne Jacker brought Steve back from the dead (he was *not* killed in the helicopter crash in Australia; he'd had amnesia), reactivated the old Steve-Rachel-Alice triangle, but failed to bring up the ratings. *Another World* plodded on; Jacker succeeded in finally integrating Bay City, but the new black characters were saddled with mediocre material. In 1983, Allen Potter, *Another World*'s first producer, replaced Rauch, and Robert Soderberg, who had taken over as headwriter for Jacker, was replaced by Dorothy Ann Purser. *Another World*, the lowest-rated hour soap, was clearly in transition, searching for the formula that would restore it to its former grandeur.

The May 4, 1984, episode celebrated the show's twentieth anniversary with the reintroduction of Jacquie Courtney as Alice Matthews Frame. There was a new optimism in the air, especially when Richard Culliton, the headwriter who had done wonderful things with *Guiding Light*, began to pull the meandering storylines together while bringing back humor, energy, and style to the show. *Another World* became popular with fans again as the show zeroed in on the star-crossed romance of Sally (Alice's adopted daughter) and the flamboyantly sullen Catlin Ewing.

However, the show did not use Courtney as effectively as hoped (Alice became instead a sympathetic ear to daughter Sally) and the actress left after a year. *Another World* also could not hold on to talented performers who played the pivotal villains Carl and Cecile ("As God is my witness, I'll never tell the truth again!") But others were groomed to fill their formidable boots, and the pleasing storylines continued around two "core" families, the blue-blood Love family and the middle-class McKinnons. Rachel and Mac still found themselves in the thick of the drama, but after two decades the Matthews family was merely a memory.

The regime of new executive producer John P. Whitesell II and headwriter Margaret DePriest brought a new head of steam to the show: the return of Mitch Blake; the casting of superstar Denise Alexander as Mary McKinnon and John Considine as the villainous Reginald Love; an exciting serial-killer mystery (similar to the Salem Strangler and Salem Slasher stories DePriest introduced on *Days of Our Lives*); and an endless parade of male pulchritude. The overload of new characters confused the audience at first, but the ratings, for the first time in years, began to climb.

Harding Lemay has written a fascinating book about his experiences on the show, *Eight Years in Another World* (Atheneum, 1981).

CAST

Rachel Davis	Victoria Wyndham 1972–
	Margaret Impert 1971
	Robin Strasser 1967–71; 1972
Mackenzie Cory	Douglass Watson 1974–
	Robert Emhardt 1973
Ada Davis	Constance Ford 1967–

Jim Matthews	Hugh Marlowe 1969–82
	Shepperd Strudwick 1965–69
	Leon Janney 1964–65
	John Beal 1964
Mary Matthews	Virginia Dwyer 1964–75
Liz Matthews	Irene Dailey 1974–86
	Nancy Wickwire 1969–71
	Audra Lindley 1964–69
	Sara Cunningham 1964
Bill Matthews	Joseph Gallison 1964–68
Pat Matthews	Beverly Penberthy 1967–82
	Susan Trustman 1964–66
Dr. Alice Matthews Frame	Jacqueline Courtney 1964–75; 1984–85
	Linda Borgeson 1981–82
	Vana Tribbey 1981
	Wesley Ann Pfenning 1979
	Susan Harney 1976–79
Dr. Russ Matthews	David Bailey 1973–81
	Robert Hover 1971–72
	Sam Groom 1966–71
	Joey Trent 1964
Grandmother Matthews	Vera Allen 1964
Janet Matthews	Liza Chapman 1964–65
Missy Palmer	Carol Roux 1964–70
Ken Baxter	William Prince 1964–65
Laura Baxter	Augusta Dabney 1964–65
Tom Baxter	Nicholas Pryor 1964
Fred Douglas	Charles Baxter 1964–71
Emily Hastings	Mona Bruns 1966
Michael Bauer	Gary Pillar (Carpenter) 1966–67
Hope Bauer	Elissa Leeds 1966
John Randolph	Michael M. Ryan 1964–79
Lee Randolph	Barbara Rodell 1967–69
	Gaye Huston 1964–67
Michael Randolph	Lionel Johnston 1975–79
	Christopher J. Brown 1974
	Glen Zachar 1974
	Tom Sabota, Jr. 1974
	Tom Ruger 1972–73
	Tim Nissen 1972
	Christopher Corwin 1971
	John Sullivan 1971
	Dennis Sullivan 1970
Marianne Randolph	Beth Collins 1980–81
	Adrienne Wallace 1977–79
	Ariane Munker 1975–77
	Tiberia Mitri 1974-75

Marianne Randolph *(cont.)*	Jill Turnball 1973–74
	Loriann Ruger 1972–73
	Tracey Brown 1971
	Lora McDonald 1971
	Jeanne Beirne 1970
Danny Fargo	Antony Ponzini 1966–67
Madge Murray	Doris Belack 1966–67
Flo Murray	Marcella Martin 1966–67
Helen Moore	Murial Williams 1966–73
Lenore Moore	Susan Sullivan 1971–76
	Judith Barcroft 1966–71
Walter Curtin	Val Dufour 1967–72
Katherine Corning	Ann Sheridan 1965–66
Peggy Harris Nolan	Micki Grant 1966–73
Sam Lucas	Jordan Charney 1967–70; 1974
Lahoma Vane Lucas	Ann Wedgeworth 1967–70
Lefty Burns	Lawrence Keith 1967-68
Dr. Dan Shearer	Brian Murray 1978–79
	John Cunningham 1970–71
Susan Matthews Shearer	Lynn Milgrim 1978–79; 1982–83
	Lisa Cameron 1969–71
	Roni Dengel 1964
	Fran Sharon 1964
Steve Frame	David Canary 1981–83
	George Reinholt 1968–75
Jamie Frame	Laurence Lau 1986–
	Stephen Yates 1983–85
	Richard Bekins 1979–83
	Tim Holcomb 1978–79
	Bobby Doran 1975–78
	Brad Bedford 1973
	Tyler Mead 1973
	Aiden McNulty 1972–73
	Seth Holzlein 1970
Willis Frame	Leon Russom 1976–80
	John Fitzpatrick 1975–76
Emma Frame Ordway	Tresa Hughes 1976–79
	Beverlee McKinsey 1972
Sharlene Frame Matthews	Laurie Heineman 1975–77
Vince Frame	Jay Morran 1978–79
Janice Frame Cory	Christine Jones 1978–80
	Victoria Thompson 1972–74
Molly Ordway	Rolanda Mendels 1975–78
Cindy Clark	Leonie Norton 1970–72
Ted Clark	Stephen Bolster 1971–73
Caroline Johnson	Rue McClanahan 1970–71
Gerald Davis	Walter Matthews 1972–73
Gil McGowan	Dolph Sweet 1972–77
	Charles Durning 1972

Robert Delaney	Nicolas Coster 1972–76; 1980
Iris Cory Bancroft	Beverlee McKinsey 1972–80
Eliot Carrington	James Douglas 1972–74
	Joe Hannaham 1972
Dennis Carrington	Jim Poyner 1978–80
	Mike Hammett 1972–78
Louise Goddard	Anne Meacham 1972–82
Vic Hastings	John Considine 1974–82
Carol Lamonte	Jeanne Lange 1974–76
Therese Lamonte	Nancy Marchand 1976
Sally Frame	Taylor Miller 1985–86
	Mary Page Keller 1983–85
	Dawn Benz 1983
	Jennifer Runyon 1981–83
	Julie Philips 1979–80
	Cathy Greene 1975–78
Beatrice Gordon	Jacqueline Brookes 1975–77
Raymond Gordon	Gary Carpenter (Pillar) 1977
	Ted Shackelford 1975–77
Olive Gordon Randolph	Jennifer Leak 1976–79
Jeff Stone	Dan Hamilton 1977–79
Burt McGowan	William Russ 1978
	Joseph Hindy 1977–78
Tim McGowan	Christopher Allport 1973–74
Clarice Hobson	Gail Brown 1975–86
Charlie Hobson	Fred J. Scollay 1977–81
Leigh Hobson	Christopher Knight 1981
Denny Hobson	James Horan 1981–82
Dr. Dave Gilcrist	David Ackroyd 1974–77
Brian Bancroft	Paul Stevens 1977–85
Ted Bancroft	Luke Reilly 1983–84
	Richard Backus 1979
	Eric Roberts 1977
Tracy DeWitt	Janice Lynde 1979–81
	Caroline McWilliams 1975
Evan Webster	Barry Jenner 1976–77
Rocky Olsen	John Braden 1975–77
(Leonard) Brooks	John Tillinger 1978–82
	John Horton 1977–78
Leueen Parrish	Margaret Barker 1978
Gwen Parrish Frame	Dorothy Lyman 1976–80
Angie Perrini Frame	Maeve Kinkead 1977–80
	Toni Kalem 1975–77
Rose Perrini	Kathleen Widdoes 1978–80
Joey Perrini	Ray Liotta 1978–81
	Paul Perri 1978
Eileen Simpson	Vicky Dawson 1978–79
Sven Petersen	Roberts Blossom 1977–78
Helga Lindeman	Helen Stenborg 1977–78

Regine Lindeman	Barbara Eda-Young 1977–78
Elena de Poulignac	Maeve McGuire 1981–82
	Christina Pickles 1977–79
Cecile de Poulignac	Nancy Frangione 1981–84; 1986
	Susan Keith 1979–81
Joan Barnard	Patricia Estrin 1977–78
Greg Barnard	Ned Schmidtke 1977–78
Vivien Gorrow	Gretchen Oehler 1978–84
Renaldo	Julius La Rosa 1980
Larry Ewing	Richard J. Porter 1978–86
Blaine Ewing	Judy Dewey 1984–85
	Laura Malone 1978–84
Buzz Winslow	Eric Conger 1978–80; 1982
Sylvie Kosloff	Leora Dana 1978–79
Kirk Laverty	Charles Cioffi 1979
June Laverty	Geraldine Court 1979
Philip Lyons	Robert Gentry 1979–81
Mitch Blake	William Grey Espy 1980–82; 1986–
Jason Dunlap	Warren Burton 1980–82
Kit Halloway	Bradley Bliss 1979–82
Dr. Rick Halloway	Tony Cummings 1980–82
Amy Halloway	Deborah Hobart 1980
Taylor Halloway	Ron Harper 1980
Miranda Bishop	Judith McConnell 1980–81
Zachary Colton	Curt Dawson 1980–81
Jerry Grove	Paul Tinder 1981–82
	Kevin Conroy 1980–81
	Michael Garfield 1979–80
Jordan Scott	J. Kenneth Campbell 1980–81
Vic Strang	Ben Masters 1982
Ilsa Fredericks	Gwyda DonHowe 1981–82
Melissa Needham	Taro Meyer 1980–82
Sandy (Alexander) Cory	Christopher Rich 1981–85
Dr. Oliva Delaney	Tina Sloan 1980–81
Diana Frame Shea	Anne Rose Brooks 1981–82
Pete Shea	Christopher Marcantel 1981–82
Loretta Shea	Anita Gillette 1982
Harry Shea	Ed Power 1981–82
Quinn Harding	Petronia Paley 1981–87
Ed Harding	Howard E. Rollins, Jr. 1982
Thomasina Harding	Pamela G. Kay 1984–86; 1987
	Shelia Spencer 1982–83
Lt. Bob Morgan	Robert Christian 1982–83
Henrietta Morgan	Michelle Shay 1982–84
R. J. Morgan	Reggie Rock Blythewood 1981–83
Mary Sue Morgan	Tisha M. Ford 1983
Anne Whitelaw	Mary Joan Negro 1981–82
Julia Shearer	Faith Ford 1983–84
	Jonna Leigh 1983

Julia Shearer (*cont.*)	Kyra Sedgwick 1982–83
Louis St. George	Jack Betts 1982–83
Reuben Marino	Jose Ferrer 1983
Cass Winthrop	Stephen Schnetzer 1982–86; 1987–
Stacey Winthrop	Terry Davis 1982–83
Marie Fenton	Lenka Peterson 1983
Gil Fenton	Tom Wiggin 1983–84
Felicia Gallant	Linda Dano 1983–
Miss Devon	Evalyn Baron 1983–84
Peter Love	Marcus Smythe 1985–
	Christopher Holder 1985
	John Hutton 1982–84
Donna Love	Philece Sampler 1987–
	Anna Stuart 1983–86
Nicole Love	Laurie Landry 1986–1987
	Kim Morgan Greene 1983–84
Marley Love	Ellen Wheeler 1984–86
Victoria Love	Ann Heche 1987–
	Rhonda Lewin 1986–87
	Ellen Wheeler 1985–86
Perry Hutchins	David Oliver 1983–85
Carl Hutchins	Charles Keating 1983–86
Roy Bingham	Morgan Freeman 1982–84
Lily Mason	Jackee Harry 1983–86
Dr. Abel Marsh	Joe Morton 1983–84
Leo Marsh	Joe Morton 1983–84
Mark Singleton	Robin Thomas 1983–85
Alma Rudder	Elizabeth Franz 1982–83
Ella Fitz	Lois Smith 1982–83
Jeanne Ewing	Melissa Luciano 1982–83
Catlin Ewing	Thomas Ian Griffith 1984–87
Maisie Watkins	Patricia Hodges 1982–87
David Thatcher	Lewis Arlt 1983–84
Jennifer Thatcher	Sofia Landon 1983
Dr. Royal Dunning	Michael Minor 1983–84
Emily Benson, R.N.	Alex (Dianne) Neil 1984–85
M. J. McKinnon	Sally Spencer 1986–87
	Kathleen Layman 1984–86
Ben McKinnon	Richard Steen 1984–85
Kathleen McKinnon	Julie Osburn 1984–86
Carter Todd	Russell Curry 1984–86
Grant Todd	John Dewey-Carter 1984–85
Nancy McGowan	Jane Cameron 1984–87
	Danielle Burns 1974–83
Wallingford	Brent Collins 1984–
Vince McKinnon	Robert Hogan 1987–
	Duke Stroud 1986
	Jack Ryland 1984–85
Hunter Bradshaw	Robert Sedgwick 1984–85

Tony the Tuna	George Pentecost 1984–86; 1987
Dee Evans	Katie Rich 1985–86
Jake McKinnon	Tom Eplin 1985–86
Bridget Connell	Barbara Berjer 1985–
Brittany Peterson	Sharon Gabet 1985–87
Zane Lindquist	Patrick Tovatt 1985–86
Michaud Christophe	Serge Dupire 1985
Daphne Grimaldi	Liliana Komorowska 1985
Daniel Gabriel	Peter Lochran 1985–86
Edward Gerald	John Saxon 1985–86
Dr. Chris Chapin	Don Scardino 1985–86
Neal Cory	Robert LuPone 1985–86
Adam Cory	Ed Fry 1986–
Michael Hudson	Kale Browne 1986–
John Hudson	David Forsyth 1987–
Reginald Love	John Considine 1986–
Mary McKinnon	Denise Alexander 1986–
Scott LaSalle	Hank Cheyne 1986–
Cheryl McKinnon	Kristen Marie 1986–
Tony Carlise	John H. Brennan 1986–87
Greg Houston	Christopher Cousins 1986–87
Chad Rollo	Richard Burgi 1986–
Sara Montaigne	Missy Hughes 1986–87
Rose Livingston	Ann Flood 1986–87
Peggy Lazaras	Rebecca Hollen 1986–
Zack Edwards	James Pickens, Jr. 1986–
Lisa Grady	Joanna Going 1987–
Dr. Alan Glaser	David O'Brien 1987

AS THE WORLD TURNS

April 2, 1956–   CBS

The top-rated soap from 1959 to 1971 and winner of high ratings and intense audience loyalty ever since, *As the World Turns* has been the most emulated and the most parodied (Carol Burnett's famous *As the Stomach Turns* skits) serial in the history of television. Procter & Gamble, who packaged the show, even took out a full-page ad in *The New York Times* in 1965 to boast of the soap opera's seemingly invincible status. How and why did this slow-moving, introspective "day-to-day story of the affections that bind and conflicts that threaten two closely related families in an American community"—as the drama described itself in 1956—strike such a responsive chord with the American public? The answer can be summed up in two words: Irna Phillips.

With the successful transference of *The Guiding Light* from radio to television in 1952, Phillips, the dominant force in serial programing, began lobbying P & G to launch her new project, a totally different concept in daytime drama, not pre-sold by radio, which would run an unheard-of thirty minutes. Early television soaps were essentially kinescope versions of radio programs—wordy, overmelodramatic fifteen-minute episodes that separated characters into neat piles of good and bad. Phillips sensed the dramatic possibilities of the new medium, but P & G remained unexcited about *As the World Turns* and only gave in to Phillips when they realized that this irascible woman was not going to abandon her pet project.

As the World Turns, which premiered the same day as the crime melodrama *The Edge of Night*, revolutionized the approach to serial drama by concentrating on a leisurely, visual emphasis on character in lieu of action. It was an approach perfectly suited to television. There were long conversations, more close-ups, flawed "good" characters, and ambiguous dialogue that had viewers guessing what was happening under the surface, and why. The cameras caught the subtleties, ironies, and domestic wit. What are now considered soap opera clichés—people chatting over continuous cups of coffee, pregnant pauses, long close-ups precipitating fade-out—were strikingly original. As more dramatic ambiguities were developed, audiences felt their loyalties divided and challenged. By the end of its first year, with Phillips and Agnes Nixon writing and Ted Corday handling the directing and production chores, the live show was a certified hit.

Set in Oakdale, a small town in Illinois, *As the World Turns* centered on two families, the Hughes and the Lowells. The Hughes family included Grandpa Hughes; his free-spirited daughter Edith; son Chris; Chris's wife Nancy; and their four children, Donald, Penny, Bob, and Susan. (Susan died in a freak accident, hit by lightning while swimming.) The Lowells included Judge Lowell, his unhappily married son Jim; Jim's wife Claire; and their daughter Ellen.

The "liberated" Edith, played by Hollywood actress Ruth Warrick, was the pivotal character early in the show's run. Her affair with Jim Lowell and her influence over her niece Penny caused emotional upheaval in both households, but the focus switched to the younger characters after Jim Lowell's death. Jim's daughter Ellen had a son (Dan Stewart) out of wedlock and gave him up for adoption, eventually claiming him years later. Ellen's best friend, Penny Hughes, took up with Jeff Baker despite her parents' warning that she was too young.

The Penny and Jeff story was enormously popular, becoming daytime's first major youth romance and creating soap opera's first stars, Rosemary Prinz and Mark Rydell. Penny and Jeff's first marriage was annulled, but they were married again, all the while beset with problems: Jeff's trial for murder, Penny's miscarriage, Jeff's alcoholism and his eventual desertion of his family. In 1962 Rydell wanted to leave the show to become a film director and it was decided that the actor was too firmly identified with the role for it to be recast. On August 23, just as a reunited Jeff and Penny were about to adopt a baby, Jeff was killed in a car accident. A storm of protest over Jeff's death erupted from viewers, with telephone calls, telegrams, and letters (one women sent ninety-seven) flooding the network. Television executives were astounded by the unprecedented response, which reminded them again how potent soap opera could be. The characters of *As the World Turns* had become like second families to millions, and *TV Guide* called the uproar the "automobile accident that shook the nation."

Meanwhile, in 1960, Eileen Fulton created a sensation as Lisa Miller, the southern vixen who was to become the center of trouble for the next twenty years. Sparks began to fly when Fulton was paired with Don Hastings (the teen idol from *Captain Video*), who played nice guy Bob Hughes. Although Lisa was guilty of many lapses, nothing made her more hated by her audience of housewives than a simple sequence in which she hired a maid to clean house and went gallivanting about town. When mother-in-law Nancy complimented Lisa on what a nice home she had made for Bob, audiences were furious. Lisa (Miller Hughes Eldridge Shea Colman McColl Mitchell) went on to become television's most famous and longest-running villainess, but over the years she has mellowed considerably. In 1965 *As the World Turns* was the first soap opera to spin off another serial. *Our Private World*, with Fulton as its star, ran briefly in prime time. Fulton returned to daytime and *As the World Turns* two years later. (See OUR PRIVATE WORLD.)

During the '60s a second family was slowly integrated into the show as the Lowells were eased out, and more members of the Stewart family—David and Ellen (Lowell) Stewart, his son Paul, her son Dan, and their daughters Carol Ann (Annie) and Dawn (Dee)—played larger parts. The show continued to flourish, even though it lost its most popular heroine in 1968 when Rosemary Prinz left to pursue other acting opportunities. But the soap was delivered a blow in 1970 when Irna Phillips left, claiming illness. Many fans believed that her real reason for leaving was to secretly help her adopted daughter Katherine develop the ABC serial *A World Apart*.

When Phillips returned to *As the World Turns* two years later, the show had slipped in the ratings. The new writers had created a complex, vaguely incestuous story in which Dan Stewart was married to Susan, by whom he had a daughter (Emmie), and in love with his brother Paul's wife Elizabeth, by whom he also had a daughter (Betsy). The conservative audience did not cotton to sympathetically presented, adulterous, star-crossed romance. Phillips "solved" the problem by simply writing out these important characters. Paul died of a brain tumor while Elizabeth fell up (!) a staircase and died. Dan was sent packing to London while Susan was married off to the impotent Dr. Bruce Baxter; their union was soon annulled and Susan was sent out of town. These melodramatic twists not only failed to win back the audience but alienated viewers even more.

With the ratings plummeting, Phillips allowed Kim, one of her best-conceived characters, to seduce her sister's husband, Bob Hughes, and make plans to raise the child alone, out of wedlock. It was one thing for Bob to be manipulated by Lisa, but it was quite another for the leading man to have feet of clay, and to sleep with his wife's sister. When P & G saw major defections in audience loyalty in the summer of 1973, they fired Phillips. The creator and guiding light of this show and half a dozen other TV serials quietly retired to write her memoirs. She died shortly before Christmas of that year.

Robert Soderberg and Edith Sommer moved over from P & G's *The*

Guiding Light to become *As the World Turns'* new headwriters. The Soderbergs brought back some old favorites, created tantalizing new characters, and quickly reestablished the show's popular appeal without changing its conservative values. Kim, fiercely independent in Phillips' reign, was turned into a more traditional (i.e., long-suffering) heroine exploited by Dr. John Dixon, a highly complex man who became obsessed with her. Kim was exquisitely played by former model and popular prime-time actress Kathryn Hays and became the ostensible star of the show for the next five years. But the acting honors belonged to Larry Bryggman, a highly respected theater actor, who turned John Dixon's often cardboard villainy into understandable, haunting desperation. Reportedly Hays and Bryggman did not initially get along offstage, but their chemistry on camera resulted in some of the most heart-breaking pantomiming that television drama has ever known. A superb storyline, in which Kim fell in love with Dr. Dan Stewart but was thwarted at every turn by John and Dan's self-destructive ex-wife Susan (the beautiful powerhouse actress Marie Masters), ran for several years.

On December 1, 1975, *As the World Turns* expanded to an hour, and received top ratings for the next three years. The continuity remained strong, with more actors staying longer in their roles than in any soap then or since. The super-constructed stories continued to build slowly to a wallop of a finish for those who were patient. In a cover story on soap operas in 1976, *Time* magazine ridiculed *As the World Turns* for being overly bland, euphemistic, and reactionary. (In 1975 Dan had been courting Kim for months and finally confessed his love for her with nary a kiss, although their hands had once touched—on a doorknob.)

Procter & Gamble was beginning to feel that their show was a dinosaur amid all the free-living, barely clothed human animals having a ball on the ABC soaps and on CBS's *The Young and the Restless*. In the summer of 1978 the Soderbergs started to fall asleep at the helm, repeating a story on alcoholism and reworking other plots. Feeling pressure to "get with it," the show added a disco set and ran an unpopular storyline about a prostitute. The famous long scenes were cut in favor of fast-moving clips. Bedroom antics increased, but as the show moved faster, it lost its focus. The Soderbergs were replaced by another husband-and-wife team, Ralph Ellis and Eugenie Hunt, who had been writing dialogue for the show. The bottom soon dropped out of the show as long-running characters were written out, parts were recast, and a slew of dull characters were introduced. Eileen Fulton's Lisa was saddled with a gothic romance lifted straight out of *Jane Eyre*, and Don Hastings' Bob was seen hobnobbing about town with a boring ballerina.

Early in 1980, with the ratings dive-bombing, Jerome and Bridget Dobson, who had successfully contemporized *The Guiding Light* and brought that show its first Emmy as Outstanding Daytime Drama, were called in for emergency surgery. In addition to imaginative storylines, the Dobsons created a series of strong male characters which the female-dominated serial desperately needed, included a willfully sexy scene almost daily, and emphasized the younger characters. The Dobsons zeroed in on Larry Bryggman's John Dixon—by this time television's longest-running villain—in a series of dramatic turns, including matrimonial rape, blindness, and a faked death. Bryggman's brilliant performance and the Dobsons' excellent writing resulted in a complete and successful face lift for Oakdale.

But not all was happy on the set. Helen Wagner, who had played Nancy Hughes since 1956, suddenly quit shortly before the show's twenty-fifth anniversary, complaining that the older characters had just about disappeared from the show anyway. (She returned a couple of years later to attend grandson Tom's wedding, and returned full-time to the show shortly afterwards.) In a rather ill-advised move the Dobsons were replaced by K. C. Collier and Tom King, who managed to turn the Dobsons' carefully constructed storyline into a convoluted, spy-laden mess. After a year, the Dobsons returned to repair the damage and put the show back on course. John Saffron and Caroline Franz proved worthy successors.

Early in 1984, Saffron was replaced by the team of Tom King and former soap actress Millee Taggart (Janet Bergman, *Search for Tomorrow*), who concentrated on the romantic problems of teenagers Betsy Stewart (daughter of Dan and Elizabeth) and Frannie Hughes (daughter of Bob and Jennifer). Later that year, headwriters Cynthia Benjamin and Susan Bedsow Horgan refocused the show, continuing the "young love" plotlines but also giving the older core characters Bob, Kim, and Lisa their first real storylines in years. In April, 1985 Bob and Kim were married after an on-and-off courtship of twelve years. Joining in the celebration were favorites from the show's past, including Nancy Hughes, son Don, and, in an appearance after 17 years, Rosemary Prinz as Penny. The renovated *As the World Turns* was bursting with confidence—once again, a thoroughbred amid a field of barking mutts.

The show truly high-stepped into the heavens with the innovations of new executive producer Robert Calhoun and headwriter Douglas Marland. While Calhoun updated the production values, Marland reactivated the show's heritage with contemporary, surprising twists and turns. The return of the magnificent fortyish foursome (with all of its heartbreaking resonance)—Kim, Bob, Lisa, and John—played brilliantly against the Tracy-Hepburnesque banter of thirtyish Tom and Margo, the romantic longings of twentyish Craig and Sierra, and the randy confusion of the teens, Lily, Dusty, Holden, and Meg.

Overseeing all the intrigue from her drawing room and hot tub was rich-bitch Lucinda Walsh, a nasty cross between Lady Windermere and Lucretia Borgia. (We've never seen a gal so hungry for affection: you didn't know if she wanted to make love to James Stenbeck or merely eat him up.) Like Lucinda, you never knew exactly where *As the World Turns* was headed—except straight to the top.

CAST

Nancy Hughes	Helen Wagner 1956–
Chris Hughes	Don MacLaughlin 1956–86
Bob Hughes	Don Hastings 1960–
	Ronnie Welch 1958–60
	Bobby Alford 1956–58

Penny Hughes	Rosemary Prinz 1956–68; 1985; 1986–87
	Phoebe Dorin 1971
Donald Hughes	Conard Fowkes 1978–80; 1985; 1986
	Martin West 1977–78
	Peter Brandon 1966–72
	James Noble 1962
	Richard Holland 1956–62
	Hal Studer 1956
Grandpa Hughes	Santos Ortega 1956–76
	William Lee 1956
Edith Hughes	Ruth Warrick 1956–60
Jim Lowell	Les Damon 1956–57
Claire Lowell Cassen	Barbara Berjer 1965–71
	Jone Allison 1964–65
	Nancy Wickwire 1960–64
	Gertrude Warner 1960
	Anne Burr 1956–59
Judge Lowell	William Johnstone 1956–78
Ellen Lowell Stewart	Patricia Bruder 1960–
	Wendy Drew 1956–60
Jeff Baker	Mark Rydell 1956–62
Janice Turner Hughes	Virginia Dwyer 1962
	Joyce Van Patten 1956–57
Dr. Doug Cassen	Nat Polen 1956–67
Dr. Tim Cole	William Redfield 1958
Louise Cole	Mary K. Wells 1958
Lisa Miller	Eileen Fulton 1960–
	Betsy von Furstenberg 1983–84
	Pamela King 1964
Alma Miller	Dorothy Blackburn 1978
	Ethel Remey 1963–77
Tom Hughes	Scott Holmes 1987–
	Gregg Marx 1984–87
	Jason Kincaid 1984
	Justin Deas 1981–84
	Tom Tammi 1980
	C. David Colson 1973–78
	Peter Galman 1969–73
	Peter Link 1969
	Paul O'Keefe 1967–68
	Richard Thomas 1966–67
	Frankie Michaels 1964–66
	Jerry Schaffer 1963
	James Madden 1963
Dr. David Stewart	Henderson Forsythe 1960–
Betty Stewart	Patricia Benoit 1960–62
Dr. Paul Stewart	Dean Santoro 1970–71

Dr. Paul Stewart (*cont.*)	Marco St. John 1969
	Garson DeBramenio 1969
	Michael Hawkins 1968
	Steven Mines 1966–68
	Edmund Gaynes 1964–67
	Alan Howard 1962–64
Dr. Dan Stewart	John Colenback 1966–73; 1976–79
	John Reilly 1974–76
	Jeffrey Rowland 1966
	Doug Chapin 1964
	Paul O'Keefe 1962–63
Franny Brennan	Toni Darnay 1963–65
Mary Mitchell	Joan Anderson 1963–65
Jim Norman	James Broderick 1962
Bruce Elliott	James Pritchett 1962
Debbie Whipple	Kimetha Laurie 1962
	June Harding 1962
Alice Whipple	Leslie Charleson 1966
	Jean McClintock 1962
Dr. Neil Wade	Michael Lipton 1962–67
Judith Wade Stevens	Connie Lembcke 1964–67
Dr. Jerry Stevens	Roy Poole 1964–65
Sylvia Hill	Millette Alexander 1964–66
Dr. Al Suker	Michael Ingram 1964–66
Martha Suker	Ann Hegira 1964
Helene Suker	Jerrianne Raphael 1964
John Eldridge	Nicolas Coster 1966
Sara Fuller	Gloria DeHaven 1966–67
Joan Rogers	Joan Copeland 1966–67
Dick Martin	Edward Kemmer 1966–70; 1975–78
	Joe Maross 1966
Otto Martin	Allen Nourse 1966–68
Carl Wilson	Martin Rudy 1966–71
Martha Wilson	Anna Minot 1966–70
Ann Holmes	Augusta Dabney 1966–67
Bill Holmes	William Prince 1966–67
Amanda Holmes	Deborah Steinberg Soloman 1966–70
Dr. Jerry Turner	James Earl Jones 1966
Dr. Bellows	P. Jay Sidney 1967
	Brock Peters 1966
Sandy McGuire	Barbara Rucker 1975–79
	Ronnie Carrol 1975
	Jill Andre 1968
	Dagne Crane 1966–71
Roy McGuire	Konrad Matthaei 1966–68
Julia Burke	Fran Carlon 1968–75
Dr. Susan Burke Stewart	Marie Masters 1968–79; 1986–87

Dr. Susan Burke Stewart (*cont.*)	Judith Barcroft 1978
	Leslie Perkins 1968
	Jada Rowland 1967–68
	Diana Walker 1967
	Connie Scott 1966–67
Dr. Michael Shea	Roy Shuman 1968–70
	Jay Lanin 1966–67
Karen Adams	Doe Lang 1968–70
Elizabeth Talbot	Judith McGilligan 1972–73
	Jane House 1969–72
Ronnie Talbott	Curt Dawson 1973
	Peter Stuart 1970
Hank Barton	Gary Sandy 1970
Dr. John Dixon	Larry Bryggman 1969–
Carol Deming	Rita McLaughlin Walter 1970–81
Simon Gibley	Jerry Lacy 1971
Meredith Halliday	Nina Hart 1970–71
Ellie Bradley	Swoozie Kurtz 1971
Miss Peterson	Margaret Hamilton 1971
	Nancy Andrews 1971
Dr. Carol Ann Stewart ("Annie")	Mary Lynn Blanks 1982–84; 1986
	Randall Edwards 1982
	Julie Ridley 1980–82
	Martina Deignan 1976–79
	Shelley Spurlock 1973–74
	Ariane Munker 1972–73
	Barbara Jean Ehrhardt 1970–71
	Jean Mazza 1969–70
Dawn Stewart ("Dee")	Vicky Dawson 1982–83; 1986
	Jacqueline Schultz 1981–82
	Heather Cunningham 1980
	Marcia McClain 1976–78
	Glynnis O'Connor 1973
	Jean Mazza 1972–73
	Simone Schachter 1971
Betsy Stewart	Lindsay Frost 1984–
	Meg Ryan 1982–84
	Lisa Denton 1981–82
	Suzanne Davidson 1972–80
	Patricia McGuiness 1971
Emily Stewart	Melanie Smith 1987–
	Colleen McDermott 1986–87
	Jenny Harris 1975–79
Kim Reynolds	Kathryn Hays 1972–
	Patty McCormack 1975–76
Jennifer Ryan Hughes	Gillian Spencer 1972–75
	Geraldine Court 1971–72
Dr. Rick Ryan	Con Roche 1972–73; 1986–87
	Gary Hudson 1978

Barbara Ryan	Colleen Zenk 1978–
	Donna Wandrey 1971–72
Dr. Bruce Baxter	Ben Hayes 1972–73
	Steve Harmon 1972
Amy Hughes	Una Kim 1986–87
	Irene Yaah-Ling Sun 1973
Marian Graham	Laurie Heineman 1973
Jay Stallings	Dennis Cooney 1973–80
Grant Colman	James Douglas 1974–81; 1986
	Konrad Matthaei 1973–74
Joyce Colman	Barbara Rodell 1974–81
Mark Galloway	Anthony Herrera 1974–75
	Stephen Bolster 1974
Natalie Bannon Hughes	Janet Zarish 1981
	Judith Chapman 1975–77
Norman Garrison	Michael Minor 1975
Tina Richards	Toni Bull Bua 1975
Mary Ellison	Kelly Wood 1975–80
Brian Ellison	Robert Hover 1975
Pat Holland Dixon, R.N.	Melinda Peterson 1976–77
Marion Connelly, R.N.	Clarice Blackburn 1976–78
Kevin Thompson	Max Brown 1978
	Michael Nader 1976–78
Nick Conway	Douglas Travis 1978
Valerie Conway	Judith McConnell 1976–79
Jane Spencer	Georgann Johnson 1977–79
Beau Spencer	Wayne Hudgins 1977–79
Melinda Gray Spencer	Ariane Munker 1978–80
Ralph Mitchell	Keith Charles 1977–79
Dr. Alex Keith	Jon Cypher 1977–79
Karen Peters	Leslie Denniston 1978
Tina Cornell	Rebecca Hollen 1978
Dr. Jeff Ward	Robert Lipton 1978–84
Bennett Hadley	Doug Higgins 1979
Dana McFarland	Deborah Hobart 1979
Ian McFarland	Peter Simon 1979–80
Brad Hollister	Peter Brouwer 1980–81
Eric Hollister	Peter Reckell 1980–81
James Stenbeck	Anthony Herrera 1980–83; 1986–87
Nels Andersson	Einar Perry Scott 1980–84
Nick Andropolous	Michael Forest 1980–82
Steve Andropolous	Frank Runyeon 1980–86
Margo Montgomery	Hillary Bailey 1983–
	Margaret Colin 1981–83
Cricket Montgomery	Lisa Loring 1981–83
Craig Montgomery	Scott Bryce 1982–87
Lyla Montgomery, R.N.	Anne Sward 1981–
	Velek(k)a Gray 1980

Maggie Crawford	Mary Linda Rapeleye 1981–85
Haley Wilson	Dana Delany 1981
Cynthia Haines	Linda Dano 1981–82
Karen Haines	Kathy McNeil 1981–84
Miranda Marlowe	Elaine Princi 1981–82
Gunnar Stenbeck	Hugo Napier 1982–84
Ariel Aldrin	Judith Blazer 1982–83
Greta Aldrin	Joan Copeland 1983
Mr. Big	Brent Collins 1983
Whit McColl	Robert Horton 1982–84
Brian McColl	Mark Pinter 1984–87
	Frank Telfer 1983–84
	Robert Burton 1982
Kirk McColl	Christian J. LeBlanc 1983–85
Diana McColl	Kim Ulrich 1983–85
Charmane McColl	Lee Meredith 1983–84
Frannie Hughes	Julianne Moore 1985–
	Terri VandenBosch 1983–84
	Helene Udy 1983
	Tracy O'Neil 1980
	Maura Gilligan 1975–78
	Kelly Campbell 1973
Burke Donovan	David Forsyth 1983
Dustin Donovan	Brian Bloom 1983–
Paul Stenbeck	Andrew Kavovit 1986–
	C. B. Barnes 1985–86
	Danny Pintauro 1983–84
Frank Andropolous	Jacques Perreault 1983–85
Tucker Foster	Eddie Earl Hatch 1982–85
Samantha Jones	Juanita Mahone 1983
Heather Dalton	Tonya Pinkins 1984–86
Marcy Thompson	Marisa Tomei 1983–85
Dr. Zach Stone	Leon Russom 1983
Stan Holden	W. T. Martin 1981–82
Richard Fairchild III	Norman Snow 1983
Lonnie	Matthew Cowles 1983
Dorothy Connors	Nancy Pinkerton 1983–84
Jay Connors	Breck Jamison 1983–86
Lucinda Walsh	Elizabeth Hubbard 1984–
Lily Walsh	Martha Byrne 1985–
	Lucy Deakins 1984–85
Juliet Hanovan	Tracy Kolis 1984
Kent Bradford	Ernest Townsend 1984
Raymond Speer	Donald May 1984
Michael Christopher	Harris Yulin 1984–85
Dr. Russ Elliot	Richard Backus 1984–85
Cal Randolph	Luke Reilly 1984–85
Lord Markham Cushing	Ross Kettle 1985
Sierra Estaben	Finn Carter 1985–

Rick Putnam	Tony Cummings 1985
Shannon O'Hara	Margaret Reed 1985–
Harriet Corbman	Sloane Shelton 1985–
Kevin Gibson	Steven Weber 1985–86
Marie Kovac	Mady Kaplan 1985
Douglas Cummings	John Wesley Shipp 1985–86
Marsha Talbot	Giulia Pagano 1985–86
Hal Munson	Benjamin Hendrickson 1985–
Holden Snyder	Jon Hensley 1985–
Iva Snyder	Lisa Brown 1985–
Emma Snyder	Kathleen Widdoes 1985–
Meg Snyder	Jennifer Ashe 1986–
Seth Snyder	Steve Bassett 1986–
Tad Channing	Larry Pine 1986
Tonio Reyes	Peter Boynton 1986–
Earl Mitchell	Farley Granger 1986–
Duncan McKechnie	Michael Swan 1986–
Beatrice McKechnie	
McColl	Ashley Crow 1986–87
Roy Franklin	Count Stovall 1985–
Dr. Casey Peretti	Bill Shanks 1986–
Sabrina Hughes	Julianne Moore 1986–
Andrew Dixon	Scott DeFreitas 1985–
	Sean Anthony 1984
	Alfie Smith 1982
	Robert Dwyer 1980
	Jason Ferguson 1976–79
Jessica Griffin	Tamara Tunie 1987–
Rod Landry	William Fichtner 1987–
Taylor Baldwin	Maggie Baird 1987–

BARE ESSENCE

February 15, 1983–June 13, 1983   NBC

Former *General Hospital* star Genie Francis's first project on her CBS contract was the two-part, four-hour TV movie *Bare Essence*, about intrigue in the perfume business. Airing in October 1982 and co-starring Linda Evans, Donna Mills, and Lee Grant, it received excellent ratings, but CBS passed on a proposed serial version. NBC picked up on the project and promoted it heavily ("Love her. Use her. Or destroy her. Everyone wants a piece of Tyger Hayes.") Despite an appealingly energetic performance by Genie Francis as Tyger (née Patricia Louise), *Bare Essence* failed to win an audience in its reincarnated form.

Produced and directed by Walter Grauman and turgidly written by Robert Hamilton, with a helpful, but tardy assist from the gifted Pat Falken Smith, *Bare Essence* was a routine story of murder and family mayhem. (One columnist called it *Bare Minimum*.) On the first episode, Chase, Tyger's new husband, was killed in a racing car accident—an accident orchestrated, one learned in the final installment, by Muffin, a jealous in-law. Such talents as Jessica Walter, as stock villainess (obviously modeled on Joan Collins's Alexis in *Dynasty*), and Jaime Lyn Bauer (Laura-lee Brooks on *The Young and the Restless*, 1973–82) were wasted in this lifeless melodrama. After cancellation, Genie Francis returned to *General Hospital* to finish up soap opera's most famous storyline.

CAST

Tyger Hayes	Genie Francis
Chase Marshall	Al Corley
Ava Marshall	Jessica Walter
Lady Bobbi Rowan	Jennifer O'Neill
Niko Theopolous	Ian McShane
Alexi Theopolous	Michael Nader
Hadden Marshall	John Dehner
Margaret Marshall	Susan French
Marcus Marshall	Jonathan Frakes
Muffin Marshall	Wendy Fulton
Barbara Fisher	Jaime Lyn Bauer
Larry Devito	Morgan Stevens
Robert Spencer	Ted LePlat
Alan	Richard Backus
Sean Benedict	Michael Woods

BEACON HILL

August 25, 1975–November 4, 1975   CBS

Modeled closely on the hit British serial *Upstairs, Downstairs, Beacon Hill* was the most touted prime-time soap since the Lana Turner–George Hamilton debacle *The Survivors*. Set in Boston after World War I, it dramatized the contrast between the lives of the Lassiters, a rich Irish family, and their servants, poor Irish immigrants. Despite a lavish production (the premiere episode cost $900,000) and an impressive audience for the opener (a whopping 43% of people watching TV were tuned in to this show), the show could not sustain viewer interest. The overly large cast and fragmented stories did not allow the audience to get its bearings, and CBS cancelled the show after only eleven episodes. Two episodes were never aired. The music was by Marvin Hamlisch, who had just picked up three Oscars for *The Sting* and *The Way We Were*. Produced by Jacqueline Babbin (later of *All My Children*), the splendid cast included many daytime drama favorites.

CAST

Benjamin Lassiter	Stephen Elliott
Mary Lassiter	Nancy Marchand
Maude Palmer	Maeve McGuire
Richard Palmer	Edward Herrmann
Brian Mallory	Paul Rudd

Fawn Lassiter	Kathryn Walker
Robert Lassiter	David Dukes
Emily Bullock	DeAnn Mears
Trevor Bullock	Roy Cooper
Betsy Bullock	Linda Purl
Rosamund Lassiter	Kitty Winn
Giorgio Balanci	Michael Nouri
Emmaline Hacker	Beatrice Straight
Mr. Hacker	George Rose
Terence O'Hara	David Rounds
Marilyn Gardiner	Holland Taylor
Maureen Mahaffey	Susan Blanchard
Kate Mahaffey	Lisa Pelikan
William Piper	Richard Ward
Grant Piper	Don Blakely

BEHIND THE SCREEN

October 9, 1981–January 8, 1982   CBS

Created by David Jacobs (*Dallas*, *Knots Landing*) and produced by Cathy Abbi (*Love of Life*), this late-night weekly serial (Fridays, 11:30, E.S.T.) was by no means the first show to use a soap opera as a setting. As early as 1949 TV's *A Woman to Remember* dramatized the backstage doings of a radio soap. Similarly, *Ryan's Hope* used the soap opera within a soap opera technique presenting the story of Barbara Wilde in 1981. Launched with an hour-long special (thirty-five-minute episodes afterwards), *Behind the Screen* was set in and out of the studios of the youth serial *Generations*.

The center of attention was its vulnerable young star Janie-Claire, whose powerful agent Evan, wheelchair-confined mother Zina, and volatile co-star Brian all wanted to dominate her. The early episodes were odd and meandering, but the last few shows, written by Ronnie Wencker-Konner, pulled the storylines together. In the final episode, which left viewers up in the air as to who poisoned starlet Joyce Daniels, Michele Lee of *Knots Landing* appeared as herself among the party guests questioned by police—who mistakenly identified her as Mary Tyler Moore.

CAST

Evan Hammer	Mel Ferrer
Janie-Claire Willow	Janine Turner
Zina Willow	Joanne Linville
Jordan Willow	Scott Mulhern
Brian Holmby	Michael Sabatino
Gerry Holmby	Joshua Bryant
Dory Holmby	Loyita Chapel
Karl Madison	Mark Pinter
Angela Aries	Claudette Nevins
Joyce Daniels	Erica Yohn

| Lynette Porter | Debbi Morgan |
| Bobby Danzig | Bruce Fairbairn |

BEN JERROD

April 1, 1963–June 28, 1963   NBC

Created by Roy Winsor, this short-lived, Hollywood-based serial about two lawyers in the small town of Indian Hill, Rhode Island, was the first soap to be regularly broadcast in color. (*Search for Tomorrow* and other CBS serials had been broadcast periodically in color as early as 1954.) Starring Michael Ryan (John Randolph, *Another World*, 1964–79), *Ben Jerrod*'s first and only case involved the defense of Janet Donelli, a secretive young socialite on trial for the murder of her husband. *Ben Jerrod* aired at 2:00 P.M., E.S.T., and premiered the same day as *The Doctors*, which immediately followed it on the NBC schedule. The show was produced by Joseph Hardy, directed by Fred Carney, and written by William Kendall Clarke. Roy Winsor served as executive producer.

CAST

Ben Jerrod	Michael M. Ryan
John Abbott	Addison Richards
Janet Donelli	Regina Gleason
Peter Morrison	Peter Hansen
Jim O'Hara	Ken Scott
Lt. Choates	Lyle Talbot
Lil Morrison	Martine Bartlett
Sam Richardson	Gerald Gordon
Emily Sanders	Denise Alexander

THE BENNETTS

July 6, 1953–January 8, 1954   NBC

Chronicling the everyday affairs of a lawyer and his wife in the small town of Kingsport, this fifteen-minute serial was broadcast from Chicago at 11:15 A.M., E.S.T. It dramatized the reactions of the Bennetts to the problems of friends and clients in daily episodes, described in capsule TV listings such as "The Bennetts are hosts to a party that threatens to end a career" or "A broken antenna brings an unexpected picture." A major storyline concerned the Bennett's next door neighbors, Blaney and Meg Cobb, who, desperate to have children, got mixed up in a phony adoption scheme. The show was produced by Ben Park, directed by John Hinsey, and written by Bill Barrett.

CAST

Wayne Bennett	Don Gibson
Nancy Bennett	Paula Houston
Speedy Winters	Vi Berwick

Blaney Cobb	Jack Lester
Meg Cobb	Beverly Younger
George Konosis	Sam Siegel
Alma Wells	Kay Westfall

BERRENGER'S

January 5, 1985–March 9, 1985   NBC

Created and produced by Diana Gould, *Berrenger's* used a posh New York department store as the backdrop for serialized romance and familial conflict. The Berrenger family included Simon Berrenger, the ruthless head of the family empire; Babs, his daughter who was bent on proving herself in the business world; Billy, his likably troublesome younger son; and Paul, his elder son, the company president who continually locked horns with Simon; and Gloria, Paul's estranged wife who managed to worm her way back into Paul's life.

The central heroine was Shane Bradley, the merchandising vice president, whose affair with Paul Berrenger jeopardized her career. Farther down the corporate ladder was Julio Morales, a Hispanic dress designer; Stacey Russell, a black department manager; Emmie Springer, an ingénue salesgirl; and John Higgins, a playboy who spent his days dressing chic mannequins and his nights undressing chic models.

Berrenger's was most notable for the reintroduction of film actress Yvette Mimieux to prime-time TV after the short-lived crime series *The Most Deadly Game* in 1970, and for the energetic performance of Andrea Marcovicci as the nasty Gloria—quite a change-of-pace from Marcovicci's popular role as feminist Dr. Betsy Chernak on *Love is a Many Splendored Thing* in the early '70s. However, *Berrenger's* found resistance to its department store melodrama and the show quickly fell into the bottom of the ratings barrel, viewers apparently deciding to shop elsewhere.

CAST

Simon Berrenger	Sam Wanamaker
Paul Berrenger	Ben Murphy
Gloria Berrenger	Andrea Marcovicci
Billy Berrenger	Robin Strand
Babs Berrenger	Anita Morris
Melody Hughes	Claudia Christian
Todd Hughes	Art Hindle
Shane Bradley	Yvette Mimieux
Julio Morales	Eddie Velez
Stacey Russell	Jonelle Allen
Cammie Springer	Leslie Hope
John Higgins	Jeff Conaway
Danny Krucek	Jack Scalia
Laurel Hayes	Laura Ashton
Max Kaufman	Alan Feinstein
Rinaldi	Cesar Romero

BEST OF EVERYTHING

March 30, 1970–September 25, 1970   ABC

Created and written by James Lipton, this serial, based on the bestselling Rona Jaffe novel and the subsequent 1959 hit movie, dramatized the adventures of three young career women in New York. The movie starred Hope Lange, Suzy Parker, and Diane Baker, with Joan Crawford as Amanda, their overbearing boss at Key Publishing. Although the soap had built-in name recognition and an appealing cast that mixed Hollywood veterans with a host of talented ingénues, ABC cancelled after a six-month run on daytime. Jacqueline Babbin produced and Jack Woods and Alan Pultz directed. Don Wallace served as executive producer on the half-hour soap, which was broadcast at 12:00 Noon, E.S.T., opposite the popular *Jeopardy* and the cult serial *Where the Heart Is*.

CAST

April Morrison	Susan Sullivan
	Julie Mannix
Linda Warren	Patty McCormack
Kim Jordan	Katherine Glass
Amanda Key	Gale Sondergaard
Violet Jordan	Geraldine Fitzgerald
Ed Peronne	Victor Arnold
Ken Lamont	Barry Ford
Johnny Lamont	Stephen Grover
Barbara Lamont	Rochelle Oliver
Kate Farrow	M'El Dowd
Randy Wilson	Ted LePlat
Gwen Mitchell	Ginnie Curtis
Anne Carter	Diane Kagan
Dexter Key	James Davidson
Joanna Key	Bonnie Bee Buzzard

THE BOLD AND THE BEAUTIFUL

March 23, 1987–   CBS

Created by William J. Bell and his wife Lee Phillip (*The Young and the Restless*), this sumptuous soap was set in and about the Los Angeles fashion industry and centered on two families, the high-powered Forresters and the middle-class Logans. (In preproduction, the show was called *Rags* and was set in Chicago, where the Bells lived for years.)

Eric Forrester, president of Forrester Creations, a leading manufacturer of women's clothing, was unhappily married to Stephanie, whom he had married after she became pregnant with their first child. Their children were: Kristen, whose beauty and youth were envied by her mother; Ridge, the Casanova-like vice president of the family business; and Thorne, who had lived his entire life in the shadow of his brother.

The Logan family was headed by Beth, who has been the sole provider for her children—Storm (Stephen, Jr.), a law student; Brooke, in college; Donna, an ambitious eighteen-year-old; and Katie, an introverted teen. Other characters included William Spencer, a widower who was extremely overprotective of his daughter Caroline; Margo Lynley, Eric Forrester's beautiful administrative assistant; Dave Reed, a cop romantically involved with Brooke Logan; and Rocco Carner, Katie Logan's street-wise pal.

Most of the early story concerned the stormy romance between virginal Caroline Spencer and the arrogant (read: ripper of bodices) Ridge Forrester. Many of the plotlines were retreads from the early days of *The Young and the Restless* (the rich family/poor family concept; the sexual attack of Caroline, similar to the Chris Brooks story; brother Ridge fighting brother Thorne over the same woman, a carbon copy of Snapper and Greg battling it out over Chris; the desertion by the father of the poor Logans similar to that of the Fosters), etc.

Fortunately, the soap was served up in the same mesmerizing style as its "mother show": beautiful people (although three of the young blond women were physically indistinguishable from one another), stunning visuals, and strong production values. What was strikingly original from the start was the performance of Susan Flannery (Emmy winner as Laura Horton on *Days of Our Lives* in 1975) as Stephanie Forrester—a fascinating alabaster sphinx of a woman.

CAST

Eric Forrester	John McCook 1987–
Stephanie Forrester	Susan Flannery 1987–
Kristen Forrester	Teri Ann Linn 1987–
Ridge Forrester	Ronn Moss 1987–
Thorne Forrester	Clayton Norcross 1987–
Beth Logan	Nancy Burnett 1987–
	Judith Logan 1987
Storm Logan	Ethan Wayne 1987–
Brooke Logan	Katherine Kelly Lang 1987–
Donna Logan	Carrie Mitchum 1987–
Katie Logan	Nancy Sloan 1987–
Grandma Logan	Lesley Woods 1987–
William Spencer	James Storm 1987–
Caroline Spencer	Joanna Johnson 1987–
Margo Lynley	Lauren Koslow 1987–
Dave Reed	Stephen Shortridge 1987–
Rocco Carner	Bryan Genesse 1987–
Mark Mallory	Michael Philip 1987–

THE BRIGHTER DAY

January 4, 1954–September 28, 1962   CBS

Irna Phillips had successfully transferred *The Guiding Light* from radio to television two years earlier and decided to do the same with *The Brighter Day*, which had been flourishing on radio since 1948. Originally set in the town of Three Rivers, the location was changed to New Hope when the show switched to television. (It was explained that Three Rivers was destroyed in a flood.) The story revolved around the Reverend Richard Dennis, his flock, and his five children: Liz (happily married, she appeared briefly in the TV version in 1956); Althea, a neurotic young woman; Grayling, an alcoholic; Patsy, a teenager; and Barbara, the baby of the family, who was nicknamed Babby.

Because Dennis was a widower, Aunt Emily (played by Mona Bruns) was seen as a mother figure, not only for the Dennis children but for the community at large. (She even wrote an advice column for *The New Hope Herald*.) Each episode opened with the words, "Our years are as the falling leaves. We live, we love, we dream, and then we go. But somehow we keep hoping, don't we, that our dreams come true on that brighter day." Initially the show ran simultaneously on radio and television, but the radio version was discontinued in 1956, the year of *The Brighter Day*'s greatest popularity. In April of that year it became the number-one daytime drama, a status it was never to achieve again.

Early storylines concentrated on Althea's dreams of becoming an actress—a career which abruptly ended when Althea was decked onstage by a falling sandbag. Experiencing wild mood swings afterwards, Althea was convinced to seek psychiatric help. Dr. Blake Hamilton told her that women like her were happier in the kitchen. "The kitchen," he declared, "is the warmest place in the house, perhaps the warmest in the world." Undaunted, Althea told her shrink to stuff it and fled New Hope for the Big Apple to become a star! Meanwhile, the family struggled with Grayling's alcoholism. (Hal Holbrook, who played Grayling for five years, used one of Grayling's drunk scenes as his successful audition to the Actor's Studio.) Grayling eventually settled down with Sandra Talbot; years later— in a storyline that would prove disastrous for *The Brighter Day*—Sandra experienced a hysterical pregnancy while Grayling enjoyed a brief affair with Nurse Marion Dorsey, who was treating Sandra.

In 1961, when the production moved from New York to Hollywood, the show expanded from daily fifteen-minute episodes to a half hour. Popular when written by John Haggart and produced by Bob Steele (the *A Woman to Remember* team), *The Brighter Day* suffered from a continual change of writers, staff, and air time. Writers included such notables as Sam Hall, Eileen and Robert Mason Pollock, and Irna Phillips, the creator. The show was first broadcast at 1:00 P.M., E.S.T., and later was aired in late-afternoon slots. CBS took over the show from Procter & Gamble and made radical changes. The meddling caused more problems for the dwindling audience, and the show was cancelled within a year. On the final episode, Walter Dennis stepped forward and bid viewers farewell as the camera pulled back and the other members of the Dennis family gradually receded into the background, becoming quiet figures onstage. "The microphones can't pick up the voices," Walter said, "and soon the picture will fade. If on occasion you think of us, we hope your memory will be a pleasant one." Mona Bruns Thomas—whose son Frankie Thomas (*Tom Corbett, Space Cadet*) said she dressed like "Whistler's Mother" throughout

The Brighter Day's run—has written a full account of her experience on this and other soaps in *By Emily Possessed* (Exposition Press).

CAST

Rev. Richard Dennis	Blair Davies 1954–62
	William Smith 1954
Emily Potter	Mona Bruns 1954–62
Althea Dennis	Anne Meacham 1960–61
	Maggie O'Neill 1960
	Jayne Heller 1956
	Brooke Byron 1954–55
Grayling Dennis	Forrest Compton 1961–62
	James Noble 1959–60
	Hal Holbrook 1954–59
Patsy Dennis Hamilton	June Dayton 1961–62
	Lois Nettleton 1954–57
Dr. Randy Hamilton	Larry Ward 1954–57
Babby Dennis	Nancy Malone 1959–60
	Mary Linn Beller 1954–59
Sandra Talbot Dennis	Nancy Rennick 1961–62
	Mary K. Wells 1960–61
	Gloria Hoye 1957–59
	Diane Gentner 1956
Peter Nino	Joe Sirola 1959–60
Walter Dennis	Paul Langton 1962
Ellen Dennis	Lanna Saunders 1960
	Patty Duke 1958–59
Rev. Max Canfield	Herb Nelson 1956–58
Lydia Canfield	Murial Williams 1956–58
Lenore Bradley	Lori March 1956–58
Adolph McClure	Frank Thomas 1960
Donald Harrick	Walter Brooke 1956–58
Steven Markley	Peter Donat 1958
Tom Bradley	Robert Webber 1958
Diane Clark	Lin Pierson 1959
Eliot Clark	Ernest Graves 1960
	Lawrence Weber 1959
Bud Clark	Charles Taylor 1959
Lois Williams, R.N.	Marian Winters 1960
Dr. Charles Fuller	Dean Harens 1961–62
Chris Hamilton	Mike Barton 1961–62
Toby Ballard	Don Penny 1962
Mort Barrows	Benny Rubin 1962
Judith Potter	Bennye Gatteys 1962

With: Jack Lemmon, William Windom, Santos Ortega, and Judy Lewis.

BRIGHT PROMISE
September 29, 1969–March 31, 1972   NBC

Created by Frank and Doris Hursley (*General Hospital*), this was a contemporary conceptual drama set in Bancroft, a midwestern college town. What distinguished it from other soaps was a willingness to tackle such issues as student unrest, sexual permissiveness, and drug addiction. The Hursleys emphasized psychiatry and the working out of problems by turning to professionals, even going as far as calling the show "group therapy."

But audiences did not warm up to this issue-oriented theater, having overdosed on relevance during the '60s. *One Life to Live* and *All My Children*, which were launched during this period, were far more successful at introducing controversial subjects, probably because Agnes Nixon was able to wrap relevance in a much more entertaining package. Broadcast at 3:30 P.M. E.S.T., *Bright Promise* also faced stiff competition from the top-rated *Edge of Night*. Hollywood leading man Dana Andrews (*Laura*, *The Best Years of Our Lives*, etc.) starred as Thomas Boswell, a widower and president of Bancroft College. When it became apparent that the show's content and themes were not panning out, the show shifted away from the professors and the 15,000 students to the town at large and the romantic problems of the Jones and Pierce families.

After *Bright Promise* was cancelled because of poor ratings, director Gloria Monty went on to work on TV movies of the week. When she returned to daytime television in 1978 to produce the ailing *General Hospital*, Monty applied the techniques of prime-time television to *General Hospital* coupled with many of the more appealing *Bright Promise* ingredients: a youthful cast, headline-grabbing storylines, and psycho-sexual melodrama without the psychiatric chatter. The combination proved a success. Monty also remembered three of *Bright Promise*'s brightest stars and *General Hospital* soon welcomed Susan Brown, David Lewis, and Anthony Geary.

CAST

Thomas Boswell	Dana Andrews 1969–70
Martha Ferguson	Susan Brown 1969–72
William Ferguson	Paul Lukather 1969–71
	John Napier 1970
David Lockhart	Anthony Geary 1971–72
Henry Pierce	David Lewis 1969–72
	Tod Andrews 1969
Sandra Jones Pierce	Pamela Murphy 1970–72
	Susannah Darrow 1969–70
Stuart Pierce	Peter Ratray 1969–72
Ann Boyd Jones	Gail Kobe 1970–72
	Coleen Gray 1969–70
Howard Jones	Mark Miller 1971–72
Isabel Jones	Lesley Woods 1971–72

Sylvia Bancroft	Regina Gleason 1971
	Anne Jeffreys 1971
Elaine Bancroft	Jennifer Leak 1971
Dr. Tracy Graham	Dabney Coleman 1971–72
Dr. Brian Walsh	John Considine 1971–72
Jody Harper	Sherry Alberoni 1971–72
Red Wilson	Richard Eastham 1969–72
Dr. Amanda Winninger	June Vincent 1971–72
Jennifer Matthews	Nancy Stephens 1969–70
Chet Matthews	Gary Pillar (Carpenter) 1969–70
Albert Porter	Peter Hobbs 1969
Alice Porter	Synda Scott 1969
Charles Diedrich	Anthony Eisley 1971
Professor Mitchell	Ivor Francis 1969–72

CAPITOL

March 26, 1982–March 20, 1987   CBS

CBS's first new soap in nine years premiered with a one-hour special on prime time (following the network's powerhouse *Dallas*) before beginning daily half-hour installments the next week. Created and initially written by Stephen and Elinor Karpf (the mini-series *Captains and the Kings*), *Capitol* focused on two feuding Washington, D.C., families, the Cleggs and the McCandlesses.

The Cleggs were headed by Sam Clegg, a political bigwig, and his second wife Myrna, a manipulative power broker. The rest of the family consisted of Sam's son Sam Clegg III (Trey), a Congressman who was being groomed for the presidency; Sam and Myrna's playboy son Jordy; their beautiful daughter Julie; and their baby-doll teenage daughter Brenda. The McCandless family was headed by Judson Tyler, whose career was ruined in the McCarthy era by the vindictive Myrna. His daughter Clarissa had married the man Myrna had coveted and had also incurred Myrna's wrath since then. Clarissa's children completed the McCandless family: Tyler, a returning Air Force hero; Wally, a mixed-up college student; Matt, a college gymnast; Thomas, a handicapped doctor; and Gillian, a teenager.

Executive producer John Conboy chose Hollywood veterans Rory Calhoun, Constance Towers, Carolyn Jones, and Ed Nelson and a group of extremely attractive but inexperienced young actors to fill out the cast. Conboy also brought the ingredients that had made his production of *The Young and the Restless* so popular—lush sets, costuming, and camerawork— and added location footage of the picturesque D.C. area to the Hollywood-based show.

Sandwiched between the popular *As the World Turns* and *The Guiding Light*, *Capitol* did extremely well in its premiere week, racking up a 5.8 Nielsen rating and a 23 share, the highest ratings ever for a soap opera's first week on any network. Unfortunately, while *Capitol* was conceptually sound, with its warring families and the star-crossed romance between

Tyler McCandless and Julie Clegg, the execution was another matter. Fans agreed that the Karpfs' day-to-day writing was weak and the acting by the young romantic leads painfully amateurish, especially noticeable in the formidable company of Constance Towers and Ed Nelson.

The Karpfs were replaced by Joyce and John William Corrington, who shifted the focus away from Tyler and Julie to another star-crossed romance, between Congressman Trey Clegg and former call girl Shelley Granger. This storyline culminated, a year after the show premiered, when Jane Daly's Shelley confessed all in a fifteen-minute monologue, and then left town. The Corringtons contrasted this well-written sequence with an overlong international intrigue story that only served to get the show even further off the track.

Things began to jell when Peggy O'Shea (*One Life to Live*) took over as headwriter. O'Shea put sex into romance, tension into the political battles, and added a touch of traditional melodrama with the introduction of the mentally disturbed Paula Denning. Characterizations grew richer and the dialogue became sharper. Natalie Wood's sister Lana came on as Fran Burke, whose secret past shook up the entire Clegg family and became the catalyst for even more manipulations by Myrna. (Marj Dusay replaced Carolyn Jones as Myrna after Jones died of cancer about a year after *Capitol*'s premiere.) With its improved writing and emphasis on the physical attractiveness of the young cast, *Capitol* by its second anniversary was the highest-rated half-hour serial on the air.

However, *Capitol*, which was set in a city which was over 70 percent non-white, had not a single black character (except for brief appearances by Tyler McCandless's military sidekick) in almost three years. This situation was partially redressed by new headwriter Henry Slesar, who introduced Vegas entertainer Lola Falana as Charity Blake, an artist's representative. Slesar (*The Edge of Night*) continued O'Shea's romantic storylines, but also sprinkled the drama with his patented crime stories, wreaking havoc for the people of Washington, D.C., and its fictional suburb Jeffersonia, Virginia.

James Lipton (*Guiding Light*'s resident hearthrob as Dr. Dick Grant in the fifties) was *Capitol*'s last headwriter, and its final year was nothing if not wild. Sloane Denning married Prince Ali of the war-torn country Baracq. Jarrett Morgan was revealed to be the presumed-dead Baxter McCandless, while Matt McCandless was told he was really Prince Marim Mahmoud, the brother of the supposedly slain Prince Ali. Out of nowhere, stalwart Senator Mark Denning turned out to be a traitor. Sam Clegg, not Trey, was revealed to be Scotty's father. And Sam's first wife, Laureen, fresh from a nuthouse and in disguise, became Scotty's new nanny! This inspired looniness was somewhat balanced by a harrowing story in which D.J. Phillips turned Kelly Harper on to drugs. Jess Walton was a standout as the strung-out Kelly.

The irony of *Capitol*, of course, was that this modern, glamorous soap never achieved the ratings that the "old hat" *Search for Tomorrow*, the show it replaced, had produced. On the final episode, furious producers refused to tie up any of the loose ends. In fact, in the final scene *Capitol*'s most beloved heroine, Sloane, faced a firing squad. "Ready," cried that nasty Abdullah, "Aim!" Fade-out: The End.

Capitol went out with a whimper; we'll never know about the bang part.

CAST

Myrna Clegg	Marj Dusay 1983–87
	Marla Adams 1983
	Carolyn Jones 1982–83
Sam Clegg II	Richard Egan 1982–87
	Robert Sampson 1982
Sam Clegg III (Trey)	Nicholas Walker 1982–87
Julie Clegg	Catherine Hickland 1983–87
	Kimberly Beck 1982–83
Jordy Clegg	Todd Curtis 1982–87
Brenda Clegg	Karen Kelly 1985–87
	Ashley Laurence 1985
	Leslie Graves 1982–84
Judson Tyler	Rory Calhoun 1982–87
Clarissa McCandless	Constance Towers 1982–87
Tyler McCandless	Dane Witherspoon 1985–86
	David Mason-Daniels 1982–85
Wally McCandless	Bill Beyers 1982–87
Dr. Thomas McCandless	Michael Catlin 1983–87
	Brian Robert Taylor 1982–83
Matt McCandless	Rod Stryker 1987
	Christopher Durham 1982–84
	Shea Farrell 1982
Gillian McCandless	Kelly Palzis 1982
Sen. Mark Denning	Ed Nelson 1982–87
Paula Denning	Julie Adams 1983–87
Sloane Denning	Deborah Mullowney 1982–87
Lawrence Barrington	Jeff Chamberlain 1982–83
Lizbeth Bachman	Tonja Walker 1982–86
Shelley Granger/Kelly Harper	Jess Walton 1984–87
	Jane Daly 1982–83
Frank Burgess	Duncan Gamble 1982
Kurt Voightlander	Wolf Muser 1983
Jeff Johnson	Rodney Saulsberry 1982–83
Danny Donato	Eddie Zammitt 1984
	Victor Brant 1983
Veronica Angelo	Dawn Parrish 1983–85
Maggie Brady	Julie Parrish 1982–85
Zed Diamond	Bradley Lockerman 1983–87
Fran Burke	Lana Wood 1983
Amy Burke	Kimberly Ross 1983
Detective Keyes	John Colenback 1983–84
Ricky Driscoll	Billy Warlock 1984–85

Frankie Bridges	Beth Windsor 1984–85
Hal Dayton	Arthur Malet 1984–85
Cheetah	Becca C. Ashley 1984–85
Chip Landry	Lindsey Richardson 1984–85
Nino Vincent	Joey Aresco 1985
Baxter McCandless	Ron Harper 1985–87
Linda Vandenberg	Lara Parker 1985–86
Vera Sweet	Valarie Reynolds 1985–86
Leanne Foster	Christine Kellogg 1985–87
Kate Wells	Cheryl-Ann Wilson 1986–87
Jenny Diamond	Catherine Hickland 1985–86
Dylan Ross	Mitch Brown 1985–87
Meredith Ross	Tawny Kitaen 1986–87
D.J. Phillips	Grant Aleksander 1986
Darlene Stankowski	Tammy Wynette 1986–87
Prince Ali	Peter Lochran 1986–87
Jeffrey Martin Sahim	Michael Evans 1986–87
Princess Yasmeen	Alisha Das 1986
Abdullah	Nick Ramus 1987
Carol Greshner	Carol Alt 1987
Angelica Clegg	Terri Hatcher 1986–87
Laureen Clegg	Janis Paige 1987

THE CATLINS

April 4, 1983–May 31, 1985   TBS

Created by C. T. McIntyre, this daytime, half-hour soap was the first serial to be broadcast daily from Atlanta on Ted Turner's cable network. *The Catlins* centered on a large, powerful Southern family: Catherine Catlin, the feisty, forthright matriarch; her son T.J., owner of Catlin Enterprises; his wife Annabelle; and their children: Matthew, a doctor; Maggie, a lawyer; Beau, a race-car driver; Jonathan, president of Catlin Enterprises; and Jennifer, who as the show opened was unjustly accused of the murder of her philandering fiancé Robert Goode.

Much of the conflict was provided by the Quinns, a nasty banking family headed by Medger Quinn, including his creepy son Seth; his son Cullen, an ex-con; and his beautiful daughter Eleanor, who was married to Jonathan Catlin. After the murder trial was played out, the show shifted from Jennifer to the battle by brothers Matt and Beau over reporter Lauren Woodward. A year after its premiere, *The Catlins* was again in the thick of a highly dramatic trial after Eleanor Quinn Catlin was killed. The serial was initially produced and written by McIntyre. The supervising producer was Heather Hill and the creative consultant was Steve Lehrman. The other writers included Sam Smiley, Craig M. Brown, Robin Grunder, and Maura Swanson.

CAST

Catherine Catlin	Mary Nell Santacroce
T. J. Catlin	Michael Forest
	J. Don Ferguson
Annabelle Catlin	Pamela Burrell
	Muriel Moore
Dr. Matt Catlin	Dan Albright
Maggie Catlin	Julie Ridley
	Victoria Loving
Beau Catlin	Peter Boynton
	Larry Jordan
Jonathan Catlin	Jerry Homan
Jennifer Catlin	Terri VandenBosch
	Jennifer Anglin
	Nancy Kennedy
Medger Quinn	Danny Nelson
Seth Quinn	Brett Rice
Cullen Quinn	McLinn Crowell
Lauren Woodward	Christina Reguli
Crissy Catlin	Nancy Leep
	Candy Howard
Robert Goode	Dirk Randall
Dirk Stack	Joe Ranier
Woody Thorpe	Charles Hill
Memphis Morgan	Justine Thieleman
Stuart Blake	Stuart Culpepper
Andrea Smith	Iris L. Roberts
Vanessa Crane	Lisby Larson

THE CLEAR HORIZON

July 11, 1960–March 11, 1961;
February 26, 1962–June 11, 1962   CBS

Created and written by Manya Starr, *The Clear Horizon*, titled *Army Wife* in preproduction, concerned the problems of astronauts and their wives stationed at Cape Canaveral, Florida. The thirty-minute soap was one of the first serials to be broadcast from California and among the first to be shot on location. On the debut show, Roy Selby, an Army Signal Corps officer, was recalled from his Alaskan post to the Pentagon and given a new commission in Florida. Presented live until it was initially cancelled, *The Clear Horizon* was taped when it made its reappearance after a year's hiatus. The producer was Charles Pollacheck and the directors were Joseph Behar and Hal Cooper.

CAST

Roy Selby	Edward Kemmer
Ann Selby	Phyllis Avery
Greg Selby	Craig Curtis

Ricky Selby   Jimmy Carter
                          Charles Herbert
Col. Theodore Adams   William Roerick
Lois Adams   Denise Alexander
Sgt. Harry Moseby   Rusty Lane
Frances Moseby   Eve McVeagh
Mitchell Corbin   Richard Coogan
With: George Gobel, Grace Albertson, Ted Knight, and Lee
Meriwether.

THE COLBYS
November 20, 1985–March 26, 1987   ABC

Two of Hollywood's biggest stars, Charlton Heston and Barbara Stanwyck, were drafted to star in this spin-off of *Dynasty*. Characters for this new show, created by Esther and Richard Shapiro and Eileen and Robert Mason Pollock, first made appearances on *Dynasty* in the spring of 1985. Later, stars from *Dynasty* (except Joan Collins) made periodic visits to Bel Air, California, where *The Colbys* was set.

Heston played Jason Colby, the kingpin of the Colby's conglomerate (which included real estate, an aerospace lab, and an oil and timber company). Stanwyck starred as Constance Colby, Jason's sister, matriarch and conscience of the family. Jason was married to the formidable Sable (*née* Sabella Scott) and they had three children: Monica, who had an unhappy affair with the very married Neil Kittridge; Bliss, who became involved with Sean McAllister, the nephew of Zach Powers, Jason's archenemy; and Miles, who married Randall Adams, an amnesia victim. Other characters included Jeff Colby, who was discovered to be the natural son of Jason, by Sable's sister, Francesca Scott Colby Hamilton Langdon (Frankie, for short). For years, Frankie had passed off Jeff as the son of Phillip Colby (Jason's brother), the black sheep of the family, who had been presumed dead in Vietnam. Clearly peeved at the revelation, sister Sable snarled, "I don't give a damn about your bastard, you little slut!"

In the first season, Randall was revealed to be Fallon Carrington, Jeff's ex-wife. Miles let Fallon go, but not before he raped her. Jeff remarried Fallon, then discovered that she was pregnant, and in the second season, the child was found to be the natural daughter of Jeff not Miles. Both Jeff and Miles were put on trial for different murders by a vengeful D.A., John Moretti. Little did they know that Zach Powers had more than a hand in their indictments—the very same Zach who was attempting to sexually console Sable after Jason insisted on a divorce so that he could marry Frankie.

In the 1986–87 season, Miles married the sneaky, slinky Channing Carter; Bliss became engaged to Kolya Rostov, a Soviet ballet dancer who had defected; and Monica fell in love with her old flame Senator Cash Cassidy and discovered that he had adopted Scott, the son she had given up for adoption years before. After the reported death of Constance Colby in Nepal, all suspicion for the murder focused on a mysterious American expatriate named Hoyt Parker, who turned out to be none other than the very alive Phillip Colby! Back in California, Jason discovered brother Phillip and fiancée Frankie in bed together. ("Frankie," Sable snapped, "you are a walking ad for adultery.") The season ended hilariously as Fallon spotted a UFO and sauntered aboard with the extraterrestrials—the Close Encounter of the Cancellation Kind.

The Colbys, despite its cult audience, was plagued with terrible ratings from the beginning, despite its prime advantage—perhaps the classiest performance by an actress ever on a prime-time soap, that of Stephanie Beacham (as Sable), who attacked the sometimes campy material as if it were an Edward Albee drawing room drama. Sophisticated, scared, and scary, this stock villainess-turned-Mother Courage knocked ostensible heroine Katharine Ross and hero Charlton Heston right off the screen. No wonder he cringed every time he heard those high-heels—clickety-clack—heading in his direction.

CAST

Jason Colby	Charlton Heston 1985–87
Constance Colby	Barbara Stanwyck 1985–86
Sable Colby	Stephanie Beacham 1985–87
Francesca Colby Langdon	Katharine Ross 1985–87
Jeff Colby	John James 1985–87
Fallon Carrington Colby	Emma Samms 1985–87
Miles Colby	Maxwell Caulfield 1985–87
Bliss Colby	Claire Yarlett 1985–87
Monica Colby	Tracy Scoggins 1985–87
Zach Powers	Ricardo Montalban 1985–87
Sean McAllister	Charles Van Eman 1985–86
Neil Kittridge	Philip Brown 1985–86
Wayne Masterson	Gary Morris 1986
Hutch Corrigan	Joseph Campanella 1985–86
Arthur Cates	Peter White 1985–87
D.A. John Moretti	Vincent Baggetta 1985–86
Channing Carter Colby	Kim Morgan Greene 1986–87
Lucas Carter	Kevin McCarthy 1986–87
Kolya Rostov	Adrian Paul 1986–87
Sen. Cash Cassidy	James Houghton 1986–87
Adrienne Cassidy	Shanna Reed 1986–87
Phillip Colby	Michael Parks 1987
Maya Kumara	Bianca Jagger 1987

CONCERNING MISS MARLOWE

July 5, 1954–July 1, 1955   NBC

NBC drafted Hollywood leading lady Louise Allbritton (*The Egg and I*) for this short-lived fifteen-minute serial (3:45 P.M., E.S.T.), which opened on the same day as the network's *First Love, Golden Windows,* and *A Time To Live.* Allbritton played Maggie Marlowe, a middle-aged New York actress who was just about to leave her career for marriage when she found that her fiancé had died. Afterwards, back at work, she began to fall in love with a married man. To make matters worse, the play Maggie chose to make a comeback in was an unqualified stinker, with ingenue Kit Christy sabotaging Maggie's performance. In a seemingly separate sub-plot, Maggie urged private detectives to continue their search for her daughter, who fourteen years earlier had been lost in France by a careless grandmother. Imagine Maggie's joy—and horror—when she discovered that the nasty Kit was you-know-who! The show was produced by Tom McDermont, directed by Larry White, and written by John Pickard and Frank Provo.

The soap is chiefly remembered for one of live TV's all-time bloopers: a phone rang when it was not supposed to. In the confusion that followed, the leading lady answered the phone, and very flustered, walked off the set—but not before announcing to her maid, "It's for you!" Louise Allbritton, who was married to journalist Charles Collingwood, was a frequent guest star on prime-time TV after the cancellation of the show. She died February 16, 1979, of cancer.

CAST

Margaret Marlowe	Louise Allbritton
	Helen Shields
Bill Cooke	John Raby
Jim Gavin	Efrem Zimbalist, Jr.
Mike Donovan	Byron Sanders
Linda Cabot	Sarah Burton
Cindy Clayton	Patricia Bosworth
Harry Clayton	John Gibson
Dot Clayton	Helen Shields
Tommy Clayton	Eddie Brien
Hugh Fraser	Lauren Gilbert
Ronald Blake	Bert Thorn
Kit Christy	Chris White
Harriet the Hat	Jane Seymour
Augusta Gorme	Meggie Leubecker
Katie Patrick	Vera Rivers

CONFIDENTIAL FOR WOMEN

March 28, 1966–July 8, 1966   ABC

This daytime effort can be considered a serial in the sense that it presented a five-part story over a week's time. Jane Wyatt, best known as Margaret Anderson on *Father Knows Best,* hosted the series. Dr. Theodore Rubin, author of a dozen books on self-help and combatting obesity, including *Forever Thin* and *Compassion and Self-Hate,* provided psychiatric commentary; the stories were based on his case files. It aired for a half hour at

2:00 P.M., E.S.T., opposite *Days of Our Lives* and the popular game show *Password*.

DALLAS

April 2, 1978–   CBS

The first major prime-time soap opera effort since *Peyton Place* closed in 1969, *Dallas* became the highest-rated serial television has ever known, the source of TV's most famous villain, the focus of a fanatical worldwide following, and the model for a host of popular imitators, including *Dynasty*, *Falcon Crest*, and its own spin-off *Knots Landing*.

Created by David Jacobs, *Dallas* was introduced to the American public with five trial episodes in the spring of 1978. Revolving around the rich Ewing clan and set outside Dallas at the Ewing ranch Southfork, the show initially pitted the Ewings against a rival family, the Barnes, who felt they had been swindled out of an oil bonanza forty years before. The Ewings included John Ross, Sr. (Jock), a former oil wildcatter; his wife Eleanor Southworth (Miss Ellie); their son J.R., an unscrupulous businessman; Sue Ellen, J.R.'s wife, a former beauty contestant; Bobby, Jock and Ellie's handsome, likable son; and Lucy, the spoiled daughter of the Ewing black-sheep son, Gary. The Barnes included Digger, who hated Jock for stealing his land and his true love, Miss Ellie; Cliff, his hot-tempered son; and Pamela, his beautiful daughter, who married Bobby and lived at the Ewing ranch.

The five trial shows were self-contained dramatic episodes, not in the serial form. In one, a pregnant Pam, taunted by J.R., fell from a barn top and lost her child. The shows did well, and *Dallas* was back in the fall of 1978, but it wasn't until the show began to feature continuing, layered storylines stretching over many episodes that *Dallas* started to take off. Viewers watched with growing interest as J.R.'s business machinations and mistresses accumulated while his wife Sue Ellen fell slowly into the arms of Cliff Barnes and, later, into alcoholism. The various complex romantic and business developments—which included Lucy ("the world's tiniest nympho," chimed *The Village Voice*) seducing ranchhand Ray Krebbs who, a couple of years later, learned that he was Jock's illegitimate son and Lucy's uncle—propelled the show into the top ten by the end of its first full season.

The Washington Post spoke for many when it called *Dallas* America's *Upstairs, Downstairs*. Richard Cohen wrote, "It's indigenous, it's well written, it's well acted, and it's dirty as hell. The chief difference between the two shows is that in *Dallas* everything takes place at breakfast, not at tea, and there is no downstairs at the ranch house."

The 1979–80 season of *Dallas* was action packed. Lucy's parents, Gary and Valene Ewing, were remarried and moved out of town to start a new life and a new show. (See *Knots Landing*). Jock was put on trial for the murder twenty-eight years before of Hutch McKinney. But on his death-bed, Digger Barnes confessed to the murder and told Pam that her real father was the dead Hutch. J.R. found that he, not Cliff Barnes, was the father of Sue Ellen's baby, John Ross. J.R. began an affair with Sue Ellen's sister, while Sue Ellen found solace with a sexy cowboy, Dusty Farlow. Dave and Donna Culver, part of a powerful political family, were introduced, and a couple of years later Donna married Ray Krebbs. After a series of death threats, J.R. was shot by an unknown assailant on March 21, 1980. It turned out to be a shot heard round the world.

Over the summer of 1980 the audience watching re-runs swelled to 40 million regular viewers in the U.S. and 300 million in fifty-six other countries. All waited for the answer posed by cover stories in *Time* and *People*: "Who shot J.R.?" Executive producer Philip Capice and producer Leonard Katzman, who wrote the show after creator David Jacobs had left, had carefully set up over a half dozen characters with motives to eliminate J.R. The whodunit caused "*Dallas* fever," a condition whose symptoms included magazine contests, Las Vegas odds-making, and a hit song. Among the obvious suspects were Sue Ellen, her sister Kristin, and Cliff, but bets were also laid on swindled banker Vaughn Leland, Lucy's ex-boyfriend Alan Beam, and Dusty—although Sue Ellen's lover had been presumed dead in a plane crash.

At the center of the brouhaha was J.R. and the man who played him, Larry Hagman. J.R. had become such an American folk hero, albeit questionably, that he received 600 votes in the Oklahoman presidential primary. Part of J.R.'s appeal was that he was totally and wittily amoral: "Once you give up integrity, the rest is a piece of cake," he once observed. Hagman, whose deliciously malevolent performance was largely responsible for the show's popularity, was in the midst of contract negotiations, which only added to the excitement. If Hagman did not return to the show, the actor could be replaced (Robert Culp was the name most mentioned), or J.R. could die from his wounds—both alternatives unacceptable to fans. Hagman took off for Great Britain (where *Dallas* had become a national craze—20 million regular watchers in a country of 56 million) as the show went into production for its fall season. But Hagman soon returned, receiving a reported $1 million-plus salary and a share of J.R. merchandising, thus delivering the dastardly J.R. from death's door and Southfork from terminal ennui.

Six different versions of the shooting had been filmed as Sue Ellen, Cliff, Kristin, Jock, Miss Ellie, and—as a joke—J.R. himself fired the pistol. On November 21, 1980, it was revealed that J.R.'s jilted mistress Kristin was the culprit—a bulletin that actually opened the evening news in the nation's capital and had Britons listening to the BBC at three o'clock in the morning for the newsflash. The episode attracted 83 million viewers in the U.S. and, with a 53.3 rating and a 76 share, the largest TV audience ever for an entertainment show. (The record was broken three years later by the final episode of *M*A*S*H*.)

Other developments in the 1980–81 season included the marriage of Ray Krebbs and Donna Culver, the marriage of Lucy to medical student Mitch Cooper, the introduction of an ambitious public relations expert Leslie Stewart (who had affairs with J.R. and his political rival), and the discovery of Pam's mother Rebecca Wentworth. On the final episode Pam, Sue Ellen, and Kristin (who was not prosecuted for the shooting) wore similar black-and-white outfits; a female body, wearing black and white, was found floating in the Ewing pool.

At the beginning of the 1981–82 season, viewers found that it was Kristin who had died in the pool. After considerable intrigue, Pam and Bobby adopted Kristin's son Christopher. A divorced Sue Ellen romanced Cliff, a crippled Dusty, and Dusty's father Clayton. Mitch Cooper's white-trash sister Afton, a would-be chanteuse, was introduced, and after sleeping around town ended up with Cliff Barnes. Mitch's marriage to Lucy ended when she found him in bed with Evelyn Michaelson, an older woman. Because actor Jim Davis (best known for his co-starring role with Bette Davis in the 1948 film *Winter Meeting*) had died over the summer, his character Jock was sent to South America on business. Later Jock was reported dead in a mining disaster.

The 1982–83 season found Jock's will driving a wedge into the Ewing family. J.R. and Bobby were at each other's throats, and Bobby's marriage was failing because of business pressures. As Pam's sister Katherine shamelessly pursued Bobby, a new character, Mark Graison, set his sights on Pam. Although Sue Ellen and J.R. remarried, J.R. continued his extramarital activities. Sue Ellen discovered him in bed with Holly Harwood, and in an alcoholic haze wrecked her car. She and Mickey Trotter—Ray Krebbs' cousin and Lucy's love interest—were injured. The season ended with still another cliff-hanger as Southfork went up in flames, trapping Ray, J.R., Sue Ellen, and John Ross inside. (*Dynasty*, *Dallas*'s soap rival, ended its season with a similar inferno.)

In the 1983–84 season all were rescued from the fire, but Mickey died in the hospital, with Ray held responsible for a mercy killing. Pam and Bobby were finally divorced and pursued other romantic interests while still in love with each other. Three celebrities were introduced to *Dallas*, although the highest-rated prime-time serial hardly needed the publicity. Christopher Atkins, the teen idol of *The Blue Lagoon*, came on as Peter Richards, John Ross's camp counselor who took a shine to Sue Ellen. Their May-December affair drove Lucy to drink and J.R. to revenge. Priscilla Presley came on as Jenna Wade (a part previously played by soap siren Morgan Fairchild), who had been Bobby's first lover. Jenna's daughter Charlie turned out not to be Bobby's child, as Jenna had once claimed, but Bobby proposed marriage to Jenna.

Near the end of the season, Alexis Smith was introduced as Lady Jessica Montford, who joined forces with J.R. to stop the wedding between her brother, Clayton Farlow, and Miss Ellie. The unstable Jessica even attempted to kill Miss Ellie; later Ellie and Clayton were finally wed. Meanwhile, after the death of her fiancé Mark, Pam discovered the extent of Katherine's treachery. On the final episode, written by Arthur Bernard Lewis, several major characters again threatened to kill J.R. An intruder entered J.R.'s office and shot at J.R.'s chair several times, but it was not J.R. who fell to the floor, but a wounded Bobby—the object of three women's affections: Jenna, Katherine, and Pam.

In the 1984–85 season, it was revealed that the scorned Katherine had intentionally shot Bobby rather than let Jenna or sister Pam get their claws into him. J.R. and Sue Ellen's *Who's Afraid of Virginia Woolf?* marriage was "on" again after Sue Ellen's cradle-robbing affair with Peter Richards. (J.R. in bed with Sue Ellen: "If it helps, you can think of him.") And two new female characters were introduced: Mandy Winger, a seductress who attended to Cliff Barnes's wounds after Afton walked out on him; and Jamie Ewing, a young woman who claimed to be a Ewing relative, the daughter of Jock's brother Jason.

But one of the most interesting developments of the season was the entrance of Donna Reed as Miss Ellie, replacing Barbara Bel Geddes, who left the show after five years because of illness. The daytime soaps had had mixed luck with replacing established talent, and the acceptance by the public of Donna Reed in such a highly identifiable role remained a question mark, especially since Bel Geddes was still being seen daily in the role, the serial having entered into syndication that season. It soon became clear, however, that Reed never caught on to the pioneer spirit of Miss Ellie, and public reaction to her performance was mixed at best. When Barbara Bel Geddes recovered from her stroke, she was convinced by producers to return to her role the next season. Donna Reed later sued CBS Entertainment and Lorimar Productions for $7.5 million, charging breach of contract.

Other developments included the arrest of Jenna Wade for the murder of her husband, Naldo Marchetta. (Although Jenna was engaged to Bobby, Marchetta blackmailed Jenna into remarriage after he kidnapped their daughter Charlie.) And J.R. was up to his usual mischief: forcing Jamie from Southfork, stealing Mandy from Cliff, and paying off doctors to convince Pam that Mark Graison was still alive and receiving unorthodox medical treatments out of the country. Later J.R., darlin', drove Sue Ellen to drink and threatened to institutionalize her if she did not grant him a divorce so he could marry Mandy. Sue Ellen again found spiritual and romantic bliss in the arms of Dusty Farlow, who had suddenly popped up on the scene after an absence of four years.

Much of the season focused on the attempt of Cliff Barnes to take over Ewing Oil on the basis of a 1930 document splitting the company equally among Digger Barnes, Jock, and Jason Ewing. Cliff married Jamie to control two-thirds of the shares, but the gambit backfired when Jack, Jamie's brother, supplied J.R. with evidence that Jock had bought back Digger and Jason's shares. The Ewings also won another court battle when Bobby proved that Jenna had been framed for Naldo's murder, the real killer being hired assassin Andre Shuman.

On the final episode of the 1984–85 season, presented in an unusual 90-minute special, Lucy remarried Mitch (who whisked her to Atlanta and off the show), Donna told Ray that she was pregnant, and Bobby realized that he loved Pam and always had. After Bobby and Pam spent the night together, a woman driving a sports car tried to run over Pam, but Bobby pushed Pam out of the way and was struck himself. The driver of the car crashed into a truck and was killed instantly. The culprit was discovered to be Katherine Wentworth, who had shot Bobby a year before.

While the other prime-time serials ended with elaborate cliff-hangers designed to keep fans guessing "what happens next," *Dallas* concluded its season with an emotionally-packed and tragic finale—an ending made necessary by actor Patrick Duffy's departure from the show. As the Ewings gathered around his hospital bed, Bobby told them, "Be a family." Then he quietly died.

Well, not exactly. IT WAS ALL A DREAM!!! Pam woke up a year later supposedly married to Mark Graison and found Bobby in her shower. Buck-naked, Bobby winked, "Good morning." Understandably, Pam Van Winkle fainted. Here's what happened: the 1985–86 season was not the best for *Dallas*. It had drifted off into stories of international intrigue (J.R.'s dealings with Angelica Nero in Greece and Pam emerald hunting in a South American jungle with Matt Cantrell). Behind the scenes, Larry Hagman was hopping mad. The show had lost its focus: where were the family conflict, sex and power struggles in and about Southfork?

Hagman convinced his good friend Patrick Duffy to return to the show and demanded that Leonard Katzman, the guiding force behind the scenes for years, be named executive producer. But how to get Duffy back into the storyline? Perhaps Bobby was revived at the hospital and kidnapped. No; it was decided that the entire season had to be wiped out. (Two practical questions never quite addressed by Lorimar: on its sister show *Knots Landing*, Bobby's brother Gary had a nervous breakdown after hearing about Bobby's death. *Knots Landing* wisely decided to ignore Bobby's sudden resurrection. Secondly, thirty-one episodes were in the can and ready for syndication: why should anyone watch these reruns when *none of it really happened*?)

In the 1986–87 season, after Bobby towel-dried himself, he remarried Pam, although he found that Jenna was pregnant with his child. J.R. got caught up with the unstable B.D. Calhoun in an illegal scheme involving Middle Eastern oil. When J.R. ratted on Calhoun, the nut kidnapped John Ross, but the child was saved by the efforts of the three Ewing brothers. Donna, who later gave birth to Ray's baby (named Margaret—after Ray's mother), worked as a lobbyist in Washington, D.C. and became romantically involved with Senator Andrew Dowling. While husband Cliff munched on an egg roll, Jamie Barnes was killed in an auto accident. Jamie's brother Jack left town, but not before Jack's ex-wife April appeared on the scene and tried to seduce every rich old codger in the vicinity of Dallas.

A mysterious man called Wes Parmalee popped up to claim he was the presumed-dead Jock Ewing. (In Pam's dream—the 1985–86 season, that is—the "Jock" character was called Ben Stivers.) Although Wes had plenty of evidence to support his claim, he fell in love with Ellie and confessed his fraud. Sue Ellen started up a lingerie company called *Valentine*, hired Mandy Winger as its top model, and attempted to get Mandy out of J.R.'s hair once and for all. As the season closed, the Justice Department and various scavengers threatened to close Ewing Oil, Jenna gave birth to Bobby's son Lucas, and Pam crashed her car right into a moving van. The car exploded into a huge fire bomb.

CAST

Ellie Ewing	Barbara Bel Geddes 1978–84; 1985–
	Donna Reed 1984–85
Jock Ewing	Jim Davis 1978–81
J.R. Ewing	Larry Hagman 1978–
Sue Ellen Ewing	Linda Gray 1978–
Lucy Ewing	Charlene Tilton 1978–85
Gary Ewing	Ted Shackelford 1979–81
	David Ackroyd 1978–79
Valene Ewing	Joan Van Ark 1978–81
Bobby Ewing	Patrick Duffy 1978–85; 1986–
Pamela Barnes Ewing	Victoria Principal 1978–87
Cliff Barnes	Ken Kercheval 1978–
Digger Barnes	Keenan Wynn 1979–80
	David Wayne 1978–79
Kristin Shepard	Mary Crosby 1979–81
	Colleen Camp 1979
Patricia Shepard	Martha Scott 1979; 1985
Rudy Millington	Terry Lester 1979
Amos Krebbs	William Windom 1980
Ray Krebbs	Steve Kanaly 1978–
Donna Culver Krebbs	Susan Howard 1979–87
Dave Culver	Tom Fuccello 1979–
Julie Grey	Tina Louise 1978–79
Liz Craig	Barbara Babcock 1978–81
Vaughn Leland	Dennis Patrick 1979–
Harve Smithfield	George O. Petrie 1979–
Dusty Farlow	Jared Martin 1979–81; 1985–86
Clayton Farlow	Howard Keel 1981–
Alan Beam	Randolph Powell 1979–80
Alex Ward	Joel Fabiani 1980–81
Dr. Elby	Jeff Cooper 1979–81
Marilee Stone	Fern Fitzgerald 1980–
Punk Anderson	Morgan Woodward 1980–
Mavis Anderson	Alice Hirson 1982–
Evelyn Michaelson	Patty McCormack 1981–82
Mitch Cooper	Leigh McCloskey 1979–82; 1985
Afton Cooper	Audrey Landers 1981–84
Arliss Cooper	Anne Francis 1981–82
Clint Ogden	Monte Markham 1981
Leslie Stewart	Susan Flannery 1981
Roy Ralston	John Reilly 1983
Jordan Lee	Don Starr 1979–
Rebecca Wentworth	Priscilla Pointer 1981–83
Katherine Wentworth	Morgan Brittany 1981–85
Holly Harwood	Lois Chiles 1982
Mark Graison	John Beck 1983–86

Mickey Trotter	Timothy Patrick Murphy 1982–83
Lil Trotter	Kate Reid 1983; 1986
Peter Richards	Christopher Atkins 1983–84
Jenna Wade	Priscilla Beaulieu Presley 1983– Francine Tacker 1980 Morgan Fairchild 1978
Charlie Wade	Shalane McCall 1983–
Naldo Marchetta	Daniel Pilon 1983–84
Paul Morgan	Glenn Corbett 1983; 1986–87
Travis Boyd	Christopher (Denny) Albee 1984
Edgar Randolph	Martin E. Brooks 1983
Martha Randolph	Joanna Miles 1984
Lady Jessica Montford	Alexis Smith 1984–85
Jamie Ewing	Jenilee Harrison 1984–87
Mandy Winger	Deborah Shelton 1984–
Eddie Cronin	Fredric Lehne 1984–85
Andre Shuman	Rod Arrants 1985
Amanda Ewing	Susan French 1985 Lesley Woods 1979
Jack Ewing	Dack Rambo 1985–87
Angelica Nero	Barbara Carrera 1985–86
Grace	Merete Van Kamp 1985–86
Nicholas	George Chakiris 1985–86
Alex Garrett	William Prince 1986
Dr. Jerry Kenderson	Barry Jenner 1985–86
Matt Cantrell	Marc Singer 1986
Ben Stivers	Steve Forrest 1986
Wes Parmalee	Steve Forrest 1986
April Stevens	Sheree J. Wilson 1986–
B.D. Calhoun	Hunter von Leer 1986–87
Sen. Andrew Dowling	Jim McMullan 1986–87
Nicholas Pearce	Jack Scalia 1987–
Casey Denault	Andrew Stevens 1987–
Lisa Alden	Amy Stock 1987–
Harrison Dandridge	Burt Remsen 1987

DARK SHADOWS

June 27, 1966–April 2, 1971   ABC

More spook opera than soap opera, this fanatically followed daytime serial about the comings and goings of the paranormal was the television rage among teenagers in the '60s. Its star, Jonathan Frid, who played Barnabas, the beleaguered vampire who'd rather quit than bite, became an overnight cult hero. Almost fifteen years after its cancellation, *Dark Shadows* is seen in syndication in more than fifty markets and a number of fan clubs still hold annual conventions with former cast members in attendance as honored guests.

The show was the brainchild of executive producer Dan Curtis, who claims to have been on a train from New England to New York, daydreaming, when the story of *Dark Shadows* was conceived. Looking out at the brooding scenery—the cliffs, mansions, and waters—Curtis noticed a young woman huddled against another window and imagined her as his heroine on the way to becoming a governess in a strange house by the ocean. He handed the idea over to writer Art Wallace, who developed the project. *Dark Shadows* was set in Collinsport, a town on the Maine coast (exterior shots were filmed in Newport, Rhode Island), and told the story of the blue-blood Collins family: Elizabeth Collins Stoddard and her daughter Carolyn; Elizabeth's brother Roger Collins and his young son David; and David's governess Victoria Winters.

Initially, *Dark Shadows* was a mild gothic romance with *Rebecca*-like touches, such as Victoria Winters' voice-over narration at the beginning of each show. (When Alexandra Moltke did not appear on a particular episode, another actress filled in.) It was taped in black and white and employed cheap, fly-apart sets that were sparsely furnished. During most of the run usually only five actors were used per episode. With former Hollywood movie queen Joan Bennett as *Dark Shadows'* ostensible star, one of its earliest plot lines centered on Elizabeth Stoddard's supposed murder of her husband years before, and her efforts to conceal it from her daughter Carolyn. Elizabeth, who was born February 28, 1917 (the writers used Joan Bennett's birthdate but sliced seven years off her age), turned out not to have killed Paul, but had been set up by blackmailer Jason McGuire.

During Art Wallace's writing tenure (Ron Sproat, Malcolm Marmorstein, and Joe Caldwell served as dialogists), *Dark Shadows* progressed at a leisurely, uninvolving pace until April 1967, when Barnabas Collins made his first appearance in Collinsport. (In syndication, *Dark Shadows* opens with these episodes.) Barnabas was first presented as a straightforward villain, terrorizing and kidnapping spunky Maggie Evans and sinking his incisors into her pale white neck at every turn. But Jonathan Frid's unusual, poignant performance struck a chord with the public, and one of the dialogue writers, Gordon Russell, began to supply Barnabas with thoughtful epigrams ("Serenity is my favorite emotion") and a guilt complex. Barnabas became troubled, philosophical, ambivalent. So distinctive and highly literary were Russell's scripts that five minutes into a particularly dramatic episode, attentive viewers could tell that it would be Russell's name appearing on the credits. He was later named headwriter.

With the show now in color, Gordon Russell's intriguing writing, and Frid's elegantly forlorn performances, *Dark Shadows* began to take off in the ratings. Frid, a Shakespearean stage actor whose only previous soap exposure was a short stint on *As the World Turns*, received 2,000 to 6,000 letters a week and became the subject of numerous magazine profiles. Barnabas was given an ally in Dr. Julia Hoffman, who attempted to cure his vampirism. Grayson Hall, who played the part, had been an Oscar nominee as the lesbian schoolteacher in *The Night of the Iguana*. Typecast afterwards, she was to Hollywood "still that crazy dyke who chased Sue Lyon all over Mexico." *Dark Shadows* changed her image as Dr. Hoffman, who fans felt carried a torch for Barnabas for years, became another audience favorite. But with Barnabas now a fascinating anti-hero, the show was without a villain. That void was filled spectacularly by Angelique (Lara Parker, in a smashing performance), a jealous witch who had turned Barnabas into a vampire two centuries earlier.

Angelique's appearance began a six-month flashback to 1795, with much of the cast playing their characters' ancestors. *Dark Shadows* doubled its audience and became the top-rated daytime attraction among females between twelve and thirty-four. Also a favorite among teenagers who were glued to the screen after school, *Dark Shadows* suddenly became a national fad that included Barnabas games, capes, bubblegum, and bad jokes. (Question: "How does Barnabas get around town?" Answer: "In his bloodmobile.") Former first lady Jacqueline Kennedy Onassis was counted among the show's enthusiasts. By 1971 Warner Paperback Library had thirty-seven *Dark Shadows* books on the market.

By the end of 1968, Frid was exhausted, having appeared almost daily for over a year and a half. A new mystery man, Quentin Collins (David Selby), was introduced in December and became *Dark Shadows*' new matinee idol, although Barnabas's storyline remained strong throughout the run. "Quentin's Theme," composed by Robert Colbert, became a hit record, and the *Dark Shadows* sound track also became a bestseller. The show again tried a fully costumed flashback, this time to 1897, with the regular cast playing different characters. Plotlines became convoluted and confusing. Dan Curtis later admitted that "story ideas were getting scarce," having tried out everything under the supernatural sun, including the creation of a Frankenstein-like fun couple called Adam and Eve as well as the concept of "parallel time." Viewership dwindled, but the fans who remained were fierce and vocal. When *Dark Shadows* was finally cancelled in 1971 to make room for *Password*, diehards picketed and even threatened to disrupt the taping of *Password*.

Dark Shadows ended so abruptly that viewers refused to let it die. The uproar was so loud that headwriter Sam Hall (husband of Grayson Hall) was compelled to wrap up the storylines in an article for *TV Guide*. Hall wrote that Roger Collins discovered that Barnabas was a vampire and attempted to drive a stake through his heart but was stopped by Angelique, who, despite her treachery, still loved Barnabas. Eventually Barnabas and Julia married, and she cured him of his bad habit. They lived happily ever after, one assumes—or as happily as a former vampire and a mad doctor could.

What made *Dark Shadows* such a cult hit, rivaling even the passion demonstrated by "The Trekkies" or the put-on nihilism displayed by the creatures haunting midnight showings of *The Rocky Horror Picture Show*? The intriguing moral ambiguity of Barnabas and the imaginative performances of Frid and Lara Parker certainly produced unresolved feelings and faithful viewing among the audience. On a sheer entertainment level, when *Dark Shadows* was not suspenseful drama, it was campy and hilarious. In 1969 critic Cleveland Amory called the serial "the worst in history, but the worse it is the better you'll love it." The overworked Frid and Grayson Hall consistently forgot their lines and strained helplessly to find their places on the teleprompter. Walls and scenery fell down, banisters swayed at a touch, coughs were heard from the crew, microphones and shadows constantly made unwelcome appearances. Wags soon dubbed the show *Mike Shadows*.

In one episode, Clarice Blackburn, as the housekeeper Mrs. Johnson, forgot her lines. A booming voice from the sidelines prompted, "Then go to the old house"—a line the frightened Blackburn quickly bellowed. In another episode, in a particularly dimly lit scene, an arm snaked in from stage right and turned on a lamp. Although the limited budget did not allow for retakes or editing, when Joan Bennett referred to Collinswood as "Hollywood," the mistake was mercifully erased.

Dark Shadows lives on in syndication, in the Warner Paperback Library novels by Marilyn Ross, and in two full-length motion pictures, both of which starred the TV regulars. Afterwards, executive producer Dan Curtis made several TV movies (nearly always using *Dark Shadows'* distinctive score) before launching the mini-series blockbuster *The Winds of War*. Director Lela Swift and John Sedwick went on to successful careers on *Ryan's Hope* and *The Edge of Night*. Gordon Russell later became headwriter on *One Life to Live*, where he created the powerful Karen Wolek story. He died shortly afterwards. Sam Hall succeeded Russell as headwriter on *One Life to Live*, just as he followed Russell on *Dark Shadows*.

Jonathan Frid made the forgettable horror film *Seizure* and returned to stage work. Grayson Hall appeared on a few soaps, most notably on her husband's *One Life to Live* as Euphemia Ralston. Lara Parker broke into movies (*Save the Tiger*) and guested on most prime-time dramatic series during the '70s, before returning to the soap scene in the sexy cable effort *A New Day in Eden*. David Selby co-starred with Barbra Streisand in *Up the Sandbox* and later joined the casts of two prime-time soaps, *Flamingo Road* and *Falcon Crest*.

Joan Bennett turned up years later on *The Guiding Light* as herself and spoke affectionately of her experience on *Dark Shadows*. Her not-so-affectionate remembrances are collected in *The Bennett Playbill* (Holt), co-written by *The Edge of Night's* Lois Kibbee. And socialite Alexandra Moltke (Isles), who received special billing as Victoria Winters, made headlines, in grand soap opera fashion, as "the other woman" in the Claus von Bülow trial for the attempted murder of his wife, Sunny. (Isles fled the country afterwards, claiming that she received numerous death threats after von Bülow's conviction. She reappeared dramatically at the last minute to testify against von Bülow in the second trial, which acquitted him.) Last but not least, Kathryn Leigh Scott, who spoke the opening line of the premiere of *Dark Shadows* in 1966, later popped up as Cecil Colby's secretary on the first season of *Dynasty*.

The immortal line which opened *Dark Shadows*? "You're a jerk!"

CONTEMPORARY CAST

Victoria Winters	Alexandra Moltke (Isles)
	Betsy Durkin
Elizabeth Stoddard	Joan Bennett
Barnabas Collins	Jonathan Frid
Roger Collins	Louis Edmonds
Carolyn Stoddard	Nancy Barrett
David Collins	David Henesy
Willie Loomis	John Karlen
	James Hall
Joe Haskell	Joel Crothers
Maggie Evans	Kathryn Leigh Scott
Sam Evans	David Ford
	Mark Evans
Jason McGuire	Dennis Patrick
Paul Stoddard	Dennis Patrick
	Joel Fabiani
Burke Devlin	Anthony George
	Mitchell Ryan
Mrs. Johnson	Clarice Blackburn
Harry Johnson	Craig Solocum
Dr. Dave Woodard	Richard Woods
	Robert Gerringer
	Peter Turgeon
Dr. Julia Hoffman	Grayson Hall
Sarah Collins	Sharon Smyth
Angelique DuVall Collins	Lara Parker
Cassandra Collins	Lara Parker
Quentin Collins	David Selby
Grant Douglas	David Selby
Daphne Harridge	Kate Jackson
Jeb Hawkes	Christopher Pennock
Sebastian Shaw	Christopher Pennock
Bruno Hess	Michael Stroka
Sabrina Stuart	Lisa Richards
Adam	Robert Rodan
Eve	Marie Wallace
Megan Todd	Marie Wallace
Hallie Stokes	Kathy Cody
Prof. Elliot Stokes	Thayer David
Count Petofi	Thayer David
Matthew Morgan	Thayer David
Tony Peterson	Jerry Lacy
Balberith	Humbert Allen Astredo
Nicholas Blair	Humbert Allen Astredo
Amanda Harris	Donna McKechnie
Olivia Corey	Donna McKechnie
Gerald Stiles	James Storm
Phillip Todd	Christopher Bernau

Chris Jennings	Don Briscoe
Tom Jennings	Don Briscoe
Amy Jennings	Denise Nickerson
Jeff Clark	Roger Davis
Ned Stuart	Roger Davis
Sabrina Stuart	Lisa Richards
Sheriff George Paterson	Alfred Sandor
	Vince O'Brien
	Dana Elcar
Roxanne Drew	Donna Wandrey
Richard Garner	Hugh Franklin
Frank Garner	Conard Fowkes
Phyllis Wick	Dorrie Kavanaugh
Laura Collins	Diana Millay
Ezra Braithwaite	Abe Vigoda
Vampire Girl Lily	Marsha Mason

1795 CAST

Barnabas Collins	Jonathan Frid
Angelique DuVall Collins	Lara Parker
Victoria Winters	Alexandra Moltke
	Betsy Durkin
Naomi Collins	Joan Bennett
Joshua Collins	Louis Edmonds
Abigail Collins	Clarice Blackburn
Daniel Collins	David Henesy
Sarah Collins	Sharon Smyth
Millicent Collins	Nancy Barrett
Lt. Nathan Forbes	Joel Crothers
Suki Forbes	Jane Draper
Jeremiah Collins	Anthony George
Josette DuPres	Kathryn Leigh Scott
Andre DuPres	David Ford
Countess Natalie DuPres	Grayson Hall
Ben Stokes	Thayer David
Peter Bradford	Roger Davis
Maude Browning	Vala Clifton
Ruby Tate	Elaine Hyman
Rev. Gregory Trask	Jerry Lacy
Dr. Noah Gifford	Craig Solocum

1897 CAST

Quentin Collins	David Selby
Valerie Collins	Lara Parker
Barnabas Collins	Jonathan Frid
Rev. Gregory Trask	Jerry Lacy
Judith Collins Trask	Joan Bennett
Charity Trask	Nancy Barrett
Minerva Trask	Clarice Blackburn

Edward Collins	Louis Edmonds
Jamison Collins	David Henesy
Nora Collins	Denise Nickerson
Edith Collins	Isabella Hoopes
Carl Collins	John Karlen
Jenny Collins	Marie Wallace
Amanda Harris	Donna McKechnie
Timothy Shaw	Don Briscoe
Evan Hanley	Humbert Allen Astredo
Beth Chavez	Terry Crawford
Count Petofi	Thayer David
Victor Fenn-Gibbon	Thayer David
Sandor Racosie	Thayer David
Magda Racosie	Grayson Hall
Dr. Julia Hoffman	Grayson Hall
Charles Delaware Tate	Roger Davis
Dirk Wilkins	Roger Davis
Garth Blackwood	John Harkins
King Johnny Romano	Paul Michael
Widow Romano	Lana Shaw
Rachel Drummond	Kathryn Leigh Scott
Lady Kathryn Hampshire	Kathryn Leigh Scott
Aristede	Michael Stroka

A DATE WITH LIFE

October 10, 1955–June 29, 1956   NBC

This fifteen-minute daytime serial about life in a small town presented different stories stretched over a period of four to six weeks. The anthology was narrated by character Jim Bradley, the editor of *The Bay City News*, and later by Jim's brother, Tom. (Bay City was later used by NBC as the setting of *Another World*.) Barbara Britton was the star of the premiere story, playing a woman who, on the eve of her marriage, discovered that her parents had adopted her. Laurie Dayton (Britton) quickly postponed her wedding and searched for "her true identity." The story ran for twenty-five episodes, but before it ran out of steam, characters who carried the major interest of the following story were introduced. Continuity was provided by the Bradley brothers, who not only played an active part in all the stories but provided editorial comment as well.

CAST

Jim Bradley	Logan Field
Tom Bradley	Mark Roberts

With: Barbara Britton, Don Hastings (Bob Hughes on *As the World Turns* since 1960), June Dayton, Dean Harens, Anthony Eisley, Dolores Sutton, and William Redfield.

DAYS OF OUR LIVES
November 8, 1965 –   NBC

"Like sands through the hour glass, so are the days of our lives." So begins each episode of this unique family serial that has examined—with relish—the sexual and psychiatric vicissitudes of the Horton family for the last two decades. "We are a bunch of horny devils," Susan Seaforth Hayes, the show's leading lady, commented in 1976. So potently active were the Hortons that by the mid '70s Macdonald Carey and Frances Reid, top-billed as family heads, found themselves playing great-great-grandparents!

Conceived by Irna Phillips, Ted Corday, and Allan Chase—who tossed around ideas one day sitting on a porch in Southampton, N.Y.—the soap was essentially Ted Corday's project, and it was under Corday Productions' umbrella that *Days of Our Lives* flourished. The Horton family consisted of Dr. Tom Horton, the chief of Internal Medicine at University Hospital in the town of Salem; his wife Alice; their son Tommy, who was reported missing in action in Korea; daughter Addie, who went to Europe, leaving behind her troublesome daughter Julie; son Bill, a surgeon; Mickey, a lawyer; and daughter Marie, a young woman unlucky in love.

Although the cast, headed by Hollywood leading man Macdonald Carey, was full of promise and the story concept strong, *Days of Our Lives* ended its first season ranked thirty-second out of thirty-four daytime series. When Ted Corday died in 1966, his widow Betty took over as executive producer and made two important decisions: to hire H. Wesley Kenney as producer-director and William J. Bell as headwriter. Bell, who had been writing dialogue for the ultraconservative *As the World Turns* for almost a decade, made a 180-degree turn with *Days of Our Lives*, creating potent, often shocking stories with strong sexual and psychiatric themes. Part grand opera, part French farce, played out in an atmosphere of somber verisimilitude, *Days of Our Lives'* plotting evolved into terrific melodrama—a tradition carried on, more or less, to the present day.

The Horton family was tossed into one bizarre crisis after another. Marie fell in love with a doctor who turned out to be her brother Tommy, the missing soldier. (In Korea, Tommy had been tortured, developed amnesia, and had extensive plastic surgery performed on his face.) Marie, understandably, fled for the convent. But the story that put the show on the map and ran for several years was a triangle—between Bill and Mickey and Mickey's wife Laura—that included rape, a subsequent child, and the accidental killing of Tommy's meddling wife, Kitty. The paternity of the child, Michael, was probably daytime TV's longest held secret. The long storyline brought great popularity to Edward Mallory and Susan Flannery, who played Drs. Bill and Laura Horton. Flannery won the Emmy for Outstanding Actress in 1975.

Meanwhile, in interwoven, gothic-like stories, two extremely popular female stars emerged: Susan Seaforth as Julie and Denise Alexander as Susan. Julie and Susan were best friends until Susan became pregnant with David Martin's child. Since Julie also loved David, it was the beginning of a bitter feud that continued through other lovers, husbands, and constant tragedy. Alexander's performance as the sensitive, confused

Susan (caught between brothers Eric and Greg Peters in a later, famous story) and Seaforth's vixenish portrayal of Julie became audience favorites, propelling both actresses into the pantheon of daytime superstars.

In 1970 Bill Hayes came on as nightclub singer Doug Williams and quickly came between Susan and Julie and later between Julie and her mother Addie, who had returned from Europe. Although the road proved rocky for Julie and Doug, they finally got together onscreen (many times) over the next decade. Offscreen, Hayes and Seaforth married in 1974. With the melodramatic storylines coming together, *Days of Our Lives* became the number-one-rated soap in 1971, knocking the powerhouse *As the World Turns* from the top peg for the first time in a dozen years.

In 1973 William J. Bell created a new soap, *The Young and the Restless*, and became that show's headwriter, but he still contributed the long-term story for *Days of Our Lives*. Pat Falken Smith, who had been Bell's associate writer for many years, took over and made the already popular show a critical success as well. The day-to-day writing was alternately dramatic, witty, warm, and wonderfully bitchy. Falken Smith often wrote the Friday shows alone, without using staff dialogists. (The show expanded to an hour on April 21, 1975.) *Days of Our Lives* began to sweep the Emmy nominations, and was recognized for Outstanding Dramatic Series every year from 1973 to 1979 (winning in 1978) and for Falken Smith's excellent writing (with story assists by Bell) every year from 1975 to 1978, winning in 1976. During this period, Macdonald Carey also won two sentimental Outstanding Actor awards, while Bill and Susan Seaforth Hayes each earned twin nominations.

In a major story on soap opera, with the Hayeses adorning the cover, *Time* in 1976 called *Days of Our Lives* daytime's "most daring drama, encompassing every trend from artificial insemination [Doug and Rebecca] to interracial romance [David and Valerie]." The then number-three-rated show was given *Time*'s highest soap opera accolade—four teardrops. (*As the World Turns*, which had regained its top-rated position, was awarded, undeservedly, only a single teardrop.) The romantic story of Julie and Doug remained predominant throughout the '70s, especially after the departure of Denise Alexander to *General Hospital*. But *Days of Our Lives* was hardly a two-character show. The Neil-Amanda-Greg romantic triangle was immensely popular, while the young audience became hooked on the complex psychological problems of Trish Clayton. Patty Weaver, who played the split-personality Trish, soared to the top of the fan magazine polls.

Falken Smith's exit in 1977 in a contract dispute marked the end of an era. Although the show had memorable moments under the three short writing stints of Ann Marcus, Ruth Brooks Flippen, and Elizabeth Harrower (the mother of Susan Seaforth Hayes), *Days of Our Lives*, like its NBC sister soap *Another World*, was fading fast. The ABC serials, faster-moving and more youth and action oriented, began to reap high ratings and huge profits. Changes were needed on the the once volatile *Days of Our Lives*, which had grown pleasantly mellow, yet often staid and colorless. In late 1979, NBC, under the leadership of Fred Silverman, insisted on a complete overhaul of the show.

Long-time executive producer H. Wesley Kenney was replaced by Al Rabin, who had been one of the soap's directors. Amid rumors of a feud between Susan Seaforth Hayes and Bill Hayes's new leading lady on the show, Brenda Benet, Rabin began phasing out backstage personnel who, he felt, were contributing to the "negativism" on the set. More importantly Nina Laemmle, the new headwriter, eliminated fourteen characters and introduced nine new ones over a period of six months in 1980. The radical surgery, dubbed the "Valentine Day Massacre" by the cast, included three deaths: Bob Anderson of a heart attack, Brooke Hamilton (a.k.a. Stephanie Woodruff) in a car crash, and Margo Horton of leukemia. Laemmle also wrote out such major characters as Linda Anderson, Phyllis Curtis, Robert LeClair, and Laura and Bill Horton. Edward Mallory had played Bill for fourteen years when he received his pink slip.

The "renovation" was a complete flop. Not only did the dismissals alienate viewers far more than expected, but the new stories were uninvolving and the new characters uninspired. (Three years later, of the nine, only Gloria Loring's Liz remained.) With Laemmle and then Michele Poteet-Lisanti and Gary Tomlin at the writing helm, *Days of Our Lives* limped along for the next two years, rated well below the ABC and CBS shows. However, in early 1982 the show staged a brief but spectacular comeback with the return of headwriter Pat Falken Smith, who had in the interim contributed to *General Hospital*'s rise to the top. Falken Smith brought back conflict, emotionally charged drama, continuity (favorite characters returned while others referred effectively to their past), and her own distinctive brand of sarcastic, sexy humor.

In the show's tradition of strong, quietly macho leading men—most notably Jed Allan's Don Craig and Josh Taylor's Chris Kositchek—Falken Smith created police sergeant Roman Brady (Wayne Northrop, fresh from prime-time's *Dynasty*) and paired him with Deidre Hall's lady psychiatrist Marlena Evans. Eventually Roman and Marlena replaced *General Hospital*'s Luke and Laura as daytime's most popular couple. While developing the "Salem Strangler" story with a series of exciting, ironic twists, Falken Smith created an emotional storyline for actress Brenda Benet in which Lee Dumonde stood by helplessly as her daughter struggled for life. The newly arrived writer had not known that Benet's own young son had died a year before and the intense hospital scenes were, perhaps, making her relive her son's death. Benet did not protest and handled the tough two weeks admirably; but beset with severe psychological problems off the set, she committed suicide shortly afterwards. *Days of Our Lives* dedicated her remaining taped shows to her memory. In her final scene Benet's unstable character Lee complained eerily of fighting for control and prepared for an uncertain future. Benet was not replaced and the part was written out; Lee was said to have left town.

Unfortunately, the show could not hold on to Falken Smith, who left once again in the same contract dispute that had clouded her departure five years before. Her associate Margaret DePriest took over as headwriter and generated tons of publicity for the show when she allowed the "Salem Strangler" to kill Marlena Evans, the soap's main romantic heroine. The victim turned out to be Marlena's twin sister (played by

Deidre Hall's twin sister), but the gambit paid off. The ratings jumped two points.

With *Days of Our Lives* slowly regaining some of its former popularity, DePriest soon turned the show into a romantic suspense story, packed with murder mysteries and romantic entanglements, which included the popular Marie-Neil-Liz triangle. Gloria Loring, who played Liz, broke precedence for a daytime TV actress in 1983 when she negotiated a contract that guaranteed outside appearances from the show, including guest shots on several NBC prime-time series. The contract ended the "daytime ghetto," a situation created by the networks to dissuade popular daytime performers from seeking work on prime time.

Capitalizing on the popularity of the "Salem Strangler" story, DePriest and her associates next created the story of the "Salem Slasher," a long, complex plot that featured several more faked deaths and mixed identities while reactivating the DiMera family as the villains. *Days of Our Lives* became NBC's highest-rated daytime drama and a fan magazine favorite, especially with a romantic-adventure story concentrating on Bo Brady (Roman's brother) and Hope Williams (Doug's daughter by Addie and Julie's sister). The focus on the younger characters caused unrest among the long-running cast members, and in the spring of 1984, Bill and Susan Seaforth Hayes, ostensible stars of the show for a combined total of more than thirty years, refused to renew their contracts, charging they had been relegated to supporting roles after bringing *Days of Our Lives* its greatest moments of popularity.

However, the show flourished with both the focus on youth and the introduction of a series of wacky, far-out characters such as electronic wizard Eugene Bradford and dress designer Calliope Jones. (On Easter Monday 1985, Calliope wore baby chick earrings and a basket bonnet containing colored eggs.) *Days of Our Lives* swept the *Soap Opera Digest* awards and its popularity grew alongside that of fan favorites Peter Reckell and Kristian Alfonso who played Bo and Hope. The love-on-the-run storylines—set amidst New Orleans Mardi Gras and British royalty— culminated with Bo and Hope's wedding on May 23, 1985.

By the time Alfonso and Reckell—as well as superstar Deidre Hall— departed the show in April 1987, plot interest in *Days of Our Lives* had already swung to other equally popular romances. Kimberly Brady hooked up with British secret agent Shane Donovan, while Kayla Brady got involved with the show's new antihero Steve "Patch" Johnson. Although villainous Stefano DiMera was killed off (again and again—the Phoenix always rises), a new character, the treacherous, sophisticated Victor Kiriakis, became the new kingpin of Salem. And later, former *General Hospital* star Genie Francis as Diana Colville was introduced as a spunky foil for the unconventional Mike Horton.

Although *Days* had the reputation of an espionage-romance serial, the show responsibly and dramatically tackled the problem of teenage sexuality (addressing the "taboo" subject of condoms months before prime-time TV did) and also introduced the Johnson family, ripped apart by domestic violence. *Days*'s fans—the fiercest and most vocal in daytime television—now really had something to crow about.

<u>CAST</u>

Dr. Tom Horton	Macdonald Carey 1965–
Alice Horton	Frances Reid 1965–
Dr. Tommy Horton	John Lupton 1965–72; 1975–79
Mickey Horton	John Clarke 1965–
Marie Horton	Lanna Saunders 1979–85
	Kate Woodville 1977
	Marie Cheatham 1965–73
Dr. Bill Horton	Edward Mallory 1966–80
	Paul Carr 1965–66
Addie Horton Olson Williams	Patricia Barry 1971–74
	Pat Huston 1965–66
Julie Olson Williams	Susan Seaforth Hayes 1968–84
	Cathy Ferrar 1967–68
	Catherine Dunn 1967
	Carla Doherty 1965–66
Ben Olson	Robert Knapp 1965
Steve Olson	Stephen Schnetzer 1978–80
	James Carroll Jordan 1972
	Flip Mark 1965
David Martin	Clive Clerk 1966–67
	Steven Mines 1966
Helen Martin	K. T. Stevens 1966–67; 1969
Susan Hunter Martin	Bennye Gatteys 1973–76
	Denise Alexander 1966–73
Tony Merritt	Ron Husmann 1966–67
	Don Briscoe 1966
	Richard Colla 1965–66
Scott Banning	Ryan MacDonald 1971–73
	Robert Hogan 1970–71
	Mike Farrell 1968–70
	Robert Carraway 1968
David Banning	Gregg Marx 1981–83
	Richard Guthrie 1975–81
	Steve Doubet 1975
	Jeffrey Williams 1972–73
	Chad Barstad 1967–69
Dr. Laura Spencer Horton	Rosemary Forsyth 1976–80
	Susan Oliver 1975–76
	Susan Flannery 1966–75
	Floy Dean 1966
Michael Horton	Michael Weiss 1985–
	Paul Coufos 1981–82
	Wesley Eure 1974–81
	Stuart Lee 1973
	Dick DeCoit 1973
	John Amour 1971–73
	Alan Decker 1971

Michael Horton (*cont.*)	Eddie Rayden 1971
	Bobby Eilbacher 1970–71
Kitty Horton	Regina Gleason 1967
Sandy Horton	Pamela Roylance 1983–84
	Martha Smith 1982
	Heather North 1967–69
Doug Williams	Bill Hayes 1970–84; 1985–87
Hope Williams	Kristian Alfonso 1983–87
	Tammy Taylor 1981
	Natasha Ryan 1975
Dr. Mel Bailey	Richard McMurray 1969–75
Dr. Phil Peters	Herb Nelson 1972–73
Anne Peters	Jeanne Bates 1972–74
Dr. Greg Peters	Peter Brown 1972–79
Eric Peters	Stanley Kamel 1972
Bob Anderson	Mark Tapscott 1972–80
Phyllis Anderson	Corinne Conley 1973–82
	Nancy Wickwire 1972
Mary Anderson	Melinda Fee 1981–82
	Barbara Stanger 1975–81
	Susan Keller 1980
	Carla Borelli 1975
	Nancy Stephens 1975
	Karin Wolfe 1972–75
	Brigid Bazlen 1972
Linda Anderson	Elaine Princi 1984–86
	Margaret Mason 1970–71; 1975–80; 1982
Maggie Simmons Horton	Suzanne Rogers 1974–84; 1985–
Trish Clayton	Patty Weaver 1974–82
Jeri Clayton	Kaye Stevens 1974–75
Jack Clayton	Jack Denbo 1976–77
Amanda Howard	Mary Frann 1974–79
Dr. Neil Curtis	Joseph Gallison 1974–
Don Craig	Jed Allan 1975–85
Robert LeClair	Robert Clary 1972–73; 1975–80; 1981–83; 1986–87
Rebecca North	Brooke Bundy 1975–77
Brooke Hamilton/	
Stephanie Woodruff	Adrienne LaRussa 1975
	Eileen Barnett 1978–80
Valerie Grant	Diane Sommerfield 1982
	Rose Fonseca 1977
	Tina Andrews 1975–77
Danny Grant	Roger Aaron Brown 1981–85
	Michael Dwight-Smith 1975
Helen Grant	Ketty Lester 1975
Paul Grant	Lawrence Cook 1975
Sharon Duval	Sally Stark 1976

Karl Duval	Alejandro Rey 1976
Larry Atwood	Fred Bier 1977–78
Dr. Marlena Evans	Deidre Hall 1976–87
Samantha Evans	Andrea Hall-Lovell 1977–80; 1982
Chris Kositchek	Josh Taylor 1977–
Stan Kositchek	Thomas Havens 1979
Jake Kositchek	Jack Coleman 1981–82
Amy Kositchek	Robin Pohle 1979
Margo Horton	Suzanne Zenor 1978–80
Lorraine Temple	Francine York 1978
Donna Temple Craig	Tracey E. Bregman 1978–80
Dr. Jordan Barr	George McDaniel 1979–80
Byron Carmichael	Bill Hayes 1979
Lee Dumonde	Brenda Benet 1979–82
Renee Dumonde	Philece Sampler 1981–83
Scotty Banning	Dick Billingsley 1981–83
	Erick Petersen 1978
Alex Marshall	Quinn Redeker 1979–87
Jessica Blake	Jean Bruce Scott 1980–82
Joshua Fallon	Scott Palmer 1982
	Stephen Brooks 1980–82
Leslie James	Dianne Harper 1980
Kellam Chandler	Bill Joyce 1980–81
Liz Chandler	Gloria Loring 1980–86
Tod Chandler	David Wallace 1985–86
	Paul Keenan 1980–81
	Brett Williams 1980
Maxwell Jarvis	Charles Bateman 1980
Stuart Whyland	Robert Alda 1981
Dr. Evan Whyland	Lane Davies 1981–82
Count Antony DiMera	Thaao Penghlis 1981–85
Stefano DiMera	Joseph Mascolo 1982–85
Daphne DiMera	Madlyn Rhue 1982–84
Sgt. Roman Brady	Drake Hogestyn 1986–
	Wayne Northrop 1981–84
Kayla Brady	Mary Beth Evans 1986–
	Catherine Mary Stewart 1982–84
Bo Brady	Peter Reckell 1983–87
Anna Brady	Leann Hunley 1982–86
Carrie Brady	Christy Clark 1986–
	Andrea Barber 1982–86
Kimberly Brady	Patsy Pease 1984–
Sgt. Abe Carver	James Reynolds 1981–
Nikki Wade	Renee Jones 1982
Gwen Davies	Ann-Marie Martin 1982–85
Woody King	Lane Caudell 1982–83
Oliver Martin	Shawn Stevens 1983
Eugene Bradford	John de Lancie 1982–86

Trista Evans Bradford	Barbara Crampton 1983
Letitia Bradford	Ruth Buzzi 1983
Melissa Anderson	Lisa Trusel 1982–
	Debbie Lytton 1978–80; 1982
	Kim Durso 1976
Pete Jannings	Michael Leon 1983–86
Tess Jannings	Melonie Mazman 1984
Larry Welch	Andrew Massett 1983–85
Delia Abernathy	Shirley DeBurgh 1982–84
Dr. Veronica Kimball	Lenore Kasdorf 1983
Foxy Humdinger	Diane McBain 1983
Maxwell Hathaway	Tom Hallick 1984
Megan Hathaway	Cheryl-Ann Wilson 1984–85
Carlo Forenza	Don Diamont 1984
Marty, the piano player	Marty Davich 1979–
Dave, the waiter	Don Frabotta 1974–
Howie Hoffstedder	Stanley Brock 1983–86
Calliope Jones	Arleen Sorkin 1984–
Jasmine	Jolina Collins 1984–85
Kate Honeycutt, R.N.	Elinor Donahue 1984–85
Shane Donovan	Charles Shaughnessy 1984–
Emma Donovan	Jane Windsor 1985–86
Shawn Brady	Frank Parker 1983; 1985–
	Lew Brown 1984–85
Caroline Brady	Peggy McCay 1983; 1985–
	Barbara Beckley 1984–85
Diane Parker	DeAnna Robbins 1984–85
	Cindy Fisher 1984
	Dana Kimmell 1983–84
Speed Selejko	Tom Everett 1985
	Robert Romanus 1984–85
Ivy Selejko	Holly Gagnier 1984–86
Prince Nicholas	
Arani II	Grey O'Neill 1985
Hart Bennett	Chip Lucia 1985
Madeline Rutherford	Sue Rihr 1985
Ian Griffith	Darby Hinton 1985
	Harrison Douglas 1985
Janey Richards	Candi Milo 1985
Savannah Wilder	Shannon Tweed 1985–
Theo Carver	Rusty Cundieff 1985
Chief Richard Cates	Rod Arrants 1985
The Dragon	Lawrence Trimble 1985
Victor Kiriakis	John Aniston 1985–
Steve "Patch" Johnson	Stephen Nichols 1985–
Jennifer Rose Horton	Melissa Brennan 1985–
Glenn Gallagher	Rob Estes 1986–87
Sylvie Gallagher	Belinda Montgomery 1986–87
Frankie Brady	Billy Warlock 1986–

Robin Jacobs	Derya Ruggles 1986–87
Britta Englund	Amy Stock 1986
Lars Englund	Ken Jezek 1986–87
Tamara Price	Marilyn McCoo 1986–87
Paul Stewart	Paul Tinder 1987
	Robert S. Woods 1986–87
Barbara Stewart	Elizabeth Burr 1986–87
Orpheus	George DeLoy 1986–87
Olivia Reed	Amy Yasbeck 1986–87
Gillian Forrester	Camilla More 1986–87
Grace Forrester	Camilla More 1987–
	Carey More 1987
Leslie Landman	Pamela Bowen 1986–87
Adrienne Johnson	Judi Evans 1986–
Jo Johnson	Joy Garrett 1987–
Justin Kiriakis	Wally Kurth 1987–
Anjelica Deveraux	Jane Elliot 1987–
Jack Deveraux	James Acheson 1987
	Joseph Adams 1987
Sen. Harper Deveraux	Joseph Campanella 1987
Diane Colville	Genie Francis 1987–

THE DOCTORS

April 1, 1963—December 31, 1982   NBC

Premiering the same day as ABC's *General Hospital*, which also used a medical setting, *The Doctors* began not as a continuing story but a daily anthology series. Each day brought a new story featuring one of the four regulars: Dr. William Scott, Dr. Elizabeth Hayes, Dr. Jerry Chandler, and Reverend Sam Shafer, the hospital's chaplain.

Created and initially produced and written by Orvin Tovrov, who wrote radio's *Ma Perkins* for two decades, the premiere story, "Whatsoever House I Enter," told parallel stories of two children in the operating room, one of whom died. The dead girl's father put aside his own grief, comforting the worried mother of the surviving child and presenting the mother with flowers he had brought for his own little girl. Other stories that followed had titles like "One Too Many" and "Button, Button" and starred such guest notables as Dyan Cannon, Mercedes McCambridge, and Sylvia Sidney. On June 20, 1963, James Pritchett played a corporation president with a bad back. On July 9 *The Doctors*, now a story-a-week serial, reintroduced Pritchett as Dr. Matt Powers, a role he was to play for almost two decades.

On March 2, 1964, *The Doctors* became a full-fledged serial with a continuing story and expanding cast. Much of the early story concentrated on Dr. Maggie Fielding, her unhappy marriage to Alec, and her romance with Dr. Matt Powers, and her bad marriage to the villainous Kurt Van Alen, who was reported killed. Elizabeth Hubbard was introduced as Althea, who was divorced from Dave Davis and had two children, Penny and Buddy—who later died of spinal meningitis. She became engaged to Matt, but he carried a torch for Maggie. The 1966–67 season brought color to the low-rated *The Doctors* and a revitalization by producer Allen Potter and writer Rita Lakin. Gerald Gordon was introduced as the gruff Dr. Nick Bellini, who was paired in an oil-and-water romance with the neurotically prim Dr. Althea Davis. Thus began *The Doctors'* greatest romance, and Gerald Gordon and Elizabeth Hubbard won Emmies for their performances in 1976.

Meanwhile, Lydia Bruce became the new Maggie Powers, and David O'Brien was introduced as ladies man Dr. Steve Aldrich. Both stayed with their roles until *The Doctors* was cancelled fifteen years later. David O'Brien became a popular matinee idol for his portrayal of the smooth-talking Steve, who was later seen sympathetically after marrying Nurse Carolee Simpson, played first by Carolee Campbell (for whom the character was named) and later by *The Secret Storm*'s Jada Rowland. (What must viewers have thought when one day playboy Dr. Steve was supposed to say to Carolee, "I just bawled out your son in the hall," but instead declared, "I just balled your son in the hallway."?) The year 1968 turned out to be *The Doctors'* best overall year, averaging 36 percent of the audience watching TV during that half hour. The show remained highly rated for the next eight years.

The Doctors enjoyed its greatest degree of popularity under the long writing regime of Eileen and Robert Mason Pollock, who later made *Dynasty* such a smash hit. By 1972, the year it won the Emmy for best daytime serial, it was often number one or two in the ratings race, periodically nosing out the great workhorse *As the World Turns*. The show remained popular for a few years, and the Pollocks moved over to *General Hospital* (where they failed to revive an ailing show). *The Doctors* went through many writing changes, including Robert Cenedella, Margaret DePriest, and Douglas Marland, who switched his allegiance to *General Hospital* and proceeded to revive that bottom-of-the-basement show.

The other-side-of-the-tracks Dancy clan was introduced and quickly insinuated themselves into everyone's lives. The unscrupulous Nola Dancy married Jason Aldrich and soon made enemies with the Aldrich matriarch, Mona Croft (played with scrupulously cool elegance by the marvelous Meg Mundy). Dr. Jerry Dancy married Althea's daughter, Penny. Handsome Luke went from one rich woman to another before settling down with the demure but troubled Missy. And in a touching story written by Elizabeth Levin, Sara Dancy, a terminal cancer patient, gave her husband, Dr. Mike Powers, the strength to go on without her.

While *The Doctors'* best stories had always been medically oriented, well-researched, and dramatically executed, the revolving door of writers avoided such subject matter for more melodramatic fare: long, drawn-out kidnapping-rapes; Perils-of-Pauline gothic tales that inevitably ended in a fire; a hurricane that wrecked half the city. Ralph and Eugenie Ellis took the same attention-grabbing hospital hostage story that had failed to attract audiences on *As the World Turns* and transferred it to *The Doctors*, with similar results. Colgate-Palmolive, and then NBC, hired and fired so many writers one needed a box score to keep up. Harding Lemay, who had made *Another World* such a critical and commercial success, served briefly, but executives did not cotton to his leisurely pacing and character-oriented plotting. With each new writer came new characters and new stories, with no conclusion provided for the old, forgotten ones. *The Doctors* lost continuity and momentum.

In another disastrous error, NBC moved the show to a noontime slot on the East Coast, pitting it against local news programs. Local affiliates began dropping the soap. In a year and a half the number of markets carrying the show dropped from 185 to 120. Amid rumors of cancellation, in 1982 Barbara Morgenroth and Leonard Kantor took over as headwriters and injected *The Doctors* with a devil-may-care irreverence. Sometimes tasteless, sometimes strikingly original stories about grave-robbing, a subsequent plague because of it, kinky sex, plastic surgery, and weird age-retardants soon spiced up the show. (This tartness also extended to the dialogue. Socialite Adrienne Hunt, complaining about the lack of culture and sophistication in the small town, remarked, "They probably still think Brecht is a hair spray.") An anti-smoking campaign was introduced and stars such as Brooke Shields (as Erich Aldrich's date), Rex Reed, James Coco, and Tony Randall came on in guest shots, just as Johnny Carson, Arlene Francis, and Van Johnson had been worked into a storyline about The National Association for Mental Health in *The Doctors'* first years.

With the soap falling to the bottom slot in daytime programming, producing a measly 1.6 rating and 7 share, *The Doctors* was given its cancellation notice in November. In its final episode, Jeff Manning and Adrienne were married. Adrienne's mother Felicia and Lt. Paul Reed were arrested for the murder of Billy Aldrich. Black songstress Ivie declared—out of left field—her love for Luke. Mike and Kit became engaged, and Matt and Maggie decided to be remarried. *The Doctors* ended its twenty-year run with Dr. Matt Powers speaking about the past, toasting the crowd and the new year with the words, "Every end brings a new beginning."

ANTHOLOGY CAST 1963–64

Dr. Elizabeth Hayes	Margot Moser
Dr. William Scott	Jock Gaynor
Dr. Jerry Chandler	Richard Roat
Rev. Samuel Shafer	Fred J. Scollay
Dr. Matt Powers	James Pritchett
Michael Powers	Rex Thompson
Dr. Maggie Fielding	Ann Williams
Dr. Johnny McGill	Scott Graham
Alec Fielding	Joseph Campanella
	Charles Braswell

Guest Stars: Sylvia Sidney, Anita Louise, Dyan Cannon, Mercedes McCambridge, Jessica Walter, Joanna Pettet, John Cullum, Madeleine Sherwood, Gary Collins, Lori March, Esther Ralston, Virginia Dwyer, Joel Crothers, Mona Bruns, Beulah Garrick, Barbara Berjer, James Farentino, Tina Louise, Patty McCormack, Judy Lewis, Bonnie Bartlett, Douglas Marland, and Jacqueline Courtney.

SERIAL CAST 1964–82

Dr. Matt Powers	James Pritchett 1963–82
Dr. Maggie Powers	Lydia Bruce 1968–82
	Bethel Leslie 1965–68
	Ann Williams 1964–65
Dr. Steve Aldrich	David O'Brien 1967–82
Carolee Aldrich, R.N.	Jada Rowland 1976–82
	Carolee Campbell 1967–76
Dr. Nick Bellini	Gerald Gordon 1966–76
Dr. Althea Davis	Elizabeth Hubbard 1964–82
	Virginia Vestoff 1969
Penny Davis	Julia Duffy 1973–77
	Jami Fields 1969
	Christopher Norris 1967
Kurt Van Alen	Byron Sanders 1964–66
Theodora Van Alen	Augusta Dabney 1980–81
	Clarice Blackburn 1966
	Carmen Matthews 1966
Greta Van Alen Powers	Lori-Nan Engler 1981–82
	Gracie Harrison 1980–81
	Jennifer Reilly 1980
	Jennifer Houlton 1971–80
	Ariane Munker 1971
	Eileen Kearney 1971
Dr. Mike Powers	Stephen Burleigh 1982
	Ashby Adams 1981–82
	James Storm 1979–81
	John Shearin 1977–79
	Armand Assante 1975–77
	Michael Landrum 1974–75
	Peter Burnell 1968–74
	Robert LaTourneaux 1967
	Harry Packwood 1966
	Rex Thompson 1964–66
Dr. Kate Bartok	Ellen McRae (Burstyn) 1965
Liz Wilson	Pamela Toll 1966–69
Nurse Brown	Dorothy Fielding 1964–66
Dr. Steve Lloyd	Craig Huebing 1964–65
Emma Simpson	Katherine Squire 1972
Dr. Karen Werner	Laryssa Lauret 1967–69; 1971–75
Dr. Dan Allison	Richard Higgs 1971
Billy Allison Aldrich	Alec Baldwin 1980–82
	Shawn Campbell 1977–79
	David Elliott 1973–77
	Bobby Hennessey 1971–72
	Mark Kearney 1970–71
Dr. Rico Bellini	Chandler Hill Harben 1975-76
	Richard Niles 1970–71
Martha Allen	Sally Gracie 1968–77

Cathy Ryker	Holly Peters 1972–73
	Nancy Barrett 1971–72
	Carol Pfander 1970–71
Toni Ferra Powers	Anna Stuart 1971–77
Barbara Ferra	Nancy Franklin 1972
Dr. John Morrison	Patrick Horgan 1970–74
Dr. Ann Larimer	Geraldine Court 1973–77
Laurie James Iverson	Marie Thomas 1973–75
Dr. Hank Iverson	Palmer Deane 1970–76
Margo Stewart	Mary Denham 1973–74
Dr. Alan Stewart	Gil Gerard 1974–76
Mona Aldrich Croft	Meg Mundy 1972–82
Jason Aldrich	Glenn Corbett 1976–81
Doreen Aldrich	Pamela Lincoln 1977–79
	Jennifer Wood 1976–77
Nola Dancy Aldrich	Kim Zimmer 1979–82
	Kathleen Turner 1978–79
	Kathyrn Harrold 1976–78
Luke Dancy	Frank Telfer 1976–82
Sara Dancy Powers	Dorothy Fielding 1977–78
	Antoinette Panneck 1976–77
Virginia Dancy	Elizabeth Lawrence 1976–78
Barney Dancy	Lawrence Weber 1977–79
Dr. Jerry Dancy	Terry O'Quinn 1981
	Jonathan Hogan 1976–77
Stacy Wells	Leslie Ray 1975–77
M. J. Match Carroll	Amy Ingersoll 1981–82
	Katherine Glass 1978–81
	Carla Dragoni 1978
	Lauren White 1975–78
Tom Carroll	Jonathan Frakes 1977–78
	James Rebhorn 1977
Eleanor Conrad	Lois Smith 1975–77
Dr. Colin Wakefield	Philip English 1978–79
H. Swenney	Peggy Cass 1978–79
Missy Roberts Dancy	Dorian LoPinto 1978–80
Viveca Strand	Nancy Pinkerton 1979–81
Dr. John Bennett	Franc Luz 1979–81
Ashley Bennett	Valerie Mahaffey 1979–81
Dr. Jack Garner	Ben Thomas 1979–81
Dr. Claudia Howard	Doris Belack 1980
Brad Huntington	Nicholas Walker 1980–81
Darcy Collins	Nana Tucker 1980–81
Alan Ross	Richard Borg 1980–81
Calvin Barnes	Larry Riley 1980–82
Natalie Bell	Jane Badler 1981–82
	Laurie Klatscher 1980–81
Danny Martin	John Pankow 1981–82
Katy Whitney	Maia Danziger 1981–82

Theo Whitney	Tuck Milligan 1981–82
Phillip Manning	James Douglas 1982
	Alvin Epstein 1981
Dr. Jeff Manning	Michael J. Stark 1981–82
Adrienne Hunt	Nancy Stafford 1982
Dr. Jean-Marc Gauthier	Jean LeClerc 1982
Ivie Gooding	Chris Calloway 1982
Kit McCormick	Hillary Bailey 1982
Dr. Murray Glover	Rex Robbins 1982
Lt. Paul Reed	Mark Goddard 1982
Hollis Rodgers	Donna Drake 1982
Erich Aldrich	Mark Andrews 1982
	Ian Ziering 1981–82
	Thor Fields 1977–81
	Keith Blanchard 1973–77
Stephanie Aldrich	Anne Rose Brooks 1982
	Renee Pearl 1981–82
	Gloria Mattioli 1980
	Bridget Breen 1977–79

Guest Stars: Brooke Shields, James Coco, Rex Reed, Tony Randall, Arlene Francis, Van Johnson, Johnny Carson, Melba Moore, Heywood Hale Broun, and Louise Lasser.

DYNASTY

January 12, 1981–   ABC

After the apocalypse: *Dynasty*.

Like a fun-loving phoenix rising from the ashes, *Dynasty*'s indestructible Carrington family takes off every Wednesday after surviving continual tragedy (presumed deaths, hurricanes, log cabin infernos), as well as withstanding yearly entrances from grown-up offspring whose births had apparently slipped the minds of their parents.

Launched with a three-hour special, this flight-of-fancy seemed at first only an ABC clone of CBS's smash hit *Dallas*, the first soap to feature nasty families jockeying for power in the oil business. However, *Dynasty*, created by Esther and Richard Shapiro, quickly left its derivative debut behind and gave its viewers full-blown family melodrama, showy costuming, witty dialogue, and colorful performances. When veteran writers Eileen and Robert Mason Pollock, with British actress Joan Collins in tow, came aboard in the second season, *Dynasty* zoomed in the ratings. By its third season, this entertaining hour of "camp," now packed with the hoariest daytime soap clichés trotted out for prime-time consumption, became ABC's biggest prime-time hit.

Dynasty was indeed about a dynasty, the fantastically rich and powerful Carrington family, who lived and sinned in a forty-eight-room mansion in Denver. The Carrington clan was headed by Blake, president of Denver Carrington, a major oil corporation. The family included Blake's new wife and former secretary, Krystle; Fallon, his spoiled and promiscuous daughter; and Steven, his homosexual son, who interestingly enough, was the moral conscience of the family. Blake's business rival was Cecil Colby, head of Colbyco and uncle to Jeff Colby, a handsome young executive who was infatuated with Fallon. Blake's other business nemesis was Walter Lankershim, an old wildcatter upon whom Blake set his Dobermans in the premiere episode. Blake's rival for Krystle's affections was Matthew Blaisdel, a geologist for Denver Carrington, who was married to the unstable Claudia and was father to the sexually precocious teenager Lindsay.

In the low-rated first season Krystle became disillusioned with her husband's business machinations and found that her only ally in the Carrington home was Steven, who continually put Joseph, the snobbish butler-valet, in his place. Fallon, after carrying on a (literal) back-seat affair with Michael, the family chauffeur, married Jeff Colby. In an argument with Steven's ex-lover Ted Dinard, Blake accidentally killed Ted and stood trial for murder. The season climaxed with the introduction of a surprise witness: Blake's black-veiled ex-wife Alexis, who had been separated from her family for a dozen years.

Under Alexis's veil was not Sophia Loren, as rumored, but Joan Collins, who had been a Hollywood ingénue in the 1954 *Land of the Pharoahs* and B-movie star in the '70s with such delights as *The Stud* and *The Bitch*. Collins' high-powered performance as the villainess Alexis quickly set off a host of female imitators in other prime-time soaps. The beginning of the 1981–82 season also saw the arrival of the formidable writing team of Eileen and Robert Mason Pollock. The Pollocks, who in the early '70s brought *The Doctors* its highest ratings, wrote out wildcatter Walter Lankershim, soft-pedaled the business angle of the drama, and killed off the Blaisdels, with the exception of the nutty Claudia. Then they bombarded viewers with every soap opera staple in the book, presented at such a fast clip that a new tragedy seemed to befall the Carrington family every five minutes.

After Blake was found guilty of voluntary manslaughter and given probation, he raped Krystle and became blind. Later he feigned his blindness in hopes of a reconciliation with the sympathetic Krystle. Fallon was told that Cecil Colby might be her natural father, hovered close to death after a car accident, had an affair with Dr. Nick Toscanni, and produced a child by husband Jeff. (Her son, Little Blake, was eventually kidnapped.) Steven, like his sister, hovered close to death after a pool accident, married Krystle's white-trash niece Sammy Jo, was falsely arrested for assault, and announced before leaving Denver that he was indeed, and irretrievably, homosexual. Troublemaker Alexis became engaged to Cecil Colby, but the night before the wedding Cecil suffered a heart attack in flagrante delicto, causing an angry Alexis to slap him repeatedly. After the rape, Krystle lost her child in a fall from a horse (caused by Alexis), fought off advances by Toscanni, and searched frantically in a hurricane for Blake when Toscanni, after a fight with Blake, left him for dead.

Dynasty's shamelessness paid off. By the end of the season it had hopped into the top ten, and it gathered even more of an audience with summer reruns. The drama, lacking even the merest hint of verisimilitude, was seen as refreshingly irreverent, fun, and funny—escapist entertainment shrewdly executed. Much of the suspense lay not in what would happen next but what Alexis and Krystle would *wear* next. The Nolan Miller creations became so popular that *Dynasty* spawned its own line of women's apparel. Later, capitalizing on that success, the show put out a men's fashion line, *Dynasty* sheets and towels, "Forever Krystle" perfume, dolls, and—in keeping with the nothing-is-sacred spirit of the show—even wall-to-wall carpeting and panty hose.

Alexis's characterization of Krystle as that "ex-stenographer" became a running gag, and their annual cat fight was eagerly anticipated. (They first tore up an apartment, then fought in a swimming pool, and later in a beauty parlor, using mud packs as weapons.) However, the height of tastelessness was yet to come. In a wickedly macabre climax to the kidnapping story, mentally unstable Claudia was sighted on a rooftop holding an infant and later dropping the bundle off the side of the building. After a slow-motion fall, the infant hit concrete and it became apparent that the baby was only a doll.

The kidnapping, which ended with Little Blake returned safely to Fallon, also served as the taking-off point for one of the 1982–83 season's major storylines. Alexis and Blake remembered when their first child Adam, born in 1955, was kidnapped and never returned. (Fallon was born in 1956, Steven in 1958.) Adam did return that season, an unscrupulous lawyer who later tried to kill Jeff with a poisonous paint. Mark Jenning, Krystle's "ex"-husband, was introduced this season. Although still legally married to Krystle, he fell into affairs with both Fallon and her mother Alexis. Also introduced was Kirby, Joseph's daughter, who married Jeff but carried Adam's baby.

The major storyline of the season concerned the disappearance of Steven in a Southeast Asia oil-rig disaster, the presumption of his death in the fire, and his eventual return to Denver—with a new face, transformed by plastic surgery. (The plastic surgery gambit, made necessary by a cast change, was first employed on *One Life to Live* in the late '60s.) Al Corley was replaced by Jack Coleman, fresh from his role as the "Salem Strangler" on *Days of Our Lives*. The season ended with Krystle and Alexis trapped in a burning cabin after threats had been made against Alexis by Blake, Mark, Joseph, Congressman Neal McVane, and Morgan Hess, a corrupt private investigator.

By the 1983–84 season, *Dynasty* was firmly entrenched as ABC's biggest hit, regularly ranked among the top five shows in prime time. After Mark rescued Alexis and Krystle, it was discovered that Joseph had set the fire to stop Alexis from telling Kirby a secret from the past. Joseph later committed suicide. Blake brought suit against Steven for custody of Steven's son Danny (by Sammy Jo) on the grounds that Steven was an unfit father, living with another gay man—his lawyer, Chris Deegan. Steven married Claudia, who had been recently released from a mental institution, and gained custody of Danny. Blake's relationship with Krystle was further strained with the introduction of Tracy Kendall, a beautiful new employee at Denver Carrington. But Blake saw through Tracy and remarried Krystle. Michael Nader (Kevin Thompson, *As the World Turns*) was introduced as Dex Dexter, who attempted to tame the shrewish Alexis.

At the end of the season, bodyguard Mark Jennings was killed when he fell or was pushed off a penthouse terrace after he and Alexis fought bitterly. ("You have delusions of adequacy," she snapped.) After Alexis shipped Kirby off to Paris, she was arrested for Jennings' murder. Diahann Carroll was introduced as Dominique Deveraux, a chic, black mystery woman who claimed to be a Carrington and who also disliked Alexis immensely. ("Wasn't there a singing nun called Dominique?" queried Alexis.) As Blake's financial empire collapsed, Fallon, suffering from intense head pains, skipped out on her remarriage to Jeff, driving dangerously off in the midst of a storm.

In the 1984–85 season, Fallon was presumed dead in a plane crash (her body unidentifiable, her ring among the wreckage) after allegedly running off with Peter de Vilbus. (At the funeral, ex-husband-fiancé Jeff looked down at the casket of his ex-wife-future-bride and barked, "You bitch!") Billy Dee Williams was introduced as Brady Lloyd, the recording executive husband of Dominique Deveraux. Dominique (née Millie Cox) claimed to be Blake's sister, the offspring of an interracial affair between her mother and Tom Carrington, who confirmed the story shortly before his death.

After representing herself in her trial for the murder of Mark Jennings, Alexis was convicted, but she managed to wriggle out of the inconvenience and marry for the third time, this time to Dex (né Farnsworth) Dexter. (Mark's killer was revealed to be the deranged Congressman Neal McVane, who gussied himself up in Alexis's Nolan Miller *hauteur*, a disguise that managed to fool eyewitness Steven.) Alexis's marital bliss was quickly complicated with the introduction of a (forgotten) daughter, Amanda, who developed a yen for Dex as she set out to prove that Blake was her natural father.

The holiday season saw two of Hollywood's biggest stars joining the show. Rock Hudson came aboard as Daniel Reece, who was smitten with Krystle and was revealed to be the natural father of Sammy Jo. And Ali MacGraw was introduced as Lady Ashley Mitchell, who set her sights on Blake. Other developments included the birth of Blake and Krystle's daughter, Krystina; the breakup of Claudia and Steven's marriage when Steven's relationship with colleague Luke Fuller seemed less than platonic; and Jeff's affair with Peter de Vilbus's widow, a bored young socialite who pronounced "ennui" as "on-you-ee."

In the fall of 1984, as the show began to attract 100 million regular viewers in 70 countries, Doubleday published *Dynasty: The Authorized Biography of the Carringtons*, introduced by co-creator Esther Shapiro. The book featured in-depth biographical profiles of the major characters, chapters on the Carrington lifestyle (lunch in the solarium, that patrician flesh worked off on the tennis courts), and a review of the busy storylines— good guy Blake's rape of wife Krystle in 1981 now conveniently forgotten.

Undaunted by such memory lapses, Blake and Krystle stayed together despite Sammy Jo and detective Morgan Hess's efforts—through compromising photos—to split them apart. After Daniel Reece's presumed

Six months after the premiere of Search for Tomorrow *in 1951, Joanne Barron (Mary Stuart) learned that her husband Keith had been killed in an automobile accident. Jo's apron is now on display at the Smithsonian. (Author's Collection.)*

Jo married Arthur Tate (Terry O'Sullivan) on May 18, 1955, as little Patti Barron (Lynn Loring) looked on. During the broadcast of the ceremony, the strategically placed bouquet hid the fact that actress Mary Stuart was eight-months pregnant at the time. (Author's collection.)

Although Jo was the focus of Search for Tomorrow *through the '50s and '60s, other heroines emerged. Among them was Grace Bolton, a young woman who was dying of a brain tumor. Jill Clayburgh, later a major film star, played Grace. Her confidant, Dr. Bob Rogers, was played by Carl Low. (CBS)*

By the '80s, Search for Tomorrow's *romantic storylines concentrated almost exclusively on young characters in various stages of dress and undress. Jo's niece, Suzi Wyatt (Cindy Gibb, seated), married the villainous Warren Carter (Michael Corbett) who seduced Suzi's best friend, Wendy Wilkins (Lisa Peluso). (Photo courtesy of the National Broadcasting Company, Inc.)*

Love of Life, *which premiered in 1951, was a morality tale of good and bad sisters. The compassionate Vanessa Dale (Peggy McCay) often comforted her nephew, Ben Harper (Dennis Parnell), who was neglected by his selfish mother, Meg. (Author's collection.)*

In 1975, Christopher Reeve—later of Superman *fame—was playing Ben Harper, who was still apparently in need of female comfort. Ben married virginal Betsy Crawford but forgot to mention he already was married to vamp Arlene Lovett (Birgitta Tolksdorf, pictured here). (Daytime TV Magazine Photo.)*

The Guiding Light *began broadcasting on television in 1952, with Theo Goetz as Papa Bauer, and Charita Bauer (the last name is a coincidence) as his daughter-in-law, Bertha. (Author's Collection.)*

The Bauer family has been the focus of The Guiding Light *for over three decades. Pictured here in 1954 is Glenn Walken (left) as young Michael Bauer, Charita Bauer as Bert, and Lyle Sudrow as Bert's troublesome husband, Bill. (Author's Collection.)*

*Jone Allison (right) played Meta, the most colorful member of the Bauer clan.
Meta ran away to become a model and later murdered her husband when he
continually browbeat their son. Competing for attention in this 1952 photo is
Susan Douglas, who played Meta's step daughter, Kathy.*

*In 1954, Nurse Janet Johnson (Ruth Warrick) dispensed medicine with one
hand while trying to take away the husband of ailing Kathy Roberts (Susan
Douglas) with the other. (Author's Collection.)*

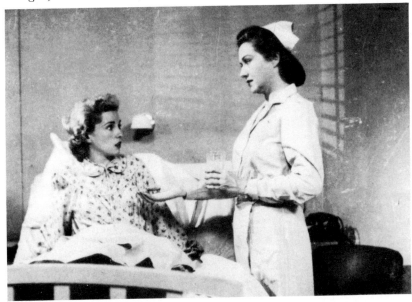

By the early '80s, The Guiding Light *had expanded to include the low-income Reardon family. To escape the humdrum reality of Springfield, Nola Reardon (Lisa Brown) often fantasized that she was in the midst of one of her favorite movies—in this case,* Now Voyager *with Quinton Chamberlain (Michael Tylo) as her co-star. (CBS.)*

Happy New Year, Guiding Light: *Judi Evans as Beth Raines, Grant Aleksander as Phillip Spaulding, Krista Tesreau as Mindy Lewis, and Michael O'Leary as Rick Bauer, 1984. (CBS)*

SERIAL SIRENS OF *1954: Halia Stoddard as nefarious Aunt Pauline on* The Secret Storm, *Nancy Coleman as suffering Helen Emerson on* Valiant Lady, *Ellen Demming as devil-may-care Meta Bauer on* The Guiding Light, *Lois Nettleton as impressionable teen Patsy Dennis on* The Brighter Day, *Frances Reid as lady lawyer Portia Manning on* Portia Faces Life, *and Dorothy Lovett as social climbing Grace Adam on* The Seeking Heart. *(Courtesy of the Broadcast Pioneers Library)*

The Brighter Day, *the story of the Reverend Richard Dennis and family, ran from 1954 to 1962. Mona Bruns (seated, left) was the always understanding Aunt Emily; Gloria Hoye (top, left) was the mysterious Sandra, who married Grayling Dennis; and Murial Williams (right) played Lydia Canfield, the loving wife of a newspaper man. (Author's Collection.)*

The TV version of Kitty Foyle *disappeared quickly in 1958, perhaps because the heroine was less Christopher Morley's working-class colleen and more Gidget Goes to Princeton. Kathleen Murray (left) headlined as the bedecked Kitty while Judy Lewis, daughter of Loretta Young, played Molly Scharf, her dateless side-kick. (Photo courtesy of the National Broadcasting Company, Inc.)*

From These Roots *was a cherished daytime drama featuring romances between theater personalities as well as on-stage musical interludes. In 1959, alcoholic actress Lynn Franklin (Barbara Berjer, right) was married to theater director Tom Jennings (Craig Huebing, left) but was in love with writer David Allen (Robert Mandan, center right) who was married to journalist Liz Fraser (Ann Flood, center left). (Author's Collection.)*

Equally loved was Young Dr. Malone *(1958–63), a poignant and often witty daytime entry. Dr. David Malone (John Connell, center) the young doctor of title, worked with his father Dr. Jerry Malone (William Prince). At home, Tracey (Augusta Dabney) faced the "empty nest" syndrome, commenting once, "Very few women pass forty without a tremor." (Photo courtesy of the National Broadcasting Company, Inc.)*

Cheesecake 1958-style: Barbara Loden as Maxine Wells, a woman with a secret past on Today is Ours. (*Author's collection.*)

Short-lived but not forgotten was The Clear Horizon, *an earth-bound melodrama about astronauts and their wives at Cape Canaveral. Pictured here in 1962 are the stars, Edward Kemmer and Phyllis Avery as Roy and Ann Selby.* (*CBS.*)

The Secret Storm *premiered in 1954, but it wasn't until 1963, when Amy Ames (Jada Rowland), who had grown up on the show, became the central heroine that the soap became a fan favorite. The spunky Amy had an affair with her history professor, Paul Britton (Jed Allan), then refused to marry him when she became pregnant. (Author's Collection.)*

The 1973 plotline that almost saved The Secret Storm *was the story in which Father Mark Reddin (David Gale) debated whether to leave the priesthood to marry Laurie Hollister (Stephanie Braxton). The steamy, controversial story brought reams of mail into CBS. (*Daytime TV *Magazine Photo.)*

On the tenth anniversary of As the World Turns *in 1966, Helen Wagner and Don MacLaughlin were still playing Nancy and Chris Hughes, cornerstones of the most popular daytime drama in history. (CBS.)*

Little did Eileen Fulton know, when she first appeared as Lisa Miller on As the World Turns *in 1960, that she would be playing the longest-running villainess in television. The object of her affection is Don Hastings, who as Bob Hughes broke free of his* Captain Video *image to become daytime TV's longest-running matinee idol. (CBS.)*

Considered by serial critics as the best actor in daytime television, Larry Bryggman also has the distinction of playing the longest-running villain in TV history, Dr. John Dixon on As the World Turns. *(CBS.)*

As the World Turns *has always excelled at presenting intriguing romantic triangles. During the mid-70s, self-destructive Dr. Susan Stewart (Marie Masters, top) was obsessed with Dr. Dan Stewart (John Reilly) who was enchanted by the elegant Kim Reynolds (Kathyrn Hays.) Marie Masters gave a harrowing performance as the alcoholic Susan. (CBS.)*

Twenty years before his starring role as J.R. Ewing on Dallas, *Larry Hagman was the romantic lead on* The Edge of Night. *In 1961, lawyer Ed Gibson (Hagman, right) married Judy Marceau (Joan Harvey), the mischievous daughter of Chief of Police Bill Marceau (Mandel Kramer, left). (CBS.)*

Opposite page: The Edge of Night, *which premiered in 1956, was a detective serial rather than a traditional soap opera. This retrospective includes (top) the first* Edge of Night *logo and the discovery of dead body in a trunk. Middle: John Larkin, who created the role of assistant D.A. Mike Karr, conferred with a crime technician and Teal Ames, who played Sara Lane. Meanwhile, Laurence Hugo, who took over the role of Mike in 1962, locked horns with reporter Nancy Pollock (Ann Flood), who was soon to become Mike's bride. Forrest Compton took over as Mike in 1971 and he and Ann Flood remained in their roles until the show was cancelled in 1984. At the bottom, nasty Stephanie Martin (Alice Hirson) turned up deader than a door nail, and lawyer Adam Drake (Donald May) successfully defended socialite Nicole Travis (Maeve McGuire), 1969. The decade-long romance between Nicole and Adam was the show's most memorable. Reruns of the program still appear on cable television. (Courtesy of the Martin Luther King Memorial Library.)*

NBC finally hit its stride with Another World, *which premiered in 1964. In 1970, girl-from-the-wrong-side-of-the-tracks Rachel Davis (Robin Strasser, right), turned the town upside down, nabbing Dr. Russ Matthews (Sam Groom) and then setting her sights on Alice Matthews' true love, Steve Frame. (Photo courtesy of the National Broadcasting Company, Inc.)*

Soap opera's most famous love story in the '70s focused on ambitious Steve Frame (George Reinholt) and sweet Alice Matthews (Jacqueline Courtney) on Another World. *(Photo courtesy of the National Broadcasting Company, Inc.)*

death in Libya, Sammy Jo inherited his vast estate with Krystle serving as executrix of his will. Unhappy with this turn of events, Sammy Jo coached her roommate Rita to impersonate Auntie Krystle. While Sammy Jo's ex-husband Steven planned to move in with Luke, musical beds again turned, Steven's ex-wife Claudia falling into brother Adam's four-poster.

As the season drew to a close on the now most popular prime-time program on the air, Amanda became engaged to Prince Michael of Moldavia, a deal sealed with Alexis's gift of herself to King Galen. (Alexis mused that as a child Amanda wished one Christmas for a country of her very own. Mama then added, "I think Santa's about to deliver!") As the Carrington family gathered for the wedding, Jeff proposed to Lady Ashley unaware that Fallon had turned up with amnesia in Los Angeles. (Pamela Sue Martin was replaced as Fallon by *General Hospital* star Emma Samms, who played her daytime and prime-time roles concurrently.) The season concluded with a terrorist attack after Amanda and Michael traded vows, machine gun fire spraying the crowd. The only sure survivor was the still-moving Jeff, who was to be the lead of a scheduled *Dynasty* spin-off in the fall, *The Colbys*—presumably leaving behind Ali MacGraw's Ashley to that Great Acting Class in the Sky.

The Moldavian catastrophe was a disaster in more ways than one. On screen, casualties included Lady Ashley Mitchell (Hallelujah!) and Steven's boyfriend, Luke. Off screen, critics and fans alike were flabbergasted at the spectacle. Defense Minister Warnick held Krystle captive in a Moldavian dungeon for weeks and tried to rape her. Alexis, tricked out in a nun's habit and a bad French accent, was traipsing across Europe to help rescue King Galen. Once freed, Krystle was kidnapped by sleazy Joel Abigore, who for weeks tried to force himself on her. Blake, sipping poisoned soup prepared by the fake Krystle, tried to rape the hapless Rita/Krystle. Linda Evans's bodice was being ripped at every turn!

Dynasty's ratings dive-bombed and *TV Guide* reported that there was talk of an apology to the nation by the show's creators! (Another major problem was that the characters of the *Dynasty* spin-off, *The Colbys*, were being introduced on *Dynasty* in the season's early episodes, shifting the show's focus away from the Carrington family.) Soon, Sammy Jo 'fessed up, Blake recovered from his poisoning, Rita and Joel were disposed of, Amanda and Prince Michael's marriage went kaput, and Alexis gave up all ideas of becoming queen of Moldavia.

After Alexis put away her tiara, she made a play for Blake, who made it clear that he wouldn't even empty her garbage. A vengeful Alexis scouted the Australian outback, brought Blake's greedy brother Ben back to Denver, and cheated Blake out of $125 million. Other developments in the 1985–86 season were Dex and Alexis's divorce when she caught him in bed with Amanda, who later attempted suicide; Alexis's sister Caress popping up with a manuscript called *Sister Dearest*; Dominique refusing to marry Garrett Boydston, Jackie's natural father; and Ben and Alexis stealing Blake's South China Sea oil leases—they bought Blake out lock, stock, and mansion. Surveying the room, Alexis snarled, "Clear out all this junk and take your blonde tramp with you!" Blake began choking the wicked witch. Meanwhile, nutty Claudia accidentally set fire to *La*

Mirage, the whole kit and caboodle went up in flames, and it was bye-bye Claudia.

In the 1986–87 season Sammy Jo and Clay Fallmont married and divorced. Later, Sammy Jo tried to work things out with Steven, but Steven continued to wrestle with his bisexuality. Adam became self-destructive after Claudia's death, found evidence that he might not be a Carrington after all, and married his Montana sweetheart Dana Waring (Leann Hunley, an Emmy winer as Anna DiMera on *Days of Our Lives*). In an accident at an oil rig, Blake was hit on the noggin and lost his memory. Alexis squired him off to a paradise resort and they reminisced about old times. When Blake regained his memory, he was much kinder to Alexis.

Meanwhile, little Krystina needed a heart transplant, and the mother of the donor, Sarah Curtis, later became obsessed with Krystina and kidnapped the child before Sarah realized she needed psychiatric help. A nasty Buck Fallmont informed Clay, who had fallen in love with Ben Carrington's daughter, that Clay was the natural son of Ben, by Buck's late wife Emily. Dominique became engaged to Nick Kimball. And, in the season finale, Matthew Blaisdel, who had been presumed dead in South America six years before, popped up in Denver to "claim" his former love, Krystle!

The once mighty *Dynasty*—which had once attracted Henry Kissinger, former president Gerald Ford, and Betty Ford to appear in a party sequence—had fallen on hard times, lucky to break into the weekly top-twenty rated shows. Will this downard spiral continue? Not if Alexis has anything to say about it: quoting the immortal Yogi Berra, she once snapped, "It ain't over 'til it's over!"

CAST

Blake Carrington	John Forsythe 1981–
Krystle Grant	Linda Evans 1981–
Fallon Carrington	Emma Samms 1985–
	Pamela Sue Martin 1981–84
Steven Carrington	Jack Coleman 1982–
	Al Corley 1981–82
Alexis Carrington	Joan Collins 1981–
Adam Carrington	Gordon Thomson 1982–
Jeff Colby	John James 1981–
Cecil Colby	Lloyd Bochner 1981–83
Sammy Jo Dean	Heather Locklear 1981–
Matthew Blaisdel	Bo Hopkins 1981; 1987
Claudia Blaisdel	Pamela Bellwood 1981–86
Lindsay Blaisdel	Katy Kurtzman 1981
Walter Lankershim	Dale Robertson 1981
Ted Dinard	Mark Withers 1981
Michael Culhane	Wayne Northrop 1981; 1986–87
Joseph Anders	Lee Begere 1981–83
Kirby Anders	Kathleen Beller 1982–84
Andrew Laird	Peter Mark Richman 1981–
Dr. Nick Toscanni	James Farentino 1981–82

Tony Driscoll | Paul Keenan 1982–84
Mark Jennings | Geoffrey Scott 1982–84
Rashid Ahmed | John Saxon 1981–84
Rep. Neal McVane | Paul Burke 1982–84; 1987
Morgan Hess | Hank Brandt 1982–
Chris Deegan | Grant Goodeve 1983–84
Tracy Kendall | Deborah Adair 1983–84
Dex Dexter | Michael Nader 1983–
Peter de Vilbus | Helmut Berger 1984
Nicole Simpson | Susan Scannell 1984–85
Dominique Deveraux | Diahann Carroll 1984–
Brady Lloyd | Billy Dee Williams 1984–85
Amanda Carrington | Karen Cellini 1986–87
| Catherine Oxenberg 1984–86
Luke Fuller | William Campbell 1984–85
Dean Caldwell | Richard Hatch 1984
Tom Carrington | Harry Andrews 1985
Daniel Reece | Rock Hudson 1984–85
Lady Ashley Mitchell | Ali MacGraw 1985
Hal Lombard | Bradford Dillman 1984
Rosalind Bedford | Juliet Mills 1984
Prince Michael | Michael Praed 1985–86
King Galen | Joel Fabiani 1985–86
Elena | Kerry Armstrong 1985
Rita Lesley | Linda Evans 1985–86
Joel Abigore | George Hamilton 1985–86
Warnick | Theodore Bikel 1985
Garrett Boydston | Ken Howard 1985–86
Jackie Devereaux | Troy Beyer 1986–87
Caress Morrell | Kate O'Mara 1986
Bart Fallmont | Kevin Conroy 1985
Clay Fallmont | Ted McGinley 1986–87
Buck Fallmont | Richard Anderson 1986–87
Emily Fallmont | Pat Crowley 1986
Ben Carrington | Christopher Cazenove 1986–87
Leslie Carrington | Terri Garber 1987–
Dana Waring | Leann Hunley 1986–
Claire Prentice | Kimberly Beck 1986–87
Sarah Curtis | Cassie Yates 1987
Dirk Maurier | Jon Cypher 1987
Gavin Maurier | Neil Dickson 1987

DYNASTY II: THE COLBYS
See: The Colbys

THE EDGE OF NIGHT

April 2, 1956–November 28, 1975;   CBS
December 1, 1975–December 28, 1984   ABC

Daytime's longest-running oddity—a mystery serial rather than traditional soap opera—*The Edge of Night* survived almost thirty years of less than outstanding ratings, a devastating time change, a jump from the CBS network to ABC, and a dwindling number of local affiliates carrying the show. But *Edge* was also the recipient of intense viewer loyalty. Fans have included Eleanor Roosevelt, P. G. Wodehouse, Tallulah Bankhead, and Cole Porter as well as regular viewers, a consistent 50 percent of whom were men—a statistic shocking to those who consider daytime drama the exclusive domain of housewives.

Procter & Gamble had been kicking around the idea of a mystery serial for some time in the early '50s, even attempting to buy the TV rights to *Perry Mason*, a successful radio show that had been cancelled in 1955 after a twelve-year run. When negotiations did not pan out, P & G merely hired *Perry Mason*'s writer Irving Vendig to create a new show with John Larkin, who played Perry on radio, as the Perry-styled smart lawyer Mike Karr. (*Perry Mason*, of course, was adapted successfully to prime time with Raymond Burr starring in the title role from 1957 to 1966.) Called *The Edge of Night* and positioned in the late-afternoon slot (4:30 E.S.T.) to reflect the show's title and sense of foreboding, the serial was presented live and was the first major daytime soap—along with *As the World Turns*, which premiered the same day—to run a half hour long.

Set in the midwestern city of Monticello—which seemed to have the highest crime and mortality rate in the U.S.—the serial revolved around the adventures of assistant district attorney Mike Karr and his wife Sara Lane. So troublesome was life in the area that *Time* wrote, "Hell is a city much like Monticello." In the first storyline Mike found himself drawn into the syndicate problems of Sara's brother Jack, played by Don Hastings, who spoke the opening line of the premiere show. Unlike other daytime serials, which gathered loyal viewers slowly, *The Edge of Night* was an immediate hit, with an audience of nine million after its first year. The serial format was perfect for the whodunit storylines, and the audience found the cops-and-robbers action (staged dramatically by producer-director Don Wallace) refreshing in the midst of the afternoon suds.

In 1961, when actress and militant vegetarian Teal Ames wanted to leave her role as Sara Karr, writer Carl Bixby, who had taken over for Irving Vendig, decided to kill the character off rather than risk recasting such an identifiable role. On Washington's Birthday Sara was killed while pushing her daughter Laurie Ann (played by John Larkin's daughter Victoria) out of the way of an onrushing car. The audience was shocked; fans tied up the CBS switchboard and bombarded the network with telegrams and letters, 8,000 in all. "Shakespeare himself did not create a more convincing cast of praiseworthy personalities," wrote one disgruntled viewer. "What perversion of common decency prompted anyone to shatter such a team?" The next day the network put Teal Ames on the air to show that the actress was indeed alive and well. Ames explained that she wanted to leave the show to pursue a theater career and to go on a speaking tour to promote organic vegetables.

Shortly afterwards John Larkin also wanted to leave the show, but this time the writers thought it wise to recast. Larkin was replaced by Larry Hugo, and the writers also built up the part of Mike Karr's junior law partner Ed Gibson, played by Larry Hagman—a future soap superstar as J. R. Ewing in *Dallas*. To fill the void created by Sara Karr's death, a new leading lady was written in. Ann Flood, former star of *From These Roots*, came on as reporter Nancy Pollack on March 22, 1962, and a month later, on April 23, Nancy and Mike were wed, thus creating one of soap opera's longest-lasting marriages. The classically beautiful, red-haired Flood had the distinction of having the longest tenure of any actor on *The Edge of Night*: over twenty-two years.

The show continued to flourish in the '60s, even through a succession of writing changes that included Lou Scofield and Margaret DePriest, Gabrielle Upton (writing under the pseudonym Gillian Houghton), and James Lipton. In 1966 Erwin Nicholson took over as producer and the next year brought color to Monticello. In 1968 veteran mystery writer Henry Slesar became headwriter, beginning a writing stint of fifteen years, the longest in the history of daytime drama. Slesar proved a master of the serial format, creating a series of bizarre, intricate plots of offbeat characters in the spirit of the irreverent detective movies of the '40s.

Slesar gave birth to a slew of memorable villainesses, including Stephanie Martin and Pamela Stewart, and a long line of fun-loving, exotically named anti-heroines, such as Brandy (née Olivia Brandeis) Henderson and Raven (née Charlotte) Alexander. Lawyer Adam Drake was paired with the spirited Nicole Travis in a sensational love story, causing actors Donald May and Maeve McGuire to soar in the fan magazine polls. In November of 1968 Slesar wrote a very unusual episode in which Adam Drake, dramatically summing up his case to a jury, was the only one to speak during the half hour. Donald May as Adam flawlessly delivered forty-two pages of monologue.

The Edge of Night continued to use up actors at a fast clip with continuous murder and mayhem plotlines. Only a handful of core characters remained through the years: Mike and Nancy, Adam and Nicole, and Bill and Martha Marceau. The political Whitney family, once written out, had been a favorite, so Slesar brought the Whitney women back years later. Lois Kibbee played the matriarch Geraldine for a decade before becoming Slesar's associate writer while continuing to play the part. Tiffany Whitney did not fare as well, finding final disappointment in a rendezvous with the sidewalk. ("Masochism is my game," she once insisted, "it wears better than backgammon.") The offbeat nature of the drama required constant turnover of actors who were able to make an impression quickly. Over the years the show employed many of the finest actors of the American stage.

In 1972 Procter & Gamble made the strategic error of moving the show to a spot earlier in the afternoon, ostensibly to create a block of P & G serials amid the less popular CBS soaps. *The Edge of Night* lost its youth audience, who had watched after school, and many of its male viewers, home from early work shifts. (The show also lost "the edge of night" concept, airing at 2:00 P.M., E.S.T.) Confronted with plummeting ratings, CBS decided to cancel the show in late 1975, but P & G balked and moved the serial to ABC in a late-aftenoon slot. *The Edge of Night* premiered on ABC on December 1, 1975, in a ninety-minute special in which Serena Faraday shot her husband on the courtroom steps and Adam Drake vowed to clear her name.

On November 11, 1976, *The Edge of Night* presented another special episode in which only Ann Flood and Forrest Compton, as Nancy and Mike Karr, appeared on camera. The show dramatized the breakup of the Karrs' marriage as Nancy, disillusioned with her husband's obsession with fighting crime, packed to leave. Superbly acted, written (by Slesar and associate writer Grace Garment), and directed (by John Sedwick), the two-character show was one of the most emotionally packed and unusual in daytime drama history. The next year brought *The Edge of Night*'s most controversial move, the writing out of Donald May after a decade as Adam Drake. Adam was shot in the back just before revealing information about the murder of Beau Richardson, the man who had broken up the Karrs' marriage. The Karrs reconciled.

With the departure of Adam Drake came the introduction of a new romantic leading man, Dr. Miles Cavanaugh, played by Joel Crothers, who had been a favorite on *Somerset*. (Although doctors were regular fixtures on all other daytime serials, this was the first regular character to be a physician on *The Edge of Night* since Dr. Hugh Campbell in the '50s.) His introduction precipitated one of the show's best storylines as Miles' wife Denise, a modern-day Hedda Gabler, wreaked havoc in the lives of Nicole and Miles. Highlighted by a bravura performance by Holland Taylor as Denise, the story climaxed with two monologues in which Denise planned "the perfect crime"—her own death at the hands of Miles. As it turned out, it was Denise's father who injected her with the fatal dose. After the fatal injection, the pain-wracked Denise murmured, "Thank you, Daddy," making her the most unforgettable in writer Henry Slesar's long line of "Daddy's girls."

Although Slesar's writing remained entertaining over the next few years— such as in the "Mansion of the Damned" storyline with actress Kim Hunter—more and more ABC affiliates dropped the show or aired the serial on a delayed basis. Youth had exploded in daytime, and *The Edge of Night* tried to keep up with the times, concentrating on young heroines like April Cavanaugh and Jody Travis. Police chief Bill Marceau (actor Mandel Kramer) was given his walking papers after twenty years and was replaced by a sexy new police chief, Derek Mallory, played by Dennis Parker, who had starred in a series of "adult" films in the '70s, such as *Take Off* and *Blonde Ambition*.

But *The Edge of Night* failed to pick up a substantial audience, even though it followed the phenomenally successful *General Hospital* in many markets. In 1983, with the show rated among the bottom soaps, Henry Slesar was replaced by Lee Sheldon, who had written for many prime-time detective series. Sheldon's first move was to kill off Nicole Cavanaugh and emphasize the younger performers. Sheldon continued in the Slesar vein, however, keeping *The Edge of Night*'s peculiar brand of irreverent wit and off-the-wall characters. His first major storyline—an evil genius attempting to take over Monticello through mass hypnosis—had overtures of science fiction. At least he did end one of *The Edge of Night*'s most baffling mysteries: why Mike and Nancy Karr, who were so in love with each other, had separate beds. After twenty years of a Procter & Gamble marriage, Nancy finally suggested to Mike, "What do you say we give up our twin beds and go all out and buy a double?"

Neither Mike and Nancy's marital intimacy nor the continuous antics of Raven Alexander Jamison Swift Whitney Whitney, the show's delightful young vixen-heroine, was enough to bring a resurgence in the show's popularity. In November 1984, ABC announced it was cancelling *The Edge of Night*, which had finished twenty-third among twenty-six daytime programs, with a 2.8 rating and a 9 percent share of the audience. Although the top-rated *General Hospital* was the show's lead-in on ABC, *The Edge of Night* was carried by less than half of the network's affiliates, so only an estimated 62 percent of the country's 84.9 million TV homes had access to it.

After twenty-eight years and seven thousand four hundred and twenty episodes of murderous and irreverent intrigue, *The Edge of Night* had fallen victim to the cruelest and most terminal of soap opera diseases: low ratings. Because Procter & Gamble hoped the show would be picked up for syndication in the future, storylines were left open as Detective Chris Egan unearthed a bizarre mystery involving Monticello's most notorious crime figures, who had supposedly died years before.

But for other characters, the drama provided "happy endings": when Jody and Preacher broke up, Preacher left town with Liz Corell and Jody discovered romantic feelings for Jeremy Rhodes; Geraldine Saxon and Del Emerson were engaged; Miles Cavanaugh and Dr. Beth Corell (a radio psychologist and the world's oldest virgin) were married; after her kidnapping by Mark Hamilton, Raven gave birth to a baby girl, Charlotte Jasmine; Didi and Calvin were expecting a child; and Nancy and Mike—exhausted from three decades of crime fighting—welcomed daughter Laurie back home.

CAST

Nancy Karr	Ann Flood 1962–84
Mike Karr	Forrest Compton 1971–84
	Larry Hugo 1962–71
	John Larkin 1956–62
Sara Lane Karr	Teal Ames 1956–61
Jack Lane	Don Hastings 1956–60
Winston Grimsley	Walter Greaza 1956–73
Mattie Lane Grimsley	Katherine Meskill 1969–71
	Peggy Allenby 1956–66
	Betty Garde 1956
Laurie Ann Karr	Linda Cook 1975–78; 1984
	Jeanne Ruskin 1973–75
	Emily Prager 1968–73

Laurie Ann Karr (*cont.*)   Kathy Cody   1967–68
                                 Kathleen Bracken
                                 Victoria Larkin
Harry Lane   Lauren Gilbert   1956–59
Cora Lane   Sarah Burton   1956–59
Dick Appleman   Michael Strong   1959
Mary Appleman   Joan Copeland   1959
Louise Grimsley Capice   Mary K. Wells   1961–70
                                 Lisa Howard   1956–61
Phil Capice   Ray MacDonnell   1961–69
                                 Earl Hammond   1957
                                 Robert Webber   1956–57
Sara Capice   Christopher Norris   1968–70
                                 Mary Breen   1961–63
Dr. Hugh Campbell   Wesley Addy   1958–59
Gail Armstrong   Millette Alexander   1958–59
Bill Marceau   Mandel Kramer   1959–79
                                 Carl Frank
                                 Frank Campanella   1968
Martha Marceau   Teri Keane   1964–75
Judy Marceau Gibson   Joan Harvey   1961–63
Ed Gibson   Larry Hagman   1961–63
Sally Smith   Mary Fickett   1961
Viola Smith   Jacqueline Courtney   1961
Austin Johnson   Lawrence Weber   1962–63
Constance Johnson   Elizabeth Lawrence   1962–63
Toby Marshall   Rita Lloyd   1962–63
Lyn Wilkins Warren   Gillian Spencer   1962–63
Emory Warren   Bill Berger   1963
Joe Pollock   Allen Nourse   1973–79
                                 John Gibson   1962–71
Rose Pollock   Virginia Kaye   1973–79
                                 Kay Campbell   1965–68
                                 Frances Reid   1964
                                 Ruth Matteson   1962–63
Lee Pollock   Tony Roberts   1965–67
                                 Sam Groom   1964
                                 Ronnie Welch   1962–64
Cookie Pollock   Fran Sharon   1962–72
                                 June Carter   1962
Carol Kramer   Elizabeth Hubbard   1963
Nathan Axelrod   Robert Mandan   1963
Beth Anderson Barnes   Nancy Pinkerton   1963–67
John Paul Anderson   Conard Fowkes   1963
John Barnes   Barry Newman   1964–65
Elizabeth McGrath   Nancy Coleman   1967
                                 Ludi Claire   1964–66
Gerry McGrath Pollack   Millee Taggart   1966
                                 Joanna Miles   1964–65

Kelly McGrath

Penny Fuller   1964
Allen Fawcett   1980–82
Joey Alan Phipps   1980

Capt. Lloyd Griffin
Kate Griffin
Irene Wheeler
Eve Morris
Andre Lazar
Tony Wyatt
Abby Cameron
Roy Cameron
Lonnie Winters
Angela Talbot
David Gideon
Victoria Dana
Orin Hillyer
Laura Hillyer
Julie Jamison
Liz Hillyer
Dr. Jim Fields
Rick Oliver
Phoebe Smith

James Mitchell   1964
Priscilla Gillette   1964
Barbara Berjer   1964
Constance Ford   1964–65
Val Dufour   1965–66
Antony Ponzini   1965–66
Margaret DePriest   1965–66
Allen Nourse   1965–66
Peter Kastner   1966
Ann Wedgeworth   1966
John Cullum   1966–67
Joanna Roos   1966
Lester Rawlins   1966–68; 1972–73
Millette Alexander   1966
Millette Alexander   1967–68
Alberta Grant   1966–74
Alan Feinstein   1969–74
Keith Charles   1966
Johanna Leister   1973–76
Laurie Kennedy
Renne Jarrett
Heidi Vaughn   1965–67

Paul Koslo
Ephraim Webster
Jessica Webster
Steve Prentiss
Harry Constable
Katherine Lovell
Adam Drake
Nicole Travis

Roy Poole   1967
Nat Polen   1967
Rita Lloyd   1967
Conard Fowkes   1967–68
Dolph Sweet   1967–68
Mary Fickett   1967–68
Donald May   1967–77
Lisa Sloan   1981–83
Jayne Bentzen   1978–81
Maeve McGuire   1968–74; 1975–77

Ben Travis

Cec Linder   1974
William Prince   1968–69

Susan Forbes
Vic Lamont
Calvin Brenner
Stephanie Martin
Pamela Stewart
Geraldine Whitney
Gordon Whitney
Sen. Colin Whitney
Tiffany Whitney
Keith Whitney
Trudy, the maid

Bibi Besch   1969–70
Ted Tinling   1969–75
Scott Glenn   1969
Alice Hirson   1969–70
Irene Dailey   1969–70
Lois Kibbee   1970–71; 1973–84
Alan Gifford   1970–71
Anthony Call   1970–71
Lucy Martin   1970–71; 1973–76
Bruce Martin   1970–71
Mary Hayden   1970–78

John, the butler	George Hall 1970–78
Dr. Charles Weldon	Ken Bruce Martin 1971
	Conrad Bain 1970
Johnny Dallas	John LaGioia 1973–77
Tracy Dallas	Pat Conwell 1974–77
Elly Jo Jamison	Dorothy Lyman 1972–73
Kevin Jamison	John Driver 1975–78
	Richard Shoberg 1972–75
Taffy Simms	Mari Gorman 1973–74
Danny Micelli	Lou Criscuolo 1973–77
Babs Micelli	Leslie Ray 1973–74
Lt. Luke Chandler	Herb Davis 1973–78
Serena/Josie Faraday	Louise Shaffer 1975–76
Mark Faraday	Bernie McInerney 1975
Timmy Faraday	Doug McKeon 1975–76
Dr. Quentin Henderson	Michael Stroka 1975–76
Brandy Henderson	Dixie Carter 1974–76
Draper Scott	Tony Craig 1975–81
Ansel Scott	Patrick Horgan 1976–77
Nadine Alexander	Dorothy Stinnette 1976–77; 1980
Raven Alexander	Sharon Gabet 1977–84
	Juanin Clay 1976–77
Steve Guthrie	Denny Albee 1976–80
Deborah Saxon	Frances Fisher 1976–81
Tony Saxon	Louis Turenne 1976–78
Beau Richardson	David Gale 1976–77
Dr. Miles Cavanaugh	Joel Crothers 1977–84
Denise Cavanaugh	Holland Taylor 1977–78
April Cavanaugh	Terry Davis 1977–81
Logan Swift	Tom Tammi 1984
	Joe Lambie 1977–81
Winter Austen	Stephanie Braxton 1979
	Lori Cardille 1978–79
Wade Meecham	Dan Hamilton 1978–79
Margo Huntington	Ann Williams 1978–80
Eliot Dorn	Lee Godart 1978–80
Cliff Nelson	Ernest Townsend 1978–84
Calvin Stoner	Irving Lee 1978–84
Star Stoner	Yahee 1978–82
Didi Bannister	Mariann Aalda 1982–84
Derek Mallory	Dennis Parker 1979–84
Jinx Avery Mallory	Susan MacDonald 1981–82
	Kate Capshaw 1981
Nola Madison	Kim Hunter 1979–80
Owen Madison	Bruce Gray 1979–80
Brian Madison	Stephen McNaughton 1979–80
Paige Madison	Margaret Colin 1979–80
Emily Michaels	Margo McKenna 1980–81
Molly Sherwood	Laurinda Barrett 1980–81

Molly Sherwood (*cont.*)	Jane Hoffman 1980
Jody Travis	Karrie Emerson 1983–84
	Lori Loughlin 1980–83
Gavin Wylie	Mark Arnold 1980–83
Martine Duval	Sonia Petrovna 1980–81
Schuyler Whitney	Larkin Malloy 1980–84
Gunther Wagner	David Froman 1981–83
Spencer Varney	Richard Borg 1981–83
Nora Fulton	Catherine Bruno 1981–82
Mitzi Martin	Lela Ivey 1981–84
Dr. Kenneth Bryson	James Hawthorne 1981
Beth Bryson	Doris Belack 1981
Valerie Bryson	Leah Ayres 1981–83
Jim Diedrickson	David Allen Brooks 1981–82
Smiley Wilson	Frank Gorshin 1981–82
Damian Tyler	Christopher Jarrett 1981–83
Johnny Gentry	Craig Augustine 1981–82
Poppy Johnson	Karen Needle 1982–83
Ian Devereaux	Alan Coates 1982–83
Camilla Devereaux	Mary Layne 1983
Dwight Endicott	Alfred Drake 1982
Eddie Lorimer	Ray Serra 1982
Buffy Revere	Elizabeth Parrish 1982
Del Emerson	Robert Gerringer 1983–84
John "Preacher" Emerson	Charles Flohe 1983–84
Robbie Hamlin	Willie Aames 1983
Peter Nevins	David Snell 1983
David Cameron	Norman Parker 1982–83
Chris Egan	Jennifer Taylor 1983–84
Moe Eberhardt	Dick Cavett 1983
Louis Van Dine	Jerry Zaks 1983–84
Alicia Van Dine	Chris Weatherfield 1983–84
Shelley Franklyn	Pamela Shoemaker 1983–84
Dr. Beth Corell	Sandy Faison 1983–84
Liz Corell	Marcia Cross 1984
Jeremy Rhodes	Michael Conforti 1984
Gary Shaw	A. C. Weary 1984
Brian Murdock	Philip Casnoff 1984
Mark Hamilton	Christopher Holder 1984
Dr. Juliana Stanhower	Amanda Blake 1984

THE EGG AND I

September 3, 1951–August 1, 1952   CBS

Television's first comedy serial was based on the Betty MacDonald book, which had sold over a million and a quarter copies by the time of the TV version. The book had been made into a successful 1947 Claudette Colbert–Fred MacMurray film and two of its characters, Ma and Pa Kettle

(Marjorie Main and Percy Kilbridge), were spun-off in nine subsequent movie comedies. Like the book and the movie, the soap zeroed in on a city slicker couple who moved to the country to fulfill the husband's fanatical desire to run a chicken farm in the northern part of Pennsylvania.

While the serial was a comedy, it was perhaps the first soap to inject a bit of social relevance into its story when producer Montgomery Ford used the show to point out a current grain shortage and the urgent need for increased planting of feed grains. Grave press releases emanated from CBS and the Department of Agriculture, warning of the crisis. Author Betty MacDonald was played by Pat Kirkland, the daughter of actress Nancy Carroll, the star of early talkies and light film dramas. Carroll joined the cast of *The Egg and I* for a week, playing Betty's mother.

The show was directed by Jack Gage and was written by Manya Starr and Robert Soderberg. It ran weekdays at noon E.S.T. for fifteen minutes, followed by *Love of Life* and *Search for Tomorrow*.

CAST

Betty MacDonald	Pat Kirkland
Bob MacDonald	John Craven
Ma Kettle	Doris Rich
Pa Kettle	Frank Twedell
Jed Simmons	Grady Sutton
Lisa Schumacher	Ingeborg Theek
Paula French	Karen Hale

EMERALD POINT, N.A.S.
September 26, 1983–March 12, 1984   CBS

TV Guide wrote: "Richard and Esther Shapiro, the creators of *Dynasty*, have grown wealthy on the premise that life is just a bowl of serial." The Shapiros' new prime-time creation was described as a "saga of power and passion" (what else?) set in the southern United States at Emerald Point, a combat-ready naval air station. The drama centered on the Mallorys, a naval family: Rear Admiral Thomas Mallory; his twenty-eighty-year-old daughter Celia, unhappily married to lawyer Jack Warren; his twenty-four-year-old daughter Kay, who was in love with lieutenant Glenn Matthews; and his twenty-two-year-old daughter Leslie, an Air Force ensign who had taken a fancy to Russian Lieutenant Alexi Gorichenko.

Mallory's adversary was wheeler-dealer Harlan Adams, who was father to Hilary, a beautiful troublemaker, and Simon, a pilot interested in Mallory's married daughter, Celia. Other characters included Tom's sister-in-law Deanna Kincaid and Maggie Farrell, a wife of a soldier who had been reported missing in action, caught between Tom and Harlan. Much of the drama centered on the trial of Lieutenant Glenn Matthews for the murder of Jeremy Novak, who had had an affair with Glenn's girlfriend Hilary. The soap, which was served up with huge dollops of romance and sex, featured a cast of familiar TV faces and former daytime soap performers, but failed to put together a winning season. Faced with unimpressive ratings, CBS decided not to renew the show.

On the final episode the demented David Marquette attempted to stop Tom and Maggie's wedding, while the festivities brought back memories of a childhood trauma for Celia. She remembered seeing Harlan Adams raping Jenny, her mother, which made it possible that one of the Mallory girls was the daughter of the unscrupulous Harlan.

The executive producers were the Shapiros and Michael Filerman. The producer was Freyda Rothstein, and the directors included Harry Fauk. The writers included the Shapiros as well as such illustrious daytimers as Jerome and Bridget Dobson and Chuck and Patti Dizenzo.

CAST

Adm. Thomas Mallory	Dennis Weaver
Kay Mallory	Stephanie Dunnam
Leslie Mallory	Doran Clark
Celia Mallory Warren	Susan Dey
Jack Warren	Charles Frank
Lt. Glenn Matthews	Andrew Stevens
Harlan Adams	Robert Vaughn
	Patrick O'Neal
Simon Adams	Richard Dean Anderson
Hilary Adams	Sela Ward
Deanna Kincaid	Jill St. John
Maggie Farrell	Maud Adams
Lt. Alexi Gorichenko	Michael Carven
Adm. Yuri Bukharin	Robert Loggia
David Marquette	Michael Brandon

EXECUTIVE SUITE

September 20, 1976–February 11, 1977   CBS

Created and written by Henry Slesar (*The Edge of Night*), this unsuccessful prime-time serial dramatized the business and romantic intrigue at Cardway Corporation, a large California conglomerate. Much of the action pitted Dan Walling, the president of the company, against Howell Rutledge, the devious vice-president, and Rutledge's equally scheming wife Astrid. Away from the office, Walling also dealt with his troublesome children: Brian, his prodigal son; and Stacey, his daughter, who was caught up in radical politics. Based on the novel by Cameron Hawley and the 1954 movie scenario by Ernest Lehman, the show was produced by Don Brinkley and Buck Houghton. The executive producers were Norman Felton and Stanley Rubin. The directors were Joseph Hardy and Charles S. Dubin. Slesar's associate writers were Barbara Avedon and Barbara Corday, who later created the series *Cagney and Lacey*.

CAST

Dan Walling	Mitchell Ryan
Helen Walling	Sharon Acker
Brian Walling	Leigh McCloskey
Stacey Walling	Wendy Phillips
Howell Rutledge	Stephen Elliott
Astrid Rutledge	Gwyda DonHowe
Mark Desmond	Richard Cox
Yvonne Holland	Trisha Noble
Malcolm Gibson	Percy Rodriguez
Hilary Madison	Madlyn Rhue
Tom Dalessio	Paul Lambert
Glory Dalessio	Joan Prather
Summer Johnson	Brenda Sykes
Anderson Gault	William Smithers
Pearce Newberry	Byron Morrow

FAIRMEADOWS, U.S.A.

November 4, 1951–April 27, 1952   NBC

This program about small-town life appeared twice and in different formats. It began as a Sunday afternoon serial starring character film actor Howard St. John (*Born Yesterday, L'il Abner*) as the owner of a general store in a small town. In 1952 it reappeared under the title *The House in the Garden* as a continuing, daily fifteen-minute part of *The Kate Smith Hour*. The latter afternoon variety hour also included another segment, *The World of Mr. Sweeney*, which later expanded to become one of TV's first comedy serials. Agnes Ridgeway wrote the show.

CAST

John Olcott	Lauren Gilbert
	Howard St. John
Alice Olcott	Ruth Matteson
Evvie Olcott	Mimi Strongin

With: Tom Taylor, James Vickery, and Hazel Dawn, Jr.

FALCON CREST

December 4, 1981–   CBS

Created by Earl Hamner (*The Waltons*), this family saga set in the vineyards of Northern California had the extraordinary luck to follow the soap powerhouse *Dallas* on Friday nights. It also starred Jane Wyman, an Oscar winner in 1948 for *Johnny Belinda*, who happened to be the ex-wife of the current President of the United States. The premiere episode racked up an impressive 21.8 rating and was ranked as the eighth most watched program of the week. Afterwards, *Falcon Crest* consistently remained among the top-ten-rated prime-time shows.

Wyman played Angela Channing, the head of Falcon Crest Wines, who schemed to swindle her nephew Chase Gioberti out of his birthright. The Channing faction of the family, headed by Angela, included her daughter Julia Cumson, who had a drinking problem; her daughter Emma, who was emotionally disturbed; and Julia's son Lance, an irresponsible Don Juan who was Angela's protégé and flunky. The Gioberti faction was headed by Chase, who had come to Falcon Crest after his father's death, and included his writer wife Maggie (played by Susan Sullivan, a favorite as Lenore Curtin on *Another World* in the early '70s); their son Cole; and their daughter Vickie.

The serial opened with the accidental death of Jason Gioberti (Angela's brother and Chase's father) during a struggle with Emma and her boyfriend. Angela, feeling Emma might be implicated in the death, packed Jason's body in a car and blew the automobile up. Most of the action in the first season centered on Angela's attempt to conceal the truth about Jason's death and her various business machinations, such as arranging her grandson Lance's marriage to Melissa Agretti, who was pregnant by Lance's cousin Cole Gioberti. In the season finale, Angela's husband Douglas argued with Angela about Emma, suffered a heart attack, and died. A shocked Emma testified that Jason's death was an accident. Although Angela and Emma were cleared, Angela, who was clearly humiliated, vowed revenge against Chase Gioberti.

The preposterous first season was followed by a crisply written second. It introduced Richard Channing (David Selby, fresh from the *Flamingo Road* flop), who was Douglas's illegitimate son and soon Angela's new nemesis. Later, it was revealed that Jacqueline Perrault (Lana Turner, in her first major TV appearance since the 1969 soap disaster *The Survivors*) was Richard's natural mother and head of a powerful syndicate. Other new characters included Darryl Clayton, who encouraged Maggie's screenwriting; Nick Hogan, who married Vickie but continued to sleep with his ex-wife Sheila; and Richard's stepfather Henri Denault, who was killed accidentally during a struggle with Richard. Most of the narrative during the second season focused on the death of Melissa's father Carlo and the subsequent framing of Cole in the murder. In the season finale, the killer was revealed to be Julia Cumson, who began to shoot indiscriminately, thus providing a corpse-laden cliff-hanger to close the season.

The 1983–84 season opened with the funeral of Jacqueline Perrault and the struggle of Chase Gioberti to recover from gunshot wounds which caused paralysis. Other developments included the introduction of Chase's cousin, Dr. Michael Ranson, who took over Chase's case when Angela's doctor friend attempted to kill Chase. Terry Hartford, Maggie's promiscuous sister, also popped up and became Michael's wife. While Maggie had to deal with her scheming sister, her son's marriage to Linda Caproni, Chase's paralysis, and Angela's constant manipulations, she had by the end of the season developed a brain tumor, which was operated on by Michael. Nutty Julia escaped from a mental institution and, dressed in a nun's habit, presumedly went up in flames when a family cabin burned to the ground. To fulfill Julia's final request, the Channings and Giobertis boarded a plane for Italy, but the plane had been sabatoged and seemed headed for a crash landing at the season's fadeout.

At the beginning of the 1984–85 season, the casualties from the plane crash included Michael Ranson (making Terry Hartford a very merry widow), Linda Gioberti (freeing Cole for other romantic entanglements), and Phillip Erickson (enabling Angela to shake the rafters for another husband and lawyer). In an embarassing exchange, actor Mel Ferrer (Phillip Erickson) charged in *TV Guide* that a power-wielding Jane Wyman had had him dropped from the show. Wyman denied the charge. New characters in the season included Greg Reardon, Angela's new hot-shot lawyer; Gustav Riebmann, who searched for Nazi treasures at Falcon Crest; Joel McCarthy, Terry Hartford's sleazy ex-husband; Lorraine Prescott, Richard Channing's stepdaughter; and the fifty-seven-year-old Italian star Gina Lollobrigida as Francesca Gioberti, Angela's half-sister.

Major developments during the season included: Cole and Melissa's stormy reconciliation; the introduction of Charlotte Pershing, Maggie's natural mother, a compulsive gambler; and Riebmann's manipulation of Emma and Julia (discovered very much alive) in his Falcon Crest takeover. The Riebmann-Nazi storyline, which was unpopular with viewers, was quickly wrapped up midseason as the cartoon villains were killed and Julia freed from her kidnappers. (Julia, apparently finding her nun digs habit forming, soon entered a convent.) Lance was convicted of attempting to kill Angela, but Melissa finally stepped forward to confess that she had paid Joel McCarthy to make Lance look bad and McCarthy went too far. As the newlywed Melissa went to prison, her cousin Robin announced that she was pregnant with bridegroom Cole's child.

Exonerated, Lance married Lorraine in the hospital after Lorraine miscarried. Shortly afterwards, Lorraine died and Lance blamed Richard Channing for setting in motion all the incidents which preceded Lorraine's accident. In a complicated business deal, Angela double-crossed Chase and Richard, leaving Chase furious and Richard bankrupt. However, the deal backfired on Angela when Cassandra Wilder, who blamed Angela for a fire that killed Cassandra's father years before, announced that she held the notes on two-thirds of Falcon Crest. When Maggie caught Chase embracing Connie Gianinni, Maggie sought comfort in the arms of Richard Channing. The season ended with one of the many characters with a motive to kill Richard detonating a bomb in Richard's mansion, thus leaving viewers in suspense whether Richard or the innocent Maggie Gioberti would survive the fiery blast.

In the 1985–86 season, we found that Richard and Maggie had escaped and that the perpetrator of the dastardly deed was the presumed-dead Pamela Lynch. But Maggie suffered temporary amnesia and took the time to write a *roman à clef* about Angela Channing and the Tuscany Valley entitled *Sudden Friendship*. Anna Rossini went berserk, set fire to Falcon Crest, and was carted off to the loony bin. Anna's daughter Cassandra also left town after announcing that she was pregnant with Richard Channing's baby. Angela was financially bailed out by old flame Peter Stavros, whom she later married.

It was also revealed that Anna's husband Dominic had had an illegitimate son by Julia, and the son was now a priest called Father Christopher. Melissa took an immediate shine to Father Chris ("I'm bad, Father," she cooed in the confessional) when her snot-nosed cousin Robin had her baby, Hope, and fought to keep the baby from Melissa and Cole. After Robin left town with the child, Melissa's panting over Father Chris didn't pan out, and her marriage to Cole went kaput, so the spitfire spotted new prey: Eric Stavros, Peter's son. Other romances included Emma's engagement to truckdriver Dwayne Cooley ("Cheeseburgers for everyone," Dwayne yelled ecstatically in a local diner) and Lance's infatuation with rock singer Apollonia (Angela called her "Babbelonia")—an affair that ended with Apollonia sending a "Dear Lance" letter from Europe.

Other developments in the season included the marriage of Terry Hartford Ranson to Richard Channing and her presentation to him of baby Michael (whose mother, Cassandra Wilder, had died in childbirth); the discovery of Jordan Roberts's split personality (engaged to Greg Reardon, her other half, "Monica," slept with Lance); and Maggie's abduction and rape by Jeff Wainwright, her book publicist. During the earthquake that followed, Jeff escaped while Terry and Dwayne were killed.

In the busy 1986–87 season, Greg called Angela to inform her that he and the now cured Jordan were married and living in Boston. Cole left for Australia, but sister Vickie returned after a three-year absence. Lance ogled ex-wife Melissa ("What do you want now," queried Melissa, "my harvest, my body, my first-born son?" Lance replied, "Your harvest. But if I can't have that, I'll take what's behind door number two.") The duo were remarried in Vegas. Emma got involved with a bogus psychic, Vince Karlotti, married him, found that he was a bigamist, and tried to commit suicide.

Richard faked a marriage to the murderous Miss Jones ("I can never call you Erin. Sounds like one of the Waltons." This was an inside joke: Earl Hamner, the creator of *Falcon Crest*, also created *The Waltons*). When Miss Jones tried to kill Chase (instead, she accidentally killed Jeff Wainwright), Richard had her shipped off to Borneo. Miss Jones's sister, Meredith Braxton, became Michael's nanny, vowed revenge, and had herself and Michael kidnapped. But the plot went awry: Miss Jones was killed in the melee, Michael was eventually returned, and Meredith got the boot.

Meanwhile, Richard found himself falling in love with Maggie, who was estranged from Chase after she chose not to have an abortion—after all, the baby could be Chase's, not Jeff's. When Kevin was born, Melissa—who had gone bonkers after the loss of Joseph to Cole—switched the blood tests, making it appear that Jeff was the father. Maggie reluctantly gave up her son for adoption, and Melissa absconded with the child. Near the season's closing, Vickie became engaged to Dan Fixx, one of Angela's flunkies, then got drunk and slept with Eric Stavros. Vickie and Eric married shortly afterwards.

Hollywood star and flamboyant whisperer Kim Novak came aboard during this season as Kit Marlowe, a woman who was running away from mobster Rolland Saunders (Robert Stack of *The Untouchables*). Kit assumed the identity of Skylar Kimball, Peter Stavros's step-daughter whom Peter hadn't seen since Skylar was fourteen years old. She fell in love with Tony Cumson, Lance's father, who was arrested for the murder of Saunders. At the trial, Peter Stavros confessed that he killed Saunders, because one of Saunders' henchmen killed the *real* Skylar. Out on bail, Peter fled the country, taking Tony and Kit with him. But before Peter left, he gave a letter to Angela containing news that would change Angela's life forever: Angela's first-born son, whom she had presumed died at birth, was none other than her archenemy: Richard Channing!

Maggie, who had begun to fall in love with Richard, and Chase, who began an affair with Gabrielle Short, discovered accidentally that Chase was the natural father of Kevin. After some detective work, the search was on to catch up with Melissa who was trying to leave the country with the baby. Melissa's car went careening off a bridge into the water below. Chase saved Kevin, then dived back in to rescue others who had been involved in the chase: Richard, Dan Fixx, and, of course, that hilarious wacko Melissa—a.k.a. Veronique, the Slumming, Singing Socialite.

CAST

Angela Channing	Jane Wyman 1981–
Chase Gioberti	Robert Foxworth 1981–87
Maggie Gioberti	Susan Sullivan 1981–
Cole Gioberti	William R. Moses 1981–
Vickie Gioberti	Dana Sparks 1986–
	Jamie Rose 1981–83
Emma Channing	Margaret Ladd 1981–
Richard Channing	David Selby 1982–
Douglas Channing	Stephen Elliott 1981–82
Julia Cumson	Abby Dalton 1981–86
Lance Cumson	Lorenzo Lamas 1981–
Melissa Agretti	Ana Alicia 1982–
Carlo Agretti	Carlos Romero 1982
Jacqueline Perrault	Lana Turner 1982–83
Henri Denault	E. G. Marshall 1982–83
Phillip Erickson	Mel Ferrer 1981–84
Diana Hunter	Shannon Tweed 1982–83
Nick Hogan	Roy Thinnes 1982–83
Shelia Hogan	Katherine Justice 1982–83
Sheriff Dan Robbins	Joe Lambie 1982–85
Chao-Li	Chao-Li Chi 1981–
Darryl Clayton	Bradford Dillman 1982–83
Gloria Marlowe	Gloria DeHaven 1982–83
Amanda Croft	Anne Jeffreys 1982–83
Dr. Michael Ranson	Cliff Robertson 1983–84
Dr. Lantry	Ron Rifkin 1983
Pamela Lynch	Sarah Douglas 1983–85
Linda Caproni Gioberti	Mary Kate McGeehan 1982–84
Terry Hartford	Laura Johnson 1983–86
Lorraine Prescott	Kate Vernon 1984–85
Francesca Gioberti	Gina Lollobrigida 1984

Gustav Riebmann	Paul Freeman 1984–85
Greg Reardon	Simon MacCorkindale 1984–86
Joel McCarthy	Parker Stevenson 1984
Charlotte Pershing	Jane Greer 1984–85
Connie Gianinni	Carla Borelli 1985
Robin Agretti	Barbara Howard 1985–86
Bradford Linton	Donald May 1985
Cassandra Wilder	Anne Archer 1985–86
Damon Ross	Jonathan Frakes 1985
Anna Rossini	Celeste Holm 1985
Apollonia	Apollonia Kotero 1985–86
Dwayne Cooley	Daniel Greene 1985–86
Father Christopher	Ken Olin 1985–86
Jordan Roberts	Morgan Fairchild 1985–86
Erin Jones	Jill Jacobson 1985–86
Meredith Braxton	Jane Badler 1986–87
Peter Stavros	Cesar Romero 1985–87
Eric Stavros	John Callahan 1986–
Kit Marlowe	Kim Novak 1986–87
Tony Cumson	John Saxon 1982; 1986–87
Jeff Wainwright	Edward Albert 1986–
Vince Karlotti	Marjoe Gortner 1986–87
Dan Fixx	Brent Cullen 1986–
Dina Wells	Robin Greer 1986–
Francine Hope	Melba Moore 1987
Gabrielle Short	Cindy Morgan 1987
Rolland Saunders	Robert Stack 1987
Liz McDowell	Lauren Hutton 1987

FARAWAY HILL

October 2, 1946–December 18, 1946   DuMont

Although receiving cities were few—just New York and Washington, D.C., at first—this DuMont effort is technically television's first network dramatic serial. (The DuMont network later expanded to include many cities on the East Coast, before ceasing operations in 1956.) *Faraway Hill* concerned the social and romantic adjustments of Karen St. John, a sophisticated New York widow, to country life—a plot device similar to *The Egg and I*, a bestselling book and subsequent TV serial. Working with a budget of $300 per episode, writer-director David P. Lewis introduced the characters by printing their names and relationships on the screen in the premiere so that viewers could get their bearings.

In subsequent episodes, presented Wednesdays for a half hour at 9:00 P.M., Lewis began the show with Karen's narration and a recap of the previous show, illustrated with slides. Although presented live, *Faraway Hill* occasionally used film shot on location—a costly endeavor that would become popular on soap operas thirty years later. The distinguished Broadway actress Flora Campbell starred as Karen, TV's first soap opera heroine. After the cancellation of the experimental serial, Campbell had roles on many other soaps, including *The Seeking Heart, Love of Life, The Edge of Night, The Secret Storm,* and the starring role as Helen Emerson on TV's *Valiant Lady* from 1954 to 1957. She died at age sixty-seven, of cancer, on November 6, 1978.

CAST

Karen St. John   Flora Campbell
With: Mel Brandt (as Karen's love interest), Hal Studer, Lorene Scott, Frederick Meyer, Ann Stell, Bill Gale, Jack Halloran, Ben Low, Vivian King, Julie Christy, and Jacqueline Waite.

THE FIRST HUNDRED YEARS
December 4, 1950–June 27, 1952   CBS

The title of this much publicized Procter & Gamble serial was supposed to suggest the most difficult years of married life, but CBS's first daytime soap opera fell short of its goal by ninety-eight and a half years. *The First Hundred Years*, produced on a budget of $8,650 per week and directed by Gloria Monty (*General Hospital*), started off with the week-long wedding of Chris Thayer and Connie Martin. Problems soon flooded in, mostly from interfering in-laws. Connie's father presented the horrified couple with a bat-infested, three-story, seven-bedroom Victorian mansion as a wedding present. Chris and Connie, hoping to settle in a modern apartment, finally accepted the white-elephant, which, according to a press release of the day, was copied from a house of the 1890s "right down to the last cupola and curlicue."

Creator-writer Jean Holloway, a prolific radio suds scripter, hoped the soap would be presented as a "slice of life" with a "sense of humor." Critics soon complained that Holloway was writing with radio conventions in mind and with no regard for the visual possibilities of TV. (Holloway also brought her radio-oriented drama to *Love of Life* almost thirty years later, contributing to that show's untimely demise in 1980.) Other viewers found it difficult to accept Jimmy Lydon [of *Henry Aldrich* fame] as a married man; he had been typecast as a gangling adolescent in too many movies in the '40s. CBS replaced the show with a TV version of the popular radio soap *The Guiding Light*.

CAST

Chris Thayer   James Lydon
Connie Thayer   Anne Sargent
      Olive Stacey
Mr. Thayer   Don Tobin
Mrs. Thayer   Valerie Cossart
Mr. Martin   Robert Armstrong
Mrs. Martin   Nana Bryant
Margy Martin   Nancy Malone

With: Nat Polen, Larry Haines, Charles Baxter, and Mary Linn Beller.

FIRST LOVE

July 5, 1954–December 30, 1955   NBC

Any TV fan who was watching soap operas in the '50s remembers this entry with great affection. Created by Adrian Samish and written by Mayna Starr, it was a provocative look at the stormy marriage of jet engineer Zach James and his wife Laurie Kennedy. Most of the problems were caused by the brooding Zach, who had been unwanted as a child and had the single-minded desire to establish himself as someone of importance. While the loving Laurie tried desperately to understand her husband, Zach sank deeper in trouble, standing trial for the murder of an aviatrix he may or may not have had an affair with. Although the cast was packed with future soap stars—Val Dufour (Emmy winner as John Wyatt on *Search for Tomorrow*), Patricia Barry (Addie Horton, *Days of Our Lives*), and Rosemary Prinz (Penny Hughes, *As the World Turns*)—a nervous NBC, which had little confidence in its early serials, cancelled the show. Actually, the soap was doomed from the start since NBC scheduled *First Love* at 3:30 P.M., E.S.T., sandwiched between two losers, *Golden Windows* and *Concerning Miss Marlowe*.

The cancellation nearly happened earlier when the three stars were almost fired for breaking up on camera. Presented live from Philadelphia, one of *First Love*'s tragic Friday fade-outs turned into high comedy when Dufour, after witnessing a plane crash, was to tell Barry and Prinz, "Chris cracked up the plane"—Chris being Prinz's husband. Instead, Dufour rushed up to the women and said, "Chris crapped." Horrified, he stopped for a moment, then, desperate, added, "on the plane." Barry giggled at the news, and when the camera panned to the supposedly bereft wife, Prinz was shaking uproariously with laughter. Viewers wrote in to say they loved the spontaneity of the obvious blooper, thus saving the stars from receiving pink slips.

CAST

Zach James	Tod Andrews
	Val Dufour
Laurie James	Patricia Barry
Matthew James	Paul McGrath
Amy	Rosemary Prinz
Chris	Frankie Thomas
Paul Kennedy	Melville Ruick
Doris Kennedy	Peggy Allenby
Judge Kennedy	Howard Smith
Mike Kennedy	John Dutra
Bruce McKee	Jay Barney
Quentin Andrews	Frederic Downs

Peggy Gordon   Henrietta Moore
Phil Gordon   Joe Warren

FLAME IN THE WIND
See A Time For Us.

FLAMINGO ROAD
January 6, 1981–July 13, 1982   NBC

Based on the novel by Robert Wilder, this was also the second TV soap whose previous incarnation was a movie starring Joan Crawford. (The first was daytime's *Best of Everything*.) Although the film centered on Lane, a former carnival girl, and her rise to prominence in a politically corrupt town, the Crawford role was relegated to supporting status in the prime-time TV version. (*Flamingo Road* was given a try-out on NBC with a successful two-hour TV movie in May 1980, before being launched in its serial version.) Instead, the focus was on the rich, spoiled Constance Weldon, her stormy marriage to the ambitious Fielding Carlyle, and Fielding's love for Lane.

Constance, a preposterous and preposterously blond spitfire, seemed bent on ripping the shirt off every man who lived in the hot town of Truro, Florida. By the end of the serial's short run, she had seduced four of the five romantic male leads, the only escapee being Skipper, her younger brother. As Constance, Morgan Fairchild (formerly Jennifer Phillips, *Search for Tomorrow*—the best shirt-ripper in the business) became a major TV personality and provided the only sparks in a dreary first season. Besides Constance's search for a good time, much of the action dealt with the rolypoly, wheeler-dealer Sheriff Titus Semple, his machinations to get Fielding elected to state senate, and his attempt to drive Lane out of town.

The show picked up in the second season as Michael Tyrone (David Selby, a matinee idol as Quentin Collins on *Dark Shadows*) was introduced, causing upheaval in all the major characters' lives. Tyrone had an affair with Lute-Mae, the owner of a bar-bordello, and found that Lute-Mae's illegitimate child was Constance. Then he had an affair with Constance, destroying her with the truth of her paternity; he subsequently drove Lute-Mae into a sanitarium; threatened the newly married Sam and Lane; and practiced voodoo against the man he hated the most, Titus Semple. In the last episode, Tyrone created his own faked murder, planning to have Titus blamed for the killing. The final scene showed Tyrone, who was presumed dead, hiding in a monastery. The executive producers of the show were Michael Filerman and Lee Rich. Rita Lakin was the writer and supervising producer.

CAST

Constance Weldon   Morgan Fairchild
Fielding Carlyle   Mark Harmon
Lane Ballou   Cristina Raines

Sam Curtis	John Beck
Sheriff Titus Semple	Howard Duff
Lute-Mae Sanders	Stella Stevens
Michael Tyrone	David Selby
Claude Weldon	Kevin McCarthy
Eudora Weldon	Barbara Rush
Skipper Weldon	Woody Brown
Elmo Tyson	Peter Donat
Julio Sanchez	Fernando Allende
Alicia Sanchez	Gina Gallego
Sande Swanson	Cynthia Sikes

FOLLOW YOUR HEART
August 3, 1953–January 8, 1954   NBC

Using some of the storylines from her radio soap *When a Girl Marries*, Elaine Carrington created this Jane Austen–style TV serial about Ardmore society. *Follow Your Heart* concerned Julie Fielding's fight to choose a husband outside her social circle, while her mother arranged a more "appropriate" marriage. However, the "follow your heart" theme was dropped and the show evolved into an adventure serial about spies and counterspies. Unfortunately, the show, which aired daily for fifteen minutes at 11:45 A.M., E.S.T., was cancelled after the twenty-third week of a planned twenty-six-week cycle. Viewers never got to see Julie being kidnapped by mobsters, her rescue by FBI agent Peter Davis, and Julie and Peter's wedding. The soap, which continued on radio for six more years, was produced by Adrian Samish and directed by Norman Morgan.

CAST
Julie Fielding	Sallie Brophy
Mrs. Fielding	Nancy Sheridan
Peter Davis	Grant Williams
Joceylyn Fielding	Laura Weber
Sharon Richard	Maxine Stuart
Sam Fielding	John Seymour
Mrs. MacDonald	Anne Seymour

FOR BETTER OR WORSE
June 29, 1959–June 24, 1960   CBS

With the exception of *Modern Romances*, anthology serials have not really worked on daytime TV. *For Better Or Worse* ran separate stories on marital discord for three weeks at a time, such as "The Case of Fred and Claire," a housewife-versus-career story. Dr. James A. Peterson, a teacher and marriage counselor, served as host and commentator. Dyan Cannon made her TV debut in "The Case of the Childish Bride" as a spoiled young woman who could not deal with the "responsibilities" of marriage. Although *As the World Turns* was the show's powerhouse lead-in, *For Better Or Worse* failed miserably, as did its replacement *Full Circle*.

CAST

Dyan Cannon, Ronald Foster, Barry Cahill, June Walker, Marge Redmond, and Peggy McCay.

FOREVER FERNWOOD
See Mary Hartman, Mary Hartman.

FOR RICHER, FOR POORER
December 6, 1977–September 29, 1978   NBC

After a seven-month hiatus to make story and cast changes, *Lovers and Friends* returned to NBC daytime in this revamped version. The setting was still Point Clair, a Chicago suburb, but the Cushings and the Saxtons were no longer neighbors. Tom King had taken over the headwriting position from creator Harding Lemay (who remained a consultant), and there were many other changes as well. The character of Edith Cushing was recast and made a widow. Austin Cushing had married Amy Gifford. Bentley Saxton and sister Tessa had suddenly become college students. Most important, the leading parts of the star-crossed lovers Megan Cushing and Bill (changed from Rhett) were recast.

While *Lovers and Friends* had moved at a leisurely pace, *For Richer, For Poorer* began with a hook and never let up: the day of Megan and Bill's wedding, Bill's ex-girlfriend told Megan that she, Connie, was five months pregnant—with Bill's child. The lives of the Cushings and Saxtons were still intertwined and in class conflict. Writer Tom King added a third family, the wealthy Brewsters, and tried to beef up the show with romance, suspense, and soap staples such as adultery, amnesia, and organized crime. In an unusual and publicized move the popular characters of Mac and Rachel Cory (Douglass Watson and Victoria Wyndham from *Another World*) were drafted for a few appearances to perk interest in the show. Although *For Richer, For Poorer* was a far livelier entry than its predecessor, NBC gave up on the show, employing much of the cast in their other soaps.

See *Lovers and Friends*.

CAST

Megan Cushing	Darlene Parks
Bill Saxton	Tom Happer
Connie Ferguson	Cynthia Bostick
Austin Cushing	Rod Arrants
Edith Cushing	Laurinda Barrett
Amy Gifford	Christine Jones
Lester Saxton	Albert Stratton
Josie Saxton	Patricia Englund

Jason Saxton	Richard Backus
Bentley Saxton	David Abbott
Tessa Saxton	Breon Gorman
George Kimball	Stephen Joyce
Eleanor Kimball	Flora Plumb
Lee Ferguson	Robert Burton
Ira Ferguson	Roy Poole
Viola Brewster	Patricia Barry
Laurie Brewster	Julia MacKenzie
Desmond Hamilton	David Knapp
Sgt. Frank Damico	Stephen Burleigh
Colleen Griffin	Nancy Snyder

THE FORSYTE SAGA

October 5, 1969–March 29, 1970   NET

This chronicle of a turn-of-the-century family, which traced the changing mores of English society from the Victorian age to the period between the world wars, was a smash hit when broadcast over the BBC in Britain. It also brought new respect to the term "soap opera" when it aired with great success over National Educational Television in the U.S. The serial was based on the novels of Nobel Prize–winning writer John Galsworthy, whose first Forsyte book, *Man of Property*, was published in 1906. That novel was the first part of a trilogy called *The Forsyte Saga*, which, in turn, was the first section of another trilogy entitled *Forsyte Chronicles*.

In 1949 MGM brought out a film based on part of the work, starring Greer Garson and called *That Forsyte Woman*. Although it was mildly successful, there were no further dramatizations until the BBC bought the rights from MGM and decided to turn the first six volumes of *Forsyte Chronicles* into a twenty-six-part serial for TV. Producer Donald Wilson and four writers, sticking close to the original material, spent more than a year adapting the work. In 1967 *The Forsyte Saga* went into production at a cost of $700,000. (Fifteen years later, the dramatically inert eighteen-hour *The Winds of War* would cost over $40 million.) Presented on consecutive Sunday evenings *The Forsyte Saga*, like the American soap *Dallas* a decade later, became a national craze, bringing in an estimated 17 million viewers weekly. The serial was subsequently seen in more than fifty countries, including New Zealand, Yugoslavia, and the Soviet Union.

In the U.S. the press greeted the show with almost unqualified praise for its addictive format and sprawling family drama, although soap fans pointed out that complex characterizations, continuity, and incisive human insight had long been a staple of American daytime drama. The arty black-and-white camera work, the period costumes and sets, and the distinctive accents blinded critics to the fact that *The Forsyte Saga* dealt essentially with the same issues—and often on the same level of treatment—as *As the World Turns*: family conflict, adultery, marital rape, jealousy, birth, death, and romantic intrigue. *The Forsyte Saga* was a stylish, well-produced serial remembered for its diverse, rich characterizations and for the brilliant performance of Eric Porter as Soames Forsyte—whose equally brilliant American counterpart is Larry Bryggman's Dr. John Dixon on *As the World Turns.*

<u>CAST</u>

Soames Forsyte	Eric Porter
Irene Heron Forsyte	Nyree Dawn Porter
Jo Forsyte	Kenneth More
Jolyon Forsyte	Joseph O'Connor
Helene Hillmer Forsyte	Lana Morris
June Forsyte	June Barry
James Forsyte	John Welsh
Winifred Forsyte Dartie	Margaret Tyzack
Monty Dartie	Terrence Alexander
Annette Lamotte Forsyte	Dallia Penn
Fleur Forsyte Mont	Susan Hampshire
Jon Forsyte	Martin Jarvis
Michael Mont	Nicholas Pennell
Boisinney	John Bennett
Aunt Ann Forsyte	Fay Compton
Swithin Forsyte	George Woodbridge

FROM THESE ROOTS

June 30, 1958–December 29, 1961   NBC

"From these roots grow branch, leaf and flower, children of the sheltering earth, ripening into the tumult of the seasons—generation unto generation."

One of the most cherished daytime dramas ever was this star-studded soap set in the New England town of Strathfield. Created by Frank Provo and winningly produced and directed by Don Wallace and Paul Lammers, the show was packed with future soap stars: Ann Flood (Nancy Karr, *The Edge of Night*); Henderson Forsythe (Dr. David Stewart, *As the World Turns*); Millette Alexander (Sara McIntyre, *The Guiding Light*); Barbara Berjer (Barbara Thorpe, *The Guiding Light*); Craig Huebing (Dr. Peter Taylor, *General Hospital*); Robert Mandan (Sam Reynolds, *Search for Tomorrow*); Billie Lou Watt (Ellie Bergman, *Search for Tomorrow*); and John Colenback (Dr. Dan Stewart, *As the World Turns*).

The drama opened with Liz Fraser returning to her hometown from Washington, D.C., to take over the family's newspaper after her father Ben, the sixty-five-year-old publisher of *The Strathfield Record*, suffered a heart attack. Liz soon found herself in the midst of a romantic storm with three attractive suitors: Bruce Crawford, her D.C. fiancé; Dr. Buck Weaver, her childhood sweetheart; and David Allen, a playwright who finally persuaded her to walk down the aisle. Other characters included Liz's thirty-seven-year-old brother Ben Jr.; Ben's wife Rose Corelli; Liz's happily married sister Emily; Emily's husband Jim Benson; Maggie Barker, who married Buck on the rebound from Liz; Lynn Franklin, a wonderful alcoholic villainess who was in love with Liz's husband David; Tom Jennings, a theater director who married Lynn; and Gloria Saxon, a gun moll.

When Leonard Stadd took over as headwriter, the serial sparked with wit and show business stories. So wonderfully theatrical were some of the characters and situations that Tennessee Williams, a fan of the show, reportedly accused his agent of selling some of his unpublished material to the soap. The most talked about episode of the run was a show within a show: a "live" *Studio One*-like TV production of *Madame Bovary*. In these sequences, actress Lynn Hamilton was shown being made-up while director Tom Jennings nervously ordered last minute changes behind the scenes. Scenes from *Madame Bovary* were then juxtaposed with Lynn's frantic costume changes and Tom choreographing the action from the control booth, thus giving the viewer a peek into the ins and outs of live television.

Although fans were crushed at the show's cancellation, the writers provided happy endings for their characters: Ben, the mayor, successfully cleaned the town of organized crime; Lyddy revealed she was pregnant; Kass, the housekeeper, received a $200,000 check for settling her husband's estate; and Liz and her family reveled in the Christmas cards their friends had sent. The refreshing serial, which integrated music into the drama a full decade before the characters on *The Young and the Restless* burst into song was produced by the usually staid Procter & Gamble and was lovingly directed by Wallace, Lammers, Leonard Valenta, and Joseph Behar. It aired for a half hour at 3:30 P.M., E.S.T.

Like other shows at the time, *From These Roots* was presented live, and an incident on June 3, 1960, fully illustrated the horrors of live television. Fifteen minutes before air time, actress Julie Bovasso, who played Rose, walked off the set and out of the building after a dispute with Lammers about a particular scene's meaning and several line readings. Barbara Searles, an associate director, was immediately drafted to replace Bovasso. Under the circumstances Searles, who read from a script hidden from the view of the camera, did remarkably well. Bovasso was fired. She later made a name for herself as a Broadway playwright and as a character actress, playing John Travolta's mother in *Saturday Night Fever* and *Staying Alive*.

CAST

Liz Fraser Allen	Ann Flood 1958–61
	Susan Brown 1959
Ben Fraser	Joseph Macauley 1961
	Rod Hendrickson 1958–61
	Grant Code 1958
Ben Fraser Jr.	Frank Marth 1958–60
Rose Corelli Fraser	Tresa Hughes 1960–61
	Julie Bovasso 1958–60
Jim Benson	Henderson Forsythe 1958–60
Emily Fraser Benson	Helen Shields 1958–61
Lyddy Benson	Sarah Hardy 1958–61

Bruce Crawford	Byron Sanders 1958–59
Dr. Buck Weaver	Len Wayland 1958–61
Maggie Weaver	Billie Lou Watt 1958–61
Stanley Kreiser	Leon Janney 1960–61
Enid Allen	Mary Alice Moore 1958–59
David Allen	Robert Mandan 1958–61
Lynn Franklin	Barbara Berjer 1959–61
Tom Jennings	Craig Huebing 1959–61
Laura Tomkins	Audra Lindley 1959–61
Peggy Tomkins Benson	Ellen Madison 1959–61
	Ursula Stevens 1959
	Mae Munro 1958–59
Nate Tomkins	Ward Costello 1958–60
Fred Barnes	Tom Shirley 1958
Jack Lander	Joseph Mascolo 1961
Gloria Saxon	Millette Alexander 1961
Hilda Furman	Charlotte Rae 1961
Jimmy Hull	John Colenback 1960–61
Luisa Corelli	Dolores Sutton 1958–60
Artie Corelli	Frank Campanella 1958–60
Frank Teton	George Smith 1960–61
Jamie	Alan Howard 1961
Richard	Richard Thomas 1961
Kass	Vera Allen 1958–61
George Weimer	Donald Madden 1961

FULL CIRCLE

June 27, 1960–March 10, 1961   NBC

Dyan Cannon made her TV debut as a guest on *For Better or Worse* and returned to daytime TV as the star of this half-hour romantic drama. She played Lisa, a young woman whose husband Loyal died under mysterious circumstances. Lisa became involved with Gary, a sexy young drifter hitchhiking on the southern East Coast, who found himself caught up in the intrigue of the Virginia town of Crowder and its first family. Bill Barrett wrote the serial, broadcast live from Hollywood and seen on the East Coast at 2:00 P.M. *Full Circle* was produced by Norman Morgan and directed by Livia Granito and Bill Howell. After cancellation, Dyan Cannon retired temporarily from show business, making headlines by marrying Cary Grant. After divorcing Grant, she made a comeback in such film comedies as *Bob & Carol & Ted & Alice* and *Heaven Can Wait*.

CAST

Lisa Crowder	Dyan Cannon
Loyal Crowder	John McNamara
Gary Donovan	Robert Fortier
Carter Talton	Byron Foulger
David Talton	Bill Lundmark

Beth Perce	Amzie Strickland
Dr. Kit Aldrich	Jean Byron
Virgil Denker	Michael Ross
Ellen Denker	Nancy Millard
The Deputy	Sam Edwards

GENERAL HOSPITAL

April 1, 1963–   ABC

From a cherished medical drama delving into the lives of Dr. Steve Hardy and Nurse Jessie Brewer to a pop culture phenomenon celebrating the wild adventures of Luke and Laura, *General Hospital* is a Cinderella story in three distinct acts. The middle act is, of course, the dreary period in the mid '70s when the show fell from a number-one spot in 1972 to near the bottom of the heap in 1977. Very close to cancellation, *General Hospital* staged an unprecedented comeback with the miraculous innovations of producer Gloria Monty. The show soon broke all records in daytime television and changed not only the face of daytime drama but even the way people view soap operas.

Premiering the same day as NBC's similarly conceived hospital drama *The Doctors*, the show was created by Frank and Doris Hursley, who had lifted *Search for Tomorrow* out of the dramatic doldrums. The Hursleys set up a tantalizing platonic relationship between a gruff but vulnerable doctor and a strong, long-suffering nurse who were the focus of activities on the seventh floor of a large metropolitan hospital. Nurse Jessie Brewer withstood constant crisis, mostly caused by her unfaithful young husband Phil Brewer. Dr. Steve Hardy, while comforting Jessie, had his own problems to deal with, mostly involving his off and on romance with ex-stewardess Audrey March. Former child star and baseball hero John Beradino as Steve and Emily McLaughlin as Jessie became the cornerstones of the show and have remained with *General Hospital* for over two decades.

Comic relief from all the physical and mental anguish on the seventh floor came in the form of Audrey's sister, the crusty head of student nurses, Lucille March. As played by Lucille Wall (star of radio's *Portia Faces Life*), Lucille was a lovable disciplinarian, forever barking at the nurses to fix their caps and to straighten up. (While other soaps in the '70s had switched to more sophisticated musical scoring, *General Hospital* still employed its antiquated organ music to amusing advantage, often punctuating Lucille's charge down the hall.) Other core characters in the early years included Dr. Tom Baldwin, his lawyer brother Lee, Lee's wife Meg, and Meg's son Scotty.

Working with a small cast and on an extremely low budget with the staff doubling on endless production chores, producer-director Jim Young did very well covering up the makeshift sets by concentrating on the strong chemistry of his cast. With the help of medical consultant Dr. Franz Bauer, the Hursleys created some exciting melodramatic medical stories, further interweaving the lives of the core characters. Jessie was defended by Lee for the murder of her elderly husband Dr. John Prentice. It was revealed that John's daughter Polly had administered the fatal dose. Jessie was ultimately reunited with Phil (who had an affair with Polly), thus triggering many more unhappy years for Jessie. Craig Huebing was introduced as psychiatrist Peter Taylor and eventually married Jessie during a period when she thought Phil was dead. (Interestingly enough, Huebing had played Phil Brewer briefly years before.)

Besides developing stories on alcoholism (Iris Fairchild) and breast cancer (Meg Baldwin), the Hursleys wrote a daring plot in which Audrey became pregnant by secret artificial insemination. The gambit paid off with a surprising burst of popularity, and when Audrey returned from Vietnam the Hursleys again wrote another highly complex pregnancy story for her. Audrey became the victim of marital rape at the hand of Dr. Tom Baldwin and hid the pregnancy and subsequent child from Steve, with whom she had reconciled. This comedy of errors was played with superb desperation by Rachel Ames (daughter of character actor Byron Foulger), and the show's ratings soared.

By 1972, with Audrey's trial for the murder of Tommy's kidnapper, *General Hospital* had supplanted *As the World Turns* and *Days of Our Lives* as daytime's highest rated drama. This was the show's highwater mark for some time; *General Hospital* fell from a 10.6 rating in 1972 to an 8.2 mark the next year, a loss of about 1.5 million viewing homes. The show continued in a steady downward skid, losing a rating point a year for several years. Perhaps the hospital setting had worn out, the stories grown stale, and the characters overexposed to too much melodrama and too many murder trials. Whatever the reasons for the audience defections, the Hursleys—and later writers Bridget (the Hursleys' daughter) and Jerome Dobson—continued to stick close to the formulas that had made the show a success in the past.

Jessie again became involved with Phil and once again was disillusioned. To appeal to younger viewers, Jessie was given guardianship of her teenage niece Carol and nephew Kent, played by Mark Hamill (who starred in *Star Wars* years later). Again Jessie was exploited by a Phil Brewer–like Teddy Holmes, who ultimately ran off with her niece. A younger version of Jessie was introduced in the form of Diana Maynard, who was exploited and raped by Phil. Later, Diana (played by Valerie Starrett, who mustered quite a fan following) married Dr. Peter Taylor, Jessie's ex-husband. This vaguely incestuous roundelay, which synthesized bits and pieces of old stories, culminated in an exciting whodunit as Phil Brewer was found dead and both Jessie and Diana were accused of his murder.

In 1975, Tom Donovan became the new producer and Richard and Suzanne Holland served briefly as headwriters. The Hollands zeroed in on actress Denise Alexander, who had been hired away from *Days of Our Lives* at great expense in 1973 but had been used ineffectively in the intervening years. Alexander's Dr. Lesley Williams became the soap's new focus, caught in a whirlwind romance with the rich, unscrupulous Cameron Faulkner. Before leaving the show the Hollands created a story that would ultimately become *General Hospital*'s salvation: Lesley's discovery that Laura, the child she thought dead years ago, was alive. Alexander's highly emotional performance laid the groundwork for Lesley's growing obsessive attachment to Laura, which years later would lead Leslie to take the rap for murder.

The next year Eileen and Robert Mason Pollock, who had done so well guiding *The Doctors* for many years, took over as headwriters and completely overhauled the show. *General Hospital* expanded from a half hour to forty-five minutes and lost over a dozen characters. To populate the New York town of Port Charles (as the once nameless city was now known), the Pollocks created a crush of new characters, including the Dante and the Webber families. The latter family consisted of Terri Webber Arnett; her brothers Doctors Rick and Jeff Webber; and Jeff's wife Monica, who was obsessively in love with Rick. The Jeff-Monica-Rick romantic triangle was not only the Pollock's strongest storyline, it was in reality their *only* plotline, and like the rest of the show, ludicrously overwritten. The gauzy love scenes smacked of desperation tactics, seemingly pulled from a Candlelight Ecstasy Romance:

Monica: You're my heaven and my hell.
Rick: You're a fever in my blood—a fever I can't live without.
Monica: We've paid our dues and we found we can't live without each other.

Someone seemed to like this particular scene since it played over and over again for months, interrupting other stupefying antics obviously mounted to pick up the ratings, such as Lesley's "satanic" fetus and Mary Ellen Dante's wild machinations to win back husband Mark from Terri Webber Arnett.

General Hospital continued to fall in the ratings and there was talk of cancellation in 1977, when the show settled near rock bottom. Irving and Tex Elman took over briefly for the Pollocks, bringing back exciting hospital drama and introducing Kin Shriner as Scotty Baldwin and pairing him with Genie Francis's Laura. (The Pollocks later became the headwriters of prime-time's *Dynasty*, pulling in a huge audience with their high-falutin' brand of camp melodrama.) Richard and Suzanne Holland were brought back as writers as ABC worked feverishly behind the scenes to save the show. As he made plans to expand the soap from an unwieldly forty-five minutes to a full hour, Fred Silverman hired the delightful Leslie Charleson, who had made such an impression on audiences in *Love Is a Many Splendored Thing*, to replace the unfortunate actress playing the pivotal role of Monica.

Daytime vice-president Jackie Smith, on the advice of Agnes Nixon, brought in Douglas Marland, who had orchestrated several youth-oriented storylines on *The Doctors*, to take over the writing chores. She then hired Gloria Monty, who had directed *The Secret Storm* for fifteen years, as the new producer. Monty took over on New Year's Day, 1978. To the horror of the budget-conscious executives, Monty immediately threw out the first week of hour-long shows, which were already taped and ready for airing. She decided that the show should be shot using prime-time techniques: out of sequence, and in small segments to be spliced together by the team of editors she soon hired.

Monty's other innovations and driving perfectionism shocked and pleased the cast and crew. Monty was appalled at the lighting, which employed the same key light on both Jessie and Audrey—if any was used at all. She corrected the lighting and hired new musicians to score the show. A new team of whiz-kid directors (Marlena Laird, Phil Sogard, and Alan Pultz— later multiple Emmy winners) employed cross-cutting and other techniques that would make *General Hospital* a technical marvel. New set designers were brought in to replace the drab scenery. (Working right through the taping, the workmen's appearance in the background became part of the story: it was explained that the hospital itself was going through a renovation.) A former acting teacher whose students had included Marlon Brando and Walter Matthau, Monty demanded the best from her cast and become notorious for her exacting acting notes and her constant finger snapping to pick up the pace.

But as any person involved in soap opera knows, all the technical innovations in the world won't save a badly written show. It was up to Douglas Marland to deliver, and deliver he did. Marland wrote a daring story in which the fifteen-year old Laura, taunted by her older lover, kills him accidentally in rage. When Laura's mother took the blame for the killing, the story of the sacrificing mother and the confused teenager really took off, hooking the young audience. Meanwhile, Marland introduced the young villainess Bobbie Spencer (energetically played by Jackie Zeman) to thwart Laura's every positive move, mostly toward Scotty Baldwin, whom both girls loved. At the center of the storm was actress Genie Francis, whose ferociously emotional, sweetly vulnerable performance as Laura dazzled viewers and co-workers alike.

Marland next developed a highly complex romance among the adults, throwing old lovers Monica and Rick together when the hospital was quarantined, much to Alan and Lesley's chagrin. The pressure-cooker drama, which combined romance with life-or-death theater, fascinated viewers, and the audience swelled. Monty and Marland had achieved the impossible, bringing *General Hospital* back from the bottom of the ratings cellar to number three in little over a year. (It was also a critical moment for the show, which now ran after Gordon Russell's gut-wrenching Karen Wolek story on *One Life to Live*. The two soaps became the most exciting back-to-back programs in television.) But disagreements brewed backstage. After the onscreen marriage of Scotty and Laura, Monty wanted immediate marital discord, in the form of romantic interference by Bobbie's brother Luke, while Marland opted for a more realistic evolvement.

After Marland's departure, *General Hospital* entered a highly controversial, but phenomenally popular period. Pat Falken Smith, famous for her exciting melodrama, bitchy dialogue, and notorious rape stories on *Days of Our Lives*, was hired as headwriter. Monty picked up the pace even more, demanding shorter scenes and more action-oriented storylines. Amid a highly complex organized crime plotline, Falken Smith and Monty made what was to become the most controversial move in the history of daytime drama. On October 5, 1979, Luke, who was convinced he would be killed in mob activity soon, forced Laura to dance with him to the throbbing music of Herb Alpert's "Rise" in his deserted disco. He then pushed Laura to the floor and raped her. Crying in fear and humiliation, Laura screamed "No!" repeatedly before the fade-out.

The married Laura had expressed interest in Luke, but from Francis's gut-wrenchingly painful performance as a rape victim afterwards, it was clear that the incident had been more than a seduction. Laura was hospitalized and attended group therapy sessions for rape victims for a while, but as the months passed it became clear that there was powerful chemistry between Genie Francis and Anthony Geary, who had created a fascinating anti-hero in Luke Spencer. *General Hospital* had become enormously popular and the stories were moving with such momentum that the show was not about to slow down by sending its new male lead to therapy or jail. Instead, the show ignored the rape issue, thus appearing to condone the incident, and later got around to calling it a "seduction." Meanwhile, at a personal appearance to promote the show, teenage fans screamed at Tony Geary, "Rape me, Luke! Rape me!"

Years later Genie Francis commented incisively: "My blood runs cold at the thought that what happened between Luke and Laura on *General Hospital* was a glorification of rape. I really don't think it was. I played a rape victim for a year and I was really proud of the work I did. Then they realized that the chemistry between Tony Geary and me was something they couldn't ignore, and they turned everything around. I was so angry. . . . I felt it negated a whole year's work. But I couldn't blame them for what happened." After he left the show, Anthony Geary came to agree with Francis that a woman falling in love with her rapist was a dangerous dramatic precedent, especially when staged in front of an impressionable teenage audience.

With the mob at their heels, Luke and Laura began a series of popular on-the-run stories, falling in love between death threats by Frank Smith, Hutch, and a transvestite killer called Sally. Although the show gave lip service to other stories, such as the machinations of Tracy Quartermaine and Heather Webber, *General Hospital* soon became known as "The Luke and Laura Show." Francis and Geary worked nearly every day and dominated the screen, a work schedule comparable only to the daily appearances by Jonathan Frid and Grayson Hall in the '60s on *Dark Shadows*, which was a half-hour show. The location shooting of the action sequences and a dance scene in a deserted department store gave *General Hospital* a reputation for fast-paced action adventure, but Gloria Monty's special genius saw all the action halt for the love story. After dozens of ten- or twenty-second scenes, nearly every day ended with a seven-minute romantic scene, frequently improvised, between Luke and Laura. The whole world stopped for these young people deeply and platonically in love.

As Anthony Geary's popularity skyrocketed, the show soared to number one and then some. *General Hospital* had captured a fanatical following and the audience continued to swell, especially among teenagers. When, in October 1980, Luke and Laura finally made love, local stations were deluged with calls from fans complaining that the scene was too short and not explicit enough. As Luke and Laura were becoming pop culture phenomenons, the show's once popular mainstays—Steve, Jessie, and Audrey—were not only relegated to supporting status but were lucky to have more than a few lines of dialogue a week. The emphasis was on youth, and the introduction of Rick Springfield (who became a rock idol during his *General Hospital* tenure) as Bobbie's new love interest Noah Drake, sent the young audience into soap opera heaven.

In 1981, Monty and ABC daytime vice president Jackie Smith, over the objections of headwriter Pat Falken Smith, decided to steer *General Hospital* in a surprising and fantastic direction. Associate writer A. J. Russell had written a science fiction story about Luke and Laura trying to prevent the mad genius Mikkos Cassadine from freezing the world! The "Ice Princess" story took off in the summer, when the kids were home from school, and soon the show captured the teenagers and young children as well. *General Hospital* turned into a cartoon drama and Geary's performance became mannered and bombastic, but audiences loved it, and the story generated reams of publicity.

In a story on *General Hospital* on September 28, 1981, with Luke and Laura adorning the cover, *Newsweek* wrote: "Sophisticates may look at a storyline like that and see a trashy, electronic comic strip. But to *GH* cultists, it smacks of nothing less than Tolstoy adapted by Fellini, with Redford and Streisand in the leads. Since the mad-scientist caper began, fan mail to the show has jumped from four bags to nine, while ratings have shot to record heights." Monty's commercial instinct had paid off and ABC was soon bringing in well over a million dollars a week profit from the show. Newspapers and magazines fell over one another to cover the story while Genie Francis and Tony Geary, and their alter-egos Luke and Laura, became household names.

The publicity snowballed and then culminated with the wedding of Luke and Laura on November 16–17, with no less than Elizabeth Taylor, as the widow Cassadine, in attendance, cursing the proceedings. The two shows reached over 14 millions homes with a 52 share of the audience— the highest ratings ever recorded in daytime television. Kin Shriner dramatically revived his role as Scotty Baldwin, Laura's ex-husband, by snatching the thrown wedding bouquet. *General Hospital* seemed in formidable shape, but there was trouble around the bend.

Writer Pat Falken Smith, who had brought such energy, wit, and excitement to the show, quit after repeated battles with producer Gloria Monty, commenting wryly: "Gloria's a genius—who runs a gestapo operation." A new writing team was put together, headed by Monty herself and Robert J. Shaw. They faced a new problem: the departure of Genie Francis as Laura. Shortly after the New Year, Laura disappeared into a fog, followed by the nefarious David Gray. With Laura presumed dead, *General Hospital* attempted to fill the void with a Laura lookalike, Laura Templeton, and there were plans to throw Laura's feisty sister Jackie and the grieving Luke into a sizzling romance. Demi Moore, who played Jackie, received the most publicity ever garnered by a newcomer to daytime, but it soon became apparent that the romance was a bust.

The writing on the show deteriorated into a convoluted mess while Gloria Monty was hospitalized, but the show continued its enormous popularity. With inflated, unheard of numbers of viewers, an audience loss of a million here and there did not matter. Joyce and John William

Corrington, the creators of *Texas*, served briefly as headwriters, but failed to put the show together. Then Anne Howard Bailey, the creator of the innovative failure *How to Survive a Marriage*, became the new headwriter. Bailey was far more successful, injecting a dose of realistic drama into the adventure stories and introducing Emma Samms, a breathtakingly beautiful actress reminiscent of a young Elizabeth Taylor, as Holly Sutton, Luke's new love interest.

With Holly in the midst of a romantic triangle between Luke and his best friend Robert Scorpio (played by Tristan Rogers, a new matinee idol whose popularity often exceeded Tony Geary's), the hilarious Quartermaines squabbling, and villains Scotty and Heather working overtime, *General Hospital* was back on its feet again. Fans had become accustomed to the yearly cloak-and-dagger storylines, and 1983 introduced a long spy plotline revolving around Dr. Grant Putnam and Natalie (a.k.a. Natasha!) Dearborn, played by Brian Patrick Clarke and Melinda Cordell, who appeared daily and carried the bulk of the show. Wags soon commented that if they had a dime for every time Natalie made a phone call in the hospital lobby or whispered conspiracies on a park bench, they would be millionaires.

However, most of the excitement occurred at the tail end of the year with the return, after almost a two-year absence, of Genie Francis as Laura to finish up soap opera's most famous love story. (This was the second time Laura came back from the "dead," the first time occurring after Lesley was told Laura had died shortly after birth.) Although *General Hospital* had sustained its number-one position in the interim, the ratings quickly leaped back to the inflated figures of 1981. "Think of Laura," a Christopher Cross tune released that summer to general disinterest, was used as Laura's theme song, and shot up on the record charts. (It was not the first hit song generated by the show. Luke and Holly's theme song "Baby, Come to Me," a Patti Austin–James Ingram duet, was a smash in previous months. "General Hospi-Tale," a campy rap song about the characters' checkered past, was popular a couple years earlier.) By Christmas, Luke and Laura were reunited, and had left Port Charles to live happily ever after.

With Luke and Laura gone, to say nothing of the departure of *General Hospital*'s fun-loving villains Heather and Scotty, Gloria Monty had her work cut out for her. In the spring of 1984, the show also lost its once pivotal romantic lead, Lesley Webber, when actress Denise Alexander's contract was not renewed after an eleven year run on the show. (Lesley was killed off in an automobile accident, causing more audience defections and protest.) *General Hospital* also cut Emily McLaughlin and Rachel Ames's appearances down to a handful a year, although each actress had been on the show for over two decades.

Monty had revolutionized daytime television, making *General Hospital* a technical marvel, but the show had stretched credibility to the limits, and the plotlines had become sluggish and repetitive. In the first six months of 1984 *General Hospital* lost over four million viewers. Since the Grant Putnam spy story had been popular with young viewers, the show pitted the real (demented) Grant Putnam against the sympathetic, imposter Grant for the attentions of the show's new heroine, Celia Quartermaine. (Brian Patrick Clarke, who played both Grants, did a remarkable job considering the circumstances, memorizing sixty to eighty script pages almost daily for months.) With *Guiding Light*, which was aired directly opposite *General Hospital*, gaining a reputation as a quality drama with attractive young performers, the number-one show for five years faced an uncertain future.

Tony Geary—with stud earring and furry beard—and Genie Francis again reprised their roles as Luke and Laura in November 1984, a ratings sweep month of prime interest to surveying advertisers. (This is why so many daytime serials bring their storylines to climax in November or February—another surveying month.) A Mexican adventure story was introduced to create new enthusiasm in the show, but Geary and Francis again departed, leaving Port Charles in the capable hands of the romantic duo Robert and Holly Scorpio. When former headwriter Pat Falken Smith returned in 1985 (her dispute with Gloria Monty settled amicably), she created a new love interest for Robert Scorpio. Anna Devane, Robert's former wife, was introduced to fill the void created by actress Emma Samms, who went on to *Dynasty*. Falken Smith also reactivated the Quartermaine family as pivotal characters, but the emphasis continued to be on espionage and romantic adventure.

Everything had changed, and nothing had changed—as Jessie answered the phone at the seventh floor nurse station.

In December 1986 the Monty–Falken Smith team went out with fireworks, their super couples—Frisco (Jack Wagner, a teen rock idol) and Felicia as well as the more mature Anna Devane and the mysterious Duke—embroiled in one adventure caper after another. It didn't matter that the Laurenton mystery was so confusing you needed some Purity water just to soothe your migraine or that the Mr. Big—head of organized crime in Port Charles—turned out to be none other than that nice Captain Burt Ramsey. The show was never more popular or more action-packed.

The new executive producer, H. Wesley Kenney, and headwriter Ann Marcus continued the fast pace, but with a more humane touch and deeper characterizations. Relief came in the form of emotionally charged medical stories, romances between the doctors and nurses, and the reintroduction of Audrey and Steve Hardy's son Tom, now grown and waving a medical degree. If anything, the show was finally living up to its title, *General Hospital*.

CAST

Dr. Steve Hardy	John Beradino 1963–
Jessie Brewer, R.N.	Emily McLaughlin 1963–
Dr. Phil Brewer	Martin West 1967–75
	Rick Falk 1966
	Craig Huebing 1966
	Robert Hogan 1966
	Roy Thinnes 1963–66
Audrey March, R.N.	Rachel Ames 1964–
Lucille March, R.N.	Lucille Wall 1963–76; 1982

Al Weeks	Tom Brown 1963–65; 1970–74
Lenore Weeks	Lenore Kingston 1963–65
Eddie Weeks	Doug Lambert 1963–65
	Craig Curtis 1963
Priscilla Longworth	Allison Hayes 1963–64
Peggy Mercer	K. T. Stevens 1963–65
Dorothy Bradley	Susan Seaforth (Hayes) 1963
Cynthia Allison	Carolyn Craig 1963
Randy Washburn	Mark Miller 1964
Angie Costello Weeks	Jana Taylor 1963–65
Dr. Tom Baldwin	Don Chastain 1976–77
	Paul Savior 1967–72
Lee Baldwin	Peter Hansen 1965–85
	Ross Elliott 1963–65
Meg Baldwin	Elizabeth MacRae 1969–70; 1972–73
	Patricia Breslin 1966–69
Scotty Baldwin	Kin Shriner 1977–83; 1987–
	Johnny Jensen 1974–75
	Don Clarke 1973–74
	Tony Campo 1972
	Teddy Quinn
	Johnnie Whittaker
Brooke Clinton	Indus Arthur 1968–73
	Adrienne Hayes 1965–68
Dr. John Prentice	Barry Atwater 1965–67
Polly Prentice	Jennifer Billingsley 1966–67
	Catherine Ferrar 1966
Chase Murdock	Ivan Bonar 1967; 1971–73; 1977
Jane Dawson, R.N.	Shelby Hiatt 1969–75
Howie Dawson	Ray Girardin 1969–74
Mrs. Dawson	Phyllis Hill 1970–75
	Maxine Stuart 1969–70
Sharon Pinkham, R.N.	Sharon DeBord 1967–73
Dr. Henry Pinkham	Peter Kilman 1969–75
Judy Clampett, R.N.	Robin Blake 1964–74
Iris Fairchild	Peggy McCay 1967–70
Beverly Cleveland	Sue Bernard 1969
Dr. Tracy Adams	Kim Hamilton 1969–70
Denise Wilton	Julie Adams 1969
Dr. Peter Taylor	Craig Huebing 1969–79
	Paul Carr 1969
Diana Taylor, R.N.	Brooke Bundy 1973–76
	Valerie Starrett 1969–77
Dr. James Hobart	James Sikking 1973–76
Dr. Lesley Williams Webber	Denise Alexander 1973–84
Augusta McLeod, R.N.	Judith McConnell 1973–75

Mary Briggs, R.N.	Anne Helm 1972–73
Teddy Holmes	John Gabriel 1972–73
	James Westmoreland 1972
Carol Murray	Anne Wyndham 1972–73
Kent Murray	Mark Hamill 1972–73
Mark Simpson	Gary Frank 1972
Dr. Joel Stratton	Rod McCary 1974–75
	Barry Coe 1974
Gordon Grey	Eric Server 1974
	Howard Sherman 1973–74
Florence Grey	Ann Collings 1974
Cameron Faulkner	Don Matheson 1975–76
Kira Faulkner	Victoria Shaw 1974–75
Beth Maynard	Michele Conaway 1975–76
Dr. Kyle Bradley	Daniel Black 1975–76
Carolyn Chandler	Augusta Dabney 1975–76
Bobby Chandler	Ted Eccles 1975–76
Samantha Chandler	Marla Pennington 1976–79
	Kimberly Beck 1975
Laura Vining	Genie Francis 1976–81; 1983; 1984
	Stacey Baldwin 1975–76
Barbara Vining	Judy Lewis 1975–76; 1978
Amy Vining	Shell Kepler 1979–
	Cari Ann Warder 1975–76
Terri Webber Arnett	Bobbi Jordan 1976–77
Dr. Rick Webber	Chris Robinson 1978–86
	Michael Gregory 1976–78
Dr. Jeff Webber	Richard Dean Anderson 1976–81
Dr. Monica Webber	
Quartermaine	Leslie Charleson 1977–
	Patsy Rahn 1976–77
Dr. Gail Adamson	
Baldwin	Susan Brown 1977–85
Heather Grant Webber	Robin Mattson 1980–83
	Mary O'Brien 1977–79
	Georganne LaPiere 1976–77
Alice Grant	Lieux Dressler 1978–83
	Camila Ashland 1976–77
Dr. Mark Dante	Gerald Gordon 1976–78; 1982–83
Mary Ellen Dante	Lee Warrick 1976–77
Dr. Gina Dante	Donna Bacalla 1978–79
	Brenda Scott 1978
	Anna Stuart 1977–78
Dr. Gary Lansing	Steve Carlson 1977–79
Howard Lansing	Richard Sarradet 1978–81
Dr. Adam Streeter	Brett Halsey 1976–77
Kathyrn Corbin	Maggie Sullivan 1977–78

Lamont Corbin	William Bryant 1978
	George E. Carey 1977
Dorrie Fleming, R.N.	Angela Cheyne 1977–80
David Hamilton	Jerry Ayres 1977–78
Dr. Alan Quartermaine	Stuart Damon 1977–
Edward Quartermaine	David Lewis 1978–
Lila Quartermaine	Anna Lee 1978–
Tracy Quartermaine	Jane Elliot 1978–80
Mitch Williams	Christopher Pennock 1979–80
Dan Rooney	Frank Maxwell 1978–
Capt. Burt Ramsey	Bob Hastings 1979–86
Susan Moore	Gail Rae Carlson 1978–83
Jeremy Logan	Philip Tanzini 1978–82
Anne Logan, R.N.	Susan Pratt 1978–82
Spence Andrews	Daniel J. Travanti 1979
Jonelle Andrews	Mary Ann Mobley 1979
Bryan Phillips	Todd Davis 1978–87
Claudia Phillips	Bianca Ferguson 1978–
Eddie Phillips	Sammy Davis, Jr. 1982
Ruby Anderson	Norma Connolly 1979–
Luke Spencer	Anthony Geary 1978–84
Barbara Jean Spencer	Jacklyn Zeman 1977–
Roy DiLucca	Asher Brauner 1978–79
Frank Smith	George Gaynes 1980
Jennifer Smith	Lisa Marie 1980
Joe Kelly	Douglas Sheehan 1979–82
Paddy Kelly	Frank Parker 1980
Rose Kelly	Loanne Bishop 1980–84
Hutch	Rick Moses 1980–81
Sally/Max	Chris Morley 1980
Richard Simmons	Richard Simmons 1979–81
Stella	Jeff Donnell 1980–
Sarah Abbott	Eileen Dietz 1980–81
Robert Scorpio	Tristan Rogers 1981–85; 1986–
O'Reilly	Billie Hayes 1981; 1985
Alexandria Quartermaine	Renee Anderson 1980–81
Dr. Noah Drake	Rick Springfield 1981–83
Tony Cassadine	Andre Landzatt 1981
Victor Cassadine	Thaao Penghlis 1981
Mikkos Cassadine	John Colicos 1981
Helena Cassadine	Elizabeth Taylor 1981
Stavros Cassadine	John Martinuzzi 1983
Tiffany Hill	Sharon Wyatt 1981–83; 1986–
Delfina	Nita Talbot 1981
Slick Jones	Eddie Ryder 1981–83
Emma Lutz	Merrie Lynn Ross 1981–84
Packy Moore	Leonard Stone 1982
Mickey Miller	Milton Berle 1981–82

Dr. Arthur Bradshaw	Martin E. Brooks 1981
Jackie Templeton	Demi Moore 1982–83
Laura Templeton	Janine Turner 1982–83
David Gray	Paul Rossilli 1982
Blackie Parrish	John Stamos 1982–84
Mike Webber	David Mendenhall 1980–86
Holly Sutton	Emma Samms 1982–85
Celia Quartermaine	Sherilyn Wolter 1983–86
Jimmy Lee Holt	Steve Bond 1983–86
Grant Andrews/Putnam	Brian Patrick Clarke 1983–85
Natalie Dearborn	Melinda Cordell 1983
Gregory Malko	Joe Lambie 1983
Dr. Hector Jerrold	Booth Colman 1983
Louisa Swenson	Danielle von Zerneck 1983–84
Dr. Tom Hardy	David Wallace 1987–
	David Walker 1982–84
	Bradley Green 1981–82
	David Comfort 1977
Jake Meyer	Sam Behrens 1983–
D. L. Brock	David Groh 1983–85
Terry Brock	Robyn Bernard 1984–
Constance Townley	Jeanna Michaels 1983
Shirley Pickett	Roberta Leighton 1983
Ginny Blake	Judith Chapman 1984–86
Lorena Sharpe	Shelley Taylor Morgan 1984–86
Amanda Barrington	Anne Jeffreys 1984–86
Vanessa Raphael	Tracy Brooks Swope 1984
Josh Clayton	James McNichol 1984–85
Steffi Brands	Elissa Leeds 1984
Frisco Jones	Jack P. Wagner 1983–
Dr. Anthony Jones	Brad Maule 1984–
Tanya Roskov	Hilary Edson 1984–87
Boris Roskov	William MacMillan 1984
Leo Russell	John Callahan 1984–85
Sylvia Whitby	Linda Borgeson 1984–85
Beatrice Le Seur	Marcella Markham 1984
Felicia Cummings	Kristina Malandro 1984–
Maria Rameriz	June Lockhart 1984–86
Sean Donely	John Reilly 1984–
Derek Barrington	Mark Goddard 1984–86
Jack Slater	Randall England 1984–85
D.A. Ken Morgan	Lloyd Haines 1984–86
Brett Madison	James Horan 1985–87
Anna Devane	Finola Hughes 1985–
Kevin O'Connor	Kevin Bernhardt 1985–86
Patrick O'Connor	Guy Mack 1985–
Buzz Stryker	Don Galloway 1985–87
Sandy Stryker	Yvette Nipar 1986–87
Robin Soltini	Kimberly McCullough 1985–

Jennifer Talbot	Martha Scott 1986
Ted Holmes	David Doyle 1986–87
The Ancient One	Keye Luke 1985
Dr. Yank Se Chung	Patrick Bishop 1985–87
Jade Soong	Tia Carrere 1985–87
Lucy Coe	Lynn Herring 1986–
Duke Lavery	Ian Buchanan 1986–
Camellia McKay	Liz Keifer 1987
Corey Blythe	George Lyter 1987–
Rosa Fernandez	Maria Rangel 1987
Dr. Greta Ingstrom	Kristina Wayborn 1987
Malcolm Rutledge	John Demos 1987
Dusty Walker	Shaun Cassidy 1987
Dr. Simone Ravelle	Laura Carrington 1987–

GOLDEN WINDOWS

July 5, 1954–April 8, 1955   NBC

Young & Rubicam presented this daytime serial focusing on the fame and fortunes of Juliet Goodwin, a twenty-two-year-old singer who left Maine to pursue a career in New York over the objections of both her father and her fiancé. In the Big Apple, Juliet found herself caught between John Brandon, her fiancé, and Tom Anderson, a man with a troubled past. While weighing the pros and cons of that dilemma, an elderly foreigner introduced himself backstage to Juliet as Fritz Lang. (An in-joke: Fritz Lang was a famous German director.) Could Fritz be Juliet's natural father? Although destined for a short run, *Golden Windows* foreshadowed show business stories on *From These Roots* and *The Young and the Restless*. The fifteen-minute soap was broadcast at 3:15 P.M., E.S.T., following *One Man's Family*. The show was produced by Mary Harris and Thomas Riley; directed by Dan Levin; and written by Corlis Wilbur and John Young.

CAST

Juliet Goodwin	Lelia Martin
Charles Goodwin	Eric Dressler
Tom Anderson	Herbert Patterson
John Brandon	Grant Sullivan
Hazel	Barbara Cook

THE GREATEST GIFT

August 30, 1954–July 1, 1955   NBC

This Adrian Samish creation introduced television's first woman doctor. The daytime soap was centered around Dr. Eve Allen, who returned home after years of medical school and a stint in the Army Medical Corps in Korea. Taking over her uncle's medical practice, a clinic in a rundown neighborhood in a small town, Eve became romantically involved with Dr. Phil Stone. While fighting "the inherent prejudices" against women doctors, Eve found herself treating the son of Ridgeton, Connecticut's most influential citizen. Legal troubles soon ensued. Produced by Al Morrison, directed by Joe Behar, and written by James P. Cavanaugh, the show aired at 3:00 P.M., E.S.T.

CAST

Dr. Eve Allen	Anne Burr
Dr. Phil Stone	Philip Foster
Betty Matthews	Athena Lorde
Harold Matthews	Will Hare
	Martin Balsam
Ned Blackman	Gene Peterson
	Ward Costello
Jim Hanson	Jack Klugman
Sam Blake	Josef Drake
Peter Blake	Henry Barnard
Mrs. Blake	Helen Warren
Peg	Margaret Heneghan
Harriet	Anne Meara

THE GUIDING LIGHT

June 30, 1952–   CBS

The longest-running drama in broadcast history, *The Guiding Light* has evolved from a radio soap about a minister and his flock in the '30s and '40s; to a fifteen-minute television entry about the German-American Bauer family in the '50s and '60s; to a half-hour drama about the romantic lives of Mike and Ed Bauer in the '70s; to, finally, a triumphant hour celebrating the domestic interaction between the various Springfield families in the '80s.

Created by Irna Phillips, *The Guiding Light* began broadcasting on NBC's Red radio network on January 25, 1937, and was supervised for Procter & Gamble by the Compton Advertising Agency. Set in the fictional city of Five Points and introduced by organ strains of Goetzl's *Aphrodite*, the drama focused on Dr. John Ruthledge (played by Arthur Peterson) and the problems of his parishioners. The soap was inspirational in tone (hence the title), and frequently entire episodes were given over to Ruthledge's sermons. These sermons, which taught that faith and patience brought happiness, proved to be so popular that a collection of them sold almost 300,000 copies.

The Guiding Light enjoyed great popularity in its first decade and employed such talents as Mercedes McCambridge (Mary Ruthledge), Sam Wanamaker (Ellis Smith), and John Hodiak (Ned Holden.) Originally broadcast from Chicago, the show was moved to Hollywood when Irna Phillips and her associates relocated to the West Coast. In the late '40s, the production was moved to New York and the setting of the drama was changed from Five Points to Selby Flats, a fictional suburb of Los Angeles, where the Bauer family lived. With all these changes came similar changes in the content of the program. The "guiding light" theme no longer had religious implications, but was reinterpreted to mean the support that a close family brings to romantic and domestic crisis.

The Bauers were a first-generation German-American family with Old World values who struggled for a better life in the U.S. They included Mama and Papa Bauer; their son Bill (originally called Willie) and his wife Bertha (called Bert); and Bill's sisters Trudy, who married and moved to New York, and Meta, a feisty young woman who would cause trouble for years. In 1950, Charita Bauer (the last name is a coincidence) joined the cast as the new Bert Bauer, replacing actress Ann Shepherd, and stayed with the show for thirty-five years.

In the beginning, Bert was an unsympathetic character, pushing her husband beyond his means and complaining selfishly for want of creature comforts. Later, after her husband Bill fell into alcoholism, Bert fought hard to keep her family together, weathering a long, stormy marriage. Eventually, she became the "guiding light" of the family, an example of goodness and a person upon whom all could depend. (The official "guiding light" of the family was Papa Bauer, played for two decades by the well-loved Theo Goetz.) Most of the early action centered on Meta Bauer, Bert's sister-in-law. On radio, Meta ran away from home, became pregnant by the caddish Ted White, and murdered Ted when he browbeat their son Chuckie. Meta offered temporary insanity as a plea and won not only her case but the heart of the reporter who covered her trial as well. She married Joe Roberts, who had a grown daughter, Kathy.

In June 1952, Irna Phillips began broadcasting *The Guiding Light* on both television and radio, but not simultaneously. In the morning the cast rehearsed and performed the show at Liederkranz Hall, live for TV. Then they walked to a studio five blocks away and performed the same show for the radio audiences. (In this way, if fans missed the show on TV or did not own a set, they could catch the radio version later in the afternoon.) The cast followed this schedule until the radio version was discontinued four years later. With the cancellation of *The Brighter Day* in 1962, *The Guiding Light* became the only soap to make a successful transfer from radio to television.

During the period when the show was broadcast on both media, the setting of the show was switched from California to the community of Springfield, located somewhere in the Midwest. The story in the '50s, written by Phillips and Agnes Nixon, focused on Meta's stepdaughter Kathy, who married Dr. Dick Grant. But the marriage was annulled when Kathy admitted that her daughter Robin was really the child of Kathy's first husband Bob Lang. After Meta's husband died of cancer, both Meta and Kathy fought over Mark Holden, a business partner of Bill Bauer. When Kathy was killed in an automobile accident in 1958, CBS was swamped with protests; Irna Phillips answered viewers with a form letter: "You have only to look around you, read your daily papers, to realize that we cannot, any of us, live with life alone. . . ."

Meanwhile, Bert attempted to keep her marriage together, bringing up two children, Michael and William Edward (Ed). Agnes Nixon, who had been Irna Phillips' associate, became headwriter, and *The Guiding Light* flourished. It was during this time that Nixon began injecting social issues and educational messages into the drama. She integrated an edifying story-line about uterine cancer, in which Bert Bauer's life was saved by its early detection. Mike Bauer grew up fast and became the show's new young hero in the early '60s. Overprotective Bert disapproved of his romance with Robin Holden, then interfered in his raising Hope, his daughter by Julie Conrad.

As Bert became the dominant force in the family, Bill became weaker and weaker, drinking more heavily and having extramarital affairs. Near the end of the decade, Bill's plane to Alaska crashed and he was presumed dead. (Bill reappeared on the scene in 1977, with teenage daughter Hillary in tow.) Bill's "death" shattered his younger son Ed, who had become a doctor. Ed also became an alcoholic and abused his wife Leslie. When Mike Bauer returned from Bay City (the fictional locale of Irna Phillips' *Another World*), he fell in love with Leslie. But Leslie became pregnant by Ed, and Mike married the scheming Charlotte Waring. A few years after Leslie gave birth to Frederick (named after Papa Bauer), she and Mike were finally united, but their happiness was short-lived; Leslie died in 1976 of injuries sustained in a hit-and-run accident.

Agnes Nixon left the show to write *Another World* in the mid '60s. Writers during *The Guiding Light*'s next decade included David Lesan and Julian Funt, Theodore and Mathilde Ferro, actor John Boruff (who had played Henry Benedict), actor James Lipton (who had played Dr. Dick Grant), Gabrielle Upton, Jane and Ira Avery, Robert Soderberg and Edith Sommer, James Gentile, and Robert Cenedella. The show began broad-casting in color in the spring of 1967 and expanded to a half hour in September 1968. Although there had been many changes on the show, the drama still had not caught up with the contemporary spirit of shows created by Irna Phillips' protégés, Agnes Nixon and Bill Bell. *All My Children* and *The Young and the Restless* became immensely popular with a mix of social issue–oriented drama and youthful romance. In 1975, Jerome and Bridget Dobson took over as *The Guiding Light*'s headwriters and successfully contemporized the drama in the following five years.

As the show expanded to a full hour in 1977, the Dobsons created a series of beautifully constructed stories, centering on a series of intricate romantic triangles—and quadrangles! They introduced the ambitious Alan Spaulding, his unhappy wife Elizabeth, and their son, Phillip. Elizabeth's best friend was free-spirited Jackie Marler, who, unknown to Elizabeth, was the natural mother of Phillip. Jackie became smitten with Mike Bauer but Mike fell in love with Elizabeth. Although Jackie did not love Alan, she married him to get close to Phillip. Alan later dumped Jackie and married Hope, Mike Bauer's daughter. And Elizabeth married Dr. Justin Marler, Jackie's ex-husband and Phillip's real father, thus completing the roundelay.

The Dobsons brought to the show not only romance but regular injec-tions of eroticism—situational sex. Roger Thorpe not only seduced Ed

Bauer's second wife Holly and his third wife Rita, but Ed's half-sister Hillary as well! Roger became soap opera's sexiest villain, and the audience refused to let him die, even after almost a decade of troublemaking. After a sensational trial for marital rape (a gambit the Dobsons would repeat on *As the World Turns*), Roger was "killed" by Holly, only to pop up again a year later to terrorize Rita and Holly. The brilliantly directed sequence in which Roger chased Rita through a carnival hall of mirrors to a recording of Barbra Streisand and Donna Summer's duet "Enough Is Enough" won *The Guiding Light* the Emmy as Outstanding Daytime Drama in 1980. Although he seemed to have more lives than a cat, Roger finally met his fate in a dramatic finish taped on location in the Dominican Republic: he fell off a cliff to his death. Thus put an end to the sensational star turn by actor Michael Zaslow, who began on the show April 1, 1971, and left exactly nine years later on April Fools' Day, 1980 (viewers never saw the body).

The Dobsons had also created a young-love storyline in which Ben married Amanda Wexler (who turned out to be Alan Spaulding's illegitimate daughter), but was still in love with his ex-wife, Evie. But the story had petered out by the time Douglas Marland took over as headwriter in 1980. Marland created his own youthful triangle: confused Morgan Richards fell in love with young Dr. Kelly Nelson but was thwarted at every turn by the devious, deprived Nola Reardon, who became obsessed with the idea of marrying Kelly. So energetic and convincing was Lisa Brown's performance as Nola that the actress, according to CBS officials, began receiving the most intense "hate" mail of any daytime performer since Eileen Fulton two decades before. For this and other compelling stories, Marland deservedly won the Emmy for Outstanding Writing in 1981.

Marland next exploited Lisa Brown's comedic flair and formidable acting skill in a series of fantasy sequences, in which the movie-mad Nola imagined herself in variations of *Now Voyager*, *Casablanca*, and *Wuthering Heights* (the movie, not the book). These highly inventive sequences and poignant storylines featuring the longings of Nola's rough but sensitive brother Tony and sister Maureen, who married Ed Bauer, brought the show renewed popularity. While the NBC dramas and the other CBS soaps kowtowed to the ABC block of powerhouse soaps, *The Guiding Light* stood up against its competition, the top-rated *General Hospital*. *The Guiding Light* consistently found a third-place spot in the ratings and topped off the 1981–82 season with wins for Outstanding Writing and for Outstanding Daytime Drama.

However, Marland and producer Allen Potter, who had taken over in 1976 after the two-decade stint of producer Lucy Rittenberg, soon found themselves at odds. When Potter dropped Marland's Emmy-award-winning friend Jane Elliot from the show after her intense, hair-raising performance as split personality Carrie Todd, Marland was furious. He filled out the remaining months on his contract and quit. The show suffered during this caretaker period, as the highly complex mystery story (Quint-Mona-Mark) collapsed into a convoluted mess. Pat Falken Smith became the new writer and attempted to straighten it out, but it became even more entangled. Falken Smith's short stay with the show was highlighted by a bizarre plot turn in which a house that was being moved crashed into the Reardon's home (thus creating room for Tony's bar, Company).

L. Virginia Browne's stint as headwriter was marked by the introduction of Grant Aleksander as Phillip Spaulding. Browne also pushed Phillip and Ed Bauer's son Rick (Frederick) to the forefront of the drama and the ratings jumped two points. By the time the *Texas* team of writer Richard Culliton and producer Gail Kobe took over in the spring of 1983, *The Guiding Light* was in a critical slump, the stories wandering, but this talented team put the show on the comeback trail, reinstating the Bauer family as the focus, finishing off the inherited, byzantine storylines with a flourish, and, best of all, introducing the most appealing young-love stories ever on daytime drama.

Headwriter Culliton, and later Pamela K. Long (also of *Texas*), transformed *The Guiding Light* back into a *family* show, constructing stories around five main families—the Bauers, Spauldings, Chamberlains, Lewises, and Reardons—who interacted in surprising and complex ways. They also created a series of well-written sequences—a senior prom, a civil war–theme ball, young lovers on the run in Manhattan—and the audience began to respond. The teenage characters were not cardboard cut-outs but flesh-and-blood figures with understandable desires and divided loyalties.

Krista Tesreau as the hilariously spoiled Mindy Lewis, Judi Evans (who nabbed an Emmy) as rape victim Beth Raines, Vincent Irizarry as the pugnacious Lujack, Michael O'Leary as the sensitive medical student Rick Bauer, and especially Grant Aleksander as the flamboyantly alienated Phillip Spaulding, all seemed poised for stardom. With these talented young actors and the likable older characters receiving equal screen time, the new *Guiding Light* had across-the-board appeal. In the first half of 1984, the show added two million viewers to its audience while the competition, the seemingly invincible *General Hospital*, lost five million as a result of Luke and Laura's departure.

The Guiding Light zoomed to the number-one spot in the ratings; the finest daytime drama over the past five years had finally, if briefly, become the most popular. And the introduction of the exquisite Beverlee McKinsey (top-billed on *Texas*) as Alexandra Spaulding brought new critical and commercial interest to the show. But trouble loomed ahead: in October 1984, the Bauers—the "tentpole" family of the show for almost forty years—were dealt a series of devastating blows. Hillary Bauer was suddenly "killed off," her brother Mike was written out of the show, and the actor playing Ed Bauer was replaced. Such changes were not reassuring to fans, who were hopeful that *Guiding Light* would be the phenomenon of the '80s.

On February 28, 1985, actress Charita Bauer died, marking the end of an era. Jerry verDorn, who played Ross Marler, made the announcement to viewers with the words, "The continuing story *Guiding Light* is dedicated to the memory of Charita Bauer, whose portrayal of Bert Bauer has illuminated our lives for over 35 years. The spirit of Charita Bauer, her strength and her courage, her grand good humor, her passion for life, and her humanity have touched us all. She has graced our lives at *Guiding Light* and will be with us always."

With only Ed and Rick left of the Bauer family, *Guiding Light* concentrated on romantic adventure stories featuring Beth and Lujack or Fletcher and Claire. Almost all of Douglas Marland's colorful characters from the turn of the decade—Nola, Quinton, etc.—were also written out or defused (Vanessa Chamberlain) as the Lewises became Springfield's first family. At the center of the Lewis family was the former Reva Shayne, who married Billy Lewis, became engaged to his brother Josh, then wed patriarch H.B. Lewis, and finally fell for Kyle Sampson, who claimed he was H.B.'s illegitimate son. Like Reva, *Guiding Light* was suddenly suffering an identity crisis.

Guiding Light's lack of focus continued through 1986 with five (!) headwriting regimes and a new executive producer. Joe Willmore brought back popular characters and performers (Christopher Bernau's Alan, Peter Simon's Ed, Robert Newman's Josh, and Grant Aleksander's Phillip) and established the Shaynes—Hawk, Sarah, Reva, Roxie, and Rusty—as the show's core family. These "have-nots" offset the aristocratic Spauldings and "new money" Lewises. Springfield also welcomed a storm of strong, young romantic pairings (headwriter Sheri Anderson's forte) and a sprinkle of intrigue. As *Guiding Light* celebrated its 50th anniversary in 1987, the various elements were beginning to jell once again. It was the end of one era and the beginning of another.

CAST

Bert Bauer	Charita Bauer 1950 (Radio)–84
Bill Bauer	Ed Bryce 1959–69; 1977–78; 1983
	Lyle Sudrow 1952-59
Papa Bauer	Theo Goetz 1949 (Radio)–73
Mike Bauer	Don Stewart 1968–84
	Robert Pickering 1968
	Gary Pillar (Carpenter) 1963–66
	Paul Prokopf 1962–63
	Michael Allen 1959–62
	Glenn Walken 1954–56
Dr. Ed Bauer	Peter Simon 1981–84; 1986–
	Richard Van Vleet 1984–86
	Mart Hulswit 1969–81
	Robert Gentry 1966–69
	Pat Collins 1959–61
Meta Bauer Banning	Ellen Demming 1953–74
	Jone Allison 1949 (Radio)–52
Joe Roberts	Herb Nelson 1952–56
Kathy Roberts Holden	Susan Douglas 1952–58
Joey Roberts	Tarry Green 1952–53
Trudy Bauer	Lisa Howard 1957–58
	Helen Wagner 1952
Grandma Elsie	Ethel Remey 1956–57

Dr. Dick Grant	James Lipton 1952–62
Laura Grant	Alice Yourman 1953–62
Marie Wallace	Lynne Rogers 1954–62
	Joyce Holden 1954
Janet Johnson, R.N.	Lois Wheeler 1954–58
	Ruth Warrick 1953–54
Mark Holden	Whitfield Connor 1956–59
Alice Holden	Lin Pierson 1958–60
	Diane Gentner 1956–58
	Sandy Dennis 1956
Robin Fletcher	Gillian Spencer 1964–67
	Ellen Weston 1962–64
	Nancy Malone 1961–62
	Abigail Kellogg 1960–61
	Judy Robinson 1959–60
	Zina Bethune 1956–58
Dr. Paul Fletcher	Bernard Grant 1956–70
Anne Benedict Fletcher	Elizabeth Hubbard 1962
	Joan Gray 1956–62
Henry Benedict	Lester Rawlins 1967
	Paul McGrath 1967
	John Boruff 1962–66
	John Gibson 1959–62
Helene Benedict	Kay Campbell 1957–64
Dr. Bruce Banning	William Roerick 1974
	Sydney Walker 1970–71
	Barnard Hughes 1961–66
	Les Damon 1956–60
Ruth Jannings Holden	Virginia Dwyer 1959–60
	Louise Platt 1958–59
Joe Turino	Joseph Campanella 1959–60
Amy Sinclair	Joanne Linville 1959
Ben Scott	Bernard Kates 1965–68
Maggie Scott	June Graham 1965–68
Peggy Scott	Fran Myers 1965–79
Jane Fletcher	Chase Crosley 1963–68
	Pamela King 1961–63
George Hayes	Philip Sterling 1963–68
Dr. John Fletcher	Erik Howell 1967–71
	Don Scardino 1965–67
	Daniel Fortas 1965
	Donald Melvin 1963–65
	Sheldon Golomb 1962
Alex Bowden	Ernest Graves 1960–66
Doris Crandall	Barbara Becker 1961–62
Julie Conrad Bauer	Sandra Smith 1962–65
Hope Bauer	Elvera Roussel 1979–83
	Katherine Justice 1977
	Robin Mattson 1976–77

Hope Bauer (*cont.*)	Tisch Raye 1975–76
	Elissa Leeds 1968–73
	Paula Schwartz 1968
	Jennifer Kirschner 1964–65
Dr. Stephen Jackson	Stefan Schnabel 1965–81
Leslie Jackson	Lynne Adams 1966–76
	Barbara Rodell 1971–73
	Kathryn Hays 1971
Dr. Jim Frazier	James Earl Jones 1966
	Billy Dee Williams 1966
Martha Frazier	Ruby Dee 1967
	Cicely Tyson 1966
Dr. Sara McIntyre	Millette Alexander 1969–82
	Jill Andre 1967–68
	Patricia Roe 1967
Dr. Joe Werner	Anthony Call 1972–76
	Berkeley Harris 1972
	Ed Zimmermann 1967–72
	Ben Hayes 1966–67
Tim (T.J.) Werner	Nigel Reed 1981–82
	Christopher Marcantel 1981
	Kevin Bacon 1980–81
	T. J. Hargrave 1974–76
Lee Gantry	Ray Fulmer 1969–71
Mildred Foss	Jan Sterling 1969–70
Charlotte Waring Bauer	Melinda Fee 1970–73
	Victoria Wyndham 1967–70
Kit Vested	Nancy Addison 1970–74
David Vested	Dan Hamilton 1971
	Peter D. Greene 1970–71
Stanley Norris	William Smithers 1971
	Michael Higgins 1970
Barbara Norris	Barbara Berjer 1971–81
	Augusta Dabney 1970
Andrew Norris	Ted LePlat 1980–81
	Barney McFadden 1975
Holly Norris	Maureen Garrett 1976–81
	Lynn Deerfield 1970-76
Ken Norris	Roger Newman 1970–75
Janet Mason	Caroline McWilliams 1969–75
Roger Thorpe	Michael Zaslow 1971–80
Adam Thorpe	Robert Milli 1972–81
	Robert Gerringer 1972
Linell Conway	Christina Pickles 1970–71
Marion Conway	Kate Harrington 1971
	Lois Holmes 1971
Karen Martin	Tudi Wiggins 1971–72
Tom Halverson	Chris Sarandon 1969–70
Flip Malone	Paul Carpinelli 1969

Claudia Dillman	Grace Matthews 1968–69
Marty Dillman	Christopher Wines 1969
	Robert Lawson 1968
Betty Eiler	Madeleine Sherwood 1971–72
Charles Eiler	Graham Jarvis 1971–72
Dr. Wilson Frost	Jack Betts 1973–74
Pam Chandler	Maureen Silliman 1974–76
Dr. Tim Ryan	Jordan Clarke 1974–76
Ann Jeffers	Maureen Mooney 1975–79
Spence Jeffers	John Ramsey 1976
Dean Blackford	Gordon Rigsby 1977–78
Rita Stapleton	Lenore Kasdorf 1975–81
Eve Stapleton	Janet Grey 1976–83
Viola Stapleton	Kate Wilkinson 1975–81
	Sudie Bond 1975
Ben McFarren	Stephen Yates 1976–82
Malcolm Granger	Ed Seamon 1976
Dr. Justin Marler	Tom O'Rourke 1976–83
Jackie Marler	Carrie Mowery 1980–82
	Cindy Pickett 1976–80
Lanie Marler	Kathleen Kellaigh 1978–79
Ross Marler	Jerry verDorn 1979–
Alan Spaulding	Christopher Bernau 1977–84; 1986–
Elizabeth Spaulding	Lezlie Dalton 1977–81
Phillip Spaulding	Grant Aleksander 1982–84; 1986–
	John Bolger 1985–86
	Jarrod Ross 1977–81
Frederick Bauer	Michael O'Leary 1983–
	Phil MacGregor 1982–83
	Robbie Berridge 1976–78
	Gary Hannoch 1972–76
	Albert Zungallo 1970–71
Hillary Bauer	Marsha Clark 1978–84
	Linda McCullough 1977–78
Simone Kincaid	Laryssa Lauret 1977–78
Katie Parker	Denise Pence 1977–85
Floyd Parker	Tom Nielsen 1979–85
Dr. Mark Hamilton	Burton Cooper 1978–79
Dr. Peter Chapman	Curt Dawson 1978–80
Diane Ballard	Sofia Landon 1977–81
Brandy Shelooe	JoBeth Williams 1977–81
	Sandy Faison 1977
Brandon Spaulding	Keith Charles 1984
	John Wardwell 1983
	David Thomas 1979
Lucille Wexler	Rita Lloyd 1978–80
Amanda Spaulding	Kathleen Cullen 1978–83
Gordon Middleton	Marcus Smythe 1978–79

Dr. Renee DuBois	Deborah May 1979–80
Ivy Pierce	Deborah May 1982–83
Dr. Greg Fairbanks	David Greenan 1979
Jennifer Richards	Geraldine Court 1980–83
Morgan Richards	Jennifer Cooke 1981–83
	Kristen Vigard 1980–81
Kelly Nelson	John Wesley Shipp 1980–84
Nola Reardon	Lisa Brown 1980–85
Bea Reardon	Lee Lawson 1980–
Tony Reardon	Gregory Beecroft 1981–85
Maureen Reardon	Ellen Parker 1986–
	Ellen Dolan 1982–86
Dr. Jim Reardon	Michael Woods 1983–85
Henry Chamberlain	William Roerick 1980–
Vanessa Chamberlain	Maeve Kinkead 1980–
	Anna Stuart 1980–81
Quinton Chamberlain	Michael Tylo 1981–85
Violet Renfield	Beulah Garrick 1981–83
Lt. Larry Wyatt	Joe Ponazecki 1979–82; 1986–
Clarence Bailey	Lawrence Weber 1982–85; 1987–
	Philip Bosco 1979
Logan Stafford	Richard Hamilton 1980–81
Chet Stafford	Bill Herndon 1980–81
Joe Bradley	Michael J. Stark 1980–81
Derek Colby	Harley Venton 1981–82
Gracie Middleton	Lori Shelle 1981–83
Trudy Wilson	Amy Steel 1980–81
Lesley Ann Monroe, R.N.	Carolyn Ann Clarke 1981–84
Carrie Todd	Jane Elliot 1981–82
Mark Evans	Mark Pinter 1981–83
Mona Enright	Leslie O'Hara 1983
Brian Lister	Richard Clarke 1982–83
Silas Crocker	Benjamin Hendrickson 1981–83
Clay Tynan	Giancarlo Esposito 1982–83
Annabelle Sims	Harley Kozak 1983–85
Commander Eli Sims	Stephen Joyce 1983
H. B. Lewis	Larry Gates 1983–
Trish Lewis	Rebecca Hollen 1981–85
Josh Lewis	Robert Newman 1981–84; 1986–
Reva Shayne Lewis	Kim Zimmer 1983–
Billy Lewis	Jordan Clarke 1983–86
Mindy Lewis	Krista Tesreau 1983–
Beth Raines	Judi Evans 1983–86
Lillian Raines	Tina Sloan 1983–
Bradley Raines	James Rebhorn 1983–85
Dr. Claire Ramsey	Susan Pratt 1983–86
Warren Andrews	Warren Burton 1983–87
Alexandra Spaulding	Beverlee McKinsey 1984–
(Brandon) Lujack	Vincent Irizarry 1983–85

Fletcher Reade	Charles Jay Hammer 1984–
Lola Fontaine	Megan McTavish 1983–84
Wayne De Vargas	Peter Brouwer 1984
Jane Hogan	Mary Pat Gleason 1983–85
Darcy Dekker	Robin V. Johnson 1984
Susan Piper	Carrie Nye 1984
Jonathan Brooks	Damion Scheller 1984–85
Roz Sharp	Carolyn Byrd 1984
Muffy Baxter	Bradley Bliss 1984
India von Halkein	Mary Kay Adams 1984–87
Roxie Shayne	Kristi Ferrell 1984–
Dr. Louie Darnell	Eric Brooks 1983–86
Emma Witherspoon	Maureen O'Sullivan 1984
Kyle Sampson	Larkin Malloy 1984–86
Andy Ferris	Victor Slezak 1984–85
Nancy Ferris	J. Smith-Cameron 1984–85
Johnny "Dub" Taylor	Maarko Maglich 1984–85
Sally Gleason	Patricia Barry 1983–
David Preston	John Martinuzzi 1984–85
Zamana	Adolph Caesar 1984
Sharina	Janet League 1984
Victoria	Kim Hamilton 1984
Gina Daniels	Annabelle Gurwitch 1984
I.Q. (Martin)	Jaison Walker 1984–86
Trevor	Norman Snow 1985
Kurt Corday	Mark Lewis 1985–86
Suzette Saxon	Frances Fisher 1985
Locke Walls	Jeremy Slate 1985
Jackson Freemont	Michael Wilding, Jr. 1985–
Charlotte Wheaton	Barbara Garrick 1985
Alicia Rohmer	Cynthia Dozier 1985
Maeve Stoddard	Leslie Denniston 1985–
Calla Matthews	Lisby Larson 1985–86
Jesse Matthews	Rebecca Staab 1985–86
Simon Hall	Shawn Thompson 1985–87
Cain Harris	Jerry Lanning 1986
Dorie von Halkein	Kimi Parks 1986–87
Dinah Morgan	Paige Turco 1987–
	Jennifer Gatti 1986–87
Cameron Stewart	Ian Ziering 1986–
George Stewart	Joe Lambie 1987–
Grace Cummings	Teresa Wright 1986
Dr. Mark Jarrett	Keir Dullea 1986
Johnny Bauer	James M. Goodwin 1986–87
Christine Valere	Ariane Munker 1986–87
Paul Valere	Robin Ward 1987
Chelsea Reardon	Kassie Wesley 1986–
Rusty Shayne	Terrell Anthony 1986–
Sarah Shayne	Audrey Peters 1986–

Lisa Cutler	Sherry Ramsey 1987
Dr. Will Jeffries	Joseph Breen 1987–
Alan-Michael Spaulding	Carl Evans 1987–

HAWKINS FALLS

June 17, 1950–August 19, 1950 (prime time);
April 2, 1951–July 1, 1955 (daytime)   NBC

What began as a Saturday night series about small-town life, combining drama, situation comedy, and music, returned to television as a daily daytime soap opera featuring some of the original cast members. Broadcast from Chicago, the setting was patterned after Woodstock, Illinois (where location footage was shot as background), and focused on Clate Weathers, the town's newspaper editor, and his gossipy readers. Among the major characters in the prime-time version were Belinda Catherwood, the town's self-appointed defender of morality; Laif and Millie Flaigle, whose happy marriage was the envy of many; and Knap and Lona Drewer, who adopted the runaway Roy. On the daytime serial, after Knap died, Lona married the town doctor, Floyd Corey. Lona and Floyd became the new focus of the show, their difficulties with children and nosy neighbors providing endless grief and amusement. NBC's biggest daytime drama hit in its early years, *Hawkins Falls* was created by Roy Winsor and written by Doug Johnson. Ben Park served as producer and director. The daytime version was initially seen at 5:00 P.M., E.S.T., but was later aired in the morning slot, at 11:00 A.M.

CAST

Clate Weathers	Frank Dane
Lona Drewer Corey	Bernadine Flynn
Dr. Floyd Corey	Maurice Copeland
	Michael Golda
Laif Flaigle	Wyn Stracke
Millie Flaigle	Ros Twohey
Elmira Cleebe	Elmira Roessler
Spec Bassett	Russ Reed
Belinda Catherwood	Hope Summers
Roy Bettert	Bruce Dane
Toby Winfield	Tom Poston

With: Ron Tomme (Bruce Sterling on *Love of Life* from 1959 to 1980), Barbara Berjer (Barbara Thorpe on *The Guiding Light* from 1971 to 1981), Phil Lord, Peter Donat, and Sam Gray.

HIDDEN FACES

December 30, 1968–June 27, 1969   NBC

NBC's answer to *The Edge of Night*, this action-oriented crime drama, created and written by *Edge*'s Irving Vendig, had the bad luck to be placed opposite CBS's powerhouse *As the World Turns*. Although the show was well produced and a favorite among the limited audience it built up, NBC only gave it six months to make a dent in *World Turns'* daytime monopoly. Most of the drama revolved around the law offices of Arthur Adams, who defended Dr. Katherine Logan, a surgeon who had accidentally caused a patient's death. Arthur and Kate soon fell in love. As lawyer Arthur Adams, Conard Fowkes found his only starring role on the soaps. Over the years he has been featured in a dozen soaps, most notably on *The Secret Storm* (as Paul Britton), *The Edge of Night* (as Steve Prentiss), and *As the World Turns* (as Don Hughes).

CAST

Arthur Adams	Conard Fowkes
Dr. Katherine Logan	Gretchen Walther
Martha Logan	Louise Shaffer
Mimi Jaffe	Rita Gam
Sen. Robert Jaffe	Joseph Daly
Mark Utley	Stephen Joyce
Nick Capello Turner	Tony LoBianco
Earl Harriman	Nat Polen
Wilbur Ensley	John Towley
Grace Ensley	Ludi Claire
Allyn Jaffe	Linda Blair

HIGH HOPES

1978   Syndicated

Taped in Toronto, this was the first soap to be broadcast simultaneously in the United States and Canada. It was aired over the CBC network in Canada and over independent stations in the U.S., premiering on most of them on April 3, 1978. *High Hopes* delved into family counseling as psychiatrist Neal Chapman solved the problems of others while his own troubles mounted. Critics complained that early episodes contained too many storylines and the viewer was bombarded with too many characters and situations. Later in the show's short run, in a buzz of publicity, Dorothy Malone of *Peyton Place* fame was added to the cast. The half-hour serial was written by Winifred Wolfe, directed by Bruce Minnix, and produced by Robert M. Driscoll.

CAST

Dr. Neal Chapman	Bruce Gray
Jessie Chapman	Marianne McIssac
Meg Chapman	Doris Petrie
Trudy Bowen	Barbara Kyle
Paula Myles	Nuala Fitzgerald
Walter Telford	Colin Fox
Louise Bates	Jayne Eastwood
Amy Sperry	Gina Dick

Dr. Dan Gerald	Jan Muszinski
Victor Tauss	Nehemiah Persoff
Carol Tauss	Dorothy Malone

HOTEL COSMOPOLITAN

August 19, 1957–April 11, 1958   CBS

When the successful series *Valiant Lady* finally ran out of steam, CBS decided to replace it with this experimental, *Grand Hotel*–style anthology serial about the various guests at a New York hotel, The Cosmopolitan. Roy Winsor created and produced the show, which was broadcast at 12 noon, E.S.T. Actor Donald Woods (playing himself) narrated the comings and goings. Henderson Forsythe, who played the house detective, went on to play Dr. David Stewart on *As the World Turns*.

CAST

Narrator	Donald Woods
House Detective	Henderson Forsythe

With: James Pritchett (Dr. Matt Powers on *The Doctors* from 1963 to 1982), Walter Brooke, Dinna Smith, John Holmes, and Tom Shirley.

THE HOUSE IN THE GARDEN
See Fairmeadows, U.S.A.

THE HOUSE ON HIGH STREET

September 28, 1959–February 5, 1960   NBC

This daytime anthology serial dramatized stories about juvenile delinquency and divorce, based on actual cases, each presented in three to five episodes. While an actor played probation officer John Collier, real psychiatrists and judges played themselves, including Dr. Harris B. Peck and Judge James Gehrig. The first case concerned a sixteen-year-old boy from a "good family" who stole a car. The guest stars included some of the finest theater actors—and future soap veterans—ever to appear on the American stage. The show was written by William Kendall Clarke, directed by Lela Swift, and produced by John Haggart.

CAST

John Collier	Philip Abbott

With: Donald Madden, Martin Balsam, Sylvia Miles, Jan Miner, Frances Heflin (Mona Kane on *All My Children* since 1970), Irene Dailey (Liz Matthews on *Another World* from 1974 to 1986), Anne Meacham (Louise Goddard on *Another World* for a decade), Leora Dana, Frances Sternhagen, Lynn Loring (Patti Barron on *Search for Tomorrow* from 1951 to 1961), Kay Medford, Patricia Bosworth, and Alan Alda (as troubled juvenile Gilbert Parker).

HOW TO SURVIVE A MARRIAGE
January 7, 1974–April 18, 1975   NBC

This women's lib serial, heavily promoted by NBC, was a bold concept in daytime drama. Unfortunately, its freshness was lost in the excruciatingly didactic and heavy-handed execution. It was a soap of ideas, not characters. Created by Anne Howard Bailey (with intense involvement by NBC's vice president Lin Bolen), *How to Survive a Marriage* opened with a ninety-minute special featuring a well-publicized, explicit bedroom scene between Larry Kirby and his mistress, Sandra.

Much of the serial focused on thirty-two-year-old Chris Kirby, her reaction to her husband's philandering, her subsequent counseling with Dr. Julie Franklin, her attempt to launch a career, and her fight for custody of her daughter Lori. (Chris eventually remarried Larry the following Valentine's Day, then promptly fell into alcoholism.) In a parallel women's lib story, Fran Bachman, a middle-aged woman, struggled with the many problems of sudden widowhood. Although the latter story was sensitively and realistically handled (the actress received over a thousand letters of condolence), the soap was weighted down by by heavy-handed dialogue, pop psychology, and preachy feminist politics. After its first year, the show landed at the bottom of the daytime barrel with a 4.9 rating. *Ryan's Hope*, which premiered right after *Marriage*'s cancellation, was far more successful in integrating feminism with traditional soap staples.

Entitled *From This Day Forth* in development, *How to Survive a Marriage* starred Rosemary Prinz as the "with it" psychiatrist Julie Franklin for its first six months. Prinz, who became daytime's first real star with her long stint as Penny Hughes on *As the World Turns*, received top billing on this show, a three-day work week, and a rumored $1,000 per episode. (Prinz left the show when Julie ran off to marry Dr. Tony DeAngelo.) The soap was taped in Studio 84, where Toscanini conducted his famous radio broadcasts with the NBC symphony (with Prinz's father playing the cello). The producers included Allen Potter, Peter Andrews, and Jeff Young. Rick Edelstein and Margaret DePriest succeeded Anne Howard Bailey as headwriter.

CAST

Dr. Julie Franklin	Rosemary Prinz
Chris Kirby	Jennifer Harmon
Larry Kirby	Michael Hawkins
	Ken Kercheval
	Michael Landrum
Lori Kirby	Cathy Greene
	Suzanne Davidson
Sandra Henderson	Lynn Lowry
Dr. Tony DeAngelo	George Welbes

Fran Bachman	Fran Brill
David Bachman	Allan Miller
Rachel Bachman	Elissa Leeds
Moe Bachman	Albert Ottenheimer
Monica Courtland	Joan Copeland
Terry Courtland	Peter Brandon
Joan Willis	Tricia O'Neil
Peter Willis	Berkeley Harris
	Steve Elmore
Dr. Max Cooper	James Shannon
Johnny McGhee	Armand Assante
Maria McGhee	Lauren White
Dr. Charles Maynard	Paul Vincent
Joshua Browne	F. Murray Abraham
Dr. Robert Monday	Gene Bua
Susan Pritchett, R.N.	Veleka Gray
Alexander Kronos	Brad Davis

THE INNER FLAME
See Portia Faces Life.

KING'S CROSSING
January 16, 1982–February 27, 1982   ABC

When prime-time's *Secrets of Midland Heights* was cancelled after only a few episodes, producers Lee Rich and Michael Filerman promised a revision of the show with a new title in the future. What emerged a year later was a completely different serial. Although the show included two of the young stars of *Midland Heights*—Marilyn Jones and Daniel Zippi—the setting had switched from the Midwest to a small college town. The focus had also changed from teenage sexual shenanigans to family domestic drama, although both serials shared gothic flourishes in their opening episodes.

Despite the presence of several former daytime stars—Michael Zaslow (Roger Thorpe, *The Guiding Light*); Mary Frann (Amanda Peters, *Days of Our Lives*); and Stephanie Braxton (Laurie Stevens, *The Secret Storm*)—the lackluster storylines and dull characters proved unattractive to prime-time viewers conditioned to the explosive drama of *Dynasty* and *Dallas*. The show revolved around the Hollister family: Paul, an alcoholic English teacher; Nan, his long-suffering wife; Carey, a spunky teenager, who found her crippled cousin Jullian hidden away in a third-floor bedroom; and Lauren, an aspiring pianist who fell in love with symphony conductor Jonathan Hardary. Sally Robinson was the writer and producer. See *Secrets of Midland Heights*.

<u>CAST</u>

Paul Hollister	Bradford Dillman
Nan Hollister	Mary Frann
Carey Hollister	Marilyn Jones
Lauren Hollister	Linda Hamilton
Louisa Beauchamp	Beatrice Straight
Jillian Beauchamp	Doran Clark
Billy McCall	Daniel Zippi
Jonathan Hadary	Michael Zaslow
Carol Hadary	Stephanie Braxton

KITTY FOYLE

January 13, 1958–June 27, 1958   NBC

Ginger Rogers won the 1940 Academy Award for the film version of the Christopher Morley novel about an Irish girl from the wrong side of the tracks who fell in love with a man from Philadelphia society. The radio version aired from 1942 to 1944. As a publicity gimmick, the television serial version conducted an extensive talent hunt, auditioning over two hundred actresses before awarding the title role to Kathleen Murray. To build suspense in the drama, Kitty was not introduced until the fifth week of the television run. The show-business newspaper *Variety* blamed its failure on the banality of the scripts, which the paper considered surprising since *One Man's Family*'s Carleton E. Morse headed up the writing team. The show was produced by Charles Irving, directed by Hal Cooper, and packaged by Henry Jaffee Enterprises. The half hour *Kitty Foyle*, which opened with panoramic location shots of downtown Philadelphia, was broadcast on the East Coast at 2:30 P.M.

<u>CAST</u>

Kitty Foyle	Kathleen Murray
Ed Foyle	Bob Hastings
Pop Foyle	Ralph Dunne
Sophie Foyle	Kay Medford
Mac Foyle	Larry Robinson
Olivia Strafford	Valerie Cossart
Wyn Strafford	William Redfield
Molly Scharf	Judy Lewis
Rosie Rittenhouse	Les Damon
Stacey Lee Balla	Marie Worsham

With: Patty Duke, Teri Keane, Karl Weber, Ginger McManus, and Lee Bergere.

KNOTS LANDING
December 27, 1979– CBS

A spin-off from *Dallas*, this prime-time serial concentrated on domestic conflict rather than the corporate greed of *Dynasty*, *Falcon Crest*, and its mother show, *Dallas*. Created by David Jacobs, it focused on the lives of Gary Ewing, the alcoholic black sheep of the millionaire Ewing family, and Valene, whom he had recently remarried. (Although Ted Shackelford played the role of Gary Ewing on *Dallas*, David Ackroyd had actually originated the role. Ackroyd later appeared on *Knots Landing* as Bill Medford, a man who grew close to Karen Fairgate after his wife committed suicide. Both actors had running parts on *Another World* in the mid '70s.) Gary and Valene Ewing moved to the community of Knots Landing in Southern California to build a new life. But their in-laws—Gary's brothers Bobby and J.R.—and their troublesome daughter Lucy dropped in from time to time.

Their neighbors, whose lives often intertwined romantically, included Karen and Sid Fairgate, who owned Knots Landing Motors, where Gary worked; Kenny and Ginger Ward, a young recording executive and his wife; and Richard and Laura Avery, an unscrupulous lawyer and his confused wife. In the second season Jane Elliot (who had made a huge impression in daytime TV as Tracy Quartermaine on *General Hospital*) and theater actor Paul Rudd were introduced as Judy and Earl Trent. While helping Earl deal with his alcoholism, Gary had an affair with the intense, long-suffering Judy. Daytime alumni Donna Mills (Laura Donnelly, a nun on *Love Is a Many Splendored Thing*) appeared on the scene, playing Abby Cunningham, Sid's divorced sister, a devious blond bombshell who first pursued Richard but then set her sights on Gary.

The third season opened with the death of Sid Fairgate, who had been hospitalized after an automobile crash. Abby began to work closely with Gary, eventually drawing him into a torrid affair. Theater legend Julie Harris was introduced as Lilimae Clements, Val's mother, who encouraged Val to write a novel about the Ewing dynasty. (The novel, *Capricorn Crude*, became an immediate bestseller.) The season ended with Val discovering Gary's infidelity and her leaving him.

The fourth season introduced three new characters: Mack (M. Patrick) Mackenzie, who married Karen after she had put her grief over Sid's death behind her; Chip Roberts, a scheming young man who ingratiated his way into Val and Lilimae's lives; and Ciji Dunne, a rock singer, whose murder was blamed on a drunken Gary. The season concluded with Val rediscovering her feelings for Gary; Chip running off to New York with Karen's daughter, Diana; and Richard deserting Laura.

In the next season Gary was cleared of Ciji's murder and married Abby, but became fascinated with a Ciji lookalike, Cathy Geary. (Lisa Hartman, who was popular with younger viewers as Ciji, returned to play the part.) Douglas Sheehan, who played Joe Kelly on *General Hospital*, joined the cast as Ben Gibson, romancing Val, who found she was pregnant with Gary's baby. Other characters introduced were Senatorial candidate Gregory Sumner and his teenage daughter Mary Frances. Sumner had a shady fling with Abby, and then managed to almost ruin Mack's career, but Sumner was under the thumb of syndicate boss Mark St. Claire, who served as the catalyst in several seemingly divergent storylines. As the season ended Abby's deviousness was exposed, and it was discovered that Gary's death had been faked (Cathy Geary's ex-husband Ray was killed instead) so St. Claire would make his final move to take over Lotus Point. In the dramatic season finale, Gary saved the pregnant Val from a bomb planted in a car, Karen was shot by St. Claire's goons, and St. Claire kidnapped Abby.

The 1983–84 season was *Knots Landing*'s most popular, a consistent top-ten rating winner, edging out such tough competition as *Hill Street Blues* and *20/20*. Its emphasis on familial conflict—such as the problems caused by Karen's pill addiction—set it apart from the other prime-time soaps. The exciting conclusion to the season, as the different storylines came together into one, was carefully planned and grew organically from the plot, unlike *Falcon Crest* and *Dynasty*, which often ended a season with an indiscriminate apocalypse. *Knots Landing* ended the year with *Soap Opera Digest* declaring it television's finest serial.

In the 1984–85 season, Sumner shot and killed Mark St. Claire, who had held Abby hostage. Gary and Abby then shared an uneasy reconciliation. After Karen was told she had probably less than a year to live following the surgery for her gunshot wound, she finally submitted to a life-or-death operation and recovered. Alec Baldwin (Billy Aldrich, *The Doctors*) was introduced as Joshua Rush, a young preacher who thought he was Lilimae's nephew, but turned out to be her son. Joshua fell in love with Cathy, but his evangelist career on Abby's cable TV super-station quickly came between the two.

Most of the story during the season zeroed in on the melodramatic story in which Valene's twins were kidnapped at birth by Abby's pal Scott Easton. Val, unable to deal with what she was told was the stillbirth of her children, later suffered a nervous breakdown and took the identity of Verna Ellers, a character in one of Valene's bestselling novels. As Verna was about to marry Parker Winslow, Gary stepped in in the nick of time and stopped the wedding. Other developments that season included the introduction of Howard Duff as powerful wheeler-dealer Paul Galveston, who turned out to be the natural father of Senator Greg Sumner. And *Knots Landing* scored a coup signing the reclusive Ava Gardner in her first television role—as Paul's widow, Ruth Galveston.

Gardner proved to be one of the highlights of an otherwise dreary prime-time soap season. Cigarette smoke enveloping her every mischievous move, Gardner's Ruth orchestrated Greg's resignation from the senate to run Empire Valley, a planned community used as a front for sophisticated satellite spying. Ruth also attempted to break up Greg and Laura with Abby's help, but Greg proposed to Laura anyway. Meanwhile, Josh and Cathy were married as Karen and Mack moved in on Dr. Mitch Ackerman, who killed himself rather than revealing where Val's babies had been placed. The season ended with the discovery of the adoptive parents, but as Val approached the Fisher's home, Harry Fisher drove off with one of the twins.

In the 1985–86 season, little Bobby and Betsy were eventually returned. Gary stepped aside, although everyone in town suspected that he was the twins' natural father. This paved the way for Ben and Valene—whom Greg Sumner refered to as "Dagwood and Blondie"—to marry. Gary later suffered a nervous breakdown after he learned of his brother Bobby's death. Then, learning of the full extent of the top-secret activities planned for Empire Valley, Gary simply blew the project up.

Jill Bennett, of the governor's office, came onto the scene and after flirting with Mack, set her eye on Gary. Jill was in fact Dottie Simpkins and was in cahoots with her brother, who called himself Peter Hollister. They sought revenge against Galveston Industries for swindling land from their family, which precipitated their father's suicide. Peter went to Greg Sumner and claimed to be his half-brother—the son of Paul Galveston and Sylvia Lean. Sylvia had had a son (who had died) by Paul, but went along with the fraud with Peter for a promised financial settlement.

Meanwhile, Joshua's career as a TV evangelist went haywire; he was preaching by day and beating his wife by night—as well as sleeping with all God's groupies under the sun. Crazed one night, Joshua lured wife Cathy up to a rooftop and tried to throw her off, but his mother Lilimae stopped him, and Joshua himself fell to his death. Afterwards, Cathy resumed her singing career and fell into an affair with Ben Gibson. But, at the last minute, Ben decided not to become road manager to Cathy, and returned to his wife, Valene.

Greg, washed up politically, began to promote Peter (Greg didn't care if Peter was his brother or not) as state senator—which pleased Abby, who knew all about Peter's secrets, in and out of bed. Karen began snooping around Empire Valley and Lotus Point after her son Eric became ill because of all the chemical leaks in the real estate projects. Greg hired Phil Harbert to throw a scare into Karen, but the plan backfired—and how!

In the 1986–87 season, Karen was kidnapped, and the unstable Phil became obsessed with her and tried to kill her several times. Eventually, Greg discovered Phil's whereabouts and saved Karen. When Karen returned home, there was a visitor, Paige Matheson, who claimed to be the daughter of Mack by the wealthy Anne Winston. (*Knots Landing* over several months used flashbacks depicting Mack and Greg's friendship and Mack's romance with Anne. Young Greg was played by William Devane's real-life son, Joshua.) Anne also arrived on the scene and tried to seduce Mack by dancing drunkenly and amusingly to "California Dreamin'." (Michelle Phillips, who played Anne, was a former member of The Mamas and the Papas.) Shortly after her fake attempted suicide, Anne left town in a huff.

Meanwhile, Greg and Laura married, and Laura gave birth to a baby girl, Meg. Abby and Gary divorced, and Gary eventually married Jill Bennett. After Peter was elected state senator, "brother" Greg was back in power. It was then Jean Hackney, supposedly with the C.I.A. but really belonging to a terrorist organization, who wanted Greg dead. ("No, I'm not happy to see you," said Greg to Jean, "and, yes, that is a gun in my pocket.") Jean blackmailed Ben into killing Greg, but Ben couldn't go through with it, and he and Greg faked the murder for Jean's benefit. Although Jean was apprehended, Ben suffered from severe anxiety attacks afterwards, and left town, telling Valene he had journalism assignments in South America.

Peter enjoyed affairs with both Abby and Paige Matheson, but when he found out that Olivia held a letter from the recently deceased Sylvia Lean, he went after Olivia too. Teenager Olivia was recovering from cocaine addiction, and Peter exploited her crush on him. Just as she was about to hand over the letter to Peter, Olivia spotted Paige coming out of Peter's shower. Olivia mailed the letter to Gary, but it was intercepted by Jill, Gary's new wife. At the end of the season, Peter was found stabbed to death with Olivia crouched over the body. Mama Abby covered up the crime and disposed of the body in a vat of concrete.

As an exasperated Eric Fairgate commented, "Living in this cul-de-sac is like living in the middle of a soap opera!"

CAST

Gary Ewing	Ted Shackelford 1979–
Valene Ewing	Joan Van Ark 1979–
Karen Fairgate	Michele Lee 1979–
Sid Fairgate	Don Murray 1979–81
Diana Fairgate	Claudia Lonow 1979–84
Michael Fairgate	Pat Peterson 1979–
Eric Fairgate	Steve Shaw 1979–
Kenny Ward	James Houghton 1979–83
Ginger Ward	Kim Landford 1979–83
Richard Avery	John Pleshette 1979–83
Laura Avery	Constance McCashin 1979–
Jason Avery	Danny Ponce 1983
	Danny Gellis 1980–82
	Justin Dana 1979–80
Abby Cunningham	Donna Mills 1980–
Brian Cunningham	Brian Green 1986–87
	Bobby Jacoby 1980–84
Olivia Cunningham	Tonya Crowe 1980–
Judy Trent	Jane Elliot 1980–81
Earl Trent	Paul Rudd 1980–81
Lilimae Clements	Julie Harris 1981–
Chip Roberts	Michael Sabatino 1982–83
Ciji Dunne	Lisa Hartman 1982–83
Cathy Geary	Lisa Hartman 1984–86
Ray Geary	Bruce Fairbairn 1984
Mack MacKenzie	Kevin Dobson 1982–
Jeff Munson	Jon Cypher 1982–83
Scooter Davis	Allan Miller 1981–83
Lt. Janet Baines	Joanna Pettet 1983
Mitchell Casey	Barry Primus 1983
Ben Gibson	Douglas Sheehan 1983–87
Gregory Sumner	William Devane 1983–

Mary Frances Sumner	Danielle Brisebois 1983–84
Jane Sumner	Millie Perkins 1983–84
Mark St. Claire	Joseph Chapman 1984
Joshua Rush	Alec Baldwin 1984–85
Scott Easton	Jack Bannon 1984
Parker Winslow	Mayf Nutter 1984–85
Paul Galveston	Howard Duff 1984–85
Ruth Galveston	Ava Gardner 1985
Dr. Mitch Ackerman	Laurence Haddon 1984–85
Shelia Fisher	Robin Ginsburg 1985
Harry Fisher	Joe Regalbuto 1985
John Coblentz	Madison Mason 1985–86
Jill Bennett	Teri Austin 1985–
Peter Hollister	Hunt Block 1985–87
Sylvia Lean	Ruth Roman 1986
Phil Harbert	Louis Gaimbalvo 1986
Jean Hackney	Wendy Fulton 1986–87
Paige Matheson	Nicollette Sheridan 1986–
Young Anne	Nicollette Sheridan 1986–87
Young Mack	Doug Savant 1986–87
Young Greg	Joshua Devane 1986–87
Anne W. Matheson	Michelle Phillips 1987
Al Baker	Red Buttons 1987

LOVE IS A MANY SPLENDORED THING
September 18, 1967–March 23, 1973   CBS

This admirable, cherished daytime effort began as a continuation of the 1952 autobiography *A Many Splendored Thing* by Han Suyin (a pseudonym) and the 1955 hit film, *Love Is a Many Splendored Thing*, which starred Jennifer Jones and William Holden. It concerned the star-crossed romance between Mark Elliott, a war correspondent, and Han Suyin, a Eurasian woman doctor, which ended with Mark's death in Korea. The soap, created by Irna Phillips, picked up the story years later as Mark and Han's daughter Mia left Hong Kong to study medicine in San Francisco.

There Mia (played by Nancy Hsueh, of Chinese-Scotch-Irish descent) met her aunt and uncle, Helen and Phillip Elliott, and the Donnelly family: Dr. Will Donnelly and his daughters Iris and Laura. Mia first dated Paul Bradley, an American Vietnam War pilot, then became seriously involved with Jim Abbott, a local doctor. These were daytime's first interracial romances, and Phillips was careful to dramatize the realities of the situation and some characters' bigoted reactions. A storm of controversy, much of it created by network officials, ensued. When CBS executive Fred Silverman ordered the storyline killed, an enraged Irna Phillips quit. The character Mia Elliott was sent packing after a six-month run.

After the shake-up, the new writers, Jane and Ira Avery, focused on a young, spectacularly attractive cast. Producer John Conboy (later of *The Young and the Restless* and *Capitol*) added superb production values—lush settings and top-notch lighting effects—a gambit so popular that it created a trend toward "beautiful people" storylines. Leslie Charleson and Donna Mills became daytime stars as the spunky Iris and the confused Laura. (Laura was initially seen in a convent, in conflict over whether or not to take her final vows. The nun story, like the interracial romance, was thought to be controversial and the storyline was dropped.) When David Birney was cast as Mark Elliott, the man who created havoc between the two sisters, the soap zoomed in the ratings. Birney's intense popularity was short-lived; he left the show, and soon after starred in the sitcom *Bridget Loves Bernie* with Meredith Baxter, who would become his wife. Leslie Charleson and Donna Mills also left the serial. Charleson was a guest star on nearly all the popular prime-time series at the time, before returning to daytime television as Dr. Monica Webber on *General Hospital*. Mills later starred as the vixen Abby Cunningham on *Knots Landing*.

After the roles of Iris, Laura, and Mark were recast (much too often), the show was refocused. Under the writing regimes of James Lipton, Don Ettlinger, and Ann Marcus, the previously WASP cast was expanded to include the Chernak family: the unconventional Betsy, her dynamic brother Peter—both doctors—and their mother Lily. The texture of the show also changed, from love story to melodrama. The families became embroiled in a barrage of organized crime, blackmail, and political corruption. Audience defections were noticeable, but the ratings were still good. CBS, which had bungled nearly all the managerial decisions, lost faith in the show.

To the fury of the soap's diehard fans, CBS notified the show on February 12, 1973, that the March 23 episode would be their last. The story concluded happily when the independent Betsy and her live-in lover Joe Taylor were wed in a traditional ceremony. In its final scene, Judson Laire, who played Dr. Will Donnelly, stepped out of character and thanked the audience for their loyalty and support. "It's hard to say good-bye after such a long acquaintance," he said, "but, who knows? Perhaps we'll live on in your memories."

CAST

Mia Elliott	Nancy Hsueh 1967
Paul Bradley	Nicholas Pryor 1967
Dr. Jim Abbott	Ron Hale 1973
	Robert Milli 1967–68
Phillip Elliott	Len Wayland 1967
Helen Elliott Donnelly	Gloria Hoye 1968–73
	Grace Albertson 1967
Mark Elliott	Tom Fuccello 1972–73
	Michael Hawkins 1970–71
	David Birney 1969–70
	Sam Wade 1968
Iris Donnelly Garrison	Bibi Besch 1971–73
	Leslie Charleson 1967–70

Laura Donnelly	Barbara Stanger 1972–73
	Veleka Gray 1970–71
	Donna Mills 1967–70
Dr. Will Donnelly	Judson Laire 1968–73
Lt. Tom Donnelly	Albert Stratton 1969–73
	Robert Burr 1967–69
Martha Donnelly/	
Julie Richards	Beverlee McKinsey 1970–71
Ricky Donnelly	Shawn Campbell 1967–73
Jim Whitman	Berkeley Harris 1970
Spence Garrison	Brett Halsey 1973
	Ed Power 1968–72
	Michael Hanrahan 1968
Nancy Garrison	Susan Browning 1969
Joe Taylor	Leon Russom 1972–73
Dr. Betsy Chernak Taylor	Andrea Marcovicci 1970–73
Dr. Peter Chernak	Vincent Baggetta 1970–73
	Michael Zaslow 1970
	(Paul) Michael Glaser 1969–70
Lily Chernak Donnelly	Diana Douglas 1970–73
Angel Allison Chernak	Suzie Kay Stone 1969–73
Sen. Alfred Preston	Don Gantry 1971–72
Walter Travis	John Carpenter 1972
Marian Hiller	Constance Towers 1971–72
Celia Winter	Abigail Kellogg 1972–73

LOVE OF LIFE

September 24, 1951–February 1, 1980   CBS

Created by Roy Winsor and John Hess, this story of two sisters, one good, one bad, ran almost three decades before being unceremoniously snuffed out in its 7,316th episode. Broadcast live from Liederkranz Hall, Studio 54, in New York, the fifteen-minute serial began daily with Charles Mountain's narration of the theme: "*Love of Life*, the story of Vanessa Dale in her courageous struggle for human dignity." And, oh, what a struggle it was for the long-suffering Van (played by well-known actress Peggy McCay), who was saddled with an amoral, hedonistic sister, Meg, whose escapades continually shocked and titillated viewers.

Set in New York City and in the small town of Barrowsville, much of the early story was entertaining melodrama: both Van and Meg were put on trial (several times) for various murders. Later, Van married lawyer Paul Raven, who successfully defended her in one of these courtroom dramas. When Meg was written out in 1956, the show was refocused, and was expanded to a half hour two years later. (In 1962, *Love of Life* was trimmed down to twenty-five minutes to make room for five minutes of CBS news; right before cancellation, in its new late-afternoon slot, the show was again expanded to a half hour.) After Paul Raven was presumed dead in a plane crash, Van was romanced by Bruce Sterling, a widower. Bruce was a teacher at a prep school in Rosehill, New York, where he and Van settled when they married in April 1959. In a bizarre turn of events, Ron Tomme, who joined the show as Bruce in January 1959, romanced Bonnie Bartlett, who was playing Van right up until the night before the wedding. When Van actually walked down the aisle, she was being played by Audrey Peters! Both Tomme and Peters remained in the roles until the show was cancelled in 1980.

The marital road for Bruce and Van was rocky, as they dealt with meddling in-laws, jealousy, and Bruce's infidelities with teacher Ginny Crandall and Dr. Jennifer Stark. The show introduced a very popular young-love storyline, the stormy romance of Tess Krakauer and Bill Prentiss, played by the offscreen husband-and-wife team Toni Bull Bua and Gene Bua. *Love of Life*, reflecting the social changes of the '60s, began to flirt with contemporary issues such as campus unrest and drug abuse, but it still fell back on stock devices such as amnesia to create conflict. "Matt Corby," the attorney who defended Tess and Bill for the murder of Tess's ex-husband John Randolph, turned out to be Paul Raven, Van's first husband, who had had extensive plastic surgery after the plane crash. Van, torn between Paul and Bruce, divorced Bruce, to the horror of viewers. A few years later Van and Bruce were remarried.

By 1973, the show had begun to fizzle, exhausting such formidable writing teams as Eileen and Robert Mason Pollock, Esther and Richard Shapiro (later creators of *Dynasty*), and Paul Roberts and Don Wallace. However, that year a new producer, Jean Arley, and new writers Claire Labine and Paul Avila Mayer—later creators of *Ryan's Hope*—re-energized the show. It was a memorable period, especially when, in January 1974, the superb Canadian actress Tudi (née Mary Susan) Wiggins joined the cast as Meg, thus reactivating the show's original good-sister-bad-sister theme. Meg joined forces with the corrupt mayor Charles Hart against Van and Bruce, who vowed to clean up Rosehill. Equally exciting was the introduction of Christopher Reeve—later of *Superman* fame—as Ben Harper, Meg's devilishly handsome and selfish son. Ben married the virginal Betsy Crawford, although he was still married to the sexy, wise-cracking Arlene Lovett. (Asked by the police if she had ever been questioned before on any arson charge, Arlene snarled, "Yeah, the Chicago fire!") In one unusually disturbing episode, the complex Meg realized the extent of Ben's deviousness and the values she had instilled in him. She began beating him over the head in a fit of familial rage, and then fell to the floor in a heap, calling her beloved grandchild a "bastard"—the first time the word was uttered on daytime TV.

With the writing stints of Margaret DePriest, and then Paul and Margaret Schneider, the bigamy triangle continued and other stories were developed, but the new-found audience began to dwindle. Written by Gabrielle Upton, *Love of Life* became more youth-oriented and contemporary, but then Jean Holloway, who had worked in soap opera's infancy, became headwriter, and the bottom fell out. Holloway wrote the show as if it were a radio serial, and her ludicrous Bambi Brewster story—a dumb hooker-with-a-heart-of-gold who traveled across the country to discover that her nutty minister father had abused her as a child (Somerset Maugham gone hogwild)—became the laughingstock of the industry.

Veteran writer Ann Marcus and producer Cathy Abbi attempted to patch things up, but the show, which had become the lowest-rated daytime program, received its cancellation notice on January 5, 1980. Hoping to be picked up by another network (à la *The Edge of Night*'s switch from CBS to ABC), the show played out the scripts as written, refusing to tie up the loose ends or provide a happy ending for the audience. Instead of a confrontation-reconciliation scene between Meg and Van or a montage of Van and Bruce's twenty-year love affair, *Love of Life* ended on February 1, 1980, with Betsy fainting while testifying at Ben's trial for assault. As the credits rolled to the Tony Bennett record "We'll Be Together Again," Larry Auerbach, who had directed the show since its beginning, walked through the empty sets. "The Lady"—as Tudi Wiggins touchingly referred to *Love of Life*—had come to an end.

CAST

Vanessa Dale	Audrey Peters 1959–80
	Bonnie Bartlett 1955–59
	Peggy McCay 1951–55
Meg Dale	Tudi Wiggins 1974–80
	Jean McBride 1951–56
Sarah Dale	Valerie Cossart 1979–80
	Joanna Roos 1968–78
	Jane Rose 1951–56
Bruce Sterling	Ron Tomme 1959–80
Ben Harper	Chandler Hill Harben 1976–80
	Christopher Reeve 1974–76
	Tommy White 1957–58
	Dennis Parnell 1951–57
Will Dale	Ed Jerome 1951–53
Matt Slocum	Burt French 1953–54
Alex Crown	Russell Thorson 1953
Jill Crown	Natalie Priest 1953
Charles Harper	Paul Potter 1951–53
Ellie Crown	Bethel Leslie 1956
	Mary K. Wells 1955–56
	Hildy Parks 1951–55
Miles Pardee	Joe Allen, Jr. 1951
Paul Raven/	
Matt Corby	Richard Coogan 1951–56
	Robert Burr 1970–72
Althea Raven	Joanna Roos 1955–57
Judith Lodge Raven	Virginia Robinson 1954–57
Hal Craig	Steven Gethers 1953–56
Jack Andrews	Donald Symington 1958
Tom Craythorne	Lauren Gilbert 1958
Tammy Forrest	Ann Loring 1956–70

Tammy Forrest (*cont.*)	Scottie McGregor 1956–57
Noel Penn	Gene Peterson 1958
Alan Sterling	John Fink 1969–70
	Dennis Cooney 1965–67
	Dan Ferrone 1964–65
	Jim Bayer 1959–64
Barbara Sterling	Zina Bethune 1965–71
	Lee Lawson 1961–65; 1970
	Nina Reader 1959–61
Dr. Tony Vento	Jordan Charney 1965
	Ron Jackson 1959–65
Vivian Carlson	Helen Dumas 1959–71
	Eleanor Wilson 1959
Henry Carlson	Jack Stamberger 1961–71
	Tom Shirley 1959–61
Guy Latimer	John Straub 1962–63
Rick Latimer	Jerry Lacy 1972–78
	Edward Moore 1970–72
	Michael Ebert 1966–70
	Paul Savior 1960–66
Hank Latimer	David Carlton Stambaugh 1970–78
	Justin Sterling 1965
Ginny Crandall	Barbara Barrie 1960
Dr. Jennifer Stark	Joan Bassie 1969–71
Link Porter	Gene Pellegrini 1961–69
Maggie Porter	Joan Copeland 1961–62
Kay Logan	Joan Copeland 1962–63
Sandy Porter	Bonnie Bedelia 1961–67
Julie Murano	Jane Manning 1965
	Jessica Walter 1962–65
Philip Holden	David Rounds 1963–65
Jason Ferris	Robert Alda 1966–67
Sharon Ferris	Eileen Letchworth 1966–67
Hester Ferris	Marie Masters 1966–67
Glenn Hamilton	Bert Convy 1963
Ace Hubbard	Jed Allan 1964
Jonas Falk	Roy Scheider 1965–66
	Ben Piazza 1965
Charles Lamont	Jonathan Moore 1966–78
	Stan Watt 1966
Diana Lamont	Diane Rousseau 1966–76
Beatrice Swanson	Jane Hoffman 1968–75
Kate Swanson	Sally Stark 1969–75
	Leonie Norton 1967–69
Bill Prentiss	Gene Bua 1967–72
	Philip Clark 1970
Tess Krakauer	Toni Bull Bua 1966–73
Mickey Krakauer	Alan Yorke (Feinstein) 1965–68

Anna Krakauer	Jocelyn Brando 1966–67
Toni Prentiss Davis	Louise Larabee 1969
	Frances Sternhagen 1967–68
John Randolph	Byron Sanders 1967–69
	Barton Stone 1967
Richard Rollins	Lawrence Weber 1969–71
Jamie Rollins	Ray Wise 1970–76
	Donald Warfield 1969–71
Joe Bond	Lincoln Kilpatrick 1968–70
Rita Bond	Darlene Cotton 1968–70
Loretta Allen	Ja'net DuBois 1970–72
Daisy Allen	Sharon Brown 1971
	Irene Cara 1970–71
Monica Nelson	Beverly Todd 1968–70
Ed Bridgeman	Hugh Franklin 1969
Sally Bridgeman Rollins	Catherine Bacon 1969–73
Candy Lowe, R.N.	Susan Hubley 1973–74
	Nancy McKay 1972–73
Dr. Dan Phillips	Drew Synder 1970–74
Vinnie Phillips	Nancy Marchand 1970–74
	Beatrice Straight 1970
Dr. Lloyd Phillips	Douglass Watson 1972–73
Link Morrison	John Gabriel 1970–72
	George Kane 1969–70
Dr. Ted Chandler	Keith Charles 1974–75
Dr. Joe Corelli	(Paul) Michael Glaser 1971–72
	Tony LoBianco 1972–73
Judith Cole	Marsha Mason 1972
Connie Loomis	Chris Chase (Irene Kane) 1962–65
Caroline Aleata	Roxanne Gregory 1976–78
	Deborah Courtney 1973–76
Eddie Aleata	John Aniston 1975–78
Jeff Hart	Charles Baxter 1973–74
David Hart	Brian Farrell 1974–75
Betsy Crawford	Margo McKenna 1978–80
	Elizabeth Kemp 1973–77
Dr. Tom Crawford	Mark Pinter 1979–80
	Richard K. Weber 1976–79
Arlene Lovett	Birgitta Tolksdorf 1974–80
Carrie Johnson	Peg Murray 1974–80
Felicia Fleming	Pamela Lincoln 1974–77
Johnny Prentiss	Trip Randall 1972–78
Dr. Joe Cusak	Peter Brouwer 1976–78
Lynn Henderson	Amy Gibson 1976–78
Ray Slater	Lloyd Battista 1975–80
Ian Russell	Michael Allinson 1976–77
Bambi Brewster	Ann McCarthy 1977–80
Mia Marriott	Veleka Gray 1977–80
Dr. Andrew Marriott	Ron Harper 1977–80

Dr. A. Marriott *(cont.)*	Richard Higgs 1977
Andy Marriott	Christian Marlowe 1977–78
Elliott Lang	Ted LePlat 1978–80
Dory Patton	Sherry Rooney 1977–78
Wes Osborne	Woody Brown 1979–80
Wendy Hayes	Elaine Grove 1977–78
Dr. Leann Wilson	Mary Ann Johnson 1979–80
Steve Harbach	Paul Craggs 1979–80
Amy Russell	Dana Delany 1979–80
Prof. Timothy McCauley	Shepperd Strudwick 1979–80

LOVERS AND FRIENDS

January 3, 1977–May 6, 1977   NBC

After establishing *Another World* as one of daytime's highest-rated soaps, writer Harding Lemay and producer Paul Rauch went to work on creating a new serial about two very different kinds of families: the wealthy Cushings and the upwardly mobile Saxtons. The Cushings included Austin, an unemployed college dropout with a drinking problem; Megan, his sister; Richard, their stockbroker father; and Edith, their socialite mother. The Saxtons included Rhett, who fell in love with Megan Cushing; his parents Lester and Josie; Jason, his brother who also vied for Megan's affections; Bentley, his younger brother; Eleanor, his social-climbing sister married to George Kimball; and Tessa, his youngest sister.

Set in Point Clair, a fashionable suburb of Chicago, *Lovers and Friends* (titled *Into this House* in development) concentrated on class conflict and psychological themes. Like *Another World*, the drama depended more on character development than plot, but *Lovers and Friends* had a far more youthful cast. (It was also taped in the Brooklyn studio adjacent to *Another World*.) When the soap did not catch on immediately, NBC decided to put it on hold for intensive revisions. The revamped version, *For Richer, For Poorer*, appeared six months later. See *For Richer, For Poorer*.

CAST

Austin Cushing	Rod Arrants
Megan Cushing	Patricia Estrin
Richard Cushing	Ron Randell
Edith Cushing	Nancy Marchand
Rhett Saxton	Bob Purvey
Lester Saxton	John Heffernan
Josie Saxton	Patricia Englund
Jason Saxton	Richard Backus
Bentley Saxton	David Abbott
Tessa Saxton	Vicky Dawson
Eleanor Kimball	Flora Plumb
George Kimball	Stephen Joyce
Desmond Hamilton	David Knapp
Amy Gifford	Christine Jones

Connie Ferguson   Susan Foster
Sophia Slocum   Margaret Barker

LOVING

June 26, 1983–   ABC

The eagerly anticipated collaboration between Douglas Marland, the celebrated former headwriter of *General Hospital* and *Guiding Light*, and Agnes Nixon, the creator of *All My Children* and *One Life to Live*, turned out happily: a classic soap opera built around contemporary themes and timeless romance. ABC's first daytime effort in nearly a decade, *Loving* quickly tackled father-daughter incest, the plight of Vietnam veterans, research into the sexually related disease AIDS, and the psychological struggles of a young priest. Like Nixon's *All My Children*, the new show effectively integrated social problems with romance, domestic drama and wit, without *All My Children*'s tendency toward caricature.

Loving was launched with a Sunday two-hour prime-time TV movie starring Lloyd Bridges and Geraldine Page, who played Johnny Forbes and Amelia Whitley, former lovers caught in the midst of a university scandal involving drugs and prostitution. Although the premiere was directed by Michael Lindsay-Hogg (*Brideshead Revisited*), it was sluggish, standard television fare, without the emotional elements that make soap opera so popular. But when the actual story began the next day, without Bridges and Page in the cast, it became apparent that *Loving* was a dramatic force to be reckoned with. While other daytime soaps were awash in a sea of international intrigue, *Loving* was refreshingly domestic, packed with familial conflict and star-crossed romance.

Loving was unafraid of going out on a limb; in one highly dramatic sequence Mike Donovan, a Vietnam veteran, became drunk at a town picnic, took center stage, and spoke bitterly about Vietnam and his troubled life afterwards. Almost a year later, *Loving* went on location at the Vietnam Veteran Memorial in Washington, D.C., for another emotion-packed set piece. James Kiberd's performances as Mike in both sequences were among the season's finest. Unfortunately, the morning slot where ABC positioned *Loving* was not attracting the viewers the network expected. There was early talk of cancellation, but *Loving* was given another chance when it was scheduled in an afternoon slot beginning in October 1984.

The show was set in the university town of Corinth on the East Coast, and centered on four families whose lives intertwined socially and romantically. The politically minded Roger Forbes was married to the beautiful blue-blood Ann Alden, and they had two children: Lorna, a hedonistic college student; and Jack, their adopted son, who fell in love with Lily Slater, an incest victim. Ann's parents were Isabelle and Cabot Alden, who had their hands full bringing up their calculating grandson Curtis. At the other end of the social spectrum was the Donovan family, which included Patrick and Rose, a retired policeman and his seamstress wife; their son Mike, a Vietnam vet and a policeman; their younger son Douglas, a college professor; and their young daughter, Stacey. Mike was married to Noreen Vochek, a nurse involved in AIDS research. Noreen's brother Jim was a priest who had to come to terms with his past. Their sister was Merrill, a television reporter, who was unlucky in love.

Two years after its premiere, *Loving* had strayed away from its original themes, many core characters being written out as the Alden family and in-laws became almost the complete dramatic focus. When Roger Forbes was reported killed in a plane crash, Ann Alden married the devious Dane Hammond, Jack's natural father. After Jack's "true love" Lily left town, Jack fell in love with Stacey Donovan, but married Ava Rescott when she became pregnant with his child. The hapless Stacey also hooked up with Tony Perelli, but her engagement was broken off when she discovered that Tony had impregnated Lorna, Jack's sister. Perhaps *Loving* needed less loving and more imagination—if not birth control information.

Loving limped along for the next few years, wracked with casting problems, with most of the original cast out on their kiesters. The wealthy Aldens stayed on and the rich/poor family concept was reactivated with the introduction of the Sowolsky family, paving the way for a star-crossed romance between Steve Sowolsky and Trisha Alden. If anything, *Loving* was the spitting image of *All My Children* in its early years, right down to the raven-haired Erica clone, Ava Rescott Forbes Alden. Like *Loving*, Agnes Nixon's *Children* and *One Life to Live* had started out slowly in the ratings, so ABC remained enthusiastic about the show's prospects.

CAST

Roger Forbes	Peter Brown 1983–84
	John Shearin 1983
Ann Alden Forbes	Callan White 1984–
	Shannon Eubanks 1983–84
Jack Forbes	Perry Stephens 1983–
Lorna Forbes	O'Hara Parker 1986–87
	Susan Walters 1983–86
Patrick Donovan	George L. Smith 1984–85
	Noah Keen 1983–84
Rose Donovan	Dorothy Stinnette 1984–87
	Teri Keane 1983–84
Douglas Donovan	Victor Bevine 1985–86
	Bryan Cranston 1983–84
Stacey Donovan	Lauren-Marie Taylor 1983–
Mike Donovan	James Kiberd 1983–85
Noreen Vochek	Elizabeth Burr 1985
	Marilyn McIntyre 1983–84
Father Jim Vochek	Peter Davies 1983–
Merrill Vochek	Patricia Kalember 1983–84
Cabot Alden	Wesley Addy 1983–
Isabelle Alden	Augusta Dabney 1983–87
	Meg Mundy 1983

Curtis Alden	Burke Moses 1986–87
	Linden Ashley 1985–86
	Christopher Marcantel 1983–85
Garth Slater	John Cunningham 1983
June Slater	Ann Williams 1983–84
Lily Slater	Britt Helfer 1987–
	Jennifer Ashe 1983–84
Billy Bristow	Tom Ligon 1983–84
Rita Mae Bristow	Pamela Blair 1983–85
Lt. Art Hindman	John Danelle 1984; 1986–
Judge Elizabeth Connors	Audrey Peters 1984
Dane Hammond	Anthony Herrera 1984–86
Shana Sloane	Susan Keith 1984–
Tony Perelli	Richard McWilliams 1984–85
	Peter Radon 1983
Clem Margolies	Richard McGonagle 1984
Warren Hodges	W. T. Martin 1984
Edy Lester	Lesley Vogel 1984
Penny O'Rourke	Emily Langworthy 1984
Jonathan Matalaine	John O'Hurley 1984–85
Ava Rescott	Roya Megnot 1984–
	Patty Lotz 1984
Millicent Whitehead	Rita Lloyd 1984
Colby Cantrell	Pamela Bowen 1984–85
Kate Rescott	Nada Rowand 1984–
Harry Sowolsky	Ed Moore 1984–
Steve Sowolsky	John R. Johnston 1984–
Keith Lane	John O'Hurley 1984–86
Gwenyth Alden	Christine Tudor 1984–
Trisha Alden	Noelle Beck 1984–
Linc Beecham	Brian Robert Taylor 1985–86
	Phil MacGregor 1985
Tug Watley	Brett Porter 1985–86
Sherri Watley	Deidre O'Connell 1985–86
	Susan Wands 1985
Rebekka Beecham	Jane Powell 1985–86
Zona Beecham	Kathleen McCall 1986
Judd Beecham	Neil Zevnik 1986
	Dan Doby 1985
Cecelia Thompson	Colleen Dion 1986–87
	Alice Haining 1985–86
	Rebecca Staab 1985
Zack Conway	John Gabriel 1986–87
Kelly Conway	Kathleen Fisk 1986–87
Rob Carpenter	Timothy Owen 1986–87
Lotty Bates	Judith Hoag 1986–
Ned Bates	Luke Perry 1987–
Eban Japes	Matthew Cowles 1986–87
Nick Dinatos	Jeff Gendelman 1986–87

Tony Benedict	Korey Mall 1987
April Hathaway	Alexandra Wilson 1987–
Clay Alden	Randolph Mantooth 1987–
Diane Winston	Jacqueline Courtney 1987–
Rick Stewart	Ron Nummi 1987–
Jenny Baylor	Mary Lynn Blanks 1986–87
Marty Edison	Isabel Glasser 1987–
Alan Howard	Steve Fletcher 1987

MARY HARTMAN, MARY HARTMAN

1976–1978   Syndicated

Called "the funniest show in the history of television" by *The Wall Street Journal* and "a genre unto itself" by *The Nation*, this pop culture phenomenon was half soap opera and half soap satire. It became a *cause célèbre* in the press, a constant topic on the cocktail party circuit, and a show that soap opera purists both loved and hated.

Starring Louise Lasser as the put-upon heroine, *Mary Hartman* was developed by Norman Lear, who bought the rights to the old radio serial *The Bickersons* in 1967 with the idea of airing a modern television version of the comic soap sometime in the future. What developed years later by veteran serial writer Ann Marcus (*Days of Our Lives*, etc.), Gail Parent (*The Carol Burnett Show*), and others was a wildly irreverent view not of soap opera but of modern life, consumerism, and television in general. The major networks vetoed the show, which in its opening episodes comically presented mass murder, exhibitionism, and impotence. Lear syndicated the show to independent stations (which sometimes edited out scenes they deemed in bad taste), beginning January 6, 1976, and airing generally in a late-night time slot.

Set in the small town of Fernwood, Ohio, *Mary Hartman* was presented in the form of the early '50s TV soaps, with long scenes and organ music cuing the emotions. In the first season Mary Hartman, the pig-tailed (Lasser wore a wig), buck-toothed, confused housewife, found herself in the midst of a comic whirlwind. Her daughter Heather was held hostage by a mass murderer; her grandfather was found to be the "Fernwood Flasher"; and her husband Tom was laid off from his job and became impotent. When Tom complained to Mary that she should become more like a woman, the perplexed Mary asked, "You mean do nothing?"

Mary's neighbors, Charlie Haggers and his wife Loretta, an aspiring country and western singer, pooh-poohed suggestions that a song from the viewpoint of the mass killer was not appropriate. Charlie said, "Of course it is. Country and western is all about real things, like murder, amputations, faucets dripping in the night." (When Mary's nymphomaniacal sister Cathy romanced a deaf mute, Loretta wrote a song entitled "How Can You Say You Love Me When You Can't Talk Back.") While trying to cope with neighbors Ed and Howard McCullough, who turned out to be lovers not brothers, and then with a high school football coach who drowned in a bowl of chicken soup in her kitchen, Mary fell in love with Sgt. Dennis Foley, a police officer who had a heart attack during a romantic clinch. With the world closing in on her—not to mention commercials reminding her that she still had "waxy yellow buildup" on her kitchen floor—Mary appeared on the *David Susskind Show* and had a nervous breakdown.

The next season introduced Gore Vidal as himself, who interviewed Mary for a new book while she became involved with the intrigue surrounding the mental hospital. But after 325 episodes Louise Lasser, who had appeared almost daily on the show, and offscreen was arrested for possession of cocaine, had had enough. She left the show as Mary ran off with Sgt. Foley. Other characters remained and more were introduced that season, and in the subsequent season, when the show was retitled *Forever Fernwood*.

Charlie Haggers had a testicle blown off in a gun accident, while Loretta developed amnesia and fell in love with Mac, a huge truck driver. Martin Mull was introduced as Garth Gimble, a wife beater who was killed by his wife—stabbed by the end of a Christmas tree. (He returned as Barth, Garth's brother, a talk show host.) Tom found a new romantic interest in Eleanor Major; Cathy became pregnant by an unknown lover; and Mary's father fell into a chemical vat, had plastic surgery, and came out looking like Tab Hunter—much to the delight of Mary's mother, Martha. Between seasons of *Mary Hartman, Mary Hartman* and *Forever Fernwood*, a TV talk show spoof entitled *Fernwood 2-Night*, using some of the same characters, ran briefly. *Mary Hartman* was seen in repeats in 1980 as part of CBS's late-night lineup, and then in syndication beginning April 4, 1983.

CAST

Mary Hartman	Louise Lasser 1976–77
Tom Hartman	Greg Mullavey 1976–78
Martha Shumway	Dody Goodman 1976–78
George Shumway	Tab Hunter 1977–78
	Philip Bruns 1976–77
Cathy Shumway	Debralee Scott 1976–78
Heather Hartman	Claudia Lamb 1976–78
Raymond Larkin	Victor Kilian 1976–78
Loretta Haggers	Mary Kay Place 1976–78
Charlie Haggers	Graham Jarvis 1976–78
Sgt. Dennis Foley	Bruce Solomon 1976–77
Merle Jeeter	Dabney Coleman 1976–78
Wanda Jeeter	Marian Mercer 1976–78
Jimmy Joe Jeeter	Sparky Marcus 1976–77
Garth Gimble	Martin Mull 1976–77
Barth Gimble	Martin Mull 1977–78
Patty Gimble	Susan Browning 1976–77
Cookie La Rue	Beverly Garland 1977–78
Eleanor Major	Shelley Fabares 1977–78
Mac Slattery	Dennis Burkley 1977–78
Penny Major	Judy Kahan 1977–78

Mae Olinski   Salome Jens   1977–78
Annie (Tippytoes) Wylie   Gloria DeHaven 1977–78
Gore Vidal   Himself   1977

MISS SUSAN
March 12, 1951–December 28, 1951   NBC

The background of this show—probably the most unusual in soap opera history—was far more dramatic than the maudlin stories that ran during its eight months on daytime TV. Susan Peters, a young Hollywood leading lady of the '40s who had major roles in *Strawberry Blonde, Meet John Doe*, and *Random Harvest*, was suddenly paralyzed from the waist down when she was shot in a hunting accident in 1945. Confined to a wheelchair, she returned to films in 1948 with *The Sign of the Ram*. Later NBC approached her to star in her own daytime drama, *Miss Susan*, later titled *Martinsville, U.S.A.*

Peters played Susan Martin, a wheelchair-bound attorney who had recently returned to practice law in her hometown of Martinsville, Ohio. Between clients, Susan worried about marrying a man who wanted a large family but who did not know that his future bride could not have children. Viewers found the story exploitive and stayed away from the show. The fifteen-minute serial was broadcast live from Philadelphia at 3:00 P.M., E.S.T., and was written by William Kendall Clarke. The thirty-year-old actress died less than a year after the cancellation of *Miss Susan*.

CAST
Susan Martin   Susan Peters
Bill Carter   Mark Roberts
Mrs. Peck   Kathryn Grill
With: Natalie Priest, Robert McQueeny, and Jon Lormer.

MODERN ROMANCES
October 4, 1954–September 19, 1958   NBC

Daytime's most successful anthology serial dramatized stories from the magazine of the same name over a single week's period. The debut story concerned a jealous young husband who suspected that his attorney was interested in his wife. Ann Flood (Nancy Karr, *The Edge of Night*) and Georgann Johnson (Ellen Grant, *Somerset*) were frequent guests, and many future daytime stars also made appearances. Initially, Martha Scott served as host and narrator; later, Mel Brandt took over; then guests such as Jayne Meadows and Margaret Truman served as narrators. H. Wesley Kenney of *Days of Our Lives* fame was one of the directors. *Modern Romances* aired daily for fifteen minutes beginning at 4:45 P.M., E.S.T.

CAST
Ann Flood, Georgann Johnson, Meg Mundy, Don Hastings, Marjorie Gateson, Millette Alexander, Phyllis Hill, Robert Mandan, Lawrence Weber, William Prince, Mary K. Wells, Augusta Dabney, and Paul Stevens.

MOMENT OF TRUTH
January 4, 1965–November 5, 1965   NBC

Before winning two Emmys for Outstanding Actor as Mac Cory on *Another World*, Douglass Watson starred in this NBC serial taped in Toronto. Watson played Dr. Robert Wallace, a professor and psychologist who found himself in the midst of social and romantic conflicts in a small Canadian town. *Moment of Truth* aired for a half hour at 2:00 P.M., E.S.T., opposite another loser, ABC's *Flame in the Wind*. It was replaced by the smash hit *Days of Our Lives*.

CAST
Dr. Robert Wallace	Douglass Watson
Nancy Wallace	Louise King
Johnny Wallace	Michael Dodds
Shelia Wallace	Barbara Pierce
Jack Williams	Stephen Levy
Vince Conway	Peter Donat
Dr. Russell Wingate	Ivor Barry
Monique Wingate	Fernande Giroux
Dr. Gil Bennett	John Bethune
Barbara Harris	Mira Pawluk
Linda Harris	Anna Hagan
Dexter	Chris Wiggins

MORNING STAR
September 27, 1965–July 1, 1966   NBC

Unlucky NBC launched two serials on the same day, *Paradise Bay* and *Morning Star*, both produced in Hollywood and in color. They were also cancelled on the same day. *Morning Star* concerned the life of Katy Elliott, a New Englander whose fiancé was killed the day before the wedding. Katy fled to New York to concentrate on a career in fashion design. Although Katy found a friend and roommate in Joan Mitchell and a boyfriend in Bill Riley, she had a difficult time leaving Springdale, Massachusetts, behind: Jan, her sixteen-year-old sister; Aunt Millie; Uncle Ed, a judge; and the memory of Greg Ross, who had died as the result of a traffic accident.

Created by Ted Corday (*Days of Our Lives*), the show was written by Carolyn Weston, a former short order cook at Frostie-Freeze who wrote romances in her spare time. (*TV Guide* labelled her "The Hickoryburger

Lady of Malibu.") The serial's promotional commercial consisted of a huge eye brimming with a teardrop and a voice booming in the background, "Cry yourself a bucketful. Watch *Morning Star*, eleven o'clock weekdays!"

CAST

Katy Elliott	Elizabeth Perry
	Shary Marshall
Bill Riley	Edward Mallory
Jan Elliott	Adrienne Ellis
Ed Elliott	Ed Prentiss
Millie Elliott	Shelia Bromley
Gregory Ross	Burt Douglas
Mike Halloran	Ted deCorda
Ann Burton	Olive Dunbar
Grace Allison	Phyllis Hill
Eve Blake	Floy Dean
Dr. Tim Blake	William Arvin
Eric Manning	Ron Jackson
Dana Manning	Betsy Jones Moreland
Stan Manning	John Stephanson
	John Dehner
Joan Mitchell	Betty Lou Gerson

NEVER TOO YOUNG

September 27, 1965–June 24, 1966   ABC

Premiering the same day as NBC's *Morning Star* and *Paradise Bay* and ABC's *The Nurses*, *Never Too Young* concentrated on a group of rambunctious teenagers at Malibu Beach—a kind of continuing *Beach Blanket Bingo*. It was a failure, but it paved the way for other youth soaps, such as *Love Is a Many Splendored Thing* and *The Young and the Restless*. In the cast were two famous prime-time teenagers, Tony Dow (Wally Cleaver on *Leave it to Beaver*) and Tommy Rettig (a child star as the first boy in the *Lassie* series). Broadcast at 4:00 P.M., E.S.T., to attract teenagers after school, *Never Too Young* was replaced by *Dark Shadows*, the cult phenomenon of the '60s.

CAST

Chet	Tony Dow
Jo-Jo	Tommy Rettig
Susan	Cindy Carol
Barbara	Pat Connolly
Frank	John Lupton
Tad	Michael Blodgett
Joy	Robin Grace
Rhoda	Patrice Wymore

Alfie   David Watson
Tim   Dack Rambo

A NEW DAY IN EDEN
1982–1983   Showtime

Cable television brought explicit language and nudity to the soap opera, but most efforts have proved transitory and have actually been long mini-series rather than open-ended stories. Showtime has been the leader in the cable soap explosion, launching *Romance*, a puerile anthology serial that dramatized stories (such as a man who hires a woman to seduce his seminary-bound son) over five episodes; Pat Falken Smith's *Lone Star Bar and Grill*, a drama about a group of Texas blue-collar workers and aspiring country and western performers; David Jacobs' *Loving Friends and Perfect Couples*, a romantic comedy about the sexual tensions in modern relationships. Even the Playboy channel got in the act with Elizabeth Levin's *Sunday Child*, about a young woman's sexual awakening, and *Love Ya, Florence Nightingale*, a continuing comedy-drama about the problems of a sex therapist, starring porno queen Marilyn Chambers. (The latter consisted of weekly peeks at Chambers' breasts as she peeled off her gray sweatshirt when greeting patients.)

By far the most successful and popular effort was *A New Day in Eden*, a Showtime creation that also aired on the Oak Media and Prism systems. Written by Douglas Marland, who had become soap opera's most sought after writer after his award winning stints with *Guiding Light* and *General Hospital*, the show dramatized the business and romantic problems of the people of Eden, a Midwestern city in the process of renovation and a sweeping urban renewal program. At the center of the action was Bryan Lewis, the president of a huge electronic company, who was threatened by Josh Collier, a troubleshooter sent to measure Eden's progress in urban renewal.

The power struggles and business machinations served as a backdrop for racier activities: an older woman-younger man romance, a deflowering in a barn, father-daughter incest, lesbianism, and a rash of rapes, murders, and mayhem on the local college campus. The producer of the thirty-three-hour serial was Gary Hoffman and the executive producer was Michael Jaffe. Much of the cast were alumni of *General Hospital*, the show into which Douglas Marland had breathed new life in the late '70s. Afterwards Marland, with Agnes Nixon, created the daytime drama *Loving*.

CAST

Bryan Lewis   Jim McMullan
Josh Collier   Steve Carlson
Miranda Stevens   Maggie Sullivan
Biff Lewis   Grant Wilson
Greg Lewis   Larry Poindexter
Clint Masterson   Jack P. Wagner
Madge Sinclair   -   Jane Elliot

Laurel Franklin   Ann Wilkinson
Betty Franklin   Lara Parker

THE NURSES

September 27, 1965–March 31, 1967   ABC

The prime-time series *The Nurses* starred Shirl Conway as Liz Thorpe, the supervising nurse at Alden Hospital, and Zina Bethune as Gail Lucas, a nurse new to the staff. It ran on CBS for three years, changing its title to *The Doctors and the Nurses* after its second season. Three weeks after its cancellation, a serial version materialized on ABC daytime. Starring as Liz Thorpe was Mary Fickett, who years later was the first daytime performer to win an Emmy, as Ruth Brent on *All My Children*. The half-hour medical soap was written by Richard Holland and produced by Doris Quinlan. A good chunk of the cast later worked for producer Quinlan on *One Life to Live*.

CAST

Liz Thorpe, R.N.	Mary Fickett
Gail Lucas, R.N.	Melinda Plank
Brad Kiernan	Lee Patterson
Dr. John Crager	Nat Polen
Dr. Paul Fuller	Paul Stevens
Pat Steele	Sally Gracie
Jake Steele	Richard McMurray
Donna Steele	Carol Gainer
Ken Alexander	Nicholas Pryor
Cora Alexander	Muriel Kirkland
Brenda McLeod	Patricia Hyland
Jamie McLeod	Judson Laire
Hugh McLeod	Arthur Franz
Vivian Gentry	Lesley Woods

With: Alan Feinstein, Leonie Norton, Polly Rowles, Darryl Wells, and Dick Van Patten.

THE O'NEILLS

September 6, 1949–January 20, 1950   DuMont

The old DuMont network was a pioneer in TV serial drama with *A Woman to Remember*, *Captain Video*, and *Faraway Hill*. This was one of the network's later efforts, a TV version of the radio soap that had run from 1934 to 1943. Airing for a half hour every Tuesday 9:00 P.M., E.S.T., it concerned the problems of Peggy O'Neill, who struggled to bring up two children without a father. Jane West and Janice Gilbert played the same characters in both the radio and TV versions. Vera Allen, the star of the show, went on to other soaps, most notably *Another World* as Grandma Matthews and *From These Roots* as Kass, the lovable Fraser family maid.

CAST

Peggy O'Neill	Vera Allen
Danny O'Neill	Michael Lawson
Janice O'Neill	Janice Gilbert
Uncle Bill	Ian Martin
Mrs. Bailey	Jane West
Morris Levy	Ben Fishbein
Trudy Levy	Celia Budkin

ONE LIFE TO LIVE

July 15, 1968–   ABC

Created by Agnes Nixon, *One Life to Live* is the most peculiarly American of soap operas: the first serial to present a vast array of ethnic types, broad comic situations, a consistent emphasis on social issues, and strong male characters. Its antagonistic characters have been viewed not as villains but rather as "have-nots" with strong motivations who emphatically believe in the American themes of hope and self-destiny.

The "one life to live" theme has served the show well through four powerful stories about double lives: Victoria Lord's split personality; Carla Gray's "passing" as white; Marco Dane's takeover of his dead brother's life; and, most brilliantly, Karen Wolek's struggle to end her secret life of prostitution and self-hatred. Karen's story became the focus for *One Life to Live*'s most memorable moment, when all the expertly choreographed stories came crashing together in the spring of 1979—perhaps the greatest week in daytime drama.

One Life to Live was created when ABC became impressed with the ratings eruption on NBC's *Another World*, written by Agnes Nixon. When ABC invited Nixon to create a serial for them, Nixon, tired of the restraints imposed by the WASPy, noncontroversial nature of daytime drama, presented the network with a startlingly original premise and cast of characters. Although the show was built along the classic soap formula of a rich family and a poor family, *One Life to Live* emphasized the ethnic and socioeconomic diversity of the people of Llanview, Pennsylvania, a suburb of Philadelphia. The concept provided for sharp class conflict and became the perfect vehicle for a series of star-crossed romances.

The powerful Lord family, which owned Llanview's newspaper *The Banner*, was headed by Victor Lord, the domineering father of two daughters, Victoria and Meredith. Viki, who was treated like the son Victor that he (presumably) had never had, became an essential part of the family business and fell in love with Joe Riley, a fun-loving, hard-drinking reporter. Joe's family were Irish-American Catholics and included his sister Eileen, who was married to Dave Siegal, a Jewish lawyer. While Victor disapproved of this romance, he was even more vehemently opposed to Merrie's attraction to Larry Wolek, a young intern at Llanview Hospital. Larry's family—sister Anna and auto mechanic brother Vince—were poor Polish-American Catholics who had struggled to put Larry through medical school.

While viewers were treated with the awe-inspiring performance of Gillian Spencer as the split-personality Viki/Niki and the appealing puppy love romance between Larry and Merrie, the show also launched a daring story in which Carla Gray passed as white and romanced both Jim Craig, a white doctor, and Price Trainor, a black intern. The controversial storyline, packed with complexities and fraught with irony, caused many local ABC affiliates to cancel the program and forced viewers to come to terms with their own prejudices. *One Life to Live* continued through the next decade to present positive images of blacks in provocative storylines.

Produced by Doris Quinlan and written by Agnes Nixon, Paul Roberts, and Don Wallace, *One Life to Live*, which preceded the popular *Dark Shadows* on most ABC stations, built up a loyal following among young viewers. The social upheaval of the '60s prepared the audience for Agnes Nixon's heralded "relevance" campaign. When Dr. Jim Craig's daughter, Cathy, became addicted to drugs, she went to a drug rehabilitation center for teenagers in New York. The soap taped sequences at Odyssey House with real addicts in group therapy sessions, forcing Cathy to recognize her problem. Later in the show, when Cathy wrote an article about venereal disease, thousands of fans wrote in requesting copies.

In its first three years, *One Life to Live* had casting problems, and the parts of Cathy, Viki, and Larry were each played by three different performers. One casting change that caused considerable comment in the industry occurred when James Storm wanted to leave his role as Larry. In the story, Larry was rescued from a flash fire in the hospital by nurse Karen Martin—whom he later married, causing more pain for Meredith Lord. Larry underwent plastic surgery, and when the bandages were removed Michael Storm, James's brother, was the new Larry! The plastic surgery gimmick proved so successful that other shows, including *Dynasty*, employed it when recasting important roles.

In the early '70s, Gordon Russell became the headwriter and zeroed in on two characters, both of whom served as antagonists to Erika Slezak's appealing, strong-minded Victoria Lord. The first was Dorrie Kavanaugh's Cathy Craig, who became famous writing on feminist issues and raising a child, by Joe Riley, out of wedlock. (When Jennifer Harmon played Cathy, the death of the baby Megan caused Cathy to go into an emotional tailspin. The show, which had explored postpartum depression, with Dr. Joyce Brothers playing herself, when Meredith Lord lost a child, was thus able to further explore mental health issues.) In 1973, Nancy Pinkerton was introduced as Dr. Dorian Crammer, a dynamic manipulator who married Victor Lord and eventually became the mistress of the Lord estate, Llanfair, when Victor died on June 16, 1976. Pinkerton's intense performance was a force to be reckoned with; Dorian remained *One Life to Live*'s pivotal character even after Pinkerton's departure.

The death of Meredith Lord in 1973 left the show without an ingénue heroine, and Jenny Wolek, a novitiate nun and cousin of the Llanview Woleks, was introduced to fill the gap. Jenny married Tim Siegel on his death bed and later became involved with the unscrupulous tennis bum Brad Vernon, who would cause Jenny much unhappiness during the next decade. (The original Brad was played with all-American sleaze-charm by Jameson Parker, later a prime-time TV star in *Simon & Simon*.) Jenny's dangerous missionary work in Latin America, as she attempted to help the poor in a military dictatorship, was integrated off and on in the drama—years before reports of the deaths of the Maryknoll nuns in El Salvador.

Although *One Life to Live* was good social drama, its initial popularity had dwindled somewhat during the early '70s, placing it well below the top ten daytime dramas. But the show got a shot in the arm when in 1975 it snagged the two biggest stars in daytime television, Jacquie Courtney and George Reinholt, who had been fired by the top-rated *Another World*, *One Life to Live*'s competition on NBC. George Reinholt was introduced as Tony Harris, who turned out to be the illegitimate son of Victor Lord. Later, Jacquie Courtney joined Reinholt as Pat Ashley, a journalist who had had a child by Tony years before. Tony and Pat's romance brought hundreds of thousands of viewers and reams of publicity to the show.

With the ratings improving, *One Life to Live*, along with the ailing *General Hospital*, was expanded from a half hour to an unusual forty-five minute format on July 26, 1976. The show introduced many new characters, including Karen Wolek, Jenny's selfish, kitten-with-a-whip sister. Kathyrn Breech played Karen as a cool, calculating tease who seduced her cousin Larry into marriage, but when Judith Light replaced Breech, Karen evolved into a self-destructive force of nature, wreaking havoc everywhere. Karen's childish search for fulfillment—in gifts from "tricks"—turned into all-out prostitution when Marco Dane, a former lover, became her pimp.

As Karen struggled to free herself from her pimp and her own self-hatred, the ratings began to climb. On January 16, 1978, *One Life to Live* expanded to a full hour as Karen and Talbot Huddleston, a rich boyfriend, argued in a speeding automobile. The car struck and killed Pat and Tony's son, Brian, then sped away. Jacqueline Courtney's powerful, week-long performance as the grieving mother was one of the year's highlights. Meanwhile, Viki had been blackmailed by Marco over pornographic pictures, and signs of her split personality of nine years earlier began to surface. The show soared to become the second-highest-rated daytime drama, just behind *All My Children*. When Marco was killed, Viki was put on trial for murder and, in the spring of 1979, all of *One Life to Live*'s storylines, planned so carefully for years by Gordon Russell, culminated with the dramatic testimony of Karen Wolek.

Viki's trial became the wildest in the show's history. Soap critics have called that week the most dramatic in soap opera, showcasing one of the most disturbing performances ever on television. As Karen, Judith Light was absolutely electric, giving the kind of bravura, theatrical performance that becomes legendary. Karen confessed her prostitution, and pointed out Talbot Huddleston as the hit-and-run killer of Brian as well as the murderer of Marco Dane. (As it turned out, Talbot had actually killed Marco's look-alike brother, Mario; Marco later assumed his brother's identity.) The repercussions from the trial, with all the characters in the show involved in one way or another, were felt for months. Light won the Emmy for Outstanding Actress in 1980, followed by another win the next year.

One Life to Live continued its Emmy streak, which began with Al Freeman, Jr. (the first black to win a daytime Emmy) in 1979, Light in 1980 and 1981, Robin Strasser in 1982, Robert S. Woods in 1983, and Erika Slezak in 1984. But the show also had its share of backstage tragedy with the deaths of Barbara Britton, who played Fran Gordon, Nat Polen, who played Dr. Jim Craig for twelve years, and Gordon Russell, the show's beloved headwriter. Sam Hall succeeded Russell (just as he had on *Dark Shadows*), and the flavor of the show began to change.

With the success of *Dallas* in mind, the show introduced the wheeling-dealing Buchanan family, who had relocated from Texas. The Buchanans included Asa, a J.R.–type patriarch; Clint, a newspaper editor, who wooed and won Viki after Joe Riley's death; and Bo, who romanced Pat but eventually married Delilah Ralston. An extended, gothic storyline about Olympia Buchanan's imprisonment by her husband culminated in a huge masquerade party and Olympia's death. (The party lasted a month!) Another unfortunate story, which pitted Pat against her psychotic sister Maggie for the affections of Clint, veered the show farther off the track.

More pleasing to long-time viewers was the renewed focus on Dorian Lord, who had married Herb Callison, the prosecutor in the Victoria Lord trial. Robin Strasser, who was the soaps' most famous villainess in the late '60s as Rachel Davis on *Another World*, had achieved what seemed the impossible: making viewers forget Nancy Pinkerton's superb performance as Dorian. Strasser's Dorian was sophisticated and sexy, a jangling body of raw nerve. Dorian mellowed somewhat with the introduction of Cassie, the daughter she had thought lost, but her machinations continued with the introduction of Michael Zaslow as David Reynolds, Cassie's father.

In the beginning of 1983, the show lost Judith Light, who left to pursue other acting opportunities, and, at the end of the year, Jacquie Courtney, whose contract was unaccountably not renewed. The soap also lost its long-time producer Joseph Stuart, who had gone on to work on ABC's *Loving*. He was replaced by Jean Arley. The ratings, although slipping a bit, remained respectable. *One Life to Live* showed signs of rejuvenation when Henry Slesar, who had written *The Edge of Night* for fifteen years, was hired as co-headwriter. The once socially charged drama had drifted into stories of international intrigue, mystery, and romance, although—perhaps as a nod to the past—the writers introduced the low-income O'Neill family, who were similar to the Wolek family of yesteryear. The entertaining *One Life to Live* rested comfortably between the top-rated shows and the lesser soaps that were struggling desperately for recognition. Still, the ratings were not good enough for ABC and in mid 1984 the network hired writers Joyce and John William Corrington (*Texas*) and producer Paul Rauch (*Another World*, during its golden age) to give Llanview a complete facelift.

The Corringtons came on like gangbusters, tossing Llanview into the midst of an organized crime war. When Samantha Vernon, the young bride of police officer Rafe Garrison, suffered "brain death" after an assault, it was discovered that Sam was pregnant. *One Life to Live* then broke new ground in television, dramatizing the transfer of the embryo to a woman who could not conceive by natural means. Afterwards, when Sam, a core character for a decade, was taken off the life support system by her father, Dr. Will Vernon, it was one of the most touching moments of the season.

The Mafia stories soon collapsed into a confusing muddle and former headwriters Sam Hall and Peggy O'Shea were called in to repair the damage. Hall and O'Shea put the show back on course again in 1985, developing a story around the memory of the show's dead patriarch, Victor Lord, and how his hand still guided the fates of the people of Llanview. When Viki's spoiled young ward, Tina Clayton, claimed to be the illegitimate daughter of Victor, Viki began to break down, eventually reverting to her split personality of fifteen years before. Viki now not only had antagonists in Tina and Dorian (who may or may not have had a hand in Victor's death in 1976), but with her free-spirited alter-ego Niki Smith as well. Although melodramatic, the break-down sequences spread over months were psychologically sound and brilliantly performed by Erika Slezak, who once again reminded one of the words of Bette Davis and Orson Welles: the best acting around continues to be in daytime drama.

Slezak deservedly took her second Emmy for her performance, and the show continued its focus on Viki: the kidnapping of baby Jessica, an eight-year memory loss, a heart-wrenching child custody case, half-sister Tina's presumed death, and a life-or-death brain operation followed by a two-week "out of body experience"! The out-of-body story was spectacularly campy. Ascending into paradise (with sets out of a Steven Spielberg movie) Viki mumbled to herself, "I've got a feeling we're no longer in Kansas anymore." However, seeing all those wonderful actors whose characters had died over the past two decades, reprising their roles, had long-time viewers in soap opera—forgive me—heaven.

Meanwhile, Clint's illegitimate son Cord—along with his mother Maria, the Burrito Barracuda—became involved with the mischievous Tina Lord, while a new core family was introduced, the politically powerful Sanders: matriarch Elizabeth, former ambassador Charles, lawyer Judith, spunky Kate, and nasty Jamie. The outstanding production (location shots in Austria and Argentina), the writing (Clint and Viki's marital vicissitudes), and directing (an erotic tango between Cord and Kate in Buenos Aires) made the show a force to be reckoned with. But why, viewers wondered, the two-year story neglect of the pivotal, fun-loving Dorian? And who on earth designed her ghastly new wardrobe? Ronald McDonald?

CAST

Victoria Lord	Erika Slezak 1971–
	Joanne Dorian 1970
	Gillian Spencer 1968–70
Meredith Lord Wolek	Lynn Benesch 1969–73; 1987
	Trish Van Devere 1968–69
Victor Lord	Les Tremayne 1987
	Tom O'Rourke 1985
	Shepperd Strudwick 1974–76
	Ernest Graves 1968–74

Tony Lord	Phillip MacHale 1977–79; 1987
	Chip Lucia 1981–83
	George Reinholt 1975–77
Dr. Dorian Cramer	
Lord Callison	Robin Strasser 1979–87
	Claire Malis 1977–79
	Nancy Pinkerton 1973–77
Dr. Larry Wolek	Michael Storm 1969–
	James Storm 1969
	Paul Tulley 1968
Anna Wolek Craig	Phyllis Behar 1978–82
	Kathleen Maguire 1977–78
	Doris Belack 1968–77
Vince Wolek	Antony Ponzini 1968–75; 1987
	Michael Ingram 1977–81
	Jordan Charney 1975–77
Joe Riley	Lee Patterson 1968–70; 1972–79;
	1987
Eileen Riley Siegel	Alice Hirson 1972–76
	Patricia Roe 1968–72
Dave Siegel	Allan Miller 1968–72
Dr. Jim Craig	Nat Polen 1969–81
	Robert Milli 1968–69
Cathy Craig Lord	Jennifer Harmon 1976–78
	Dorrie Kavanaugh 1972–76
	Jane Alice Brandon 1971–72
	Amy Levitt 1970–71
	Catherine Burns 1969–70
Carla Gray	Ellen Holly 1968–81; 1983–85
Sadie Gray	Lillian Hayman 1968–86
	Esther Rolle 1971
Dr. Price Trainor	Peter DeAnda 1968–70
	Thurman Scott 1968
Lt. Jack Neal	Jack Crowder 1969–70
	Lon Sutton 1969
Bert Skelly	Herb Davis 1969–72
	Wayne Jones 1969
Dr. Ted Hale	Terry Logan 1968
Dr. Marcus Polk	James Douglas 1985–86; 1987
	Norman Rose 1969–74
	Donald Moffat 1968
Dr. Joyce Brothers	Dr. Joyce Brothers 1972
Dr. Steve Hardy	John Beradino 1969
Karen Martin Wolek,	
R.N.	Niki Flacks 1968–70
Julie Siegel Toland	Leonie Norton 1974–76
	Lee Warrick 1969–74
Tim Siegel	Tom Berenger 1975–76
	William Cox 1970–71

Tim Siegel (*cont.*)	William Fowler 1969
Tom Edwards	Joseph Gallison 1969–71
Dr. Kate Nolan	Peggy Wood 1969
Millie Parks	Millee Taggart 1969–70
Artie Duncan	John Cullum 1969
Marcy Wade	Francesca James 1970–71
Steve Burke	Bernard Grant 1970–75
Jack Lawson	Jack Ryland 1972–73
	David Snell 1970–72
Dr. Mark Toland	Tommy Lee Jones 1971–75
Wanda Webb Wolek	Marilyn Chris 1972–76; 1980–
	Lee Lawson 1977–79
Captain Ed Hall	Al Freeman, Jr. 1972–
	David Pendleton 1975
Joshua Hall	Guy Davis 1985–86
	Todd Davis 1977
	Laurence Fishburne 1973–76
Hubcap	Scott Jacoby 1973–74
Danny Wolek	Joshua Cox 1986
	Timothy Owen (Tim Waldrip) 1983; 1985
	Ted Demers 1984
	Steven Culp 1983–84
	Eddie Moran 1976–79
	Neail Holland 1974–76
Earl Brock	Kevin Conway 1973
Ben Howard	Albert Hall 1973
Melinda Cramer	Sharon Gabet 1987–
	Jane Badler 1977–81; 1983
	Patricia Pearcy 1973–74
John Douglas	Donald Madden 1974–75
Matt McAllister	Vance Jefferis 1974–75
Susan Barry	Lisa Richards 1974–75
Rachel Wilson	Nancy Barrett 1974
Ben Farmer	Rod Browning 1974–75
Laszlo Braedeker	Walter Slezak 1974
Dr. Alex Blair	Peter Brouwer 1975
Jenny Wolek	Brynn Thayer 1978–86
	Katherine Glass 1975–78
Karen Wolek	Judith Light 1977–83
	Kathryn Breech 1976–77
Sister Margaret	Dorothy Lyman 1975
Sheliah Rafferty	Christine Jones 1975
Patricia Ashley	Jacqueline Courtney 1975–83
Maggie Ashley	Jacqueline Courtney 1979
Paul Kendall	Tom Fuccello 1977–79
Brian Kendall	Stephen Austin 1976–78
Dr. Will Vernon	Anthony George 1977–84
	Bernie McInerney 1977

Dr. Will Vernon (*cont.*)	Farley Granger 1976–77
Naomi Vernon	Teri Keane 1976–77
Brad Vernon	Steve Fletcher 1978–86
	Jameson Parker 1976–78
Samantha Vernon	Dorian LoPinto 1981–84
	Julie Montgomery 1976–81
	Susan Keith 1979
Dr. Peter Jansen	Jeffrey David Pomerantz 1976–79; 1987
	Denny Albee 1980–82
	Robert Burton 1980
Lana McClain	Jacklyn Zeman 1976–77
Marco Dane	Gerald Anthony 1977–86
Rebecca Lee Abbott	Mary Gordon Murray 1979–86
	Jill Voight 1977–78
Richard Abbott	Jeffrey Byron 1986
	Robert Gribbon 1980–81
	Keith Langsdale 1980
	Luke Reilly 1977–78
Gwendolyn Abbott	Joan Copeland 1978–79
Ina Hopkins	Sally Gracie 1978–84
Edwina Lewis	Margaret Klenck 1978–85
Dr. Jack Scott	Arthur Burghardt 1978–80
Dr. Pamela Shepherd	Kathleen Devine 1978
Talbot Huddleston	Byron Sanders 1977–78
Adele Huddleston	Lori March 1978–79
Greg Huddleston	Paul Joynt 1978–79
Tina Clayton	Andrea Evans 1978–81; 1985–
	Marsha Clark 1985
	Kelli Maroney 1984
Bonnie Harmer	Kim Zimmer 1978
Dick Grant	A. C. Weary 1978; 1983
Adam Brewster	John Mansfield 1978–79
Gretel Cummings	Linda Dano 1978–80
Katrina Karr	Nancy Snyder 1978–83
Herb Callison	Anthony Call 1978–
Dr. Ivan Kipling	Jack Betts 1979–82; 1985
Faith Kipling	Mary Linda Rapeleye 1979–80
Fran Gordon	Willi Burke 1979
	Barbara Britton 1979
Mick Gordon	James McDonnell 1979–80
Clint Buchanan	Clint Ritchie 1979–
Bo Buchanan	Robert S. Woods 1979–86
Asa Buchanan	Philip Carey 1979–
Olympia Buchanan	Taina Elg 1980–81
Mimi King	Kristen Meadows 1979–82; 1985–86
Lucinda Schenk	Arlene Dahl 1981–84
Chuck Wilson	Jeremy Slate 1979–

Johnny Drummond	Wayne Massey 1980–84
Ted Clayton	Mark Goddard 1981
	Keith Charles 1980–81
Marcello Salta	Stephen Schnetzer 1980–82
Rafe Garrison	Ken Meeker 1980–
Steve Piermont	Robert Desiderio 1981–82
	Richard K. Weber 1981
Chip Warren	Sammy Davis, Jr. 1980; 1981; 1983
Cassie Reynolds	Holly Gagnier 1986–
	Ava Haddad 1983–86
	Cusi Cram 1981–83
Gary Corelli	Jeff Fahey 1982–85
Georgina Whitman	Nana Tucker Visitor 1982
	Ilene Kristen 1982
Astrid Collins	Marilyn McIntyre 1982
Paul Martin	William Mooney 1978–79; 1982
Helen Murdoch	Marie Masters 1982
Euphemia Ralston	Grayson Hall 1982
Drew Ralston	Matthew Ashford 1982–83
Delilah Ralston	Shelly Burch 1982–
Echo DiSavoy	Kim Zimmer 1983
Giles Morgan	Robert Gentry 1983
Eva Vasquez	Judith McConnell 1983
David Reynolds	Michael Zaslow 1983–86
Simon Warfield	Tim Hart 1983–84
Hawk	John Gibson 1984
Alec Lowndes	Roger Hill 1983–84
Courtney Wright	Phylicia Ayers-Allen 1983–84
Anthony Makana	Nicolas Coster 1983–84
Laurel Chapin	Janice Lynde 1983–85
Trent Chapin	David Beecroft 1984–85
Maxie McDermott	Christine Ebersole 1983–84
Molly McDermott	Dody Goodman 1984
Harry O'Neill	Frank Converse 1984–85
	Arlen Dean Snyder 1984
Connie O'Neill	Terry Donahoe 1985–86
	Liz Keifer 1984–85
Joy O'Neill	Julie Ann Johnson 1985–86
	Kristen Vigard 1984–85
Didi O'Neill	Barbara Truetelaar 1984–87
Mark Pemberton	Ed Power 1984
Michelle Boudin	Dana Barron 1984–85
Dr. Elston Pepper	Orson Bean 1984
Leo Coronal	Abe Vigoda 1984
Rob Coronal	Ted Marcoux 1984–86
Alex Crown (Coronal)	Roy Thinnes 1984–85
Aristotle Descamedes	Steven Hill 1984–85
Jinx Rollins	Elizabeth Burrelle 1984–85

Brian Beckett	Grainger Hines 1984–85
Ken Romak	Dean Hamilton 1984–85
Jesse Wilde	John Vickery 1984–85
Clover Wilde	Pamela Shoemaker 1985–86
Lydia Farr	Marianne Tatum 1985
Nikos Pappas	Simon Page 1985
Aida York	Pamela Gien 1985
Gulietta	Fabiano Udenio 1985–86
Mitchell Laurence	Roscoe Born 1985–86; 1987
Michael James Woodward	Grant Goodeve 1985–86
Pamela Stuart	Christine Jones 1985–87
Pete O'Neill	James O'Sullivan 1985–87
Lisa Baron	Laura Carrington 1985–86
Tracy James	Kristen Allen 1985–86; 1987
Jon Russell	John Martin 1986–
Judith Sanders	Louise Sorel 1986–87
Charles Sanders	Peter Brown 1986–87
Jamie Sanders	Mark Philpot 1986–
Kate Sanders	Marcia Cross 1986–
Elizabeth Sanders	Lois Kibbee 1986–
Cord Roberts	John Loprieno 1986–
Maria Roberts	BarBara Luna 1986–87
Allison Perkins	Barbara Garrick 1986–87
Tom Dennison	Lee Patterson 1986–
Mari Lynn Dennison	Tammy Amerson 1986–
Rick Gardner	Richard Grieco 1986–87
Max Holden	James De Paiva 1987–
Steve Holden	Russ Anderson 1987–
Gabrielle Medina	Fiona Hutchison 1987–
Cyndy London	Cynthia Vance 1987–
Lee Halpern	Janet Zarish 1987–
Virgil/Gilbert Lange	John Fiedler 1987–
Geoffrey McGrath	Don Fischer 1987–
Sandra Montagne	Judith Chapman 1987

ONE MAN'S FAMILY

November 4, 1949–June 21, 1952   NBC (prime time);
March 1, 1954–April 1, 1955   NBC (daytime)

One Man's Family, created by Carleton E. Morse, was the longest-running
serial in radio history, airing from 1932 to 1959, with 3,256 episodes having
been broadcast. Television saw two versions of the chestnut, the first
presented at night in half-hour weekly segments; the later version presented in fifteen-minute daily segments airing at 3:00 P.M., E.S.T. Like
the radio show, they told the story of Henry and Fanny Barbour and
their five children, who lived in the Sea Cliff section of San Francisco.
The TV versions did not pick up on the 1949 radio story, which by then

had focused on the Barbour children, but, instead, used the 1932 story in a 1949 setting.

Thus the eldest son Paul, a fifty-three-year-old veteran of World War I on the radio show, became a thirty-five-year-old veteran of World War II on TV. Hazel, the oldest daughter, who had married and had twins, reverted back to a twenty-eight-year-old spinster who yearned for marriage. Claudia, a rebellious romantic, and Cliff, Claudia's twin who had married three times, became students at Stanford University. The youngest, Jack, a thirty-two-year-old father of six daughters (including a set of triplets), reverted to adolescence on TV. The setting back of the clock a generation made for some interesting casting: Anne Whitfield, who played the nineteen-year-old Claudia on TV, played Claudia's grown daughter Penelope on the radio during the same period. The alumni from the TV show include Eva Marie Saint, Tony Randall, Mercedes McCambridge, and Frankie Thomas, who went on to star as the title character in *Tom Corbett, Space Cadet.*

Most of the conflict on the television versions concerned Fanny Barbour's striving to strike a delicate balance between Henry's strict, old-fashioned values and her children's assertion of their independence. On TV, Claudia (Eva Marie Saint) married adventurer Johnny Roberts, but her happiness was short-lived. When Johnny was reported wounded in the South Sea islands, Claudia and her father-in-law flew to be at Johnny's side. After stock footage established that they were 20,000 feet over the Pacific, actor Ralph Locke, who played Johnny's father, went totally blank. After struggling with his lines for a few moments on the live show, he barked at Saint, "Well, if you can't say anything, I'm leaving!" He then proceeded to walk off the set and, presumably, off the plane to his death. (Locke was back in his seat the next day.) Carleton E. Morse produced, directed, wrote, and cast the show—everything, in fact, except designing the costumes, which were provided by Lord & Taylor.

PRIME-TIME CAST   1949–52

Henry Barbour	Bert Lytell 1949–52
Fanny Barbour	Marjorie Gateson 1949–52
Paul Barbour	Russell Thorson 1949–52
Hazel Barbour Herbert	Lillian Schaaf 1949–52
Claudia Barbour	Eva Marie Saint 1950–52
	Nancy Franklin 1949–50
Cliff Barbour	James Lee 1949–52
	Bill Idelson 1949
	Frankie Thomas 1949
Jack Barbour	Richard Wigginton 1951–52
	Arthur Cassell 1949–50
Bill Herbert	Walter Brooke 1950–52
	Les Tremayne 1950
Beth Holly	Susan Shaw 1950–52
	Mercedes McCambridge 1949–50
Teddy Lawton	Madeline Belgard 1951–52
Judge Glenn Hunter	Calvin Thomas 1949

Johnny Roberts	Michael Higgins 1949–51
Mrs. Roberts	Mona Bruns 1950–51
Mr. Roberts	Ralph Locke 1950–52
Sir Guy Vance	Maurice Manson 1952
Joe Yarborough	Jim Boles 1950–52
Mac	Tony Randall 1950–52

DAYTIME CAST 1954–55

Henry Barbour	Theodore von Eltz
Fanny Barbour	Mary Adams
Paul Barbour	Russell Thorson
Claudia Barbour	Anne Whitfield
Hazel Barbour	Linda Leighton
Clifford Barbour	James Lee
Jack Barbour	Martin Dean
Johnny Roberts	Jack Edwards

OUR FIVE DAUGHTERS

January 2, 1962–September 28, 1962   NBC

The star of this family-oriented daytime serial was Esther Ralston, who was nicknamed "The American Venus" after her 1926 film triumph and was one of the highest-paid actresses of the silent era. Ralston had made over a hundred movies, co-starring with the likes of Clara Bow, Tom Mix, and Gary Cooper, but her career slacked off and she retired from the screen in 1941. She married and divorced three times, lost much of her money, and finally became a saleswoman at B. Altman & Company. (When told she looked like the old star Esther Ralston, she always denied her identity.) After appearing on the daytime courtroom drama *The Verdict Is Yours*, in which she impressed producer Eugene Burr, she was offered a comeback in Burr's new soap opera, *Our Five Daughters*.

On the show the fifty-nine-year-old actress played Helen Lee, wife of Jim, and mother of five young daughters. In the opening episodes Jim was critically injured and hung on as an invalid, throwing the family into crisis. Written by Leonard Stadd and directed by Paul Lammers, the soap tried to emulate *As the World Turns* with a sharp emphasis on family life. But the ingredients did not jell and the show was cancelled on the same day as the long-running *The Brighter Day*. Jacqueline Courtney, who played the daughter most traumatized by her father's accident went on to become a daytime superstar as Alice Matthews on *Another World*. *Our Five Daughters* aired for a half hour daily at 3:30 P.M., E.S.T., following daily episodes of *Young Dr. Malone*.

CAST

Helen Lee	Esther Ralston
Jim Lee	Michael Keene
Mary Lee	Wynne Miller
Barbara Lee	Patricia Allison

Jane Lee	Nuella Dierking
Marjorie Lee	Iris Joyce
Ann Lee	Jacqueline Courtney
Uncle Charlie	Robert W. Stewart
Don Weldon	Ben Hayes
Mary Weldon	Wynne Miller
George Barr	Ralph Ellis
Greta Hitchcock	Janis Young
Pat Nichols	Edward Griffith

OUR PRIVATE WORLD
May 5, 1965–September 10, 1965   CBS

Eileen Fulton was daytime's brightest star in the mid '60s, and so it was natural that her character was chosen to be spun-off *As the World Turns* as the central character of a new CBS prime-time serial. *Our Private World*, titled *The Woman Lisa* in development, was designed to compete with the enormously popular ABC soap *Peyton Place*. Created by Irna Phillips and William J. Bell, the show was written by Robert J. Shaw and directed by Tom Donovan. It dramatized the adventures of Lisa Miller Hughes in Chicago after her unhappy life in the small town of Oakdale, Ohio.

In Lisa's last scene on *As the World Turns* she was boarding a train to Chicago; the opening scene on *Our Private World* saw her on the train, which was pulling into Chicago, as she dumped her wedding ring into an ashtray. Lisa moved in with a middle-class family, got a job in the admitting room of a local hospital, and became involved with the socially prominent Eldridge family of Lake Forest, a Chicago suburb. At the onset storylines for both shows were interwoven, but as more characters were introduced, the focus of the new show moved away from Lisa. The twice-a-week serial—seen Wednesday and Friday at different times, which may have confused viewers—concluded with another major character, Sandy Larson, facing a murder charge. Fulton returned to *As the World Turns* for ten weeks to wrap up her storyline, as Lisa married the wealthy John Eldridge.

CAST

Lisa Hughes	Eileen Fulton
John Eldridge	Nicolas Coster
Helen Eldridge	Geraldine Fitzgerald
Tom Eldridge	Sam Groom
Eve Eldridge	Julienne Marie
Dr. Tony Larson	David O'Brien
Sandy Larson	Sandra Smith
Franny Martin	Pamela Murphy
Brad Robertson	Robert Drivas
Dick Robertson	Ken Tobey
Ethel Robertson	Grace Albertson

Pat   Catherine Dunn
Sgt. Clark   Michael Strong

PAPER DOLLS

September 23, 1984–December 25, 1984   ABC

Morgan Fairchild (*Flamingo Road*) returned to the soap scene in this witty prime-time serial set in the cutthroat fashion world. Fairchild played Racine ("Racy" for short; no last name), the lean, mean head of a prestigious Manhattan modeling agency. The wicked-tongued Racine guided the careers of two sixteen-year-old models, the fresh-faced Laurie Caswell and the self-destructive Taryn Blake.

As counterpoint to Racine was Grant Harper (Lloyd Bridges of *Seahunt*), the stoic tycoon of Harper Cosmetics. His family included his second wife Marjorie; son Wesley, who allied himself professionally and romantically with Racine; daughter Blair, a thirty-year-old model; and son-in-law David Venton, who was married to Blair and who resorted to loansharking to save his floundering sportswear company. Other characters included Julia Blake, Taryn's stage-door mother; Dinah Caswell, Laurie's concerned mother; Michael, Dinah's husband and Laurie's stepfather; Sara Frank, a lawyer; Mark Bailey, her journalist husband; Christopher York, a porno star turned model; and Sandy Paris, Racine's aide-de-camp.

Paper Dolls, created by Jennifer Miller and Leah Markus, received poor ratings and was perhaps saved from an immediate cancellation by a series of rave reviews from *People* magazine, which urged viewers to give the serial a fair shake. The soap was certainly amusing whenever Morgan Fairchild appeared, and the writers worked overtime to provide the formidable Fairchild with dozens of sophisticated one-liners. When roving reporter Mark Bailey walked in on a semi-nude Racine, he asked, "Do you want me to wait outside until you're decent?" Racine responded, "How much time do you have?" As one of the characters noted, "She's done well for a girl named off a map of Wisconsin."

CAST

Racine	Morgan Fairchild
Grant Harper	Lloyd Bridges
Marjorie Harper	Nancy Olson
Wesley Harper	Dack Rambo
Blair Harper Venton	Mimi Rogers
David Venton	Richard Beymer
Laurie Caswell	Terry Farrell
Dinah Caswell	Jennifer Warren
Michael Caswell	John Bennett Perry
Sara Frank	Anne Schedeen
Mark Bailey	Roscoe Born
Julia Blake	Brenda Vaccaro
Taryn Blake	Nicollette Sheridan

John Waite	Himself
Christopher York	Don Bowren
Sandy Paris	Jonathan Frakes
Jake Larner	John Reilly
Colette Ferrier	Lauren Hutton

PARADISE BAY

September 27, 1965–July 1, 1966   NBC

Paradise Bay and *Morning Star* debuted on the same day and were cancelled on the same day several months later. *Paradise Bay*, set and produced in California, concerned the Morgan family and the troubled young people they encountered. On the premiere episode, the body of Sally Baxter, who had died of a head wound, was washed up on the shore of the bay, shocking the beach community. Film actor Keith Andes (*The Farmer's Daughter, Clash by Night*, etc.) starred as Jeff Morgan, a radio-station manager. Other characters included Jeff's wife Mary, who found Sally's diary; their daughter Kitty, who joined a rock group, to the chagrin of her parents; Duke Spaulding, who was arrested for Sally's murder; and newspaper editor Walter Montgomery, who blasted Duke Spaulding in a series of editorials. The show was created by Ted Corday, Jerry D. Lewis, and John Monks, Jr. The writers included Lewis, Monks, Manya Starr, and Irving Vendig. *Paradise Bay* was broadcast for a half hour daily at 11:30 A.M., E.S.T., between *Morning Star* and the game show *Jeopardy*.

CAST

Jeff Morgan	Keith Andes
Mary Morgan	Marion Ross
Kitty Morgan	Heather North
Duke Spaulding	Dennis Cole
Walter Montgomery	Walter Brooke
Lucy Spaulding	June Dayton
Estelle Kimball	K. T. Stevens
Carlotta Chavez	Alice Reinheart
Chuck Lucas	Craig Curtis
Judge Grayson	Frank M. Thomas
Judge Ellis	Mona Bruns
Fred Morgan	Steven Mines
Charlotte Baxter	Paulle Clarke
June Hudson	Susan Crane

PAUL BERNARD, PSYCHIATRIST

1972   Syndicated

Created and produced by Michael Spivak, this Canadian-based serial dramatized therapy sessions between a psychiatrist and his female patients. Among the topics discussed were depression, loneliness, and parental interference. Each patient was brought back at least once a month, after intensive therapy, to measure progress. *The New York Times* called the understanding Dr. Paul Bernard "a veritable Canadian Mountie of the analytic profession." Produced in cooperation with the Canadian Mental Health Association, at least 195 episodes were syndicated to the U.S. Several of the actresses who played the patients were in other Canadian soaps seen in the U.S., *High Hopes* and *Strange Paradise*.

CAST

Dr. Paul Bernard   Christopher Wiggins
With: Tudi Wiggins (Meg Hart on *Love of Life* from 1974 to 1980), Marcia Diamond, Shelley Sommers, Phyllis Maxwell, Gale Garnett, Arlene Meadows, Mick Moore, Paisley Maxwell, Dawn Greenhalgh, Nuala Fitzgerald, Vivian Reis, and Barbara Kyle.

PEYTON PLACE

September 15, 1964–June 2, 1969   ABC

The first major prime-time serial since *One Man's Family* in 1949, *Peyton Place* was a smash hit, gathering up to 60 million Americans per episode in front of the TV set to watch the back-biting and sexual intrigue taking place in a small New England town. Based on the bestselling novel (over 9 million copies sold) by Grace Metalious, and the Lana Turner film, the TV version of *Peyton Place* netted $62 million in profits for ABC, produced 514 episodes for additional revenue in syndication, catapulted Mia Farrow and Ryan O'Neal to stardom, and, in 1972, spawned a daytime soap, *Return to Peyton Place*.

"Televison's first situation orgy," as Jack Paar called the serial, was created by Paul Monash, who produced the show throughout its five-year history. However, upon viewing the pilot, which ABC felt too closely resembled the 1957 movie, the network called in Irna Phillips as a consultant. Phillips vetoed the Selena Cross incest story—Selena raped by her father-in-law—but proposed another incest story in which Allison fell in love with her half-brother. This in turn was vetoed by Monash. Out of their disputes and collaboration came *Peyton Place*'s scenario. Unlike the novel and movie, the soap dropped the other-side-of-the-tracks Cross family and changed Michael Rossi's profession from high school principal to doctor, thus propelling the handsome newcomer into the center of the drama. (Old Doc Matt Swain of the book was then relegated to the soothsaying editor of the town paper.)

Dr. Rossi found himself in the midst of two cleverly interweaving stories. The first concerned Betty Anderson's pregnancy, her subsequent miscarriage, and her loveless marriage to the rich Rodney Harrington (Ryan O'Neal), who was carrying a torch for the virginal Allison (Mia Farrow). The second story concerned Allison's mother, Constance Mackenzie, who fell in love with Michael Rossi while attempting to protect her daughter from the truth of her paternity (Allison's real father was in prison). These stories proved so popular that in the second season the twice-weekly serial was seen three times a week, sometimes landing all three episodes in the top five in the weekly ratings race.

Because of Mia Farrow's well-publicized adventures with Frank Sinatra aboard the ship *Summer Breeze*, her character was written in and out of the show. First, Allison was hospitalized, in a coma, for a couple of weeks. Then, when Farrow married Sinatra and declared that she was not going to return to the show, Allison mysteriously disappeared from *Peyton Place*. (Mia Farrow, who was described by a co-worker as "too fey for words," divorced Sinatra two years later, the same year as her starring role in *Rosemary's Baby*. Also, in 1968, on *Peyton Place* a Mia Farrow-lookalike, Jill Smith—played by professional gossip-astrologer Joyce Jillson—turned up with a baby she claimed was Allison's.) But the other major storylines continued. Constance married Elliott Carson, Allison's natural father, when he returned after eighteen years in prison. Betty (Barbara Parkins), who had married Rodney in October 1964, next married Steven Cord (April 1966), who had defended Rodney in a murder trial. In April 1968, Betty remarried Rodney.

Peyton Place went through fifty writers and employed sixty regulars (and hundreds of others) to play out the never-ending crises that befell the town of 9,875 people. For most of the series Dorothy Malone received top billing. When she fell ill in September 1965, Lola Albright stepped in temporarily until Malone returned to the show the next year. Ed Nelson was top-billed when the characters of Constance and Elliott Carson were written out in 1968. After *Peyton Place* was cancelled, Dorothy Malone was later seen in the syndicated daytime soap *High Hopes*. Ryan O'Neal, who had stayed with the show for its entire run and had married co-star Leigh Taylor-Young, began his successful movie career with *Love Story*. Barbara Parkins, who was to star in a projected spin-off called *The Girl from Peyton Place*, instead went on to feature roles in films such as *Valley of the Dolls* and *The Kremlin Letter*. Ruth Warrick, who garnered an Emmy nomination for her role as Hannah Cord, has starred as Phoebe Tyler on *All My Children* since 1970.

Peyton Place ended without attempting to tie up several loose ends, causing viewers to wonder whether Dr. Rossi was cleared in the murder of Fred Russell, whether the pregnant Rita Harrington had a boy or girl, and whether the paralyzed Rodney ever got out of his wheelchair. Audiences got partial answers to those questions and others when the show materialized as a daytime serial, with three of the prime-time stars still in the cast. *Return to Peyton Place* ran from 1972 to 1974.

In 1977, a TV-movie, *Murder in Peyton Place*, aired, bringing back five regulars in their original roles. Dorothy Malone, Ed Nelson, Tim O'Connor, Christopher Connelly, and Joyce Jillson. It concerned the intrigue surrounding the deaths of Rodney Harrington and Allison Mackenzie (he had found her after eleven years!) in a car accident as they returned home. Another TV-movie, *Peyton Place: The Next Generation*, aired in May 1985. The drama, which also brought back a number of serial regulars, dealt with the return of Allison Mackenzie's illegitimate daughter Megan to Peyton Place. Megan brought back with her mother

Allison, who was catatonic after a rape years before. (Producers obviously forgot they had killed off Allison in 1977.) Megan, fathered by Rodney Harrington, fell in love with Dana Harrington, presumably also Rodney's child. But Betty Harrington finally stepped forward to confess that Steven Cord was Dana's natural father, thus providing a blissful reunion for Dana and Megan.

See *Return to Peyton Place*.

CAST

Constance Mackenzie	Dorothy Malone 1964–68
	Lola Albright 1965
Allison Mackenzie	Mia Farrow 1964–66
Dr. Michael Rossi	Ed Nelson 1964–69
Leslie Harrington	Paul Langton 1964–68
Rodney Harrington	Ryan O'Neal 1964–69
Norman Harrington	Christopher Connelly 1964–69
Betty Anderson	Barbara Parkins 1964–69
George Anderson	Henry Beckman 1964–65
Julie Anderson	Kasey Rogers 1964–69
Steven Cord	James Douglas 1964–69
Hannah Cord	Ruth Warrick 1965–67
Martin Peyton	George Macready 1965–68
	Wilfred Hyde-White 1967
Eli Carson	Frank Ferguson 1964–69
Elliott Carson	Tim O'Connor 1965–68
Rita Jacks Harrington	Patricia Morrow 1965–69
Ada Jacks	Evelyn Scott 1965–69
Eddie Jacks	Dan Duryea 1967–68
Dr. Claire Morton	Mariette Hartley 1965
Dr. Vincent Markham	Leslie Nielsen 1965
David Schuster	William Smithers 1965–66
Doris Schuster	Gail Kobe 1965
Kim Schuster	Kimberly Beck 1965
Stella Chernak	Lee Grant 1965–66
Joe Chernak	Don Quine 1965
Gus Chernak	Bruce Gordon 1965–66
Dr. Russ Gehring	David Canary 1965–66
John Fowler, D.A.	John Kerr 1965
Marian Fowler	Joan Blackman 1965–66
Lee Webber	Steven Oliver 1966
Chris Webber	Gary Haynes 1966–67
Sandy Webber	Lana Wood 1966–67
Ann Howard	Susan Oliver 1966
Adrienne Van Leyden	Gena Rowlands 1967
Rachel Welles	Leigh Taylor-Young 1966–67
Marsha Russell	Barbara Rush 1968–69
Carolyn Russell	Elizabeth Walker 1968–69
Fred Russell	Joe Maross 1968–69
Susan Winter	Diana Hyland 1968–69

Rev. Tom Winter	Bob Hogan 1968–69
Dr. Harry Miles	Percy Rodriguez 1968–69
Alma Miles	Ruby Dee 1968–69
Lew Miles	Glynn Turman 1968–69
Jack Chandler	John Kellog 1966–67
Joe Rossi	Michael Christian 1968
Jill Smith Rossi	Joyce Jillson 1968

PORTIA FACES LIFE
April 5, 1954–July 1, 1955   CBS

On radio from 1940 to 1951 with Lucille Wall (later Lucille March, *General Hospital*) in the title role, *Portia Faces Life* concerned the trials and tribulations of a lady lawyer presumably named after the Shakespearean heroine in *The Merchant of Venice*. The less than successful TV version initially starred Frances Reid (Alice Horton on *Days of Our Lives* since 1965) as Portia Blake Manning and was written by Mona Kent, who was one of the writers of the radio version. On the premiere episode Portia attempted to help a woman in trouble with a gambling debt. Portia's husband, Walter, who owned *The Parkerstown Herald*, found his role as "breadwinner" was continually upstaged by Portia's brilliance in the courtroom. Sensing his growing bitterness was party girl Dorie Blake, who set her sights on the chauvinistic Walter. The fifteen-minute serial, airing at 1:00 P.M., E.S.T., changed its name to *The Inner Flame* on March 14, 1955, but the title change did not help. Tony Mottola punctuated Portia's activities with his background guitar solos.

CAST

Portia Manning	Fran Carlon 1954–55
	Frances Reid 1954
Walter Manning	Karl Swenson 1954–55
	Donald Woods 1954
Shirley Manning	Ginger McManus 1955
	Renne Jarrett 1954
Dickie Blake	Charles Taylor 1954–55
Dorie Blake	Jean Gillespie 1954
Kathy Baker	Elizabeth York 1954
Bill Baker	Richard Kendrick 1954
Morgan Elliott	Byron Sanders 1954
Karl Manning	Patrick O'Neal 1954
Phoebe Faraday	Sally Gracie 1954–55
Tony Faraday	Mark Miller 1954–55
Ruth Byfield	Mary Fickett 1954–55

RETURN TO PEYTON PLACE
April 3, 1972–January 4, 1974   NBC

The 1957 film hit *Peyton Place*, starring Lana Turner, was followed up four years later with Carol Lynley in *Return to Peyton Place*, so it seemed inevitable that after the success of the prime-time TV version of *Peyton Place*, its continuation would also pop up. Daytime's *Return to Peyton Place* had many things going for it: a built-in audience, familiar characters and setting, and the return of three of the stars of the prime-time serial: Pat Morrow, Frank Ferguson, and Evelyn Scott. After a well-publicized search for an actress to play the pivotal role of Allison Mackenzie (which had made Mia Farrow a major star), producer Don Wallace and writer James Lipton chose Kathy Glass, who had appeared on their failed soap *The Best of Everything*. (Glass, a brunette, dyed her hair blond for the role; she later became popular as Jenny Wolek on *One Life to Live*.)

Although patriarch Martin Peyton had died in the prime-time version, he was miraculously brought back to life in daytime. Other new characters included the troubled Selena Cross—a major character in the novel but nonexistent in the prime-time version—who married Dr. Michael Rossi. Like the movie sequel, the daytime sequel focused on Allison's problems, which were never-ending: after all the trouble with Rodney, she married Benny Tate and became mixed up with drugs thanks to Jason Tate, Benny's twin brother, who passed himself off as Benny!

However, all the problems were not on the screen. The show was plagued by casting problems, and nearly all the major roles were recast within a year. Robert Cenedella became the new headwriter and George Paris took over as producer. Gail Kobe, the associate producer, remarked astutely years later that to daytime audiences *Return to Peyton Place* was that "dirty" little show, while its opposition, *One Life to Live*, was a family show, dramatizing familial conflict and young love. The once "daring" drama of the '50s and '60s, about a smutty small town in New England, did not adapt well to the conventions of daytime TV. It was replaced by the women's-lib serial *How to Survive a Marriage*, another unusual daytime entry that failed.

See *Peyton Place*

CAST

Constance Mackenzie	Susan Brown 1972–74
	Bettye Ackerman 1972
Allison Mackenzie	Pamela Shoop 1973–74
	Katherine Glass 1972–73
Elliott Carson	Warren Stevens 1972–74
Eli Carson	Frank Ferguson 1972–74
Dr. Michael Rossi	Guy Stockwell 1972–74
Selena Cross Rossi	Margaret Mason 1972–74
Ada Jacks	Evelyn Scott 1972–73
Rita Jacks Harrington	Patricia Morrow 1972–74
Norman Harrington	Ron Russell 1972–74
Rodney Harrington	Yale Summers 1972–74

Rodney Harrington (*cont.*)	Lawrence Casey	1972
Betty Anderson		
Harrington	Lynn Loring	1973–74
	Julie Parrish	1972–73
Leslie Harrington	Stacy Harris	1972–73
	Frank Maxwell	1972
Martin Peyton	John Hoyt	1972–73
Hannah Cord	Mary K. Wells	1972–74
Steven Cord	Joseph Gallison	1972–74
D. B. Bentley	Mary Frann	1973–74
Benny Tate	Ben Andrews	1972–73
Jason Tate	Ben Andrews	1973
Zoe Tate	Lesley Woods	1972–73

RITUALS

September 10, 1984–September 6, 1985   Syndicated

Set in the fictional college town of Wingfield, Virginia, this half hour soap, taped in Hollywood, was the first dramatic nighttime serial to be syndicated widely. The show was the brainstorm of Ken Corday (the son of Ted Corday, who created *Days of Our Lives*) and Charlene Keel, who wrote the pilot based on her novel of the same name. Syndicated by Telepictures and produced by Jorn Winther (*All My Children*), the drama opened with the death of Katherine Chapin and the effect of the matriarch's tape-recorded will on family and friends.

The Chapin family included Patrick, head of the family and owner of both Wingfield Mills and Chapin Industries; his daughter Taylor Chapin, who had been married five times and showed up at her mother's funeral stepping out of a helicopter and holding a racehorse's victory wreath; Patrick's young playboy son Brady; and Taylor's resentful daughter Julia. The middle-class Gallagher family consisted of Eddie and Sara; their son Tom, a police officer; Eddie's much younger brother Mike, an artist who taught at Haddon Hall, a women's college; and Noel, a waitress at the private school. Other characters included Carter Robertson, the unscrupulous president of Haddon Hall; Robertson's wife Christina, who had an affair with Patrick Chapin shortly before his death; Logan Williams, a writer who had been romantically snubbed by Taylor Chapin when they were younger; Dakota Lane, an actress; and Lacey Jarrett, a teacher who married Mike Gallagher.

The expensive production (an initial $15 million investment) fared badly with viewers, averaging a 2.1 rating and a 6 share in 90 markets. But Metromedia and Telepictures remained enthusiastic about the venture and ran an unusual publicity contest in February 1985 in which viewers were urged to guess which main character was to be murdered and who would pull off the dastardly deed. (The victim turned out to be Eddie Gallagher, the culprit his daughter Noel, the motive, years of abuse.)

Shortly before her father, Ronald Reagan, was reelected as President, Patti Davis appeared briefly on the show as femme fatale Marissa Mallory.

When she allegedly failed to show up for rehearsal on time, Davis was replaced by Janice Heiden, who had played split personality Lana Holbrook on *General Hospital*. About the same time the show lost its leading lady when JoAnn Pflug quit, saying that as a born-again Christian she could not play the required racy love scenes opposite George Lazenby (the James Bond of *On Her Majesty's Secret Service*).

The writers included Gene Palumbo, L. Virginia Browne, and John William Corrington, and Joyce Corrington. One of the directors was Edward Mallory, who played Dr. Bill Horton on *Days of Our Lives* from 1966 to 1980. Location footage was shot in North Carolina.

CAST

Patrick Chapin	Dennis Patrick
Taylor Chapin	Tina Louise
	JoAnn Pflug
Julia Fields	Andrea Moar
Brady Chapin	Jon Lindstrom
	Marc Poppel
Carter Robertson	Monte Markham
Christina Robertson	Christine Jones
Eddie Gallagher	Greg Mullavey
Sara Gallagher	Laurie Burton
	Lorinne Vozoff
Tom Gallagher	Kevin Blair
Mike Gallagher	Kin Shriner
Noel Gallagher	Karen Kelly
Lacey Jarrett	Philece Sampler
Dakota Lane	Mary Beth Evans
	Claire Yarlett
Cherry Lane	Sharon Farrell
Logan Williams	George Lazenby
Diandra Santiago	Gina Gallego
Marissa Mallory	Janice Heiden
	Patti Davis
Bernhardt	Cameron Smith
Patty Dupunt	Winifred Freedman
Clay Travis	Michael Welden
C. J. Fields	Peter Haskell
Lt. Lucas Gates	Antony Ponzini
Lisa Thompson	Wesley Ann Pfenning
Maddie Washington	Lynn Hamilton
Lucky Washington	Randy Brooks

THE ROAD OF LIFE

December 13, 1954–July 1, 1955   CBS

The radio version of *The Road of Life* had been popular since 1937 when Irna Phillips and Procter & Gamble decided to bring the drama to television. Replacing *The Seeking Heart*, the serial focused on three generations of two families, the Brents and the Overtons, and their long feud in the town of Merrimac. Don MacLaughlin and Virginia Dwyer, who had starred on the radio version, repeated their roles as Dr. Jim Brent and Jocelyn McLeod, the foster daughter of rich Malcolm Overton.

Since this was a medical drama (remembered chiefly for its opening: "Dr. Brent, . . . call surgery. Dr. Brent, . . . call surgery"), poor Jocelyn was afflicted with every dread disease known to man and some never known, including "rubimortis" and the dreaded "Meniere's syndrome." On the short TV version, spiteful Sybil Overton was furious that happily-married Jim Brent did not return her affections. She had Jocelyn arrested for "technically" kidnapping Sybil's child, then had Jocelyn classified as an "undesirable alien" when Jocelyn returned from Samoa after medical treatments. In one of his earliest TV roles, Jack Lemmon had a short run on the show as a supposedly nerves-of-steel surgeon. His stint is chiefly remembered for a tense operating room scene in which he turned to a nurse and barked, "Give me the hypodermic nerdle!"

Although *Road of Life* was cancelled on television in less than a year, it continued on radio until 1959. MacLaughlin later starred for over a quarter century as Chris Hughes on *As the World Turns*. Dwyer played Mary Matthews on *Another World* from 1964 to 1975. The show was written by Charles Gussman, produced by John Egan, and directed by Walter Gorman, who was Dwyer's off-screen husband. Nelson Case served as the narrator. It ran daily for fifteen minutes at 1:15 P.M., E.S.T., following *The Inner Flame*.

CAST

Dr. Jim Brent	Don MacLaughlin
Jocelyn McLeod Brent	Virginia Dwyer
Malcolm Overton	Harry Holcombe
Sybil Overton Fuller	Barbara Becker
Conrad Overton	Charles Dingle
Aunt Reggie Ellis	Dorothy Sands
Francie Brent	Elizabeth Lawrence
John Brent	Bill Lipton
Frank Dana	John Larkin
	Chuck Webster

With: Jack Lemmon, Hollis Irving, and Michael Kane.

ROAD TO REALITY

October 17, 1960–March 31, 1961   ABC

While NBC created and cancelled one daytime drama after another in an attempt to sabotage CBS's stranglehold on the audience, ABC sensibly stayed out of the firing line. Their first effort was modest, a serial dramatizing group therapy sessions. Written from actual transcripts of real group therapy sessions of five to ten participants, the show starred John Beal as Dr. Lewis, the moderator of the group. (Beal later became the first Jim Matthews on *Another World*.) Broadcast for a half hour beginning at 2:30 P.M., E.S.T., *Road to Reality*'s road to reality began and ended with its stiff competition, *Art Linkletter's House Party* and *The Loretta Young Theater*.

CAST

Dr. Lewis   John Beal

With: Eugenia Rawls, Robert Drew, Judith Braun, Kay Doubleday, James Dimitri, and Robin Howard.

ROMANCE THEATRE

1982–1983   Syndicated

Hosted by Louis Jourdan, this syndicated show presented different Harlequin Romance–type stories, each over a five-day period. The stories invariably focused on a career woman caught between two handsome men. The quality of the drama was uneven, usually weighed down by cardboard characters, cartoonish dialogue, and plots that depended heavily on coincidences, misunderstandings, and other false complications. One exception was the unusually well written character study "Image of Passion," starring James Horan (Denny Hobson on *Another World*) as Jake Jordan, a male stripper-turned-actor who can't cope in the pressure-cooker environment of Hollywood. *Romance Theatre* was produced by Bill Glenn and directed by Rudy Vejar.

CAST

James Horan, Lyle Waggoner, Paul Rossilli, Paul Keenan, and Tudi Wiggins.

RYAN'S HOPE

July 7, 1975–   ABC

Although never the winner of extraordinary ratings, *Ryan's Hope* became ABC's prestige soap—the winner of unanimous critical acclaim and more Emmy awards than any other daytime serial. The story of a struggling Irish-American family who ran a bar in New York City celebrated the American Dream, the hopes of immigrants John and Maeve Ryan for their five children, the clash between old-fashioned ideals and the pressures of modern society, and the rampant, unresolved emotions that family and love relationships inevitably produce.

Created by Claire Labine and Paul Avila Mayer, *Ryan's Hope* began with an idea by ABC who wanted the team to write a new soap called *City Hospital*, after seeing the miraculous surgery the two had performed on CBS's ailing *Where the Heart Is* and *Love of Life*. Labine and Mayer countered with an offer of a story centering on a large Irish family who run a bar across the street from a New York hospital. A year later, they presented ABC with a 200-page "bible" that contained background information on the family and the first two years of story. ABC wanted to call the show *A Rage to Love*, but when it was unable to clear the rights to its use, Labine and Mayer prevailed with their more appropriate title, *Ryan's Hope*.

In March 1975, *Ryan's Hope*, ABC's first soap in five years, went into production. It had already broken several soap opera rules by identifying the setting as a real city and the religious affiliation of the Ryans as Roman Catholic. Following the lead of *One Life to Live*, the show was an amalgam of ethnic types. Labine and Mayer created not villains and passive ingenues, but strong-minded, opinionated characters who stood up against adversity and each other. More importantly, the show was more interested in "moments" than in story: long dialogue scenes between daughter and mother, lovers dreaming of their future; and brothers and sisters squabbling among themselves, remembering real and imagined slights and resentment. It was close to the original concept of *As the World Turns* but with sharper dialogue and an eagerness to delve into the darker side of basically good people.

At the head of the family was Johnny Ryan, an Irish immigrant who was born in 1917 and was a teenage rum-runner during Prohibition, then briefly a boxer, before returning to Ireland to marry the sixteen-year-old Maeve. They settled in New York, opened a pub, and raised five children: Frank, a lawyer with political ambitions, who married Delia Reid and raised a son, Johnno; Cathleen, who married and had two children, Maura and Deirdre; Mary, a headstrong, aspiring journalist; Pat, a doctor at Riverside Hospital; and Siobhan, the family free spirit.

At the outset, Frank was slated to die after being pushed down a flight of stairs by his childish wife Delia. But ABC interceded, and Labine and Mayer did a major overhaul in their story. The early, realistically poignant scenes as the family gathered around while Frank's life hung in the balance set the tone of the show for years to come. *Ryan's Hope* was shockingly well written, with dialogue that cut to the bone. In one memorable monologue, Maeve alternately lamented and celebrated her son as she watched Frank struggle for his life. "I've known how to share his joy all these years," she said. "What I don't know is how to share his dying."

As Maeve Ryan, Helen Gallagher won the Emmy for Outstanding Actress the next year and again the following year. The show was also inundated with nominations and awards, winning the honor for Outstanding Series in 1977 and 1979, and Outstanding Writing in 1977, 1978, 1979, 1980, 1983, and 1984. But the show also had its share of bad luck— the worst recasting problems within memory—causing untold continuity problems and audience unrest. Helen Gallagher and Bernard Barrow, as Maeve and Johnny, in the serial's first eight years saw fifteen performers playing four of their children: four as Mary, four as Frank, four as Pat, and three as Siobhan. (Only one actress has thus far played the happily married Cathleen, a recurring cameo role.)

The stories over the years have been deeply romantic, pitting feisty Mary Ryan with the hard-boiled reporter Jack Fenelli, causing many strongly articulated arguments on feminism and social mores. Frank and Pat Ryan's love for the Coleridge sisters, Jillian and Faith, was continually thwarted by the machinations of the immature but highly lovable Delia.

Jillian's romance with Frank finally culminated in marriage after almost nine years. After her divorce from Frank, Delia married Pat, which sent his childhood sweetheart, Dr. Faith Coleridge, into the arms of other men. When her marriage to Pat did not pan out, Delia married Jill and Faith's brother, Dr. Roger Coleridge, who understood and enjoyed her chicanery.

In 1979, Mary was killed by organized crime after investigating the Mafia. Her death triggered years of Mafia stories and a shift to Siobhan as the show's central heroine. Siobhan became deeply involved in criminal activity when she married Joe Novak, a member of one of the most notorious crime families. By the end of the '70s, it seemed that Labine and Mayer had tried every romantic variation among their small cast of characters and had exhausted, with beautifully written dialogue scenes, such issues as abortion, marriage versus career problems, and premarital sex.

Perhaps in desperation, Labine and Mayer began to crib bits and pieces of their plots from movies such as *The Godfather* (the machine gun attack on Ryan's Bar), *On a Clear Day* (Delia's E.S.P.), *Raiders of the Lost Ark* (the archeological adventures of Aristotle Benedict-White), and, most ridiculously, *King Kong* (Delia's kidnapping by a gorilla!). On the other hand, the backstage story of Barbara Wilde, a soap opera actress—a soap within a soap—was fun and fraught with ironies, but the storyline was never developed.

With the ratings, which had been respectable during the late '70s, falling, ABC replaced Labine and Mayer with their associate writer Mary Ryan Munisteri. The new headwriter once again emphasized the Siobhan-Joe romance and the organized crime theme. Less attention was paid to the Ryan family, and a new family, the wealthy Kirklands, were introduced. With the soap meandering aimlessly, ABC brought Labine and Mayer back in early 1983. They wrote out the Kirklands and pushed the Ryan family back into the forefront of the drama. The original actors who had played Pat and Delia were brought back, and, in an unusual move, Kate Mulgrew, the original Mary Ryan, taped a number of scenes in which the daydreaming Maeve and Jack finally came to terms with Mary's death.

With the show suddenly resembling its old self, Labine and Mayer came up with their best story ever, the entrance of Charlotte Greer (Judith Chapman in a mesmerizing performance) and her family, who were bent on avenging an old Irish feud. But the story, which included romance, adventure, and potent domestic drama, was wrapped up quickly and Charlotte left town. Shortly afterwards, ABC again replaced the show's writers. (Labine and Mayer later nabbed their sixth Emmy for the Charlotte Greer story.) Pat Falken Smith, who engineered *General Hospital*'s top ratings, took over and emphasized the Coleridge family and their new relatives, especially Maggie Shelby, Jill's half-sister; Siobhan's star-crossed romance with Joe; and a gaggle of new, younger characters. During the annual St. Patrick's Day celebration, in which Maeve always sang "Danny Boy," Cathleen's eighteen-year-old daughter Maura, who called herself "Katie," was introduced into the drama. *Ryan's Hope*, now focusing on the dreams of the third generation of Ryans, was a serial in transition.

With a crippling time change and more affiliates across the country dropping the show, *Ryan's Hope*'s ratings plummeted. The Dubujak family became predominant as Siobhan married the suave Max, who was later revealed to be the head of an organized crime syndicate and, still later, was presumed dead after a particularly nasty spill. Siobhan once again became involved with Joe Novak, who had already been presumed dead twice before! The Ryans had their share of trouble, too, with the introduction of John Ryan's illegitimate son, Dakota Smith. Then there was the overnight aging of Ryan Fenelli—who married *Tigerbeat* cop-heartthrob Rick Hyde—while Johnno Ryan, who now called himself John Reid Ryan, showed up at the bar carting along an infant son, Owney.

As always, there were moments of beauty and clarity, and with the umpteenth return of co-creator Claire Labine as headwriter in March 1987, *Ryan's Hope* was certainly not going down for the count without grace and dignity—as well as a pungent side dish of good old Irish blarney.

CAST

Maeve Ryan	Helen Gallagher 1975–
Johnny Ryan	Bernard Barrow 1975–
Frank Ryan	John Sanderson 1985–
	Geoffrey Pierson 1983–85
	Daniel Hugh-Kelly 1977–81
	Andrew Robinson 1976–77
	Michael Hawkins 1975–76
Mary Ryan Fenelli	Kate Mulgrew 1975–77; 1983
	Nicolette Goulet 1979
	Kathleen Tolan 1978–79
	Mary Carney 1978
Dr. Pat Ryan	Malcolm Groome 1975–78; 1983–
	Patrick James Clarke 1982–83
	Robert Finoccoli 1979
	John Blazo 1978–79
Siobhan Ryan	Carrell Myers 1986–87
	Marg Helgenberger 1982–86
	Ann Gillespie 1981–82
	Sarah Felder 1978–80
Delia Reid Ryan	
Ryan Coleridge Crane	Ilene Kristen 1975–78; 1982–83; 1986–
	Robin Mattson 1984
	Randall Edwards 1979–82
	Robyn Millan 1979
Bob Reid	Earl Hindman 1975–84
John Reid Ryan	Jason Adams 1986–
	Tim Shew 1985
	Jadrien Steele 1975–85
Ryan Fenelli	Yasmine Bleeth 1985–
	Jenny Rebecca Dweir 1980–84
	Kerry McNamara 1979–80

Jack Fenelli	Michael Levin 1975–
Dr. Roger Coleridge	Ron Hale 1975–
Jillian Coleridge	Nancy Addison 1975–87
Dr. Faith Coleridge	Karen Morris-Gowdy 1978–83
	Catherine Hicks 1976–78
	Nancy Barrett 1976
	Faith Catlin 1975–76
Dr. Ed Coleridge	Frank Latimore 1975–76
Dr. Nell Beaulac	Diana van der Vlis 1975–76
Dr. Seneca Beaulac	John Gabriel 1975–85
Marguerite Beaulac	Anne Revere 1976
	Gale Sondergaard 1976
Dr. Bucky Carter	Justin Deas 1975–78
Dr. Marshall Westheimer	William Kiehl 1975–83
Dr. Clem Moultrie	Hannibal Penney, Jr. 1975–78
Ramona Gonzalez	Rosalinda Guerra 1975–76
Nick Szabo	Michael Fairman 1975–76
Reenie Szabo	Julia Barr 1976
Jumbo Marino	Fat Thomas 1977–79
Sister Mary Joel	Pauline Flanagan 1984–
	Jacqueline Brookes 1982
	Natalie Priest 1977–78
	Nancy Coleman 1976
	Sylvia Sidney 1975
Martha McKee	Dorrie Kavanaugh 1976–77
	Tovah Feldshuh 1976
Cathleen Ryan Thompson	Nancy Reardon 1976; 1978
Art Thompson	Gregory Abels 1976
Tom Desmond	Thomas MacGreevy 1977–79
Poppy Lincoln	Dianne Thompson Neil 1979
Dave Feldman	Joseph Leon 1977–79
Nancy Feldman	Nana Tucker Visitor 1979
	Megan McCracken 1978
	Lisa Sutton 1978
Bill Woodard	Wesley Addy 1977–78
Rae Woodard	Louise Shaffer 1977–84
Kimberly Harris	Kelli Maroney 1980–81; 1982–83
Michael Pavel	Michael Corbett 1980–81
Kevin McGuinness	Malachy McCourt 1979–84
Father McShane	John Perkins 1976–
Alicia Nieves	Ana Alicia 1977–78
Angel Nieves	Jose Aleman 1977–78
Annie Colleary	Pauline Flanagan 1979–81
Ethel Green	Nell Carter 1979
Wes Leonard	David Rasche 1979–83
Thatcher Ross	Patrick Horgan 1979
Dan Fox	Peter Ratray 1979
Chester Wallace	Robert LuPone 1980
Tiso Novotny	Dan Clarke 1979–80

Joe Novak   Walt Willey   1986–87
                                 Michael Hennessy   1983–84
                                 Roscoe Born   1981–83
                                 Richard Muenz   1979–80
Ken George Jones   Trent Jones   1980
Barry Ryan   Richard Backus   1980–81
Lilly Darnell   Kathryn Dowling   1980
                                 Christine Ebersole   1980
Rose Melina   Rose Alaio   1980–81
Matthew Pearse   Tom Aldredge   1981–82
Crimmins   Ron Tomme   1981
Orson Burns   Robert Desiderio   1981–82
                                 Nicolas Surovy   1981
Sgt. Jim Speed   Mackenzie Allen   1981–82
Carol Baker   Lori Cardille   1982
Mitch Bronsky   James Sloyan   1982
Alexi Vartova   Leonard Cimino   1982
                                 Dominic Chianese   1981
Elizabeth Jane Ryan   Maureen Garrett   1981–82
Ox Knowles   Will Patton   1982
Barbara Wilde   Judith Barcroft   1981–82
Aristotle Benedict-White   Gordon Thomson   1981–82
Spencer Smith   Lester Rawlins   1981
Hollis Kirkland   Peter Haskell   1982–83
Catsy Kirkland   Christine Jones   1982–83
Amanda Kirkland   Ariane Munker   1983
                                 Mary Page Keller   1982–83
Leigh Kirkland   Felicity LaFortune   1983–85
Sydney Galloway   Marilyn McIntyre   1982
Sydney Price   Robin Greer   1983–85
Charlotte Greer   Judith Chapman   1983
Neil MacCurtain   Roy Poole   1983
Una MacCurtain   Kathleen Widdoes   1983
Lt. Bill Hyde   David Sederholm   1983–85
Rick Hyde   Grant Show   1984–87
Bess Shelby   Gloria DeHaven   1983–87
Maggie Shelby   Cali Timmins   1983–
Jacqueline Novak   Gerit Quealy   1983–87
Max Dubujak   Daniel Pilon   1984–87
Stamford Hutchinson   Deveren Bookwalter   1983–84
Laslo Novotny   Fred Burstein   1984–85; 1987
Ken Graham   Corbin Bernsen   1984–85
Dave Greenberg   Scott Holmes   1984–85
Pru Shepherd   Traci Lin   1984–85
Katie Thompson   Julia Campbell   1984–85
                                 Lauren O'Bryan   1984
Rico   Richard Berk   1984
Jeremy Winthrop   Herb Anderson   1984
Matthew Crane   Harve Presnell   1984–85

Stephen Latham   Franc Luz   1984
Charles Whitehall   David O'Brien   1984–85
Elizabeth Maxwell   Gwyn Gilliss   1985
Tiger Bennett   Duncan Gamble   1985
Chantal Dubujak   Marisa Paven   1985
Gabrielle Dubujak   Susan Scannell   1985
Chessy Blake   Susan Scannell   1985
Ferdie   Frank O'Brien   1985
D. J. LaSalle   Christian Slater   1985
Gloria Tassky   Francine Tacker   1985
Betty Sherman   Betty Alley   1985
Devlin Kowalski   Leslie Easterbrook   1985–87
Dakota Smith   Christopher Durham   1985–
Melinda Weaver Ryan   Nancy Valen   1985–87
Maura   Kate Mulgrew   1986
Dr. Evan Cooper   Irving Allen Lee   1986–
Diana Douglas   Tracey Ross   1986
Chris Hannold   Lydia Hannibal   1986–
Hower Dowd   Keith Charles   1986–
Lizzie Ransome   Catherine Larson   1986–
Mark D'Angelo   Peter Love   1986–
Concetta D'Angelo   Lois Robbins   1987–
Zena Brown   Tichina Arnold   1987–
Emily Hall   Cynthia Dozier   1987–
Ben Shelby   James Wlcek   1987–

SANTA BARBARA

July 30, 1984–   NBC

Created by Jerome and Bridget Dobson, *Santa Barbara* was the second daytime soap to be launched in an hour format. Moving into the same time slot that the failed *Texas*, the first serial created hour-long, had occupied, *Santa Barbara* had many things going for it. The most obvious was the Dobsons, who had begun their spectacularly successful writing career on *General Hospital* in the early '70s. (Bridget Dobson is the daughter of Frank and Doris Hursley, the creators of *General Hospital*.) After maintaining good ratings on that show, the Dobsons were snatched up by Procter & Gamble to spruce up *Guiding Light*. They worked wonders on that show for five years, then created miracles on *As the World Turns*, becoming the most sought after team of writers in daytime television.

Set in Santa Barbara (where the Dobsons used to live), the drama traced the lives and loves of four families: the blue-blood Lockridges, the powerful Capwells, the middle-class Perkins, and the Andrades, a low-income Hispanic family. Overseeing all the intrigue was eighty-six-year-old theatrical legend Dame Judith Anderson as Minx, widow to T. MacDonald Lockridge ("T for Tiger," she growled in the premiere episode). The serial opened with a party in 1979 in which Channing Capwell, Jr., was murdered after an argument with his sister Kelly's fiancé, Joe Perkins. The

scene jumped forward to an engagement party for Kelly and the oppor-
tunist Peter Flint in 1984 at which it was learned that Joe Perkins, Capwell's alleged killer, had been set free. The release caused havoc among
the seaside community, particularly for Kelly Capwell, who was torn
between Joe and her memory of Channing's death.

Although the show was taped in new $12 million production facilities
in Burbank, the Santa Barbara–based Dobsons served as executive producers along with director Jeffrey Hayden (husband of Eva Marie Saint).
The expensive production (even Augusta Lockridge's doberman sported
a diamond collar) promised to give the powerhouse competition a run for
their money, although *Santa Barbara*'s rivals were, ironically, *Guiding Light*,
the drama the Dobsons loved writing, and *General Hospital*, the show that
started it all for the two. In its premiere week the glamorous new soap
about Beautiful People—almost all with blonde hair and uneven acting
ability—ran opposite the ratings-grabbing Olympic games; its first episode
only received a 4.2 rating and 13 share. However, NBC remained high
on the soap and planned to invest over $30 million on *Santa Barbara* in its
first year.

When the audience proved uninterested in a romantic mystery story
that featured such daring daytime subjects as transvestism (the mysterious
Dominic revealed to be Sophia Capwell) and male prostitution, the network ordered emergency surgery on the soap. While the production staff
backstage was reshuffled, the writers came up with the idea of getting rid
of some of the bad actresses by creating a mass murderer with a weakness
for sleek blond beauties. Other dull characters were disposed of with an
earthquake story that caused unparalleled sorrow for the people of Santa
Barbara. But for the erotically disposed Augusta, the initial rumblings
proved pleasurable: in bed with her scalawag of a husband she murmured,
"Darling, you're making the earth move for me."

After the shake-up, *Santa Barbara* suddenly blossomed into a sophisticated comedy adventure story in 1985 as the Dobsons finally revealed
Channing's murderer. (Sophia, wanting to scare Lionel with what she
thought was an unloaded pistol, instead accidentally shot her son.) The
Dobsons soon found their footing with two dazzling anti-heroes: Lionel
Lockridge, whose roguish charm was exceeded only by his penchant for
mischief, and the envious, cryptic Mason Capwell, whose ironic self-
knowledge provided the city with a one-man greek chorus, commenting
dryly on all the drawing-room intrigue.

Sensibly, *Santa Barbara* also continued the satin-sheet antics of Augusta,
who was pictured in a fantasy sequence in bed with four half-naked studs
feeding her champagne, steak tartare, and kisses—and not necessarily in
that order. Augusta was perhaps the first soap opera character ever to
receive a letter from the White House. When Augusta was temporarily
blinded on the show, the President, who apparently was unaware that
Augusta Lockridge was a fictional character, wrote, "Nancy and I are
sorry to learn about your illness. Our thoughts and prayers are with you.
God bless you."

By 1987, this delicious black comedy had become a cult hit and the
slowly rising ratings began to reflect that status. *Santa Barbara* was su-

perbly romantic in its star-crossed love story of the WASPy Eden and the Hispanic Cruz. (In a great erotic fast dance, Eden shook her blonde mane like a stoned-out Lady Godiva.) It certainly was dramatic (the death of Mason's "salvation," Mary Duvall, proved to be an extremely unpopular event with viewers—probably the biggest boo-boo in the Dobsons' career). Most emphatically, the show was downright hilarious: Mason making love to Gina in an ambulance, Gina cooking hot dogs on a hibachi at C.C. and Sophia's outdoor wedding, and Gina deadpanning to Santana's supposed allergy to flour, "Doesn't that get in the way of making tortillas?"

That Gina! In just one episode she poisoned Mason's food with lighter fluid, called Kelly a "slut," tried to set up Eden for murder by dressing up like her and pulling the plug on the comatose C.C. When Gina was kicked out of the Capwell mansion, she stripped off all her clothes in front of the family. (After she slammed the door, you half expected to hear her cry "taxi!") As Bridget Dobson noted, "There is a slight bit of perversity in us. That's me. That's my husband. We're ambivalent people. We always strive for purity and always miss!"

CAST

Minx Lockridge	Dame Judith Anderson 1984–
Lionel Lockridge	Nicolas Coster 1984–
Augusta Lockridge	Louise Sorel 1984–86
Warren Lockridge	Scott Jenkins 1986–87
	John Allen Nelson 1984–86
Laken Lockridge	Susan Marie Snyder 1987–
	Julie Ronnie 1984–85
C. C. Capwell	Jed Allan 1986–
	Charles Bateman 1984–86
	Paul Burke 1984
	Peter Mark Richman 1984
Channing Capwell, Jr.	Robert Wilson 1984–85
Mason Capwell	Lane Davies 1984–
Kelly Capwell	Robin Wright 1984–
Ted Capwell	Todd McKee 1984–
Sophia Capwell	Judith McConnell 1984–
	Rosemary Forsyth 1984
Eden Capwell	Marcy Walker 1984–
John Perkins	Robert Alan Browne 1984
Marisa Perkins	Valorie Armstrong 1984–86
Jade Perkins	Melissa Brennan 1984
Joe Perkins	Mark Arnold 1984–85
	Dane Witherspoon 1984
Amy Perkins	Kerry Sherman 1984–86
Ruben Andrade	Ismael Carlo 1984
Rosa Andrade	Margarita Cardova 1984–
Santana Andrade	Gina Gallego 1985–87
	Margaret Michaels 1985
	Ava Lazar 1984
Danny Andrade	Rupert Ravens 1984–86

Peter Flint	Stephen Meadows 1984–85
Cruz Castillo	A Martinez 1984–
Dr. Ramirez	Alejandro Rey 1984
Peaches Delight	Virginia Mayo 1984
Summer Blake	Jonna Leigh 1984
Brick Wallace	Richard Eden 1984–87
Elizabeth Peale	Lauren Chase 1985
Gina Demott	Robin Mattson 1985–
	Linda Gibboney 1984–
Brandon Demott	Brandon Call 1985–87
	Scott Curtis 1984–85
Jackie Parks	Martina Deignan 1985
Sgt. Clifford T. Monroe	Joe Lambie 1985
Marcello Armonti	Wolf Muser 1985
Maggie Gillis	Suzanne Marshall 1985
Lindsay Smith	Joel Bailey 1985
Ginger Jones	Paula Kelly 1984–85
Hank Judson	Victor Bevine 1985
J. Stanfield Lee	Joel Crothers 1985
Carmen Castillo	Carmen Zapatta 1985–86
Julia Wainwright	Nancy Grahn 1985–
Christy Duvall	Tricia Cast 1985
Mary Duvall	Harley Kozak 1985–86
Steve Bassett	Ashby Adams 1985
Mark McCormack	Jon Lindstrom 1985–86
Kirk Cranston	Robert Newman 1986
	Joseph Bottoms 1985–86
Nick Hartley	David Haskell 1985–86
Dylan Hartley	Page Moseley 1985–86
Michael "Pearl"	
Bradford III	Robert Thaler 1985–
Brian Bradford	Kyle Secor 1986–87
Courtney Capwell	Julia Campbell 1986–87
Madeline Capwell Laurent	Terry Davis 1986–87
David Laurent	Brian Matthews 1986
Halley Benson	Stacy Edwards 1986–
Lily Light	Lynn Clark 1986–87
Keith Timmons	Justin Deas 1986–
Victoria Lane	Kristen Meadows 1986–
Martin Ellis	John Wesley Shipp 1986
Paul Whitney	Stoney Jackson 1986–87
Jane Wilson	Jane Sibbett 1986–87
Caroline Wilson	Lenore Kasdorf 1986–87
Alice Jackson	Marie-Alise Recasner 1986–87
Gus Jackson	David Fonteno 1986–87
Jake Morton	Rick Edwards 1986–
Jeffrey Conrad	Ross Kettle 1986–
Dr. Alex Nikolas	Michael Durrell 1987–
Elena Nikolas	Sherilyn Wolter 1987

Cain   Scott Jaeck 1987–
Carmen Castillo II   Marisol Rodriguez 1987–

SCARLETT HILL

1965–1966   Syndicated

A kind of mini–*Grand Hotel*, this little-known serial premiered in New
York on September 20, 1965, and had a short syndicated run. The show
dramatized the lives of various people residing at a hotel in Scarlett Hill,
New York. Kate Russell, the landlady, managed to be in on all the intrigue,
including Dr. David Black's proposal to the young heroine, Janice Turner.

CAST

Janice Turner	Suzanne Bryant
Dr. David Black	Gordon Pinsent
Kate Russell	Beth Lockerbie
Walter Pendelton	Ivor Barry
Ginny	Lucy Warner
Sidney	Alan Pearce
Harry	Ed McNamara

SEARCH FOR TOMORROW

September 3, 1951–March 26, 1982   CBS;
March 29, 1982–December 26, 1986   NBC

One of the longest-running dramas in television history, *Search for To-
morrow* centered on one woman, Joanne Gardner Barron Tate Vincente
Tourneur, or, as millions know soap opera's most beloved heroine, Jo.
The thirty-five-year history of this show was a richly resonant one, reflecting social change (note Jo's progressively ethnic surnames) and, through
Jo and Mary Stuart, the actress who played her since the show's beginning,
holding out hope and optimism to its audience. But the times also pushed
Jo to the background, which might explain the show's steady decline in
the '80s, ultimately placing it at the bottom of the ratings race.

  Search for Tomorrow began with an idea by Roy Winsor, who developed
the theme, story, and characters for the Biow Company, eventually selling
the project, once titled *Search for Happiness*, to Procter & Gamble. While
in New York, Winsor met with advertising executive Richard Krolik and
his fiancée Mary Stuart, who had been a Hollywood starlet in her teens
and had returned to Manhattan to pursue a stage career. "I found her to
be attractive and warm," said Winsor, reminiscing three decades later. "I
suggested that she would make a fine leading lady for *Search*, and then
and there I offered her the role." Looking back on that lucky meeting,
Stuart remembered being skeptical about the job offer, saying, "But then
I didn't believe [Hollywood producer] Joe Pasternak either when he said,
'I'm going to make you a star, little girl.' "

  The elements soon jelled; Stuart was hired at a salary of $500 a week, and the other parts were cast quickly by Winsor and director Charles Irving. *Search* was scheduled to be launched in May 1951, then postponed until Labor Day. On September 3, television watchers received their first peek at what was to become an American institution. In the first fifteen-minute program, broadcast live from Liederkranz Hall (at a spartan production budget of $1,605.15 an episode), Jo allayed Patti's singsong cries of "But, Mommy, where is Daddy? Where is Daddy?" with a lullaby. The story, created by Winsor and written the first thirteen weeks by Agnes Nixon, was deceptively simple, as outlined by this CBS press release:

"CBS TV's *Search for Tomorrow* is the compelling story of the Barron family—father, mother, daughter-in-law, and grandchild. It is the story of an American family dominated by the 'old-fashioned' elders, successful and secure. . . . . Son, Keith Barron, a year out of the Navy, and his wife, Joanne, come into conflict with the elder Barrons when they balk at following in the old man's footsteps. Keith's sister Louise is a sympathetic ally, as is young Dr. Ned Hilton. Keith's sudden death embitters his parents, who then turn their unhappiness upon their son's widow."

Joanne was to have been a widow at the outset, but the writers decided it would be far more effective to present her first as a young housewife, putting up with day-to-day problems and a meddling mother-in-law, before tragedy struck. After six months, Keith (Johnny Sylvester, who changed his name to John Sylvester White and later appeared as the bumbling principal on *Welcome Back, Kotter*) died after an automobile accident. Stuart's muted exquisite performance as the grieving widow was perfect for Jo, whose character conception was of a young woman able to offer compassion to her neighbors while facing her own problems with courage and dignity. Unlike radio heroines, whose lives were mired in romantic fantasy, Jo was a woman with whom viewers could identify. Jo's hope for the future—her search for tomorrow—as she comforted Patti, fought to make ends meet, and dealt with Keith's bitter parents, had struck a chord with the public. *Search for Tomorrow*, Jo, and Mary Stuart were an immediate hit, or, as a succinct Roy Winsor said later, "box office from day one." By the end of 1951, *Search* had an audience of five million viewers.

As counterpoint to the domestic drama, the show introduced Jo's light-hearted next-door neighbors, Marge and Stu Bergman, and their daughter Janet, who became Patti's best friend. Melba Rae and Larry Haines as the Bergmans became favorites; their comic touches, unusual for soap opera, were welcome additions over the next two decades. When Melba Rae died in 1971, the show did not replace her with another actress. Instead, Stu became a widower in the story. Larry Haines, who continued in his role, later won a record three Emmies as the lovable Stu. (Originally in the story, the Bergmans had a son named Jimmy. One day he went upstairs to take a nap and was soon forgotten. A decade later this adolescent Rip Van Winkle was resurrected by new writers who magically changed Jimmy from Stu's son to his nephew!)

Early storylines focused on Jo's attempt to carve out a life for herself and Patti despite interference from Irene Barron, Keith's mother, who sued for custody and then kidnapped Patti. Later, Jo fell in love with

Arthur Tate and became proprietor of Motor Haven, a motel eventually expanded to include a restaurant. Jo had continual run-ins with Mortimer Higbee, a wheeler-dealer who attempted to take over Motor Haven. For years, Higbee's schemes and alliances with the steely Irene Barron and alcoholic Sue Tate (who posed as Arthur's ex-wife) brought Jo nothing but years of unhappiness and courtroom litigation. These courtroom scenes were invariably broadcast in color—a first for daytime TV—and provided the springboard for some of Jo's more weightier homilies: "In our search for tomorrow, we are often disappointed in what we find, for we have built today on the quicksand of trouble."

Jo and Arthur were finally married May 18, 1955, but the ceremony was not without comic overtones. Mary Stuart was eight months pregnant at the time and had to be photographed only from the bust up. (Stuart shocked the employees of a boutique offscreen while shopping for the wedding outfit she would wear on TV.) When Stuart became pregnant again the next year, the decision was made to write the pregnancy into the story—a first in daytime television. (Lucille Ball had her pregnancy written into *I Love Lucy* in 1953, but had the luxury of being on film. *Search for Tomorrow* was live and was at the day-to-day mercy of Mother Nature.) Stuart gave birth to a healthy boy, whom she named Jeffrey. The show taped the two together in the hospital so that millions could share in Jo's joy after giving birth to a son, whom the show called Duncan Eric.

But joy turned to horror when Stuart caught wind of what the new writers had up their sleeve for Jo. Irving Vendig, who had written the show since the end of 1951, had left to create the detective serial *The Edge of Night* in 1956. The writing reins were temporarily turned over to Charles Gussman, and then *Search for Tomorrow* went through a complete production overhaul when the ratings began to slide. Frank Dodge became the new producer and Dan Levin the director. Stuart found herself butting heads with Levin at every turn, and became livid when writers Frank and Doris Hursley, who had been given top billing over the show's star, decided to "kill off" Duncan Eric to drive up the ratings.

Despite Stuart's protestations—her own child had been used to play Duncan Eric—the boy was hit by a speeding auto on a Monday and died after a week of shows lingering on his life-or-death surgery. "It ended and was forgotten," said Stuart years later, "and perhaps you think I was a fool to feel so strongly. It was, after all, only a story. Perhaps that is the substance of daytime; it is never quite a story." (Mary Stuart was proved correct and on dramatically strategic grounds: *Search* in the '80s could have desperately used a handsome leading man with roots in the show's heritage.) While Jo had remained a pivotal character throughout the '50s—putting up with Arthur's alcoholism, his affair with Jo's sister Eunice, and constant interference by Arthur's relatives—after Duncan Eric's death, the dramatic emphasis shifted to Jo's daughter Patti and Patti's friend Janet Bergman.

Teenage Janet married Bud Gardner, who was later presumed dead in an accident. By the time Bud (played by George Maharis) returned, Janet had married Dr. Dan Walton, by whom she later had three children,

Gary, Liza, and Danny. (Chuck, Janet's son by Bud, apparently got lost in the shuffle.) Stu, Janet's father, was implicated in Bud's "second" death—this time for real—but was cleared with the help of Jo.

Patti also had her share of teenage trouble, first caught in the midst of a devastating affair with a married man, then confined to a wheelchair after an auto accident. However, doctors could not find anything physical to cause the paralysis; and when crazy Ted Ashton, who had driven the car that had "crippled" Patti, held Patti and Jo captive—the third time in four years Jo had been held at gunpoint—Patti rose dramatically from her wheelchair, causing Ted to drop the gun. For the first ten years, Patti was appealingly played by Lynn Loring, who learned to read by stumbling aloud through everyone's part in daily rehearsals. But shortly after her graduation from high school, Loring left the show to try her luck in California. She returned to daytime as Betty Harrington in *Return to Peyton Place*. After her marriage to actor Roy Thinnes (Dr. Phil Brewer, *General Hospital*), she became a film executive, producing such TV movies as *The Making of A Male Model* and features such as *Mr. Mom*.

After Lynn Loring's departure, the role of Patti was played by an estimated thirty actresses—some with extremely brief tenures—including such future soap notables as Nancy Pinkerton (Dorian Lord, *One Life to Live*), Brooke Bundy (Diana Taylor, *General Hospital*), and Melinda Cordell (Natalie Dearborn, *General Hospital*). Mary Stuart said later, "I remember distinctly fading out on a Tuesday in a scene with a tall, blond Patti and fading back in on a Wednesday with a short brunette. Unfortunately, my first line upon entering the darkened room was, 'Patti? Patti, is that you?' I thought it was funny but nobody else did." (For a list of the actresses who played Patti the longest, see the cast list at the end of this entry.)

After the Hursleys left the show to create *General Hospital*, *Search for Tomorrow* went through a series of writing changes. Over the next ten years the headwriters included Julian Funt and David Lesan, Leonard Kantor and Doris Frankel, Lou Scofield, and Robert Soderberg and Edith Sommer. Although abortion, alcoholism, and impotence were discussed on *Search for Tomorrow* during the socially aware '60s, the show mostly steered clear of controversy and kept close to the romantic intrigue that had always been its bread and butter.

In 1962, Mary Stuart became the first daytime performer to be honored with an Emmy nomination. A few years later, Jo embarked on what was to become the show's most memorable romance. Wealthy Sam Reynolds attempted to take over Tate Enterprises, and Arthur began to feel the pressure. On January 24, 1966, Arthur, Jo's husband of over a decade, suffered a heart attack and died. Jo partially blamed Sam for Arthur's death and fought his romantic overtures for years. Once together, however, Jo and Sam's happiness was short-lived. Sam's wife, Andrea Whiting Reynolds, refused to give him a divorce.

As the show began to be broadcast in color in April 1967 and finally expanded to 30 minutes in September 1968, the Andrea Whiting story brewed and finally came to a head in a spectacular trial. Andrea (theater legend Joan Copeland, in a hair-raising performance) broke down on the witness stand and all her years of villainy—seen in flashbacks—came pouring out. The repercussions from the trial were felt for years, not least by Andrea's son Len, who fell into depression and dropped his plans to marry Patti. After an affair with Grace Bolton (Jill Clayburgh), Len finally did marry Patti and adopt his and Grace's son, Chris. (Fifteen years later, Patti still had not been told that her adopted child was Len's natural son.)

In the early '70s, *Search for Tomorrow* continued with romance-crime themes, but when the husband-and-wife team Ralph Ellis and Eugenie Hunt came aboard as headwriters, the melodrama became tempered with a large dollop of feminism. Jo's sister Eunice longed for a career despite the objections of her lawyer husband John Wyatt. Eunice's stepson Scott Phillips fell in love with fellow law student Kathy Parker. When Kathy became pregnant, she had an abortion because a child would have interfered with her career. Even Jo, now over forty, had become "with it." Her costuming and hair style had taken a more relaxed flavor over the years, but her conservative values had also slowly and subtly changed. She soon was seen strumming a guitar and singing folk songs along with her adopted son, Bruce.

Following Sam Reynolds's death, Jo married Dr. Tony Vincente on October 22, 1972. Marie Cheatham was introduced as the sarcastic, sexy nurse Stephanie Wilkins in January 1974 and for the next decade Stephanie and Jo found themselves at odds over anything and everything. As Jo and Stephanie battled over Tony Vincente (to interest older viewers) and Kathy and Scott fought over her career (to pique the interest of the younger married viewers), *Search for Tomorrow* began a series of "young love" stories, perhaps in reaction to the success of beautiful teenager storylines on *The Young and the Restless*. Janet Bergman's daughter Liza took up with young composer Steve Kaslo, who suffered from leukemia, while Steve's sister Amy became pregnant by Jo's son Bruce.

While attempting this three-tier demographic story structure, *Search for Tomorrow* went through a slew of headwriters, including Theodore Apstein, Gabrielle Upton, Ann Marcus, Peggy O'Shea, Irving and Tex Elman, Robert J. Shaw, and Henry Slesar (who wrote the Steve Kaslo death scene). The ratings, though often excellent during this period, fluctuated consistently, and continuity suffered. Joyce and John William Corrington took over in 1978 and wrote in the Sentell family, and for the next few years *Search for Tomorrow* became "The Travis and Liza Show." Adventure became the name of the game as Travis (who had the same permed hairdo that Luke on *General Hospital* seemed to have patented) and Liza played out mysteries in such exotic locations as New Orleans, a deserted island in the Caribbean, and Hong Kong.

The show enjoyed a quick burst of popularity with these stories, but the adventures were an end in themselves, producing none of the complications that perpetuate domestic drama. Jo married for the fourth time, this time to a Sentell relative, gambler Martin Tourneur. After putting up with various shenanigans from the playboy Martin, Jo did what in the '50s would have been unthinkable: she divorced him! As the ratings continued to fall, the show went through still more writing changes, including stints by Linda Grover, Harding Lemay, and Don Chastain. (Symptomatic of the bad writing and network indifference, Stu's wife Ellie was written out with the incredibly "cute" explanation that she had run off with the temperamental cook!) After experimenting with time changes and then giving up, feeling that the show was a dinosaur, CBS cancelled the show in 1982, replacing *Search* with the "beautiful people" soap, *Capitol*.

On March 29, 1982, *Search for Tomorrow* moved over to NBC. (*The Edge of Night* was the first soap to jump networks, switching from CBS to ABC in 1975.) The show, which had had a respectable 7.1 rating on CBS, was greeted with a paltry 3.6 on NBC. The move cost the show three million viewing homes. With the cancellation of *Texas* and *The Doctors* on NBC later that year, *Search for Tomorrow* fell into last place in the ratings race. With such writers as David Cherrill, the Ellises (again), Gary Tomlin, Madeline David and Jeanne Glynn, and Glynn and Caroline Franz, the show attempted to dig out of the cellar by concentrating on the attractive younger characters, Jo's niece Suzi, and Stephanie's daughter Wendy, and the object of their joint affection, Warren Carter, a handsome, scheming businessman. Later writers "killed off" Travis Sentell (Rod Arrants—the first male soap star to appear on the cover of *TV Guide*) and wrote in almost a dozen post-teenage characters.

Joanna Lee, who had won an Emmy for *The Waltons*, became the new executive producer and attempted to upgrade the production values and spice up the storylines. While NBC seemed clearly uninterested in promoting the show, *Search* created its own publicity after a videotape of one of their shows was stolen. Instead of retaping, *Search* went on live on August 4, 1983—NBC's first live daytime drama episode since 1966. (Don Pardo introduced the show "Live from New York: it's *Search for Tomorrow*" in the same whimsical—and inappropriate—manner he adopted to introduce *Saturday Night Live* comedy shows.) The following year, *Search* was the recipient of reams of publicity when it presented a special episode on February 16, 1984. Presented with only two commercials, the episode dramatized the "acquaintance" rape of Sunny Adamson by her co-worker Jack Benton.

Although Jo had been pushed into the background since the advent of the Sentells, the show received its highest ratings on NBC when Jo was kidnapped. Although the melodramatic aspects of the story no doubt attracted viewers, writer Gary Tomlin (who had previously played Jo's adopted son Bruce) set up a tantalizing situation in which Jo had to pretend to be the mother of her kidnapper. By having Jo play along with her captor, *Search for Tomorrow* exploited the emotions of the generation who had grown up with Jo, considering her the ideal mother who would always extend reassurance and hope for the future.

Afterwards, Jo again faded into the background and Mary Stuart was relegated to weekly appearances. "The decline of the present version of the program," said creator Roy Winsor in 1984, "can be traced to its loss of theme and the loss of the integrity of Joanne Barron." The secret to *Search for Tomorrow*'s future, ironically enough, was in its past.

The show kept plugging away over the next two years with the reintroduction of Jo's daughter Patti (after an absence of almost a decade), a catastrophic flood, and a romantic mystery shot on location in Ireland.

But the writing was on the wall: *Search for Tomorrow* never recovered from its switch from CBS to NBC and never found its old viewers or a new audience. The show's rating for its final week was 3.3.

Search ended on a happy, optimistic note, befitting its title: Hogan married Patti; Sunny announced her engagement to Bela and the news that she was expecting a visit from the stork; Estelle was reunited with her daughter, T.R.; Liza met a Travis lookalike; Quinn popped the question to Kat and the spunky Irish lass accepted; and Stu and Jo reaffirmed their thirty-five-year friendship.

On the porch, Jo stared at the stars and Stu asked, "What is it, Jo? What are you searching for?"

"Tomorrow," Jo replied. "And I can't wait!"

CAST

Joanne Gardner Barron	Mary Stuart 1951–86
Patti Barron	Jacqueline Schultz 1985–86
	Tina Sloan 1976–77
	Leigh Lassen 1969–75
	Melinda Plank 1967–69
	Melissa Murphy 1966–67
	Gretchen Walther 1965–66
	Trish Van Devere 1965
	Patricia Harty 1964–65
	Abigail Kellogg 1961–64
	Nancy Pinkerton 1961
	Lynn Loring 1951–61
Keith Barron	Johnny Sylvester 1951–52
Irene Barron	Bess Johnson 1951–54; 1960–61
Victor Barron	Cliff Hall 1951–54
Louise Barron	Sara Anderson 1951–52
Frank Gardner	Eric Dressler 1957–58
	Harry Holcombe 1957
Stu Bergman	Larry Haines 1951–86
Marge Bergman	Melba Rae 1951–71
Janet Bergman	Millee Taggart 1971–82
	Marian Hailey 1971
	Nancy Franklin 1965–66
	Fran Sharon 1961–65
	Sandy Robinson 1956–61
	Ellen Spencer 1951–56
Tom Bergman	Robert LuPone 1983
	Mitch Litrofsky 1981–83
	John James 1977–78
	Ray Bellaran 1973–77
	Peter Broderick 1968–71
Jimmy Bergman	Peter Lazar 1962
Monica Bergman	Barbara Baxley 1962
Jessie Bergman	Nydia Westman 1959–60
	Joanna Roos 1958–59

Dr. Ned Hilton	Coe Norton 1951–54
Arthur Tate	Terry O'Sullivan 1952–66
	Karl Weber 1955–56
Hazel/Sue Tate	Mary Patton 1953–54
Mortimer Higbee	Ian Martin 1953–55
Nathan Walsh	Mark Lenard 1959–60
	Richard Derr 1959
	Frank Overton 1959
	George Petrie 1954–58
	David Orrick 1953
Eunice Gardner Wyatt	Ann Williams 1966–76
	Marion Brash 1957–61
Rose Peterson	Constance Ford 1955–56
	Nita Talbot 1954–55
	Lee Grant 1953–54
Wilbur Peterson	Don Knotts 1953–55
Allison Simmons	Anne Pearson 1959–65
	Nina Reader 1958–59
Cornelia Simmons	Doris Dalton 1958–60
Rex Twining	Laurence Hugo 1958–59
Bud Gardner	George Maharis 1960–61
	Anthony Cannon 1960
	Tony Ray 1959–60
Harriet Baxter	Vicki Viola 1959–60
Pearl March	Sylvia Field 1959–60
	Isabel Price 1959
Fred Metcalf	David O'Brien 1965–66
	Donald Madden 1964
	Tom Carlin 1961–64
Agnes Metcalf	Katherine Meskill 1961–64
Slim Davis	Wayne Rogers 1959
Hester Walsh	Kay Medford 1959
Dr. Dan Walton	Ron Husmann 1971–72
	Philip Abbott 1961–63
	Martin E. Brooks 1960–61
Dr. Gary Walton	Stephen Burleigh 1978–79
	Robert Bannard 1978
	Richard Lohman 1976–78
	John Driver 1973–74
	Tommy Norden 1971–73
Liza Walton Sentell	Louan Gideon 1985–86
	Sherry Mathis 1978–85
	Hope Busby 1977–78
	Meg Bennett 1974–77
	Kathleen Beller 1971–74
	Denise Nickerson 1971
Danny Walton	John Loprieno 1985–86
	Cain Devore 1983
	Neil Billingsley 1975–77

Sue Knowles	Audra Lindley 1962
Marion Gill	Jane McArthur 1962–64
Dr. Everett Moore	Martin E. Brooks 1962–64
Isabel Moore	Lenka Peterson 1962–64
Dr. Brad Campbell	George Kane 1962–64
Helen	Sandy Duncan 1964
Geoffrey Crane	Geoffrey Lumb 1964
Dr. Len Whiting	Dino Narizzano 1964–72; 1976
	Jeffrey David Pomerantz 1974
Andrea Whiting	Joan Copeland 1968–72
	Lesley Woods 1967
	Virginia Gilmore 1965–67
Sam Reynolds	Roy Shuman 1971–72
	George Gaynes 1971
	Robert Mandan 1965–70
Dr. Bob Rogers	Carl Low 1965–79
Emily Rogers Hunter	Kathryn Walker 1972–73
	Louise Shaffer 1967–68
	Pamela Murphy 1966–67
Dr. Nick Hunter	Ken Kercheval 1965–67; 1972–73
	Terry Logan 1968
	Stephen Joyce 1968
	Burr DeBenning 1965
Walter Haskins	Douglass Watson 1967–68
	Ernest Graves 1967
Cal Foster	Colgate Salisbury 1966–68
Doug Martin	Ken Harvey 1968–73
Althea Franklin	Dody Goodman 1968
Ida Weston	Vera Allen 1969–72
Jill Carter	Barbara Baxley 1969
Larry Carter	Hal Linden 1969
Dr. Peter Murphy	Charles Siebert 1969–71
Grace Bolton	Jill Clayburgh 1969–70
Ellie Harper Bergman	Billie Lou Watt 1968–81
Magda Leshinsky	Lilia Skala 1969–70
Erik Leshinsky	Christopher Lowe 1969–77
Lauri Leshinsky	Kelly Wood 1969–73
Scott Phillips	Peter Ratray 1977–78
	Peter Simon 1969–77
Kathy Parker Phillips	Courtney Sherman 1971–78; 1983–84
	Nicolette Goulet 1979–82
Dr. Tony Vincente	Anthony George 1970–75
	Robert Loggia 1973
	Lawrence Weber 1970
Marcy Vincente	Jeanne Carson 1970–71
Al Franklin	Al Fann 1970
John Burroughs	Adam Wade 1970
Claire Hart	Peggy Whitton 1970–71

Dick Hart	Michael Zaslow 1970–71
Jim McCarven	Michael Shannon 1970
Bruce Carson	Joel Higgins 1975–78
	Steve Nisbet 1974–75
	Gary Tomlin 1973–74
	Michael Maitland 1973
	Robby Benson 1971–73
Dr. Wade Collins	John Cunningham 1971–77
Helen Collins	Natalie Schafer 1971–72
William Collins	Ralph Clanton 1971–72
Clay Collins	Brett Halsey 1975
John Wyatt	Val Dufour 1973–79
Sarah Fairbanks	Susan Sarandon 1972
George Joslyn	Kipp Osborne 1972
Melissa Hayley Weldon	Linda Bove 1972–73
Dr. Matt Weldon	Robert Phelps 1972–73
Karl Devlin	David Ford 1972–73
Frank Ross	Andrew Jarkowsky
Marian Malin	Pat Stanley 1972–73
Walter Pace	Tom Klunis 1976–77
	Edward Grover 1976
	Wayne Tippit 1975
Jennifer Pace Phillips	Morgan Fairchild 1973–77
	Robin Eisenman 1973
Dave Wilkins	Dale Robinette 1974–75
Stephanie Wilkins Wyatt	Louise Shaffer 1984–86
	Marie Cheatham 1974–84
Wendy Wilkins	Lisa Peluso 1977–85
	Andrea McArdle 1974–77
Suzi Martin	Terri Eoff 1984–86
	Elizabeth Swackhamer 1983–84
	Cynthia Gibb 1981–83
	Stacey Moran 1976–79
	Amy Arutt
	Kristin Carl
Raney Wesner	Katherine Squire 1974
Dr. Walter Osmond	Byron Sanders 1974
Ralph Haywood	Drew Snyder 1976
	James O'Sullivan 1974
Karen Dehner	Kathleen Denzina 1975
Hal Conrad	Vince O'Brien 1974–75
	Ben Hammer 1974
Dr. Carolyn Hanley	
Walton	Marilyn McIntyre 1976–80
	Gayle Pines 1973–74
Steve Kaslo	Michael Nouri 1975–78
Amy Kaslo Carson	Anne Wyndham 1975–78
	Pamela Miller 1975
Robin Kennemer	Lane Binkley 1975

David Sutton   Lewis Arlt   1976–77
Chris Delon   Paul Dumont   1976
Gwen Delon   Barbara Babcock   1976
Gail Caldwell   Sherry Rooney   1976–77
Kitty Merritt   Donna Theodore   1977
Meredith Hartford   Tina Orr   1977–78
Dr. Greg Hartford   Robert Rockwell   1977–78
Evelyn Reedy   Lenka Peterson   1977
Dr. Allen Ramsey   Conard Fowkes   1977
Fay Chandler   Kathleen Devine   1977
Donna Davis   Leslie Ray   1977–78
Kylie Halliday   Lisa Buck   1977–78
Chance Halliday   George Shannon   1977–78
Ted Adamson   Wayne Tippit   1978–82
                         Malachi Throne   1978
Sunny Adamson   Marcia McCabe   1978–86
Laine Adamson   Megan Bagot   1978–79
Tod Adamson   Kevin Bacon   1979
Nick D'Antoni   Jerry Lanning   1978–79
Mark D'Antoni   Christopher Goutman   1978–79
Simon D'Antoni   Gregory Sutton   1979
Travis Sentell   Rod Arrants   1978–84
Mignon Sentell   Anita Keal   1978–79; 1981
Lee Sentell   Douglas Stevenson   1979–82
E. N. Sentell   Jay Garner   1979
Rusty Sentell   David Gale   1982
Gen. Roger Tourneur   William Robertson   1978–79
Martin Tourneur   John Aniston   1978–84
Tante Helene LeVeaux   Jane White   1979
Prince Antonio Stradella Robert Desiderio   1979–80
Renata Corelli Sutton   Sonia Petrovna   1979–80
Cissie Mitchell   Patsy Pease   1979–82
Beau Mitchell   Danny Goldring   1979–80
Sylvie Descartes   Maureen Anderman   1981
Zach Anders   Shawn Stevens   1981
Spencer Langley   Timothy Patrick Murphy
                         1980–81
Brian Emerson   Jay Acovone   1983–84
                         Gene Pietragallo   1981–83
                         Larry Joshua   1981
                         Paul Joynt   1980
Dr. Winston Kyle   Nicholas Courtland   1979–80
Dr. Jamie Larsen   Patricia Estrin   1979–80
Garth Taper   David Gautreaux   1980–81
Dr. Max Taper   Don Chastain   1980–81
Aja Doyan   Susan Monts   1982–83
Dane Taylor   Marcus Smythe   1981–83
Warren Carter   Michael Corbett   1982–85
Kristen Carter   Susan Scannell   1982–84

Vargas   John Glover   1983–84
Rhonda Sue Huckaby   Tina Johnson   1983–84
Ringo Altman   Larry Fleischman   1982–84
Keith McNeil   Craig Augustine   1982–83
Andie McNeil   Stacey Glick   1982–83
Jenny Deacon   Linda Gibboney   1982–83
Michael Kendall   Tom Sullivan   1982–83
Steve Kendall   Steve Lundquist   1985
                                     Philip Brown   1982–83
Lloyd Kendall   Robert Reed   1986
                                     Joe Lambie   1985–86
                                     Peter Haskell   1983–85
Alec Kendall   Robert Curtis Brown   1984–85
Chase Kendall   Robert Wilson   1985–86
                                     Kevin Conroy   1984–85
Rebecca (T.R.) Kendall   Jane Krakowski   1984–86
Dr. Barbara Moreno   Olympia Dukakis   1983
Josh Moreno   Damion Scheller   1983
                                     Josh Freund   1983
Angela Moreno   Jennifer Gatti   1983
Hogan McCleary   David Forsyth   1983–86
Cagney McCleary   Matthew Ashford   1984–86
Kate McCleary   Maeve McGuire   1986
                                     Jo Henderson   1984–85
Adair McCleary   Susan Carey-Lamm   1985
                                     Page Hannah   1984–85
Justine Calvert   Leslie Stevens   1984–85
Jack Benton   Patrick James Clarke   1983–84
Mildred P. Lascoe   Shelia MacCrae   1984
Cord Tourneur   Martin Vidnovic   1984
Victoria Windsor   Marian Woods   1984
Mr./Mrs. Tony Nargo   Tom Aldredge   1984
Kentucky Bluebird   Will Patton   1984–85
Brett Hamilton III   Brett Porter   1984–85
Big Bigelowe   Malachy McCourt   1984–85
Andrew Ryder   Adam Storke   1985–86
Sailor   Richard Gates   1985
Bela Garody   Lee Godart   1985–86
                                     Paul Espel   1985
Estelle Kendall   Domini Blythe   1985–86
Quinn McCleary   Jeffrey Meek   1985–86
Evie Stone   Joanna Going   1986
                                     Colleen Dion   1985–86
Wilma Holliday   Anita Gillette   1986
David Glenn   Jack Betts   1986
Jerry Henderson   Tim Loughrin   1986
Ella Hobbs   Ann Flood   1986
Judge Jeremiah Henderson   William Prince   1986
Matt McCleary   Patrick Tovatt   1986

| Kat Fitzgerald | Mary Jo Keenen | 1986 |
| Zophie | June Havoc | 1986 |

THE SECRET STORM
February 1, 1954–February 8, 1974   CBS

Created by Roy Winsor and directed by Gloria Monty (who orchestrated *General Hospital*'s comeback in the late '70s), this highly dramatic serial about family secrets and sweaty passions—a story motivated by characters whose emotions were often uncontrollable—enjoyed a run of two decades and one week. Originally entitled *The Storm Within* (until it was learned that an antacid was to be a major sponsor), *The Secret Storm* was set in Woodbridge, New York, and centered on Peter Ames and his troubled family.

Instead of moving slowly toward a tragic climax, *The Secret Storm* opened in the midst of tragedy, as Peter's wife Ellen, who had been injured in an automobile accident, suddenly died. Peter was left to care for their children: teenagers Susan and Jerry and nine-year-old Amy. The opening episodes were shocking to many viewers not yet used to the immediacy of television, and the gambit proved an effective hook, capturing a large early audience and building a loyal following from that base. With such writers as William Kendall Clarke and Orin Tovrov at the helm, *The Secret Storm*'s first decade found Peter falling into depression, drinking heavily, and finding his every positive move thwarted by Ellen's nefarious sister, Pauline. While Jerry was caught up with a criminal element and was sent to reform school, strong-minded Susan married Alan Dunbar, who had criminal connections. Later, Susan became intrigued with Jeff Nichols, until it was learned that Jeff was writing a tell-all novel based on the Ames family.

In 1963, Jane and Ira Avery took over the writing chores, and in the next three years, *The Secret Storm* saw its heyday, the high-water mark in its popularity. Much of the action focused on the youngest Ames, Amy, then seventeen years old. Jada Rowland, who was eleven years old when the show premiered in 1954, said later that she was hired because she looked so "pathetic." Although self-deprecating, Rowland was correct up to a point; Amy had always been an audience favorite as the perpetually lost child. However, with the Averys' regime, Rowland made the transition from child actress to the show's central romantic heroine. Amy fell in love with Kip Rysdale, and in a series of seductions and betrayals she had a child out of wedlock by history professor Paul Britton, married and divorced Kip, and then married Paul.

On the set, the cast and crew had problems of their own. *The Secret Storm* was produced in Liederkranz Hall right next to the *Captain Kangaroo* set, and animals frequently made unwanted guest appearances on the *Storm* set. Jada Rowland remembered a cow chasing director Gloria Monty down a hall. "A llama once spat at me," Rowland recalled, "and I had an elephant eat my purse. The day the cow got loose, Gloria thought it was a bull. She locked herself in the control room and called the studio manager to come save her." But even the control room was not sacred, David O'Brien (Kip Rysdale) remembered. "Once, somebody put a chimpanzee in [there]. Everybody had a lot of fun playing tricks on Gloria. She was always slightly on the ragged edge of hysteria. She was a terribly good director, but anything that had fur and crawled around made her hysterical."

Meanwhile, sympathetic Valerie Hill (played by the striking actress Lori March) came on the scene, married Peter, and became "the refuge from the storm" for the Ames family. It was during this time that the soap added a narrated coda at the end of each episode: "You have been watching *The Secret Storm*, the story of the Ames family and of deep-rooted emotions, and how these emotions are stirred up into becoming 'the secret storm.'" After the Averys left, the show sputtered with the writing of John Hess and Lou Scofield, but perked up when Don Ettlinger took over. A wonderful villainess, Belle (Marla Adams), was introduced, causing trouble for Amy at every turn, first snatching Amy's husband Paul. Tiring of Paul, Belle divorced him and married Dan Kincaid, a candidate for governor. Amy fell in love with Dan's son Kevin, but Kevin was shot by one of his father's underworld cronies and became paralyzed from the waist down.

In 1968, movie star Joan Crawford made a well-publicized visit to the show. When her adopted daughter Christina, who played the selfish Joan Kane, was hospitalized, Joan Crawford suggested that she, Crawford, step in for Christina. The idea was a bit ludicrous—a sixty-four-year-old woman playing a twenty-four-year-old housewife—but CBS officials jumped at such a potential ratings-winning gambit. The Oscar-winning actress taped all her scenes in a single weekend, for which she was paid $585, which Crawford donated to her hairdresser. The scenes were aired over a four-day period, and afterwards the character was temporarily written out.

When Christina Crawford watched the shows, she was horrified to discover that her mother was clearly intoxicated during the taping. Joan Crawford's biographer, Bob Thomas, confirms this, describing the star's consumption of vodka, brought to the set in a Pepsi-Cola cooler, as "prodigious." The entire episode is described in full in Christina Crawford's book *Mommie Dearest* (Morrow, 1978) and dramatized in the subsequent Faye Dunaway movie. As for Joan Crawford's appearance on the show, those who remember her performance retain the image of a graying woman hanging on to an illusion—stiff, scared, vulnerable. After her appearance, two Joan Crawford films were tried out briefly in TV serial form, *Best of Everything* in 1970 and *Flamingo Road* in 1981.

The next year, CBS gained control of the show from American Home Products, and creator-consultant Roy Winsor and director Gloria Monty left. *The Secret Storm* became plagued with recasting and continuity problems, enduring one writing change after another. Gabrielle Upton (writing under the pseudonym Gillian Houghton; at that time she used her real name only for screenwriting chores) became headwriter, followed by actress Bethel Leslie (Dr. Maggie Powers, *The Doctors*) and Gerry Day, then Robert Cenedella, and Frances Rickett.

The Ames family was put on the back burner—later to the point of obscurity—and the core audience withstood still more changes and far-out stories, even tolerating a plotline about a haunted house. Amy was artificially inseminated with the sperm of Dr. Brian Neeves, a bit of information that did not go unnoticed by Amy's handicapped husband Kevin, who left Woodbridge for London. The show got some mileage in the press about the "daring" romance between Laurie and a Catholic priest, Father Mark Reddin. (At first, outraged mail ran 80 percent against the romance. Later, the mailed shifted to 90 percent who wanted to see Laurie and Mark married.) However, CBS, who had mismanaged the show for five years, decided to cancel the show in the last weeks of 1973, when the ratings placed *The Secret Storm* in last place among daytime programs.

A storm of indignation erupted, perhaps the largest outpouring of protest caused by a soap opera's cancellation. Angry letters and petitions flooded CBS, switchboards lit up, and letters began appearing in local newspapers all over the country. The serial was turned back to American Home Products, which attempted to sell the show to ABC and NBC. When the two networks passed on the idea, the company entered an unusual syndicated deal with 140 stations across the country. But at the last moment, the deal fell through. *The Secret Storm* was replaced, ignominiously, by the game show *Tattletales*.

In its final episodes, complicated storylines were wrapped up at breakneck speed: Laurie killed off an attacker; Mark made his mind up to leave Laurie and return to the priesthood; Joanna Morrison found that she did not have cancer; and Brian gave up romantic designs on Amy while Kevin returned to Woodbridge. In the show's final scene, Kevin rose from his wheelchair and walked unsteadily toward Amy, who covered him with kisses. Then Valerie and the children Lisa and Danielle came in and joined the reunion. *The Secret Storm* had begun in tragedy and ended in celebration.

CAST

Amy Ames	Jada Rowland 1954–74
	Lynne Adams 1971–73
	June Carter 1960
	Beverly Lunsford 1958–60
Peter Ames	Lawrence Weber 1966–68
	Ward Costello 1964–66
	Cec Linder 1962–64
	Peter Hobbs 1954–62
Susan Ames	Judy Lewis 1964–71
	Mary McGregor 1968–69
	Frances Helm 1964
	Mary Foskett 1958–64
	Norma Moore 1958
	Rachel Taylor 1956–57
	Jean Mowry 1954–56
Jerry Ames	Stephen Bolster 1968–69
	Peter White 1965–66
	Wayne Tippit 1959–65
	Ken Gerard 1957–59

When playwright Harding Lemay took over as headwriter, Another World *evolved into a sophisticated drawing-room drama. Among the expert stage performers hired was Irene Dailey (right), who as Liz Matthews in 1975 attempted to keep the bitchy Rachel (Victoria Wyndham) from hurting Alice. (Photo courtesy of the National Broadcasting Company, Inc.)*

Violence is rarely gratuitous on serial drama, almost always growing organically from the plot and occurring at the climax of a long storyline. Here Mitch Blake (William Grey Espy) attempted to stop Janice Frame (Christine Jones) from killing Rachel in a brilliantly directed 1981 sequence taped on location in the Caribbean. (Photo courtesy of the National Broadcasting Company, Inc.)

After his Oscar nomination for Ragtime, *Howard E. Rollins, Jr. joined the cast of* Another World *in 1982 as Ed Harding. With him is Petronia Paley as his sister, Quinn. (Photo courtesy of the National Broadcasting Company, Inc.)*

Over the years, Rachel Davis (Victoria Wyndham, right) changed from villainess to vindicated heroine. She married Mac Cory (Douglass Watson, center right) and within a ten-year period, divorced him, remarried him, and then divorced him once again. In 1983, Rachel, apparently deciding the third time was a charm, again married Mac, this time in a double ceremony as Mac's son Sandy (Christopher Rich, left) wed Blaine Ewing (Laura Malone). (Ken Sherber/Kacey Assoc.)

In September 1967, Days of Our Lives *was in the midst of a dramatic trial as young Susan Hunter (Denise Alexander) was accused of the murder of her husband, David Martin, after he had caused the death of their child. With the help of her doctor, Tom Horton (Macdonald Carey, right), and her lawyer, Mickey Horton (John Clarke), Susan was acquitted on the grounds of temporary insanity. (Photo courtesy of the National Broadcasting Company, Inc.)*

Singer Bill Hayes joined Days of Our Lives *in 1970 as Doug Williams and quickly became embroiled in a romantic triangle with Susan (Denise Alexander, left) and Julie Olson (Susan Seaforth). A few years later, Hayes and Seaforth married both on and off the screen. (Photo courtesy of the National Broadcasting Company, Inc.)*

Dr. Marlena Evans (Deidre Hall) married lawyer Don Craig (Jed Allan) on March 6, 1979. (Photo courtesy of the National Broadcasting Company, Inc.)

Days of Our Lives *once again became a favorite among young fans in 1984 when Hope Williams (Kristian Alfonso) fell for antihero Bo Brady (Peter Reckell). (Photo courtesy of the National Broadcasting Company, Inc.)*

In 1972, NBC's The Doctors *won the first Emmy awarded for outstanding daytime drama. From left to right: James Pritchett as Dr. Matt Powers, Gerald Gordon as Dr. Nick Bellini, Lydia Bruce as Dr. Maggie Powers, David O'Brien as Dr. Steve Aldrich, and Elizabeth Hubbard as Dr. Althea Davis. (Photo courtesy of the National Broadcasting Company, Inc.)*

Heeeere's Johnny! In 1964, Johnny Carson appeared on The Doctors *on behalf of the then current campaign for the National Association for Mental Health. With him is Ann Williams, who then played Dr. Maggie Powers. (Author's collection.)*

ABC's Dark Shadows, *about a 200-hundred-year-old vampire who would rather quit than bite, was one of the most unusual in soap opera history. Barnabas Collins (Jonathan Frid) poses in 1968 in front of an 18th century painting of himself. (Wagner International Photos.)*

Relaxing on the set of Dark Shadows *is Jonathan Frid (left) and Louis Edmonds, who played Barnabas and Roger Collins. Buried in her script is former movie queen Joan Bennett, brushing up on her part as Elizabeth Stoddard. (Wagner International Photos.)*

A Peyton Place *scrapbook, 1965. Left to right, top row: Betty and Julie Anderson (Barbara Parkins and Kasey Rogers); Nurse Choate (Erin O'Brien-Moore); Rodney, Leslie, and Norman Harrington (Ryan O'Neal, Paul Langdon, and Christopher Connelly). Second row: Ada and Rita Jacks (Evelyn Scott and Patricia Morrow); David, Kim, and Doris Schuster (William Smithers, Kimberly Beck, and Gail Kobe). Third row, top: Matthew Swain (Warner Anderson). Bottom: Rev. Jerome Bedford (Ted Hartley). Middle: Constance and Elliot Carson and Allison Mackenzie and Eli Carson (Dorothy Malone, Tim O'Connor, Mia Farrow, and Frank Ferguson). Far right: Dr. Michael Rossi (Ed Nelson). (Courtesy of the Martin Luther King Memorial Library.)*

ABC's One Life to Live *was the first soap to consistently and successfully mix social issues into serial drama. Carla Gray (Ellen Holly) had passed for white but later accepted her black heritage. She married Captain Ed Hall (Al Freeman, Jr.) in 1973, as her mother Sadie (Lillian Hayman, in glasses) and young ward Josh (Larry Fishburne) looked on. (Daytime TV Magazine Photo.)*

Joe Riley (Lee Patterson) remarried Viki (Erika Slezak) in 1974. After Joe died in 1979, actor Lee Patterson showed up on the soap in 1986 as Tom Dennison, Joe's twin brother! (Daytime TV Magazine Photo.)

Another famous alumnus from One Life to Live *is Jameson Parker, who gave a striking performance as the selfish Brad Vernon. Joining forces with him in 1976 was the equally dynamic Nancy Pinkerton, the first actress to play one of daytime's all-time favorite villainesses, Dorian Lord. (Daytime TV* Magazine *Photo.)*

Ina Hopkin's boarding house became a haven for social outcasts on One Life to Live *in 1980. From left to right: Sally Gracie as the understanding Ina, Gerald Anthony as former pimp Marco Dane, Margaret Klenck as ambitious reporter Edwina Lewis, and Judith Light as former prostitute Karen Wolek, who attempted to break from her destructive past. Judith Light deservedly won two Emmies for her smashing performance. (*Daytime TV *Magazine Photo.)*

Writer Agnes Nixon (center), with five serial creations, is undoubtedly the single most influential force in contemporary daytime drama. Sharing the spotlight at a 1976 party are All My Children *stars Ruth Warrick (left) and Kay Campbell (right), actresses with a combined total of over a half century of soap opera work. (*Daytime TV Magazine *photo.)*

All My Children *went on location to St. Croix in 1978 for the* From Here to Eternity–*inspired honeymoon of Tom Cudahy (Richard Shoberg) and Erica Kane (Susan Lucci). (ABC.)*

ABC's Ryan's Hope, *about an Irish family who ran a bar in New York City, became the most critically acclaimed serial on the air after its premiere in 1975. From left to right: Kate Mulgrew as the spirited Mary Ryan, Helen Gallagher as the understanding Maeve Ryan, and Bernard Barrow as the lovably temperamental Johnny Ryan. (Daytime TV Magazine Photo.)*

Was Dallas *really America's prime-time answer to successful British imports such as* The Forsyte Saga *and* Upstairs, Downstairs? *Sue Ellen (Linda Gray): "Tell me, J.R., which slut are you staying with tonight?" J.R. (Larry Hagman): "Does it matter? Whoever she is, she'll be more interesting than the slut I'm looking at right now." (Courtesy of the Martin Luther King Memorial Library.)*

Lady Georgina (Lesley-Anne Down) wed the Marquis of Stockbridge (Anthony Andrews) on the final episode of Upstairs, Downstairs *in 1977. (LWT International.)*

The Young and the Restless *was a revolutionary soap, featuring potent social issues and flawlessly beautiful young performers in a rapturous presentation. On January 11, 1974, almost a year after the show's premiere, rape victim Chris Brooks (Trish Stewart) married Snapper Foster (William Gray Espy), as Greg Foster (James Houghton), Laurie Brooks (Jaime Lyn Bauer, right), and Jill Foster (Brenda Dickson, far right) looked on. (CBS.)*

Is that really Tom Selleck? On The Young and the Restless *in 1974, Laurie Brooks (Jaime Lyn Bauer) shaved off Jed Andrews (Selleck)'s moustache because it "tickled." (*Daytime TV Magazine Photo.)

General Hospital *had been popular with fans since its premiere in 1963, but when Luke and Laura were tossed into a series of love-on-the-run stories, the show took off into the ratings stratosphere. In the 1981 "Ice Princess" story, Robert Scorpio (Tristan Rogers), Laura (Genie Francis), and Luke (Anthony Geary) stole aboard the Cassadine yacht to save Port Charles from being destroyed by the evil Mikkos Cassadine. (ABC.)*

None other than Elizabeth Taylor turned up as Mikkos Cassadine's widow, Helena, who befriended Luke Spencer (Anthony Geary) but secretly cursed his marriage to Laura. (ABC.)

Luke (Anthony Geary) and Laura (Genie Francis) wed in a ceremony broadcast November 16–17, 1981. The two episodes were the highest-rated programs in the history of daytime television. (ABC.)

Although Texas *lasted only two years, it is remembered fondly for the many witty scenes between Iris Carrington (Beverlee McKinsey) and her maid, Vivien (Gretchen Oehler), who was continually appalled at her mistress's machinations. (Photo courtesy of the National Broadcasting Company, Inc.)*

Theater legend Dame Judith Anderson starred as the irrepressible matriarch Minx Lockridge in NBC's Santa Barbara, *which premiered in 1984. Louise Sorel (left) played her daughter-in-law, Augusta, and Julie Ronnie (top) played her granddaughter, Laken. (Photo courtesy of the National Broadcasting Company, Inc.)*

The Young and the Restless *began the trend of barely clothed males traipsing across the screen, a tradition continued by the Hollywood-based* Capitol, *which premiered in 1982. Capitol's executive producer John Conboy bragged that lifeguard Matt McCandless (Christopher Durham) would stay shirtless the entire summer. He did. (Jacky Winter/Copyright* Playgirl *Magazine 1984.)*

Joan Collins, John Forsythe, and Linda Evans starred in Dynasty, *one of the many popular prime-time serials that popped in the last decade. Although* Dynasty *was essentially a camp version of daytime drama, when Joan Collins, as the formidable Alexis, told a business and romantic suitor, "Nobody takes me to the cleaners and to bed in the same night," the show entered into a world of its own. (Courtesy Richard & Esther Shapiro Prods. and Aaron Spelling Prods.)*

Jerry Ames (*cont.*)	Warren Berlinger 1954–57
	Robert Morse 1954
Ellen Ames	Ellen Cobb-Hill 1954
Grace Tyrell	Eleanor Phelps 1970–72
	Margaret Barker 1969
	Marjorie Gateson 1954–69
Judge J. T. Tyrell	Russell Hicks 1954
Pauline Rysdale	Halia Stoddard 1954–70
Bruce Edwards	Ed Bryce 1955–56
	Biff McGuire 1955
Jane Edwards	Marylyn Monk 1958
	Virginia Dwyer 1955–56
	Barbara Joyce 1955
Alan Dunbar	Liam Sullivan 1971
	James Vickery 1957–67
Myra Lake Ames	June Graham 1959–63
	Joan Hotchkis 1958
Ezra Lake	Don McHenry 1959–63
	Wendell Phillips 1958
Bryan Fuller	Carl King 1958–59
Joe Sullivan	Frank Sutton 1960–61
	James Broderick 1960
Arthur Rysdale	Frank Schofield 1966–67
	John Baragrey 1962–64
	Lester Rawlins 1962
Kip Rysdale	Edward Griffith 1964–68
	David O'Brien 1963–64
	Don Galloway 1962
Jeff Nichols	James Pritchett 1960–61
Kate Lodge Ames	Polly Childs 1962
Hope Ames	Pamela Raymond 1966
Valerie Hill Ames	Lori March 1964–71
Janet Hill	Bibi Besch 1966–67
Bob Hill	Edward Winter 1969
	Justin McDonough 1967–68
	Roy Scheider 1967
Ann Wicker	Diana Muldaur 1965
Chuck Bannister	John Cunningham 1965
Paul Britton	Linden Chiles 1970
	Conard Fowkes 1969–70
	Ryan MacDonald 1966–67
	Edward Kemmer 1965–66
	Jed Allan 1964–65
	Nicolas Coster 1964; 1968–69
Brooke Lawrence	Julie Wilson 1966
George Bennett	Dan Frazer 1966
Marian Bennett	Gloria Hoye 1966
Wendy Porter	Julie Mannix 1966–68
	Rita McLaughlin 1966

Dr. Tony Porter	Arlen Dean Snyder 1966–68
Frank Carver	Robert Loggia 1972
	Jack Ryland 1971
	Laurence Luckinbill 1967–68
Mary Lou Carver	Joanna Miles 1967–68
Erik Fulda	George Reinholt 1967–68
Belle Clemens	Marla Adams 1968–74
Dan Kincaid	Bernard Barrow 1970–74
Kevin Kincaid	David Ackroyd 1971–74
	Dennis Cooney 1970–71
Tom Kane	Coe Norton 1968
Mrs. Borman	Elspeth Eric 1968
Nick Kane	Keith Charles 1968–70
Joan Borman Kane	Christina Crawford 1968–69
	Joan Crawford 1968
Archie Borman	Ken Kercheval 1968
Judge Sam Stevens	Terry O'Sullivan 1968–69
Ken Stevens	Joel Crothers 1969–71
	Gordon Gray 1968–69
Jill Stevens Clayborn	Barbara Rodell 1969–70
	Audrey Johnstone 1968–69
	Irene Bundle 1968
Hugh Clayborn	Peter MacLean 1970
Laurie Hollister	Stephanie Braxton 1970–74
	Linda DeCoff 1969
Nola Hollister	Mary K. Wells 1971
	Rosemary Murphy 1969–70
	Rita Morley 1968–69
Wilfred Hollister	Alexander Clark 1969
	Barnard Hughes 1968–69
Aggie Parsons	Jane Rose 1970–71
Dr. Ian Northcote	Alexander Scourby 1972–73
	Gordon Rigsby 1969–71
Owen Northcote	Gordon Rigsby 1969–71
Mary Lou Northcote	Clarice Blackburn 1970
Kitty Styles	Diane Ladd 1971–72
	Diana Millay 1971
Joanna Morrison	Ellen Barber 1973–74
	Audrey Landers 1972–73
Robert Landers	Dan Hamilton 1972–74
Rev. Mark Reddin	David Gale 1972–74
Stace Reddin	Gary Sandy 1973–74
Jessie Reddin	Frances Sternhagen 1973–74
Dr. Brian Neeves	Keith Charles 1973–74
	Jeffrey David Pomerantz 1972–73
Niele Neeves	Betsy von Furstenberg 1973–74
Doreen Post	Linda Purl 1973–74
Sean Childers	James Storm 1971

Cory Boucher	Terry Kiser	1971
Lisa Britton	Judy Safran	1971–74
	Terry Falls	1970
	Diane Dell	1969
Keefer	Troy Donahue	1970

SECRETS OF MIDLAND HEIGHTS
December 6, 1980–January 24, 1981   CBS

Lorimar Productions, which brought *Dallas* and other soaps to television, produced this prime-time serial aimed at the teenage audience. The premiere episode opened with a young couple in a romantic clinch, steaming their car windows. The scene switched to injured college jock Burt Carroll pulling his girlfriend, Lisa Rogers, into his hospital bed. The next scene zeroed in on Holly Wheeler and Teddy Welsh, whose parents were having a clandestine affair, as Holly pleaded with Teddy to help her lose her dreadful virginity. And so on. *Secrets of Midland Heights* catered exclusively to teenage fantasies: sadistic, gothic uncles; *Animal House*–type frat parties; hay rides; hypocritical parents; etc. Unfortunately, CBS aired the program at 10:00 P.M., E.S.T., on Saturday, when it was unlikely to hook a teenage audience. The show, written by David Jacobs and produced by Jacobs, Lee Rich, and Michael Filerman, was revised and renamed in 1982 as *Kings Crossing*, employing some of the same performers.
See KINGS CROSSING.

CAST
Holly Wheeler	Marilyn Jones
	Linda Grovernor
Martin Wheeler	William Jordan
Dorothy Wheeler	Bibi Besch
Prof. Nathan Welsh	Robert Hogan
Teddy Welsh	Daniel Zippi
Burt Carroll	Lorenzo Lamas
Lisa Rogers	Linda Hamilton
Margaret Millington	Martha Scott
Guy Millington	Jordan Christopher
Ann Dulles	Doran Clark
John Gray	Jim Youngs
Prof. Calvin Richardson	Mark Pinter

THE SEEKING HEART
July 5, 1954–December 10, 1954   CBS

Still another Procter & Gamble effort, this fifteen-minute daytime serial centered on John Adam, a doctor who worked closely with the police, and his unsatisfied wife, Grace. Adam's assistant was Dr. Robinson McKay, who realized there was something terribly wrong with her boss's marriage.

As John and Robin allied themselves professionally, they fought romantic feelings for one another. Written by Welbourn Kelley, directed by James Yarborough, and produced by Minerva Ellis, *The Seeking Heart* was seen daily at 1:15 P.M., E.S.T. It was replaced by Irna Phillips' *The Road of Life*.

<u>CAST</u>

Dr. John Adam   Scott Forbes
Grace Adam   Dorothy Lovett
Dr. Robinson McKay   Flora Campbell
With: Judith Braun, James Yarborough, and Audrey Christie.

SOAP

September 13, 1977–April 20, 1981   ABC

Before a single episode was aired, *Soap*, a supposed parody of daytime soap operas that endeavored to take *Mary Hartman, Mary Hartman* one step further, found itself the center of controversy. ABC received over 30,000 letters of protest prompted by organized religious groups, and, under mounting pressure, 15 out of 195 ABC affiliates declined to carry the prime-time serial. However, *Soap*'s initial ratings were quite high despite the tongue lashing by the Catholic Church and various Protestant groups and the critical lashing from the press.

Time wrote that "potentially affecting sexual shenanigans dissolve into mean-spirited locker-room jokes." The Catholic *Commonweal* thought the show "unremittingly juvenile," and *The New Yorker* noted, "There's a lot of random anger floating around." But others found *Soap*, which featured comic treatments of homosexuality, transsexualism, senility, exorcism, nymphomania, impotence, as well as such soap staples as organized crime, amnesia, and adultery—a breakthrough in television.

Created, produced, and written by Susan Harris, the satirical soap serial was set in Dunn's River, Connecticut, and the story centered, like most soap operas, on two families: the wealthy Tates and the middle-class Campbells. The Tate household included Chester, a businessman with a roving eye; Jessica, his dingbat wife; Corrine, their sexy daughter; Eunice, their diffident daughter; Billy, their smart-aleck teenage son; "The Major," Jessica's father, who thought he was still in the midst of World War II; and Benson, the wisecracking black cook-butler, who served as a one-man Greek chorus, commenting on the proceedings. (Benson became such a popular character that he was given his own comedy series, which did not employ the serial format, in 1979. The Tates had to hire a new butler, called Saunders.)

Jessica's sister was Mary Campbell, who was married to Burt, a blue-collar worker. Between them, they had four sons from previous marriages: Danny, who was involved in organized crime; Jodie, who was gay and thinking of a sex-change operation; Chuck, a ventriloquist who thought his dummy Bob was a real person; and Peter, a tennis jock who spent more time in bed with his students than on the courts.

Most of the first season's action focused on the investigation into the death of Peter, who was killed while taking a shower. Jessica was arrested and convicted for the murder, but at the beginning of the second season, her husband Chester confessed to the crime. Subsequent developments included Eunice's marriage to Dutch, an ex-convict; Jodie's conversion to heterosexuality; Corinne's marriage to a priest; Danny's romance with the spoiled daughter of a crime syndicate chieftain; Jessica's fling with a South American revolutionary; Burt's kidnapping by aliens; and Mary's affair with Burt's clone.

Many soap opera fans detested *Soap* because its satirizing of daytime serials was on a simplistic, often infantile, level. Ironically, the conventions of soap opera were instrumental in *Soap*'s success. Each episode ended with a series of elaborate cliff-hangers as the narrator comically asked life-or-death questions, which only served as an effective hook to reel in audiences week after week. And using the serial format, the situations and dialogue took on a sharper, funnier edge since the audience was aware of the different characters' complicated, accumulated histories. *Soap* again achieved popularity after cancellation when it was syndicated in 1981.

CAST

Jessica Tate	Katherine Helmond 1977–81
Chester Tate	Robert Mandan 1977–81
Corrine Tate	Diana Canova 1977–80
Eunice Tate	Jennifer Salt 1977–81
Billy Tate	Jimmy Baio 1977–81
The Major	Arthur Peterson 1977–81
Benson	Robert Guillaume 1977–79
Mary Dallas Campbell	Cathyrn Damon 1977–81
Danny Dallas	Ted Wass 1977–81
Jodie Dallas	Billy Crystal 1977–81
Burt Campbell	Richard Mulligan 1977–81
Peter Campbell	Robert Urich 1977
Chuck/Bob Campbell	Jay Johnson 1977–81
Saunders	Roscoe Lee Browne 1980–81
Father Tim Flotsky	Sal Viscuso 1978–79
The Godfather	Richard Libertini 1977–78
Elaine Lefkowitz	Dinah Manoff 1978–79
Claire	Kathryn Reynolds 1977–78
Carol David	Rebecca Balding 1978–81
Dutch	Donnelly Rhodes 1978–81
Sally	Caroline McWilliams 1978–79
Alice	Randee Heller 1979
Millie	Candance Azzara 1978
Leslie Walker	Marla Pennington 1979
Polly Dawson	Lynne Moody 1979–81
Dr. Alan Posner	Allan Miller 1980–81
Gwen	Jesse Welles 1980–81
Detective Donahue	John Byner 1978–80

El Pureco Valdez   Gregory Sierra   1980–81
Maggie Chandler   Barbara Rhoades   1980–81

SOMERSET

March 30, 1970–December 31, 1976   NBC

In 1970, NBC's *Another World* split into two half-hour serials, *Another World–Bay City* and *Another World–Somerset*. The latter show borrowed three characters from Bay City—lawyer Sam Lucas, his southern belle wife Lahoma Lucas, and Missy Palmer Matthews—and placed them fifty miles out of the city in the town of Somerset, population 25,000. Initially, Robert Cenedella wrote both soaps, and characters traveled freely between the two shows. In 1971, Harding Lemay took over the headwriting chores of *Another World* while *Another World–Somerset*, then called *Somerset*, was developed independently.

Cenedella concentrated on the effect the powerful Delaney family, who owned the town's mainstay, Delaney Brands, had upon the rest of the community, most notably the Grant and Cooper families. Sam Lucas's law partner was Ben Grant, who was married to Ellen. They had two teenage children, Jill and David. Laura Delaney, the dipsomaniacal heiress to the family fortune, married Rex Cooper, who brought up Laura's son Tony (by the nefarious Harry Wilson) as his own. The Delaneys (except perhaps India, a fascinating demi-goddess) never sparked the audience's imagination and the family was phased out.

When Henry Slesar became headwriter in 1971, the business intrigue and the young love stories (such as the star-crossed romance between Tony Cooper and Jill Grant) were discarded for crime and mystery stories. Slesar, who was also writing *The Edge of Night* at the time, introduced one of the most bizarre families in soap opera history, the wealthy but eccentric Moores and their many in-laws. Just who was dressing up in the middle of the night as a clown and lacing the anemic gothic heroine Andrea Moore's eggnog with poison? Was it Andrea's brother Dana, who made vague noises about becoming a writer? Her regal mother Emily, whose frosty exterior hid an even more frosty interior? Emily's insipid, fortune-hunting husband Philip? His weird, lurking son Carter? Carter's neurotic, skittish sister Zoe? Or her handsome, brooding husband Julian, a classical pianist who never tickled the ivories?

The long, well-written storyline was a fanciful conceit, but the smiling clown who haunted the family mansion for months was so insidious and unsettling that the show took on a terrifying, surrealistic air. As it turned out, Zoe—played by the remarkable theater and film actress Lois Smith—was unmasked as Jingles. She wanted Andrea out of the way because she feared her husband Julian had fallen in love with the young heroine. Afterwards, Julian decided he wanted to be a newspaper editor, and a grateful, smitten Andrea bought the local paper for him. For the next five years, through seven different writing regimes, Julian's romantic adventures, and the newspaper he worked for, were the focus of the show. Joel Crothers had been kicking around in the soaps with major roles on *Dark*

Shadows and *The Secret Storm*, but as the unlucky Julian he became one of television's most ingratiating matinee idols. After *Somerset* was cancelled, Crothers joined the cast of *The Edge of Night* as Dr. Miles Cavanaugh, a similar romantic hero.

Julian's next wife was Chrystal Ames, a former gun moll with the syndicate, who was murdered by Zoe. After finally saying good-bye to Andrea, Julian became involved with the beautiful Eve Lawrence, who was in the midst of crisis: her daughter Heather was dating Greg Mercer, who Eve realized was Heather's half-brother! When the uptight Eve was unable to provide the solace he needed, Julian married the seductive Kate Thorton. When the spoiled Victoria Paisley told Julian that Kate's "miscarriage" was an abortion, Julian divorced Kate. He tried to rekindle his romance with Eve, the love of his life, but it was too late: Eve had married Vicky's brother Ned. Sensibly, Julian fell into a stormy affair with amoral Vicky.

Meanwhile, the return of Ellen Grant and her daughter Jill Farmer (their husbands had been killed in an auto accident in Europe) triggered new stories. Jill had a series of unfortunate romances while her mother—in a move that was unusual for soap opera of the day—became involved with Dale Robinson, a handsome young man half her age. (Jameson Parker, who became a star with the detective series *Simon & Simon*, played Dale.) *Somerset*'s final storyline concentrated on Julian's attempt—with the help of two bright young reporters, Steve Slade and Carrie Wheeler—to expose organized crime in the town. By the final show, Mr. Big was caught, Steve recovered from surgery and asked Carrie to marry him, Julian reconciled with Vicky, and Heather told husband Jerry that she was going to have a baby. The final shot gathered Jerry and Heather, Julian and Vicky, and Carrie around Steve's hospital bed—all of Somerset smiling at the New Year's fadeout.

Somerset suffered from that fatal soap opera disease, the executive hot potato: too many writing, producing, cast changes; no clear-cut theme; no core family; and far too many short, fantastic plots that did not allow the audience to get its bearings. In short, there was no confidence in the show. In the 1975–76 season, *Somerset* ranked fourteenth out of fifteen daytime serials, with an average rating of 5.9, edging out only new-kid-on-the-block *Ryan's Hope*. It was replaced by Harding Lemay's *Lovers and Friends*, which utilized visiting characters from *Another World*, as *Somerset* had done in its beginning. The formidable headwriters included Cenedella, Slesar, Roy Winsor, Winifred Wolfe, A. J. Russell, and Robert J. Shaw.

CAST

Lahoma Lucas	Ann Wedgeworth 1970–73
Sam Lucas	Jordan Charney 1970–73
Missy Matthews	Carol Roux 1970
Ellen Grant	Georgann Johnson 1970–76
Ben Grant	Edward Kemmer 1970–74
Jill Grant Farmer	Susan MacDonald 1970–72; 1974
Mitch Farmer	Richard Shoberg 1971–72

David Grant	Phillip MacHale 1976
	Tom Callaway 1975–76
	Ron Martin 1970–74
Jasper Delaney	Ralph Clanton 1970
Robert Delaney	Nicolas Coster 1970–72
Peter Delaney	Len Gochman 1970–72
India Delaney	Marie Wallace 1970–72
Laura Delaney Cooper	Dorothy Stinnette 1970–73
Rex Cooper	Paul Sparer 1970–76
Tony Cooper	Barry Jenner 1974–76
	Ernest Thompson 1972–74
	Douglas Chapin 1970–71
Ginger Kurtz Cooper	Fawne Harriman 1973–76
	Renne Jarrett 1972–73
	Meg Wittner 1972
Jessica Buchanan	Wynne Miller 1970–72
Randy Buchanan	Gary Sandy 1970–72
Julian Cannell	Joel Crothers 1972–76
Zoe Cannell	Lois Smith 1972–73
Andrea Moore	Harriet Hall 1972–74
Dana Moore	Christopher Pennock 1972–73
Emily Moore Matson	Lois Kibbee 1972–73
Philip Matson	Frank Schofield 1972–73
Carter Matson	Jay Gregory 1972–73
Chrystal Ames	Diahn Williams 1973
Eve Lawrence	Bibi Besch 1973–76
Heather Lawrence	Audrey Landers 1974–76
Dr. Jerry Kane	James O'Sullivan 1974–76
Greg Mercer	Gary Swanson 1974–76
Sgt. Ruth Winter	Holland Taylor 1973–74
Doris Hiller	Gretchen Wyler 1973–74
Mark Mercer	Stanley Grover 1974
Edith Mercer	Judith Searle 1974
Kate Cannell	Tina Sloan 1974–76
Victoria Paisley	Veleka Gray 1975–76
Ned Paisley	James Congdon 1975–76
Leo Kurtz	Gene Fanning 1972–73
	George Coe 1971
Dr. Stan Kurtz	Michael Lipton 1970–74
Dr. Teri Martin Kurtz	Gloria Hoye 1973–76
Carrie Wheeler	JoBeth Williams 1975–76
Steve Slade	Gene Bua 1976
Sarah Briskin	Molly Picon 1976
	Dorothy Blackburn 1976
Tom Conway	Ted Danson 1974–76
	Michael Nouri 1974
Dale Robinson	Jameson Parker 1976
Avis Ryan	Sigourney Weaver 1976

STRANGE PARADISE

1969   Syndicated

One of the first syndicated daily serials, *Strange Paradise* was an obvious attempt to cash in on the popularity of the gothic *Dark Shadows*. Taped in Ottawa, Canada, but produced from the U.S. by Krantz Films, the half-hour serial was seen on fifty-one U.S. stations beginning in September 1969. The setting was the Caribbean island of Maljardin, and the show featured voodoo, ghosts, a Jekyll-and-Hyde leading man, and various other hair-and hell-raisers. *The New York Times* wrote of the spooky serial that it "qualifies as kookiness gone amok." The story centered on Jean Paul Desmond, who had accidentally called up the spirit of his ancestor Jacques Eloi DeMonde while attempting to bring his dead wife Erica back to life. Erica eventually broke out of her dry-ice casing to terrorize the island. Harding Lemay, who later brought *Another World* to the top of the ratings, was among the unfortunate writers.

CAST

Jean Paul Desmond	Colin Fox
Jacques Eloi DeMonde	Colin Fox
Erica Desmond	Tudi Wiggins
Helena	Tudi Wiggins
Tim Stanton	Bruce Gray
Dr. Alison Carr	Dawn Greenhalgh
Dan Forest	Jon Granik
Holly Marshall	Sylvia Feigel
Elizabeth Marshall	Paisley Maxwell
Rev. Matt Dawson	Dan MacDonald
Quito	Kurt Schiegl
Huaco	Patricia Collins
Dinah	Trudy Young

THE SURVIVORS

September 29, 1969–September 17, 1970   ABC

After forty-five motion pictures and seven husbands Lana Turner (née Julia Jean Mildred Frances Turner) at forty-nine years of age turned her attention to unconquered territory: television. Her vehicle, *The Survivors*, was one of the most expensively produced efforts ever on TV—$8 million slated for its first season—and one of the medium's all-time flops. It began as an idea of bestselling novelist Harold Robbins, who saw the show as an updated, American *Forsyte Saga* dramatized in one-hour chapters over a two-year period. (Ironically, Robbins had written the trashy bestseller *Where Love Has Gone*, a *roman à clef* about the stabbing of gangster Johnny Stompanato by Lana Turner's daughter Cheryl. Turner said she decided to let bygones be bygones.) On the basis of a nine-page synopsis—later fleshed out into a hundred-page story bible—Robbins received a contract that could have earned him over $5.5 million.

Robbins' story of two feuding banking families, however, was soon tossed out in favor of a more traditional soap opera narrative about the internal conflicts of a wealthy family. In its first ten months of filming, *The Survivors* had unloaded, in addition to Robbins, three producers, a director, a costume designer, and a story editor. The trouble-plagued production exploded when Turner complained of having to wear paste jewelry. (Fifty thousand dollars had been allocated for her wardrobe budget.) When the producer turned a deaf ear to her plea for authenticity, she slapped him. He promptly slapped her back—twice, on either cheek— and was equally promptly dismissed. Years later, in her autobiography, Turner charged that the producer had been drinking and was verbally abusing her and the costume designer.

The highly publicized premiere, playing up the glamour of its stars— Turner, George Hamilton, and Kevin McCarthy—brought in a respectable audience. But faced with savage reviews and a dwindling audience (a 10 rating with a 15 share by its fourth week), ABC decided to cut its losses and cancel after fifteen of the twenty-six planned episodes. The show was replaced by *Paris 7000*, starring George Hamilton, the only survivor from *The Survivors*. *The Survivors* returned for summer repeats in the summer of 1970 and turned up later in syndication. In 1982 Turner was still receiving small residual checks for the syndicated show, which was still playing somewhere outside the U.S. The same year, Turner was seen in a recurring role on the prime-time soap *Falcon Crest*.

The story of *The Survivors* focused on the Carlyle family, which included Baylor Carlyle, a banking czar; his son Duncan, a playboy; and his daughter Tracy, who was married to the philandering Philip Hastings. The Carlyles became entangled with South American politics and revolutionaries, which prompted the revelation that Jeffrey Hastings, Tracy's son, was also the son of Riakos, Tracy's old flame. Perhaps they should have filmed the backstage brouhaha instead.

The producers were Richard Caffey and William Frye; the directors included Michael Ritchie, who went on to direct *Smile, The Candidate*, and other feature films.

CAST

Tracy Carlyle Hastings	Lana Turner
Philip Hastings	Kevin McCarthy
Jeffrey Hastings	Jan-Michael Vincent
Baylor Carlyle	Ralph Bellamy
Duncan Carlyle	George Hamilton
Riakos	Rossano Brazzi
Belle	Diana Muldaur
Jonathan	Louis Hayward
Miguel Santerra	Robert Viharo
Marguerita	Donna Baccalla
Jean Vale	Louise Sorel
Sen. Mark Jennings	Clu Gulager

Tom Steinberg   Robert Lipton
Rosemary Price   Pamela Tiffin

TEXAS

August 4, 1980–December 31, 1982   NBC

A spin-off from NBC's ninety-minute *Another World*, *Texas* was the first daytime serial to originate in a sixty-minute format. (*Another World* mercifully retreated back to an hour.) Created by producer Paul Rauch, who had surrounded the cast of *Another World* with the most lush production values daytime had ever known, and Joyce and John William Corrington, who successfully renovated the staid *Search for Tomorrow*, *Texas* evolved from a story the Corringtons were working on about the antebellum South, called *Reunion*. But Fred Silverman, then president of NBC, told them to change direction, with the rumored promise that if the new soap was a hit in daytime, it would be moved to prime time, in the same ballpark as CBS's *Dallas*.

But *Texas* was nothing like *Dallas*. *Another World*'s most loved-hated villainess, Iris Cory Carrington Delaney Bancroft, saw a softening of her personality when transplanted to Houston. She was soon tossed into a fairy-tale romance with long-lost beau Alex Wheeler, who was the head of Houston's World Oil. (At forty, Beverlee McKinsey, who had played Iris for eight years, was anxious for a change and was threatening to leave *Another World*. She received an unprecedented billing on the new show: "*Texas*—starring Beverlee McKinsey.") While the production was elegant, the story moved at a snail's pace and the female cast, with the exception of the classy Beverlee McKinsey and the feisty Carla Borelli (as the Scarlett O'Hara–like Reena Cook), was the weakest in memory. Before the first year had ended, nearly all of the original female cast had been replaced or let go.

The reviews were uniformly bad, but *TV Guide* noted that *Texas* had its moments, most notably in the sexy costuming (Reena always seemed on the verge of spilling out of her dress) and the bitchy wit. (When Reena, still spilling, said, "I've still got my wits about me, honey," the response was, "Oh, is that what they're calling them now?") *Texas* perked up with the introduction of Iris's ex-husband Eliot Carrington (Daniel Davis, in a highly theatrical performance), a survivor of a Cambodian prison camp. When Eliot found that his son Dennis was really the natural son of Alex Wheeler, Eliot went berserk, constantly (and dramatically) flashing back to his Cambodian experiences, eventually attempting to kill Alex Wheeler.

After the Corringtons left as headwriters, two new writing regimes were introduced, first Dorothy Ann Purser and Samuel D. Ratcliffe, and then Paul Rader and Gerald Flesher. Iris went back to being her conniving old self and son Dennis also went through a personality change. The writing was sometimes interesting, but no one bothered to start a major storyline for Kin Shriner, who had been grabbed at great expense from a starring role on *General Hospital*. Desperation set in as the show actually launched a science fiction storyline. After Beverlee McKinsey left the show, the soap got a new logo, *Texas: The New Generation*. The stories became more youth-oriented and so derivative of *General Hospital*'s love-on-the-run plotlines that the scriptwriters actually allowed Lurlene, one of the show's nuttier characters, to ask about one turn of events, "You mean like Luke and Laura?" To escape the stranglehold of *General Hospital*, which aired directly opposite it, NBC moved *Texas* to a late-morning time slot.

Texas improved dramatically when Pamela K. Long, who had been playing Ashley Linden on the show, took over as headwriter. With the innovative producer Gail Kobe, a former soap actress, Long brought family drama, humor, romance, tighter plotting and pacing to the show. Two romantic triangles became immensely popular: Justin-Ashley-T.J. and Reena-Grant-Judith, the first complicated by the paternity of Ashley's son Gregory; the second by Reena's longstanding ambivalence about Justin. When the two-year-old *Texas*, which had a small but loyal audience, was cancelled on New Year's Eve 1982, it provoked the most protest mail NBC had ever received for a daytime or prime-time show.

In the final episode, Judith got out of her wheelchair and gave up her hold on Grant, thus enabling Grant to be united with Reena. The complex Justin (Jerry Lanning, in a consistently superb performance) welcomed his and Ashley's new daughter to the family. Vicky, who had lost her TV station KVIK, threw a New Year's Eve party and gave a deliberately ambiguous speech: "We have accomplished some pretty wonderful things here. Wherever you may go, you can look back on our experience here as something very special. And remember it with pride." Billy Joe led the cast in singing "Auld Lang Syne," and amid cheers, Justin proudly toasted the crowd, "To Texas!"

In the fall of 1983, *Texas* was seen in half-hour repeats on Ted Turner cable station TBS, beginning with the episodes in which Eliot attempted to kill Alex Wheeler during Iris and Alex's wedding. The repeats ended in the summer of 1984 with the episodes in which Iris, Dennis, and Paige were implicated in the murder of Chris Shaw. Gail Kobe and Pamela K. Long became *Guiding Light*'s new producer and headwriter, transforming that show into the most exciting serial of the 1983–84 season.

CAST

Iris Carrington	Beverlee McKinsey 1980–81
Dennis Carrington	Jim Poyner 1980–81
Eliot Carrington	Daniel Davis 1980–82
Alex Wheeler	Bert Kramer 1980–81
Grant Wheeler	Donald May 1981–82
Reena Cook	Carla Borelli 1980–82
Dr. Kevin Cook	Lee Patterson 1980–81
Victoria Bellman	Elizabeth Allen 1980–82
Striker Bellman	Clifton James 1981–82
	Robert Gerringer 1980–81
Justin Marshall	Jerry Lanning 1980–82
Paige Marshall	Lisby Larson 1980–82
Ginny Marshall	Barbara Rucker 1980–82

Mike Marshall	Stephen D. Newman 1980
Barrett Marshall	Stephen D. Newman 1981
Dr. Courtney Marshall	Catherine Hickland 1980–81
Dawn Marshall	Dana Kimmell 1980
Kate Marshall	Josephine Nichols 1980–82
Elena Dekker	Caryn Richmond 1980–82
Rikki Dekker	Randy Hamilton 1980–82
Max Dekker	(Charles) Jay Hammer 1981
	Chandler Hill Harben 1980–81
Terry Dekker	Shanna Reed 1980–81
Maggie Dekker	Shirley Slater 1980–81
Billy Joe Wright	John McCafferty 1980–82
Nita Wright	Ellen Maxted 1980–82
Dr. Bart Walker	Joel Colodner 1980–81
Samantha Walker	Ann McCarthy 1980–81
Clipper Curtis	Scott Stevenson 1980
Princess Jasmin Cehdi	Donna Cyrus 1980
Sheik Cehdi	Mitch Gred 1980
Col. Ahmed Al Hassin	Maher Boutros 1980
Ryan Connor	Philip Clark 1980–82
John Brady	James Rebhorn 1981–82
Vivien Gorrow	Gretchen Oehler 1981–82
Jeb Hampton	Kin Shriner 1980–81
Bernie Stokes	Michael Medeiros 1981–82
Chris Shaw	Benjamin Hendrickson 1981
Peter Parnell	Ned Schmidtke 1981
Ashley Linden	Pamela K. Long 1981–82
Gregory Linden	Damion Scheller 1981–82
Allison Linden	Terri Garber 1982
	Elizabeth Berridge 1981–82
T. J. Canfield	David Forsyth 1981–82
Mildred Canfield	Lori March 1982
Burton Canfield	Lawrence Weber 1982
	Donald Crabtree 1982
Lacey Wheeler	Lily Barnstone 1981
Brette Wheeler	Harley Kozak 1981–82
Mark Wheeler	Michael Woods 1982
	Ernie Garrett 1981–82
Judith Wheeler	Sharon Acker 1982
George St. John	Christopher Goutman 1982
Joe Foster	Tom Wiggin 1981
Bubba Wadsworth	Stephen Joyce 1981–82
Phil Roberts	Berkeley Harris 1981–82
Joel Walker	Charles Hill 1980
Ruby Wright	Dianne Thompson Neil 1981–82
Lurleen Harper	Tina Johnson 1981–82
Beau Baker	Robert Burton 1981–82
Miles Renquist	Philip English 1981–82
Mr. Hannibal	Richard Young 1981–82

Rev. Hunt Weston	Michael Longfield 1982
Margaret Ellington	Mady Kaplan 1982
Doris Hodges	Mary Pat Gleason 1982
Mavis Cobb	Dody Goodman 1982
Stella Stanton	Virginia Graham 1982

THESE ARE MY CHILDREN

January 31, 1949–February 25, 1949   NBC

This fifteen-minute soap, broadcast live from Chicago, was the first continuing daytime drama on a major network. Created and written by Irna
Phillips, *These Are My Children* was obviously based on her earliest, autobiographical radio soaps, *Painted Dreams* and *Today's Children*. Airing on
the East Coast at 5:00 P.M. daily, the serial concerned a widow who ran
a boarding house and struggled to make ends meet for her three children
and new daughter-in-law, Jean. To say this early experiment did not go
over well with critics is a major understatement. A review in *Television
World* concluded with, "There is no place on television for this type of
program, a blank screen is preferable." Norman Felton, who directed the
show, later produced two prime-time soaps, *Dr. Kildare* and *Executive Suite*.

CAST

Mrs. Henehan	Alma Platts
Patricia Henehan	Jane Brooksmith
Penny Henehan	Martha McClain
John Henehan	George Kluge
Jean Henehan	Joan Arlt
Aunt Kitty Henehan	Margaret Heneghan
Kay Carter	Eloise Kummer
Mrs. Berkovitch	Mignon Schreiber

THREE STEPS TO HEAVEN

August 3, 1953–December 31, 1954   NBC

New York City was the setting for this romantic daytime serial about the
adventures of Poco (née Mary Jane) Thurmond, a small-town girl who
dreamed of becoming a model. Created by Irving Vendig (*The Edge of
Night*), produced by Adrian Samish, and directed by Gordon Rigsby and
Norman Morgan, the show dramatized Poco's career problems and her
romance with Bill Morgan, a writer, who lived in the same brownstone
boarding house. Bill's mental problems (traumatic war memories), the
seductive Jennifer Alden, and gangster Vince Bannister got in Poco's way,
but the irrepressible heroine finally got Bill down the aisle. *Three Steps to
Heaven* was broadcast at 11:30 A.M., sandwiched between two other soap
failures, *The Bennetts* and *Follow Your Heart*. Don Pardo (*Jeopardy*) was the
announcer.

CAST

Poco Thurmond	Kathleen Maguire
	Diana Douglas
	Phyllis Hill
Bill Morgan	Mark Roberts
	Gene Blakely
	Walter Brooke
Angela	Ginger McManus
Jennifer Alden	Lori March
Mike	Joe Brown, Jr.
Charlotte Doane	Mona Bruns
Alice Trent	Laurie Vendig
Chip Morrison	Robert Webber
Vince Bannister	John Marley
Jason Cleve	Lauren Gilbert
Uncle Frank	Frank Twedwell
Nan Waring	Beth Douglas
Beth Waring	Madeline Belgard

A TIME FOR US

December 28, 1964–December 16, 1966   ABC

Premiering as *Flame in the Wind*, this half-hour daytime serial about young star-crossed love and class conflict changed its title June 28, 1965. Also changed was the name of the main family, from the ethnic Skerba to the WASPy Driscoll, thus eliminating part of the class conflict and emphasizing the romance. Produced by Joseph Hardy and written by Don Ettlinger, *A Time for Us* called upon none other than Irna Phillips for story ideas. Tom Donovan (*General Hospital*) was among the directors. The soap aired at 2:00 P.M., E.S.T., opposite *Moment of Truth* and the game show *Password*.

The main characters included Linda Driscoll, an actress who jilted Steve Reynolds; Jane Driscoll, her sister, who fell in love with Steve; Al Driscoll, their father, who ran a construction business; Martha Driscoll, Al's wife; Steve Reynolds, who worked for Al and was caught romantically between his daughters; Roxanne Reynolds, Steve's mother, who was a troublesome divorcée; Jason Farrell, Roxanne's rich and shallow father; Miriam Bentley, a busybody who teased Jason about his wife's unfaithfulness; and Dave Simon, a medical student who was Steve's best friend. Steve eventually married Jane.

CAST

Al Driscoll	Roy Poole
Martha Driscoll	Lenka Peterson
Linda Driscoll	Joanna Miles
	Jane Elliot
	Barbara Rodell

Jane Driscoll	Beverly Hayes
	Margaret Ladd
Steve Reynolds	Tom Fielding
	Gordon Gray
Roxanne Reynolds	Maggie Hayes
Craig Reynolds	Frank Schofield
Jason Farrell	Walter Coy
Leslie Farrell	Rita Lloyd
Kate Austen	Kathleen Maguire
Chris Austen	Richard Thomas
Louise Austen	Josephine Nichols
Paul Davis	Conard Fowkes
Miriam Bentley	Lesley Brooks
Dave Simon	Terry Logan
Pam	Leslie Charleson

A TIME TO LIVE

July 5, 1954–December 31, 1954   NBC

This fifteen-minute soap, broadcast from Chicago and seen on the East Coast at 10:30 A.M., centered on proofreader Julie Byron, who dreamed about becoming a reporter on a big eastern daily newspaper. She fulfilled her ambition and acquired a boyfriend, reporter Don Riker, in the bargain. In a newspaper investigation series, Julie set out to clear Greta Powers' name, although Greta's defeatism nearly caused Julie to ruin her own career. The show was created and produced by Adrian Samish. The writer was William Barrett, later of the Dyan Cannon serial *Full Circle*.

CAST

Julie Byron	Pat Sully
Madge Byron	Vi Berwick
Don Riker	John Himes
	Larry Kerr
Carl Sherman	Jack Lester
Dr. Clay	Dana Elcar
Chick Buchanan	Len Wayland
Daphne	Toni Gilman
Greta Powers	Zohra Alton
Justine Powers	John Devoe

TODAY IS OURS

June 30, 1958–December 26, 1958   NBC

Patricia Benoit was familiar to TV audiences as Nancy Remington, the nurse who married Wally Cox on *Mr. Peepers* in 1954. Four years later she starred as divorcée Laura Manning, the assistant principal of Bolton Central High School, in this daytime drama. Other characters included

Nicky, her twelve-year-old son, who felt neglected by Laura's ex-husband Karl; and Glenn Turner, architect of the new school wing, who first clashed with Laura, then fell in love with her.

Created and written by Julian Funt and David Lesan, *Today Is Ours* was cancelled after six months and was replaced by *Young Dr. Malone*, which incorporated some of *Today Is Ours'* characters and storylines. The soap aired daily for a half hour at 3:00 P.M., E.S.T., followed by *From These Roots*. Lucy Ferri and John Egan served as producers.

CAST

Laura Manning	Patricia Benoit
Nicky Manning	Peter Lazar
Karl Manning	Patrick O'Neal
Leslie Manning	Joyce Lear
Glenn Turner	Ernest Graves
Betty Winters	Nancy Sheridan
Maxine Wells	Barbara Loden
Adam Holt	John McGovern
Rhoda Spencer	Audrey Christie

UPSTAIRS, DOWNSTAIRS
January 6, 1974–May 1, 1977   PBS

It is estimated that about one billion viewers in forty countries watched *Upstairs, Downstairs* before the concluding fifty-second episode in 1977. Produced by BBC on the heels of the successful *The Forsyte Saga*, the serial chronicled the fortunes of the Bellamy family, who lived upstairs at 165 Eaton Place in London, and the foibles of their domestic staff, who worked downstairs.

The show spanned the Edwardian age (King Edward VII visited the Bellamys in one episode); World War I; the tumultuous '20s; the Wall Street crash; 1930 and the long-anticipated weddings of Hudson, the butler, to Mrs. Bridges, the cook, and Lady Georgina to her marquis. (Lesley-Anne Down, who played Georgina, later became an international film star; Anthony Andrews, who played the marquis, later starred in the television classic *Brideshead Revisited*.) The British serial became so popular in the U.S. that CBS created an American version in 1975. The highly touted but unappealing *Beacon Hill*, about Irish-American gentry and their Irish immigrant servants in Boston during the '20s, barely lasted three months.

The idea for the serial originated with Eileen Atkins and Jean Marsh. (The latter played Rose, the maid.) It was developed and produced by John Hawkesworth, who wanted to create a microcosm of British society by using the Bellamy family, counterpointed by the downstairs staff, to gauge the changing social and political mores of the times. In a rave review, *The New York Times* called *Upstairs, Downstairs* "soap opera" but of "superb vintage"—forgetting to mention the fact that American soaps had often used a rich family-poor family counterpoint to reflect contemporary social change long before *Upstairs, Downstairs.*

   The executive producer was Rex Firkin and the script editor was Alfred Shaughnessy. The writers included Hawkesworth, Shaughnessy, Rosemary Anne Sisson, Jeremy Paul, and Anthony Skene. The directors included Bill Bain, Cyril Coke, Derek Bennett, Lionel Harris, and Christopher Hodson. The show spawned two books: a novel, *Upstairs, Downstairs* (Doubleday) by John Hawkesworth; and Mollie Hardwick's *The World of Upstairs, Downstairs* (Holt), an illustrated social history of the period that, unlike the novel, had nothing to do with the serial's fictional characters.

CAST

Richard Bellamy	David Langton
James Bellamy	Simon Williams
Virginia Bellamy	Hannah Gordon
Hazel Bellamy	Meg Wynn Owen
Elizabeth Bellamy	Nicola Pagett
Lady Marjorie Bellamy	Rachel Gurney
Rose	Jean Marsh
Angus Hudson	Gordon Jackson
Edward	Christopher Beeny
Daisy	Jacqueline Tong
Kate Bridges	Angela Baddeley
Aunt Prue	Joan Benham
Sarah	Pauline Collins
Lady Georgina	Lesley-Anne Down
Frederick	Gareth Hunt
Lily	Karen Dotrice
Ruby	Jenny Tomasin
Alfred	George Innes
Emily	Evin Crowley
The Marquis	Anthony Andrews
King Edward VII	Lockwood West

VALIANT LADY

October 12, 1953–August 16, 1957   CBS

The only thing this TV serial had in common with its radio version was its title. The radio version, which had an initial run from 1938 to 1946 and a subsequent outing from 1951 to 1952, dramatized Joan Barrett's struggle to keep her "brilliant but unstable husband" firmly on the "pathway to success." The TV version, which was broadcast from New York live between 12:00 and 12:15 P.M., E.S.T., concerned another valiant lady, Helen Emerson. Included in Helen's family were her inventor husband Frank, their nine-year-old daughter Kim; their nineteen-year-old son Mickey, who was in love with Bonnie, a married woman; and their seventeen-year-old daughter Diane, who eloped with a divorced man but returned unwed to await Helen's consent to the marriage.

When Helen was widowed in the first year, much of the story concerned her struggle to adjust to loneliness and the family's lower standard of living. When Helen wasn't worrying about money, she stewed over her children's many problems. When Mickey (played by James Kirkwood, who later won a Pulitzer Prize for *A Chorus Line*) put his foot down to the overbearing Lewis Wilcox, father of Mickey's fiancée, a proud Helen finally gave her seal of approval to the marriage of Mickey to Roberta. Afterwards, Helen enjoyed a semi-tempestuous courtship with Governor Lawrence Walker, making it legal on Valentine's Day, 1957.

Screen star Nancy Coleman (*King's Row, Mourning Becomes Electra*) starred as Helen for the first year, but left the show complaining about the fast-paced world of soap opera ("I have no chance for a social life."). On December 13, 1954, Flora Campbell, the star of TV's first network soap opera *Faraway Hill*, took over as Helen and stayed with the mildly successful show the rest of its run. The serial was created by Allan Chase (who also co-created *Days of Our Lives*); produced by Leonard Blair and Carl Green; written by Charles Elwyn; and directed by the talented trio, Herb Kenwith (producer of *Diff'rent Strokes*), Ted Corday (co-creator of *Days of Our Lives*), and Ira Cirker (*Another World*).

CAST

Helen Emerson	Flora Campbell 1954–57
	Nancy Coleman 1953–54
Frank Emerson	Jerome Cowan 1953
Kim Emerson	Bonnie Sawyer 1954–57
	Lydia Reed 1953–54
Mickey Emerson	James Kirkwood, Jr. 1953–57
Diane Emerson Soames	Lelia Martin 1956–57
	Sue Randall 1955–56
	Dolores Sutton 1954–55
	Anne Pearson 1953–54
Hal Soames	Earl Hammond 1954–55
Bonnie Withers	Shirley Egleston 1955
	Joan Loring 1954–55
Captain Chris Kendall	Lawrence Weber 1954–55
Elliott Norris	Terry O'Sullivan 1955
Joey Gordon	Martin Balsam 1955
Linda Kendall	Frances Helm 1955
Roberta Wilcox	Betty Cakes 1956–57
Gov. Lawrence Walker	John Graham 1956–57

With: Margaret Hamilton and Ann Louise.

THE VERDICT IS YOURS

September 2, 1957–September 28, 1962   CBS

This daytime courtroom drama was not really a continuing story, except that each case could stretch over nine episodes before coming to a conclusion. It contained many of the ingredients that make soap operas popular, and although the shows were unscripted, the drama could be considered an anthology serial. Veteran actors were handed a short outline of the situation and were expected to improvise when cross-examined. There was a short rehearsal that consisted of a quick camera runthrough to time the show. To decide the case, twelve members of the studio audience were selected to play jurors.

Often the actresses—the weepier the better—and the prosecutors—played by real lawyers—got carried away, losing themselves totally in the situations. Most of the time the actress became hysterical and would have to be calmed down before continuing, but one time a lawyer became so angry with the way his case was going that he stormed out of the courtroom, leaving three minutes of air time to fill. Jim McKay (later of ABC's *Wide World of Sports*), who played a court reporter, feverishly ad-libbed the show's final minutes. Legal groups across the country applauded the program's realism. *TV Guide* found it "contrived" but "fascinating." Eugene Burr produced the show, and Robert Simon was the legal advisor. A prime-time version ran briefly on CBS in 1958. The daytime *Verdict Is Yours* was the half hour lead-in at 3:00 P.M., E.S.T., for two popular fifteen-minute soaps, *The Brighter Day* and *The Secret Storm*.

CAST

Court Reporters	Jim McKay
	Bill Stout
	Jack Whittaker
Court Bailiff	Mandel Kramer

With: Esther Ralston (*Our Five Daughters*), Forrest Compton (Mike Karr on *The Edge of Night* 1971 to 1984), Audrey Peters (Vanessa Sterling on *Love of Life* 1959 to 1980), and Ellen McRae (who later changed her name to Ellen Burstyn).

WAY OF THE WORLD

January 3, 1955–October 7, 1955   NBC

Although anthology serials, which dramatize different stories over a period of days, never caught on with daytime audiences, NBC had great faith in the format. *Way of the World* presented stories adapted from women's magazines over a period of a week or more, as the storyline merited. An actress played the part of hostess Linda Porter, who introduced the show as offering "a variety of plays reflecting the emotions and reactions of the world in which we live." "In the Defense of Eve Peterson," for example, dramatized an actress's reaction to her husband's death. Another story found a group of survivors from a plane crash stranded, a la *Lifeboat*, in the wilds of Newfoundland, and dramatized the changes the frozen wasteland made upon them: a rich woman saw the emptiness of material possessions and a man decided to give himself up to face a murder charge. *Way of the World* was broadcast of 10:30 A.M., E.S.T., ignominiously following *Ding, Dong School*. The writers included William Kendall Clarke, Harry W. Junkin, and Anne Howard Bailey.

CAST

Linda Porter   Gloria Louis

With: Claudia Morgan, Phillip Reed, Anne Burr, Margaret Hamilton, Gloria Strook, Lilia Skala, Constance Ford (Ada Davis on *Another World* since 1967), Addison Powell, Kathleen Maguire, Thomas Tryon (film star turned bestselling novelist), Meg Mundy, Ethel Remey, William Prince, Louise Allbritton, Margaret Heneghan, and Gena Rowlands (as Paula Graves).

WHERE THE HEART IS

September 8, 1969–March 23, 1973   CBS

Created by Margaret DePriest and Lou Scofield, former writers of *The Edge of Night*, this was a wonderfully bizarre daytime serial centering on sexual intrigues in the Hathaway and Prescott families. Everybody in the suburban town of Northcross, Connecticut, seemed to be simultaneously in love with two or three other individuals; pregnant or working on it; living with each other out of wedlock (risqué for soap operas of the day); or cheating on their lovers with their spouses! Even the stalwart Kate Hathaway, who was always to be counted upon in a crisis, took to hearing Joan of Arc voices, falling into schizophrenic fantasies, wearing Frederick's of Hollywood scanties, and dancing lewdly in front of children.

Fans remember the sexual roundelay of this show with hilarious affection chiefly because of the top-notch acting by a strong cast headed by James Mitchell (a multiple Emmy nominee as Palmer Cortlandt on *All My Children*), the lush direction of Richard Dunlap and Bill Glenn (who took their formidable talents to *The Young and the Restless*), and the sharp writing of Pat Falken Smith, Claire Labine, and Paul Avila Mayer. Although the ratings were quite good—a 6.8 when the cast was informed of the show's cancellation on February 12, 1973—CBS felt that the masses were not cottoning to the revelry, and that the cult audience the show was attracting was not what the advertisers wanted. Cancelled the same day as *Love Is a Many Splendored Thing*, it was replaced by the even more avant garde *The Young and the Restless*.

The story was a triumph of well-played farce: Julian Hathaway, a widowed English professor, married Mary, who was really in love with Julian's son Michael. Villainess Vicky Lucas exploited the situation by getting pregnant by the unhappy Michael and marrying him. After Vicky lost her baby, she vindictively pushed Mary, also pregnant, down a flight of stairs. Vicky was then committed to a mental institution, only to make a major comeback later. After divorcing the bitchy Vicky, Michael married the equally bitchy Liz Rainey. Liz had an affair with Michael's father, Julian, and became pregnant. Next, Liz made Mary think that Julian was carrying on with Loretta Jardin, a recovering alcoholic and a student of Robert Browning.

As the cancellation date grew closer, the storylines started to wind up with breathtaking dexterity. Liz admitted that she got pregnant "on purpose," and Julian, unimpressed by her audacity, suggested she pack her bags. Michael divorced Liz and remarried his ex-wife Vicky, who had been released from the institution. Meanwhile, Steve had married Julian's sister, Kate Hathaway. While suffering from amnesia, Steve became involved with Ellie Jardin, who was later murdered. Steve and Kate adopted Ellie's mute son, Peter, who later died in a fire. Other characters involved in the major storylines included Allison Jessup, Julian and Kate's sister; Dr. Hugh Jessup, Allison's husband; and Christine Cameron, who had an illegitimate child by Hugh Jessup. In 1972, Despo, the Andy Warhol star, had a two-week running role.

CAST

Julian Hathaway	James Mitchell 1969–73
Mary Hathaway	Diana Walker 1969–73
Michael Hathaway	Gregory Abels 1969–73
Vicky Lucas Hathaway	Lisa Richards 1972
	Robyn Millan 1969–71
Ed Lucas	Joseph Mascolo 1970–72
	Charles Cioffi 1969–70
	Mark Gordon 1969
Allison Jessup	Louise Shaffer 1969–73
Roy Archer	Stephen Joyce 1969–70
Dr. Hugh Jessup	David Cryer 1970–73
	Rex Robbins 1970
Ben Jessup	Daniel Keyes 1969–72
Kate Hathaway Prescott	Diana van der Vlis 1969–73
Steve Prescott	Ron Harper 1970–73
	Laurence Luckinbill 1969–70
Christine Cameron	Delphi Harrington 1969–73
	Terry O'Connor 1969
Dr. Joe Prescott	William Post, Jr. 1970–73
Terry Prescott	Ted LePlat 1971–72
	Douglas Ross 1970–71
Nan Prescott	Katherine Meskill 1970–72
Earl Dana	Bernard Barrow 1969–70
Howard Snowden	Thomas McDermott 1969
Amy Snowden	Clarice Blackburn 1971–73
Lois Snowden	Jeanne Ruskin 1970–72
Stella O'Brien	Bibi Osterwald 1969–72
Arthur Saxton	Bernard Kates 1969–71
Helen Wyatt	Meg Myles 1970–71
Tony Monroe	David Bailey 1969–70
Ruth Monroe	Nancy Franklin 1969–70
Ellie Jardin	Zohra Lampert 1970–71
Peter Jardin	Michael Bersell 1970–73
Loretta Jardin	Alice Drummond 1971–73
Margaret Jardin	Rue McClanahan 1971–72
	Barbara Baxley 1971
John Rainey	Peter MacLean 1971–73
Liz Rainey Hathaway	Tracy Brooks Swope 1971–73

Adrienne Harris	Priscilla Pointer 1972–73
Laura Blackburn	Marsha Mason 1971
Athena Stefanopolis	Despo 1972
Daniel Hathaway	Joseph Dolen 1972–73
Dr. Hollis Forbes	Joseph Gallison 1972
Jeffrey Jordan	Geoffrey Scott 1972
Robert Jardin	Keith Charles 1972

A WOMAN TO REMEMBER
February 21, 1949–July 15, 1949   DuMont

For many years *A Woman to Remember*, broadcast over the DuMont network on the East Coast, was considered to be television's first continuing serial. However, several efforts predate that effort. In 1946 there was a single-day airing of the radio serial *Big Sister* in Chicago, and the same year a thirteen-part series called *War Bride* was run on a G.E. station in Schenectady. Three weeks before the premiere of *A Woman to Remember*, NBC presented on its TV network Irna Phillips' *These Are My Children*, which lasted all of four weeks. Another DuMont serial, *Faraway Hill*, which premiered in 1946, is now thought to be TV's first network soap.

Most of the confusion seems to have arisen from some magazine articles and books that have placed *A Woman to Remember*'s premiere in 1947. Actually, the show premiered during the daytime, Monday, February 21, 1949. On Monday, May 2, 1949, the serial was switched to an evening slot, airing daily on the DuMont network from 7:30 to 7:45 P.M., E.S.T. It was cancelled Friday, July 15, 1949. *A Woman to Remember* was about— of all things—a *radio* serial. The heroine was Christine Baker, a radio soap opera star whose romantic and professional activities were often thwarted by her scheming rival Carol Winstead. Other characters included Steve Hammond, Christine's love interest; Bessie Thatcher, Christine's actress friend; and Charley Anderson, a sound man.

Charley Anderson was played by Frankie Thomas, who later found serial stardom as the lead in *Tom Corbett, Space Cadet*. His mother, Mona Bruns, who had a small part on *A Woman To Remember*, described the behind-the-scenes rehearsals and tapings as extremely hectic. The studio bathroom served as dressing room, the ventilation was poor, the sets were cluttered and the backdrops crude, and the actors were badly paid. One day when the air conditioning broke down completely and five technicians passed out from heat exhaustion, Bruns had the line on the show "I just had a tooth pulled." On the air, she said, "I've just had a pooth tulled." But her blooper diverted the actors's attention and none of the performers, who were trying very hard not to laugh, fainted.

John Raby, the male lead, remembered playing a scene with an actress who panicked on the air and attempted to bolt from the set. Raby grabbed her, pushed her into a chair, and kept her pinned there. "I can *guess* what you came to tell me," he said desperately. Then he proceeded to say her lines along with his own. Raby claims that afterwards he ran to the bathroom and threw up. *A Woman to Remember* was taped in a studio in

Wanamaker's department store on a budget of $1,750 a week with a three hour rehearsal period and only one camera filming the action. But from such humble beginnings, soap opera would blossom. The show was created and written by John Haggart. Bob Steele served as the producer and director. The show, which followed *Captain Video* on DuMont, was presented without a sponsor.

<u>CAST</u>

Christine Baker	Patricia Wheel
Steve Hammond	John Raby
Carol Winstead	Joan Catlin
Bessie Thatcher	Ruth McDevitt
Charley Anderson	Frankie Thomas

With: Mona Bruns and Frank Thomas, Sr.

WOMAN WITH A PAST
February 1, 1954–July 2, 1954   CBS

Constance Ford has long been regarded as one of the finest American actresses. After a critically acclaimed career in the theater, she was seen on screen as Sandra Dee's memorably mean mama in *A Summer Place*, in the Warren Beatty film *All Fall Down*, and in the Joan Crawford hospital drama *The Caretakers*. She is best remembered, however, for her dazzling, intense performances on prime-time television during its Golden Age and afterwards: *Kraft Theater; Alfred Hitchcock Presents; The Untouchables; Naked City; East Side, West Side; Twilight Zone; Dr. Kildare;* and *Perry Mason*.

In 1954, Ford starred in her own daytime serial, *Woman With a Past*, which premiered the same day as *The Secret Storm*. She played Lynn Sherwood, a New York dress designer involved in a myriad of romantic adventures. Other characters included Diane, Lynn's seven-year-old daughter; Pegs, Lynn's sister, a school teacher; Steve, Lynn's romantic interest; and Sylvia, Lynn's ruthless rival. Sylvia used her rich husband to back Lynn's dress shop and tried to get Sylvia to shy away from Steve. Meanwhile, Sylvia's convict husband arrived in town with his vodka and tonic-sipping girlfriend, Tiffany Buchanan, to claim daughter Diane. The serial was created and written by Mona Kent. It aired for a quarter hour daily at 4:00 P.M., E.S.T., followed by *The Secret Storm*. Afterwards, Ford played Rose Peterson on *Search for Tomorrow* and Eve Morris on *The Edge of Night* before settling down in 1967 on *Another World* as Ada Davis (Downs McGowan Hobson), where she has been delighting audiences ever since.

<u>CAST</u>

Lynn Sherwood	Constance Ford
Diane Sherwood	Barbara Myers
	Felice Camargo
Pegs	Ann Hegira
Steve Rockwell	Gene Lyons

Sylvia Rockwell	Geraldine Brooks
	Mary Sinclair
Gwen	Jean Stapleton
Tiffany Buchanan	Linda Laubach

A WORLD APART

March 30, 1970–June 25, 1971   ABC

Created by Irna Phillips' adopted daughter Katherine, *A World Apart* was obviously based on the life of Irna Phillips, who served as story editor for the show. The story concerned Betty Kahlman, a never-married soap opera writer who, like Irna Phillips, adopted two children. When Betty married Russell Barry, the show focused on the problems of a middle-aged couple coping with the generation gap. The theme was people striving to understand one another but often finding themselves "a world apart." For a time the married leads were played by William Prince and Augusta Dabney, who were married offscreen. (They had previously played a married couple on *Young Dr. Malone*.)

The Sims family were supposed to serve as a foil for the somewhat stormy Kahlmans, but the Sims still had their share of misunderstood youth. The understanding Dr. Ed Sims and his ultra-conservative wife Adrian found themselves butting heads at every turn with daughter Becky, especially when Becky fell under the spell of flower children Bud Whitman and Julie Stark. The soap opera angle (as Betty confided in associate serial writer Meg Johns and lawyer T. D. Drinkard, who reviewed Betty's scripts for accuracy) was played down later in the run as Betty found her new marriage a happy one.

Creator Katherine L. Phillips also served as headwriter, followed by Richard and Suzanne Holland. The show was produced by Tom Donovan, and the bright cast was directed by Donovan and Walter Gorman. *A World Apart* was seen on the East Coast at 12:30 P.M., opposite *Search for Tomorrow*, which was pulling in huge ratings at the time.

CAST

Betty Kahlman Barry	Augusta Dabney
	Elizabeth Lawrence
Patrice Kahlman	Susan Sarandon
Chris Kahlman	Matthew Cowles
Russell Barry	William Prince
Dr. Ed Sims	James Noble
Adrian Sims	Kathleen Maguire
Becky Sims	Erin Connor
Nancy Condon	Susan Sullivan
Jack Condon	Stephen Elliott
Dr. John Carr	Robert Gentry
T. D. Drinkard	Tom Ligon
Meg Johns	Anna Minot
Oliver Harrell	David Birney

Matt Hampton	Clifton Davis
Olivia Hampton	Jane White
Linda Peters	Heather MacRae
Dr. Nathaniel Fuller	John Devlin
Louise Turner	Carol Williard
Fred Turner	Nicolas Surovy
Bud Whitman	Kevin Conway
Dr. Neil Stevens	Albert Paulsen
Julie Stark	Dorothy Lyman

THE WORLD OF MR. SWEENEY

June 30, 1954–December 31, 1955   NBC

After a season as a continuing skit on *The Kate Smith Hour, The World of Mr. Sweeney* became a regular prime-time serial in the summer of 1954, broadcast live from New York 7:30 to 7:45 P.M., E.S.T., on Tuesdays, Wednesdays, and Fridays. On October 4, 1954, it became a daily daytime comic serial, airing at 4:00 P.M. It starred veteran character actor Charles Ruggles (*Charley's Aunt, Bringing Up Baby*) as Cicero P. Sweeney, owner of a general store and the insistent sage and raconteur in the small town of Mapleton. The other regulars included Cicero's daughter Marge (Helen Wagner, who later played Nancy Hughes on *As the World Turns* from 1960 to today) and Marge's son Kippie. *TV Guide* called the show the kind of "genuine solid TV fare that the medium has been neglecting in the past few years in favor of more hoopla, more noise and a good deal of more pretense." It was produced by Sam Schiff and directed by Alan Neuman.

CAST

Cicero P. Sweeney	Charles Ruggles
Marge Franklin	Helen Wagner
Kippie Franklin	Glenn Walken
Alice Franklin	Mimi Strongin
Liz Thompson	Helen Warnow
Sue Thompson	Susan Odin
Timmy Thompson	Jimmy Baird
Abigail Millikan	Betty Garde
Ed	Bob Hastings
Henrietta	Janet Fox
Eva	Lydia Reed

THE YOUNG AND THE RESTLESS

March 26, 1973–   CBS

More than *General Hospital, The Young and the Restless* must be considered the most revolutionary serial of the '70s—a soap that broke all the rules, both in style and story content. Created by William J. Bell and Lee Phillip, the drama featured both Cinderella-like romantic fantasy and characters bursting into song, tempered by large doses of contemporary social controversy. Perhaps even more innovative was the rapturous presentation: a lush atmosphere of swirling background music, imaginative lighting effects, sweeping camera movements, extremely attractive young people, creamy orange lipsticks, and semi-nudity.

The Young and the Restless took off like a rocket and remained consistently among the most popular daytime shows. This show set off a rash of muscular leading men traipsing about in boxer shorts and towels on other shows. It also started the trend for more youthful, sexier female apparel. After just three years on the air, the half-hour show had snagged the Emmy for Outstanding Series, the number-one spot in the ratings, and reams of publicity in the fan magazines. It had also produced the biggest soap stars of the day: Trish Stewart, William Grey Espy, and Janice Lynde—all of whom eventually left the show and were replaced by other, almost equally popular performers.

Set in Genoa City, Wisconsin, *The Young and the Restless* centered on two families, the rich Brooks, who ran the city newspaper, and the low-income Fosters, who struggled against economic adversity. Stuart Brooks and his stylish wife Jennifer had four beautiful, talented daughters: Leslie, a concert pianist; Lauralee, a free-spirited novelist (*Naked at Dawn*, *In My Sister's Shadow*, etc.); Chris, a reporter; and Peggy, a student. Liz Foster, a hard-working domestic, was the understanding mother of Snapper (William Jr.), a doctor; Greg, a young lawyer; and Jill, a beautician.

Of course, with such a classic soap structure, the show inevitably highlighted a strong, star-crossed romance between Chris and Snapper, which was complicated by both Stuart Brooks' disapproval and Chris's hesitation in participating in premarital sex. While such vivid discussions of sex were highly unusual for soaps, *The Young and the Restless* stepped further into controversy with an extended rape storyline and trial when George Curtis (played by the then unknown Tony Geary) attacked Chris Brooks. Other shows had touched on rape, mostly in marital situations, but no other soap had delved into the issue with such thoroughness, exploring the legal, emotional, psychological, and social ramifications of the act.

The Young and the Restless continued its relevance campaign for years, dramatizing such social issues as euthanasia (Liz Foster pulling the plug on her suffering husband), alcoholism (Kay Chancellor), inner city medical and legal care (Snapper and Greg Foster), obesity (Joann Curtis), breast cancer (Jennifer Brooks), mental illness (Leslie Brooks), father-daughter incest (Nick Reed and daughters Casey and Nikki), eating disorders (Traci Abbot), vasectomy (Victor Newman), problems of the handicapped (Carole Robbins), and, again, rape (this time, Peggy, Chris's younger sister).

While the show was often successful in delving into such issues, the presentation could often be heavy-handed, with the young characters barking out statistics. (Question: "Did you know *one out of ten* girls is a mother before the age of eighteen?" Answer: "Wow! That's a mindblower! What can we do?") The show was far more successful when it took care to integrate information into the drama, such as when Snapper and Dr. Casey Reed amusingly and sensually demonstrated the Heimlich manuever.

Through the years, the focal point of many of these stories was Kay Chancellor, a lonely, bitter socialite whose parade had passed her by. Kay attempted to drown her sorrows in stableboys and vodka, but with the help of her son Brock and her friend Liz, Kay ultimately came to appreciate herself and make a comeback in life. A deep friendship with Joann, a woman with a weight problem (in one grotesque episode Joann angrily devoured a macaroni casserole and a sheetcake), evolved into a relationship with positive homosexual overtones. With the audience reaction over-whelmingly negative, the lesbian storyline—the first real homoerotic plot in daytime television—was quickly truncated, marking the first time *The Young and the Restless* backed away from controversy. In 1984, Kay was again the focus of an unusual storyline. Actress Jeanne Cooper, who had played Kay since the end of 1973, opted to have cosmetic surgery; the show taped Cooper's operation, airing the explicit footage as Kay followed Cooper's lead in an extremely well done onscreen story about plastic surgery.

While social controversy was certainly part of *The Young and the Restless*, it was the fairy-tale romances of Laurie and Leslie Brooks that brought about such fierce audience loyalty. The sisters fought tooth and nail over mystery man Brad Eliot for years, then found themselves butting heads over Lance Prentiss, a wealthy jet-setter. Thus began the show's most memorable romances, a relationship as complex as it was alliterative: Leslie loved Lance but Lance married her lusty sister Laurie. Lance's brother Lucas married Leslie when Leslie became pregnant with Lance's child. But Lucas, married to Leslie, loved Laurie. . . . The stories were played out on lush, international settings, with swooning romanticism and beau-tiful characters bursting into songs such as Cole Porter's "It's All Right With Me" and Harold Arlen's "The Man That Got Away."

As viewers continued to be intoxicated with the show's escapist romantic fantasy, Jaime Lyn Bauer's Laurie emerged as the soap's central heroine. (One of Laurie's early victims was played by Tom Selleck. Their eventual romantic clinch, as Selleck's Jed Andrews stepped out of a shower into the awaiting arms of Laurie, has been called the most erotic sequence ever on daytime television.) Laurie had mellowed from her naughty early days and garnered a large share of audience sympathy over the years. Jaime Lyn Bauer's departure from the show in 1982 marked a renewed focus on the younger characters.

Laurie's mantle of naughtiness was inherited by a new character, fun-loving Nikki Reed. After marrying and divorcing Greg Foster, Nikki embarked on a career as a stripper, and *The Young and the Restless* showcased her talent in a series of wild burlesque shows. (Having a mostly female audience, the soap was also quick to employ the stripping services of John Gibson, a Chippendale nightclub dancer and former *Playgirl* pin-up. Gib-son's character, Jerry Cashman, was later involved in an extended storyline with Kay Chancellor.) Like Laurie, Nikki soon mellowed with the love of a new mystery man, Victor Newman, a man attempting to escape his unhappy past.

Victor and Nikki's romance was packed with so much intrigue that clips from *The Young and the Restless* were shown in the comedy film *Mr.*

Mom, in which a househusband became addicted to soap operas. This was not the first time a clip from *The Young and the Restless* was used effectively in the movies. In the acclaimed 1976 melodrama *Taxi Driver*, an alienated Robert De Niro (who had once appeared on *Search for Tomorrow*) watched a romantic scene between Jill Foster and Brock Reynolds before smashing the TV set with his foot.

By the turn of the decade, headwriter Bell had introduced members of two new families, anti-hero Jack Abbott and the adventurous teenager Paul Williams. By now, most of the Brooks and Foster families had been written out, and with the expansion of the show to an hour, Bell reinstated his original rich family/poor family concept by moving the new families to the forefront of the drama. The wealthy Abbott family was headed by John Abbott, the owner of Jabot Cosmetics, who became the new husband of Jill Foster. John's children by his ex-wife, Dina, who had deserted the family years before, were Jack, a scheming playboy; Ashley, a beautiful, ambitious businesswoman; and Traci, an overweight college student. Their middle-class counterparts were Carl and Mary Williams, a policeman and his wife, and their children Paul, Steve, and Patty—the latter exploited by the busy Jack Abbott.

In 1982, John Conboy, the producer who had brought so much stylistic excellence to the show, left to work on the new CBS serial *Capitol*. Bell and H. Wesley Kenney became the new executive producers and together brought a new sharpness to the show, not only reactivating the original theme, but modernizing and improving the often-dated "hip" dialogue, which had always weighed down the drama. Through the years, the male characters consistently employed the same speech pattern and phrases ("My God, man!" was a favorite) while Laurie and Nikki constantly referred to "something heavy going on." *The Young and the Restless*, which had been always expertly plotted, had a new, sophisticated sound and appeal.

A year after the renovation, the still highly rated show nabbed the Emmy as Outstanding Daytime Drama. With the appealing new leads and with song once again integrated into the show, the daily tear-stained drama had a rock-solid following. By 1984, it deposed *General Hospital* from the top spot in daytime. The show celebrated its zoom to the top with the wedding of Nikki Reed to Victor Newman, the show's most eligible bachelor. The four Brooks sisters returned for the festivities, as did several other favorite characters from the past, including Casey Reed, Kay Chancellor's ex-husband Derek Thurston, and Kay's sexy, Bible-thumping son, Brock Reynolds.

By 1985, *The Young and the Restless* was in formidable shape, ironically avoiding the young love trend it had started years ago. Instead, the show focused on the problems of three older women: Dina Abbott's attempt to conceal her past; JoAnna Manning's desire to reconcile with her daughter; and Kay Chancellor's alcoholism and struggle for self-respect.

More unusual was the development of the show's first black storyline. Other soaps had featured romances between blacks, but these love stories were invariably presented in a careful, realistic manner with social points woven into the drama. But *The Young and the Restless* showered its two black lovers with the same lush, swirling, fairy-tale romanticism that characterized all the show's best love stories. Tyrone and Amy's adventures could just as well have been written for whites. Then the show made a 180-degree turn when Tyrone was forced to go undercover and disguise himself as a white man. The drama switched back and forth intriguingly from fairy tale to social document—the entertaining one-two punch which always fascinated fans of *The Young and the Restless*.

The show once again took the Emmy's top prize in the 1985–86 season and ran neck and neck, weekly, in the ratings with *General Hospital*, daytime's consistently highest rated drama. There was sheer irony here: *General Hospital* was fast, furious, frenzied while *The Young and the Restless* moved at a snail's pace, often humorlessly, redundantly. But the atmosphere remained luxurious, the stories strong, the performers indolently gorgeous. There were tears (Nikki's debilitating illness), candlelight romance (Victor-Ashley), corporate intrigue (Jack-Jill-John), and relevance (teenage pregnancy, baby selling, the influence of suggestive rock lyrics).

Best of all was the continuation of Jill and Kay's feud—now daytime's longest storyline—complete with thirteen-year-old flashbacks (the original footage, not re-creations) and a custody battle over Jill's son Phillip. The show reverberated with emotion, continuity, regret. *The Young and the Restless* is a soap opera and a half.

CAST

Lauralee Brooks	Jaime Lyn Bauer 1973–82; 1984
Leslie Brooks	Victoria Mallory 1977–82; 1984
	Janice Lynde 1973–77
Chris Brooks	Trish Stewart 1973–78; 1984
	Lynne Topping 1979–82
Peggy Brooks	Pamela Peters 1973–81; 1984
	Patricia Everly 1979
Jennifer Brooks	Dorothy Green 1973–77
Stuart Brooks	Robert Colbert 1973–83
Liz Foster Brooks	Julianna McCarthy 1973–
William Foster, Sr.	Charles Gray 1975–76
Dr. Snapper Foster	David Hasselhoff 1975–82
	William Grey Espy 1973–75
Greg Foster	Howard McGillin 1981–82
	Wings Hauser 1977–81
	Brian Kerwin 1976–77
	James Houghton 1973–76
Jill Foster	Jess Walton 1987–
	Brenda Dickson 1973–80; 1983–87
	Deborah Adair 1980–83
	Bond Gideon 1980
Brad Eliot	Tom Hallick 1973–78
Barbara Anderson	Deidre Hall 1973–75
Sally McGuire Rolland	Lee Crawford 1973–74; 1981–82
Pierre Rolland	Robert Clary 1973–74

Marianne Rolland	Lilyan Chauvin 1974
Jeff, the stableboy	Rod Arrants 1974
Kay Chancellor	Jeanne Cooper 1973–
Phillip Chancellor	Donnelly Rhodes 1974–75
	John Considine 1973–74
Brock Reynolds	Beau Kayzer 1974–80; 1984–86
Dr. Bruce Henderson	Paul Stevens 1975–76
	Robert Clarke 1975
Dr. Mark Henderson	Steve Carlson 1975–76
George Curtis	Anthony Geary 1973
Frank Martin	Jay Ingram 1973
Warner Wilson	Rick Jason 1973
Jed Andrews	Tom Selleck 1974–75
Gwen Sherman	Jennifer Leak 1974–75
Sam Powers	Barry Cahill 1974
Jerry Frazier	Michael Gregory 1974
Maestro Faustch	Karl Bruck 1974–85
Fran Whittaker	Susan Brown 1975
Jack Curtis	Anthony Herrera 1975–77
Joann Curtis	Kay Heberle 1975–78
Ron Becker	Dick DeCoit 1976–77; 1984
Nancy Becker	Cathy Carricaburu 1977–78
Karen Becker	Brandi Tucker 1977–78
Lance Prentiss	Dennis Cole 1981–82
	John McCook 1976–80
Vanessa Prentiss	K. T. Stevens 1976–80
Lucas Prentiss	Tom Ligon 1978–82
Derek Thurston	Joe LaDue 1977–80; 1984
Suzanne Lynch	Ellen Weston 1979–80
Nikki Reed	Melody Thomas 1979–
	Erica Hope 1978–79
Dr. Casey Reed	Roberta Leighton 1978–81; 1984–
Nick Reed	Quinn Redeker 1979
Linda Larkin	Susan Walden 1979
Scott Adams	Jack Stauffer 1979
Rose DeVille	Darlene Conley 1980; 1986–87
Walter Addison	Paul Savior 1980
Jonas	Jerry Lacy 1979–81
Paul Williams	Doug Davidson 1979–
Mary Williams	Carolyn Conwell 1980–
Carl Williams	Brett Hadley 1980–
Steve Williams	David Winn 1980
Patty Williams	Andrea Evans 1983–84
	Lilibet Stern 1980–83
	Tammy Taylor 1980
April Stevens	Cynthia Eilbacher 1979–82
	Janet Wood 1979
Dorothy Stevens	Melinda Cordell 1980–82
Wayne Stevens	William Long, Jr. 1980–82

Victor Newman	Eric Braeden 1980–
Julia Newman	Meg Bennett 1980–84; 1986–
Michael Scott	Nicholas Benedict 1980–81
Douglas Austin	Michael Evans 1980–85; 1987–
Eve Howard	Margaret Mason 1980–84
Jerry Cashman	John Gibson 1981–82
Filipe Ramirez	Victor Mohica 1980–81
Jack Abbott	Terry Lester 1980–85
John Abbott	Jerry Douglas 1982–
	Brett Halsey 1980–82
Ashley Abbott	Eileen Davidson 1982–
Traci Abbott	Beth Maitland 1982–
Dina Abbott	Marla Adams 1983–86
Danny Romalotti	Michael Damian 1981–
Gina Roma(lotti)	Patty Weaver 1982–
Earl Bancroft	Mark Tapscott 1982–83
Allison Bancroft	Lynn Wood 1981–83
Kevin Bancroft	Christopher Holder 1981–83
Carolyn Harper	Mimi Maynard 1982
Andy Richards	Steven Ford 1981–87
Diane Jenkins Richards	Alex Donnelley 1982–84; 1986
Robert Laurence	Peter Brown 1981–82
Claire Laurence	Suzanne Zenor 1982
Angela Laurence	Liz Keifer 1982
Pam Warren	Kristine DeBell 1982
Cindy Lake	DeAnna Robbins 1982–83
Brian Forbes	Jay Kerr 1982–83
Tony DiSalvo	Joseph Taylor 1983
Eric Garrison	Brian Matthews 1983–85
Dr. Sharon Reaves	Velek(k)a Gray 1983
Ruby	Velek(k)a Gray 1983
Rick Darrows	Randy Holland 1983–84
Lauren Fenmore	Tracey E. Bregman 1983–
Neil Fenmore	James Storm 1983–86
Frank Lewis	Brock Peters 1982–85
Amy Lewis	Stephanie E. Williams 1983–
Jazz Jackson	Jon St. Elwood 1983–86
Tyrone Jackson	Phil Morris 1984–86
Mamie Johnson	Marguerite Ray 1982–
Tim Sullivan	Scott Palmer 1983–85; 1986–
Carole Robbins	Christopher Templeton 1983–
Marc Mergeron	Frank M. Bernard 1983–84; 1987
Dr. Alan Jacobs	Jack Wells 1984
Joe Blair	John Denos 1983–87
Cricket Blair	Lauralee Bell 1983–
Lindsey Wells	Lauren Koslow 1984–86
Shawn Garrett	Grant Cramer 1984–86
	Tom McConnell 1984
Boobsie Caswell	Joy Garrett 1984–85

Cora Miller	Dorothy McGuire 1984
Brent Davis	Bert Kramer 1984–85
	Jim McMullan 1984
JoAnna Manning	Susan Seaforth Hayes 1984–
Joseph Anthony	Logan Ramsey 1984–85
Alana Anthony	Amy Gibson 1985
Jared Markson	Linwood Dalton 1984–85
Matt Miller	Robert Parucha 1985–87
Brad Carlton	Don Diamont 1985–
Michael Crawford	Colby Chester 1985–87
Faren Connor	Colleen Casey 1985–87
Esther Valentine	Kate Linder 1982–
Nathan (Kong) Hastings	Nathan Purdee 1985–
Phillip Chancellor III	Thom Bierdz 1986–
Nina Webster	Tricia Cast 1986–
Ellen Winters	Jennifer Karr 1986–87
Evan Sanderson	John Shearin 1986–87
David Kimble	Michael Corbett 1986–
Dr. Steven Lassiter	Rod Arrants 1986–
Skip Evans	Todd Curtis 1987–
Rex Sterling	Quinn Redeker 1987–

YOUNG DR. MALONE

December 29, 1958–March 29, 1963   NBC

When *Today Is Ours* floundered in the ratings, NBC replaced the serial with the TV version of *Young Dr. Malone* (which had been broadcast on radio since 1939), incorporating into the new soap a few characters from the cancelled *Today Is Ours*. The focus of the new show was a father-and-son doctor team, practicing at Valley Hospital in Denison, Maryland. In the radio version, however, the show continued with a different plotline, since the elder Dr. Malone was working at the Three Oaks Hospital.

With seven million viewers tuned in daily, *Young Dr. Malone* enjoyed a relatively long and successful run, considering the nervous state of NBC management at the time. William Prince and Augusta Dabney, married offscreen, played the married Dr. Jerry and Tracey Malone. Their children were David, the young Dr. Malone, and Jill Malone Renfrew, who was unhappily married to Larry Renfrew, a compulsive gambler. Tracey and sister Faye, who married Dr. Stefan Koda, were the daughters of the powerful Emory Bannister. Emory was saddled with an avaricious second wife, Clare, who provided the show with most of its excitement. Clare was a classic villainess who committed adultery, lost her baby, went blind, married Lionel Steele, sank into insanity, was committed to a sanitarium, tricked her way out . . .

Young Dr. Malone was an innovative serial which combined realistic medical dilemmas—a malpractice suit against Jerry, a midlife crisis for Tracey when baby Jonathan died—with large dollops of humor. (Playboy Dr. Ted Powell continually prowled the hospital halls for prey. Spotting a pretty nurse fixing her stocking, he exclaimed, "What a tempting and toothsome sight!") Producers strived for maximum action and the show had more camera shots and movement than any other soap of the day. But it would take *General Hospital* fifteen years later to really start a technical revolution in daytime.

Created by Irna Phillips, the show included writers Charles Gussman, Julian Funt, and Richard Holland. The strong cast was directed by Walter Gorman, James Young, and Tom Donovan. Doris Quinlan, Lucy Ferri, and Carol Irwin served as producers.

Historical footnote: Lionel Steele was soap opera's first "ambivalent" villain. He was determined to take over Emory Bannister's plant, Denison Foundry; then he allied himself with the wicked Clare and married her. Later, he realized that he had values and scruples in contrast to the conscienceless Clare, who possessed neither. Former producer Lucy Ferri Rittenberg gives more than a little credit to director Walter Gorman for the brilliant performances of Martin Blaine and Lesley Woods as Lionel and Clare.

CAST

Dr. Jerry Malone	William Prince 1958–63
Tracey Malone	Augusta Dabney 1959–63
	Virginia Dwyer 1958–59
Dr. David Malone	John Connell 1958–63
Jill Malone	Sarah Hardy 1962–63
	Freda Holloway 1959–62
	Kathleen Widdoes 1958–59
Emory Bannister	Judson Laire 1959–61
Clare Bannister Steele	Lesley Woods 1959–63
Lionel Steele	Martin Blaine 1959–63
Lisha Steele	Patty McCormack 1962
	Susan Hallaran 1960–61
	Michele Tuttle 1960
	Zina Bethune 1959
Faye Bannister	Chase Crosley 1961–62
	Lenka Peterson 1959–61
Dr. Stefan Koda	Michael Ingram 1959
Dr. Eileen Seaton	Emily McLaughlin 1959–60
Peter Brooks	Robert Lansing 1959
Phyllis Brooks	Barbara O'Neill 1959
Dr. Ted Powell	Peter Brandon 1959–63
Clara Kershaw	Joyce Van Patten 1959–60
Larry Renfrew	Dick Van Patten 1961–62
Ernest Cooper	Nicholas Pryor 1959
	Robert Drivas 1959
Fran Merrill	Patricia Bosworth 1959
Jody Baker	Stephen Bolster 1959–60
Gail Prentiss	Joan Hackett 1959–60
Dr. Fred McNeill	Hugh Franklin 1962–63
Marge Wagner	Teri Keane 1963

Erica Brandt	Ann Williams 1962–63
Dr. Matt Steele	Nicolas Coster 1962–63
	Franklyn Spodak 1961
	Eddie Jones 1961
Miss Long	Mary Fickett 1961
Gig Houseman	Diana Hyland 1961–62
Rick Hampton	Louis Edmonds 1962

THE YOUNG MARRIEDS

October 5, 1964–March 25, 1966   ABC

After launching *General Hospital*, ABC produced this Hollywood-based daytime serial about the marital problems of four suburban couples: Susan and Dan Garrett, Ann and Walter Reynolds, Lena and Jerry Karr, and Liz and Matt Stevens. Created by James Elward, *The Young Marrieds* was written by Elward and Frances Rickett. The producers were Richard Dunn and Eugene Burr, and the directors were Frank Pacelli and Livia Granito. The cast was headed by Peggy McCay, the original Vanessa Dale on *Love of Life*, and included two future *Days of Our Lives* stars: Susan Seaforth, who later married her leading man Bill Hayes, and Brenda Benet, who took her own life in 1982. *The Young Marrieds* aired from 3:30 to 4:00 P.M. on the East Coast (opposite the highly rated *Edge of Night*), following *General Hospital*.

CAST

Susan Garrett	Peggy McCay
Dan Garrett	Paul Picerni
Ann Reynolds	Susan Brown
Walter Reynolds	Michael Mikler
Jerry Karr	Pat Rossen
Lena Karr Gilroy	Norma Connolly
Roy Gilroy	Barry Russo
Matt Stevens	Scott Graham
	Charles Grodin
Liz Forsythe Stevens	Floy Dean
Irene Forsythe	Constance Moore
Aunt Alex	Irene Tedrow
Jill McComb	Brenda Benet
	Betty Connor
Buzz Korman	Les Brown, Jr.
Carol West	Susan Seaforth (Hayes)

PART TWO

Who's Who
in Soap Opera

ALEXANDER, DENISE

Born November 11, 1939, New York, New York.
Susan Martin, Days of Our Lives;
Dr. Lesley Webber, General Hospital;
Mary McKinnon, Another World

Probably the most consistently popular romantic heroine in the history of television soaps, Denise Alexander began her career as a child acting in radio shows such as *A Tree Grows in Brooklyn*, *I Remember Mama*, and *Perry Mason*, eventually racking up credits in 5,000 radio episodes. On stage, she starred on Broadway as Evelyn Munn in the revival of Lillian Hellman's *The Children's Hour* and appeared with Ethel Waters in *A Member of the Wedding*. She broke into films in 1956 playing Marie Gioia opposite Sal Mineo in *Crime in the Streets*. But television began to claim her almost exclusively, and she eventually guested on over 200 shows, including *Father Knows Best*, *I Remember Mama*, *Ben Casey*, *Twilight Zone*, *Dobie Gillis*, *The Virginian*, *The Danny Kaye Show*, and *Combat*.

On daytime television, she got her first regular soap job in 1960 on *The Clear Horizon*. She played Lois Adams on the Hollywood-based serial about astronauts and their families for two years, then had a stint as Emily Sanders on the short-lived NBC soap *Ben Jerrod*. Alexander attended college at USC and UCLA, majoring in English, and for a time quit acting, trying her hand at selling real estate. In 1965 she had a brief stint on *General Hospital* playing Lorna Hill. (She also had appeared on the pilot of *General Hospital* two years earlier.) Then Alexander joined the cast of *Days of Our Lives* in March 1966 and created a sensation as Susan Martin. The actress soon became a regular fixture at the top of the fan magazine polls, and *Days of Our Lives* soared to the number-one-rated daytime drama. For seven years her character was involved in a never-ending series of melodramatic turns—mental instability, serious illness, rape, murder, etc.— but Alexander tore into the role with exquisite emotionalism and gothic beauty that kept viewers riveted.

She left the show in 1973 with a lucrative offer from *General Hospital* to play Dr. Lesley Williams. At the time, she received the highest salary ever paid to a daytime actress. Miscast for several years on *General Hospital*—as Lesley was operatically burdened with frigidity, a psychopathic husband, and a child who aged ten years overnight—Alexander was pivotal in the show's comeback in 1978. In a storyline written by Douglas Marland, Lesley took the rap for her daughter's murder of David Hamilton, culminating in Lesley's trial and Rick's alienation from her. Alexander's appealing performance in this plotline and in the subsequent Rick-Lesley-Monica romantic triangle was just as important as the Luke and Laura love story in bringing *General Hospital* to number one in the ratings.

She has been voted *Daytime TV*'s Best Actress in 1972, 1973 and 1980, and has been on that magazine's top-ten poll more weeks than any other performer. She also received an Emmy nomination for Outstanding Actress in 1976. Off the *General Hospital* set, Alexander has also worked as a photojournalist for *Ladies Home Journal* and other magazines. For the Katharine Hepburn film *Olly, Olly, Oxen Free*, directed by Richard Colla (the never-married Alexander's long-time companion), she served as still photographer and production coordinator.

In 1982 she also co-produced and co-starred in *Shaft of Love* for Showtime Cable. The soap opera comedy featured such daytime drama favorites as Tony Geary, Kin Shriner, Morgan Fairchild, Ed Nelson, and Susan Flannery. In March 1984, Alexander left *General Hospital* in a contract dispute after an eleven-year run on the show. Her fans were outraged when the character of Lesley was not merely written out but killed off in an automobile accident, leaving little chance of Alexander's return to the show. Fans picketed the ABC studios in protest, and perhaps in reaction to the popular actress's departure, *General Hospital*'s ratings continued to slide.

In August 1986, Alexander made headlines with her return to daytime. The part of Mary McKinnon on *Another World* was the kind of juicy role that allowed the actress to run the gamut from slapstick to high tragedy. Alexander was in the driver's seat again, and fans could not have been happier.

BAUER, CHARITA

Born December 20, 1922, Newark, New Jersey.
Died February 28, 1985, New York, New York.
Bert Bauer, The Guiding Light

Combining the radio and television versions of *The Guiding Light*, Charita Bauer had the distinction of playing a single character for the longest period of time in the history of soap opera, edging out Mary Stuart's Joanne on *Search for Tomorrow* by a year. She joined the radio cast of *The Guiding Light* in 1950 and continued to play Bert Bauer—the last name is a coincidence—when the show made its successful transition to television two years later. She played the part for over three decades, enduring— by accident, she modestly claimed—countless regimes and production changes.

She began her acting career as a child, making her debut at nine on Broadway in Christopher Morley's *Thunder on the Left*. Spotted in a play produced by the Professional Children's School, which Bauer attended, the young actress began to work regularly in children's radio shows, playing such diverse parts as a Chinese boy, a mosquito, and a blind hillbilly. She was the original Little Mary in Clare Boothe Luce's acclaimed all-female comedy *The Women*, which ran for two years on Broadway with Bauer playing every performance. Other theater roles followed in *Madame Capet, Your Loving Son, Life of Reilly*, and *Good Morning Corporal*.

Her career in radio soap operas flourished, with appearances as Lanette in *Our Gal Sunday*, Mary Aldrich in *The Aldrich Family*, Gail Carver in *Lora Lawton*, Maude Mason in *Maude's Diary*, Susan Wakefield in *The Right to Happiness*, Fran Cummings in *Second Husband*, and Mille Baxter in *Young Widder Brown*. In the 1949–50 TV season the actress was seen Sunday nights as Mary Aldrich in the comedy hit *The Aldrich Family*. Then she joined the radio cast of *The Guiding Light* in 1950 as Bert Bauer, the role

she would forever be identified with. When the radio show started broadcasting on daytime TV (it played simultaneously on radio and television
from 1952 to 1956, when the radio version was discontinued), Charita
Bauer as Bert Bauer, the young married heroine, was pivotal in several
storylines. She continued as a central heroine throughout the '50s and
'60s, but by the early '70s, with Bert's sons Michael and Ed as young
romantic leads, she was relegated to supporting status.

In 1978 Bert was involved in her first major storyline in years, as her
troublesome, alcoholic husband Bill reappeared after an absence of ten
years. Bauer's performance, as Bert went from shock to anger to forgive-
ness, was one of the season's highlights. The next year the actress was
presented with the Outstanding Mother Award by the National Mother's
Day Committee for heading up two families, each with a son named
Michael. (Her offscreen son, Michael Crawford, was born in 1946; her
soap son was born in 1952 while the show was on radio.) In 1983 she
appeared in the prime-time TV movie *The Cradle Will Rock* just when *The
Guiding Light* began focusing once again on Bert and the Bauer family.
After finishing up an excellent storyline that year in which Bert befriended
a dying man, Bauer was awarded an Emmy for Lifetime Achievement.
Later that year, the actress underwent major surgery when part of her
leg had to be amputated. In the spring of 1984, she came back to the show
in an emotion-packed storyline repeating her offscreen adjustment to an
artifical limb.

Her health failing, Bauer made her last appearance on the show December 10. On February 28, 1985 this great lady of American drama died,
leaving behind a legacy of thirty-five years of almost unparalleled achievement. That she passed away amid so little fanfare is no doubt due to the
perplexing snobbery still accorded soap opera by much of the media.
However, the lack of press attention was perhaps strangely appropriate
since Charita Bauer led her life with quiet modesty, considering her work
as part of an ensemble, and pointing to other soap pioneers for the enormous success of television serials.

Her acting was also deceivingly simple, a brisk, technically astute playing style which exuded so much warmth that in later performances her
characterization seemed to bask in nothing less than a Chekhovian brand
of heartbreaking merriment. She had ceased to be a mere actress playing
a part. And the slogan "Bauer Power" used backstage to represent the
family's resilience to adversity was not merely boastful: the Bauers had
come to represent the American family who were "making it." As Bert,
Charita Bauer had become a national treasure, a "guiding light" for generations of Americans.

BELL, WILLIAM J.

Born March 6, 1927, Chicago, Illinois.
Creator, The Young and the Restless;
Creator, The Bold and the Beautiful;
Co-Creator, Another World;
Co-Creator, Our Private World

Famous for his vivid handling of once taboo soap opera subjects—such as rape, incest, and lesbianism—Bill Bell grew up around Chicago, a devoted fan of the radio serials *Our Gal Sunday* and *The Romance of Helen Trent.* After attending the University of Michigan and then DePaul University, he worked for CBS, handling both production and writing chores. He switched to advertising, becoming an account executive on the Sara Lee account and many others. He met Irna Phillips, who asked him to write dialogue for *The Guiding Light* in 1957, a stint that impressed Phillips so much she switched Bell to *As the World Turns* the next year.

For nearly a decade Bell co-wrote the top-rated show with Phillips, and he helped to create *Another World* in 1964. The next year he and Phillips decided to spin off one of their most popular characters, Lisa Hughes, to become the center of a twice-weekly prime-time serial. *Our Private World,* starring Eileen Fulton, ran during the summer of 1965. After its cancellation, Bell became headwriter for the Hollywood-based *Days of Our Lives,* which had been floundering in its premiere year. Bell quickly brought the show into the ratings war with an emphasis on psychiatric melodrama contrasted with romantic fantasy. Two complex rape-seduction stories became enormously popular, creating stardom for Denise Alexander, Susan Seaforth, and Susan Flannery. *Days of Our Lives* soared to a number-one spot in 1971.

With his wife, TV hostess Lee Phillip, he created *The Young and the Restless* for CBS in 1973. (Bell married Phillip in 1954. She had her own afternoon variety show in the fall of 1963; it followed *Edge of Night* and *The Secret Storm.*) *The Young and the Restless* was unlike any previous daytime drama, focusing almost exclusively on extremely attractive players in various states of undress, and encased in an atmosphere of fanciful romanticism one moment, social controversy the next. The new show became an immediate hit. While continuing to write the long-term story for *Days of Our Lives* for years, Bell broke one taboo after another on *The Young and the Restless,* tackling such social problems as father-daughter incest, euthanasia, alcoholism, bulimia, and the new sexual freedom. For his work on *Days of Our Lives* he, with Pat Falken Smith, won an Emmy for Outstanding Writing in 1976, and garnered nominations in 1977 and 1978. For *The Young and the Restless* he was nominated for Outstanding Writing in 1975, 1976, 1979, 1986, and 1987 while the show took the prize for Outstanding Drama Series in 1975, 1983, 1985, and 1986. Bell became executive producer of *The Young and the Restless* in 1982.

In March 1987, Bell and his wife, Lee Phillip created *The Bold and the Beautiful,* a soap set in and out of the fashion industry. While continuing to serve as executive producer and headwriter on *The Young and the Restless,* Bell also served in the same capacity on the new show.

BERADINO, JOHN

Born May 1, 1917, Los Angeles, California.
Dr. Steve Hardy, General Hospital

Top-billed on *General Hospital* for over two decades, John Beradino began his acting career as a child, appearing as an extra in the *Our Gang* comedies during the '20s. Convinced that his son would be a major star, Beradino's father financed a starring vehicle for the boy. The movie was never finished, and young Beradino turned to the baseball diamond to fulfill his father's dreams of stardom. By age fifteen Beradino was playing with semi-professional baseball teams on Sundays while playing with his high school football squad during the week.

He won a football scholarship to the University of Southern California in 1936, but he soon left school to join the Texas Baseball League. That led to a successful career from 1939 to 1947 with the St. Louis Browns, interrupted by a stint with the Navy during World War II. While still playing baseball he began to work with the Pasadena Playhouse, which led to the sports star being dubbed "Hollywood John." Because of Beradino's acting background, club owner Bill Veeck, in a publicity stunt, insured Beradino's handsome mug for $1 million.

In 1948 Beradino was traded to the Cleveland Indians at double his previous salary, playing second base in the Indians' victory in the World Series over the Boston Braves. After four years with the Indians, he joined the Pittsburgh Pirates. A leg injury in 1952 forced him out of baseball and back into acting. (His baseball career, with a lifetime batting average of .249, was not forgotten. His face still decorates bubblegum baseball cards.) He got some TV guest shots, and from 1953 to 1956 he was featured on the syndicated espionage series *I Led Three Lives*. He found film work in *The Killer Is Loose* and *The Scarface Mob* and more TV work in shows such as *The Untouchables*, *Laramie*, and *Cheyenne*. This led to a starring role as Sgt. Vince Cavelli in *The New Breed*, a police drama that ran in the 1961–62 season.

When Beradino's wife died in 1962, the actor, with two children to support, began to look for a steadier acting job. He joined the premiere cast of *General Hospital* as the sometimes gruff, immensely likable Dr. Steve Hardy in 1963 and has played the part ever since. In 1964 he met his future wife, Marjorie Binder, a TWA stewardess, whom he married in 1971. Two years later the Beradinos had a daughter, Katherine Anne, and in the following year produced a son, John Anthony. In the early '70s Beradino, a leader in the fight for recognition of daytime drama, began lobbying for long overdue Emmy Awards for daytime performers and technical personnel. As part of his campaign he placed ads in *Variety* and *The Hollywood Reporter*, challenging any film or prime-time actor to do the work soap opera people do every day. No one accepted the challenge.

When daytime drama was finally recognized by the Academy of Television Arts and Sciences, Beradino was rewarded for his work on *General Hospital* by three straight nominations for Outstanding Actor in 1974, 1975, and 1976. During his long tenure on *General Hospital* (only he and

Emily McLaughlin remain from the original cast), Beradino has occasionally moonlighted, first as his *General Hospital* character Dr. Steve Hardy on *One Life to Live*, called to Llanview to consult on the Meredith Lord case. He was also seen in two prime-time TV movies, *Moon of the Wolf* and *Don't Look Back*, the story of Satchel Paige, the first black pitcher in baseball, who was Beradino's teammate in that World Series win in 1948.

BRYGGMAN, LARRY

Born December 21, 1938, Concord, California.
Dr. John Dixon, As the World Turns

Acclaimed by critics and fellow performers as the best actor in daytime television, Larry Bryggman attended school in San Francisco as a drama major and soon found himself spending all of his time on stage. His first professional acting job was in a local production of his favorite play, *Death of a Salesman*, playing Biff opposite Mildred Dunnock, who had originated the female lead on Broadway. He did theater work in Pennsylvania and Boston—interrupted by an engagement with the Army—earning credits in *Tiny Alice, More Stately Mansions, Who's Afraid of Virginia Woolf?*, and *Brecht on Brecht*.

In New York he performed in a bill of one-act plays, for which he received rave reviews and the notice of casting agents. He did a stint on *Love Is a Many Splendored Thing*, which led to his role as Dr. John Dixon on *As the World Turns* in 1969. For a while Bryggman's John Dixon was seen only in the background, but then Irna Phillips, who was again writing the show, put him opposite Kathryn Hays's Kim. The actors clicked and Phillips—and the Soderbergs who followed her—began to put Bryggman and Hays together in scene after scene. As the ambitious Dixon, the actor quickly transcended the villainous aspects of the role, infusing the part with wit, irony, intensity. For audiences, Dixon became not the man-you-love-to-hate but the man-you-shake-your-head-over as Dixon always ended up drowning in the trouble he started.

Outside of *As the World Turns* Bryggman found constant work in the theater, disproving the notion of a "soap ghetto"—the impossibility of daytime TV actors carrying out dual acting careers. He was seen in *Waiting for Godot, Play Strindberg, The Cherry Orchard, Irma La Douce* with Elke Sommer, *Ulysses in Nighttown* with Zero Mostel, *The Lincoln Mask* with Eva Marie Saint, and other plays. He co-starred on Broadway with friend Al Pacino in *The Basic Training of Pavlo Hummell* and *Richard III*, which led to a major part in Pacino's 1979 film . . . *And Justice for All*.

In 1980, when the Dobsons began to write *As the World Turns*, Bryggman's role again expanded. He was given a new leading lady, Jacqueline Schultz (whom he later married offscreen) and was seen almost daily. The Dobsons threw out the conservative values of the previous writers and replaced them with sophisticated, often daring, psychological drama with the show's most complex character, John Dixon, as its focal point.

Bryggman's performance in several well-written storylines showcased the actor at the top of his craft. He found his work being compared to the best of American acting, recalling the standards of the Golden Age of Television and the new level of excellence in film set by Brando, De Niro, and Pacino. His concentration and attention to subtext, complemented by surprising line readings and inventive stage business, earned him consistent praise from co-workers, and he was rewarded with Emmy nominations for Outstanding Actor in 1981 and 1982. During these busy years, Bryggman still found time to moonlight in the 1982 film *Hanky Panky*, which starred Gene Wilder and Gilda Radner. In 1984, Bryggman finally was recognized by the Television Academy with an Emmy as Outstanding Actor. He was again nominated in 1985, 1986, and again took the top prize in 1987.

CAREY, MACDONALD

Born March 15, 1913, Sioux City, Iowa.
Dr. Tom Horton, Days of Our Lives

A double Emmy winner for his role as the kindly patriarch of the unstable Horton clan, Macdonald Carey had a long and prodigious career in theater, radio, and film before joining the premiere cast of *Days of Our Lives* in 1965. Educated at the University of Iowa and the University of Wisconsin, he sang and acted on radio, launching a successful career in soap operas. He played Dick Grosvenor in *Stella Dallas*, Ridgeway Tearle in *John's Other Wife*, Jonathan Hillery in *Just Plain Bill*, Ted Clayton in *Ellen Randolph*, Dr. Lee Markham in *Woman in White*, and Hickory in *Young Hickory*.

After a well-received stint in the 1941 Broadway production of *Lady in the Dark*, Carey became a contract player in Hollywood for Paramount, acting leads and second leads. During the '40s he was seen in *Dr. Broadway*, *Wake Island*, *Suddenly*, *It's Spring*, *Dream Girl*, *Streets of Laredo*, *The Great Gatsby*, and other films. Free-lancing in the '50s, he was featured in *Excuse My Dust*, *Let's Make It Legal*, *Stranger at My Door*, and as Patrick Henry in *John Paul Jones*.

He began to appear on television during the early '50s with guest shots on *GE Theatre* and *U.S. Steel Hour* and starred in his own short-lived series *Dr. Christian* in 1956. He had better luck with his starring role as Herbert L. Maris, defender of the innocent, on *Lock Up* in 1959. When the syndicated series was cancelled in 1961, Carey guest-starred on nearly all of the popular prime-time shows of the period, including *Mr. Novak*, *Burke's Law*, *The Outer Limits*, *Ben Casey*, and *Lassie*.

On November 8, 1965, he began his top-billed role on *Days of Our Lives*, opening every episode for the last two decades with the words, "Like sand through the hour glass, so are the days of our lives." For his work as Dr. Tom Horton, Carey has been nominated for an Emmy as Outstanding Actor in 1968, 1973, 1974, 1975, and 1976, winning the award in 1974 and 1975. Taking periodic breaks from daytime television, he has appeared in many prime-time series, including *Owen Marshall*, *McMillan and Wife*, and *Police Story*. He has also published a book of poetry, *Out of Heart*.

COLLINS, JOAN

Born May 23, 1933, London, England.
Alexis Morrell Carrington Colby Dexter, Dynasty

As Alexis Carrington in *Dynasty*, Joan Collins became the Evita of prime-time, a Medea with lip gloss, who both used and loved her children while she enticed and swatted lovers to and from her bosom. Collins's acting career has been as busy as her personal life has been randy, as she has apparently collected a gallery of male slaves with the uncompromising greed of a Nana.

The half-Jewish, raven-haired beauty grew up in London, dodging Nazi air raids and later attending the Royal Academy of Dramatic Art. (Among her fellow students was David McCallum.) She did stage work and then, still a teenager, acted in ten British films, beginning with *Lady Godiva Rides Again* in 1951. After a stormy seven-month marriage to Maxwell Reed, a film star of British pirate epics, Collins snagged a Hollywood contract and the lead in *The Land of the Pharaohs*. During the '50s she starred in a series of forgettable Hollywood efforts, but managed to make an impact in such films as *The Virgin Queen* with Bette Davis, *The Girl in the Red Velvet Swing* with Farley Granger, *Seawife* with Richard Burton, *The Wayward Bus* with Jayne Mansfield, and *Rally Round the Flag, Boys* with Paul Newman and Joanne Woodward.

Offscreen, Collins made good use of the time she was on suspension by Fox studio for refusing inappropriate vehicles; she romanced, among others, Sydney Chaplin, Nicky Hilton, Arthur Loew, and the son of the President of the Dominican Republic. After a volatile affair with the husband of future TV star Cloris Leachman, Collins found solace in the arms of Warren Beatty, to whom she became engaged. With her career on the skids and Beatty's star on the ascent, the pair eventually split after Collins had an abortion. She later married Anthony Newley, who had become a major Broadway star, but divorced him seven years later, citing infidelities on both sides; Ryan O'Neal was Collins's achilles heel.

When Elizabeth Taylor fell ill during preproduction of *Cleopatra*, Collins, who had often been compared to Taylor, was called by Fox to replace Taylor in the lead. Taylor pulled through, and the experience soured Collins on the cavalier, often callous games played by Hollywood. The actress returned to England and starred in a series of terrible movies, including *Empire of the Ants* and *Up in the Cellar*, which co-starred none other than Larry Hagman. (Alexis and J.R. together!) In the late '70s, Collins staged a comeback in the saucy B-films *The Stud* and *The Bitch*, produced by Collins's third husband and based on the novels of her sister, Jackie (*Hollywood Wives*) Collins.

After a pleasant guest stint on *Starsky and Hutch*, Collins was offered a continuing role in the prime-time TV serial *Dynasty*, which had done poorly in its first season. With Collins's dramatic appearance as Alexis in her ex-husband's trial for the murder of their son's male lover, the ratings shot up. They continued to climb as Alexis clawed her way to the top of the corporate ladder, leaving executives spewing venom and then sending lovers to their graves after a night of prime-time passion. Collins nabbed a Golden Globe Award, and her extremely popular character set off a host of imitators on day and nighttime soap operas. *Dynasty* became the second-highest-rated series, often supplanting *Dallas* as number one, and Collins perhaps replaced Larry Hagman as the character Americans most loved to hate.

During 1983, Collins starred in the top-rated TV movie *The Making of a Male Model*, which was produced by Lynn Loring, who had grown up on daytime television as Patti Barron on *Search for Tomorrow*. Later that year, Collins posed semi-nude for *Playboy*, and the issue containing the photos of the fifty-year-old star became one of the highest-selling in the publication's history.

The following year, she published a revised version of *Past Imperfect*, her 1978 bestselling British memoir. *Past Imperfect* (Simon and Schuster, 1984) was not as explicit as the British version and deleted most of the salty expletives from the leading-lady dialogue as well as cutting short the descriptions of romances with Harry Belafonte and others. Nevertheless, the American version, which included a number of colorful behind-the-scenes anecdotes from the *Dynasty* set, became an immediate bestseller. In 1984, Collins was nominated for an Emmy for Outstanding Actress in recognition of her wicked performance on *Dynasty*. The next year the actress starred in the appropriately titled mini-series *Sins*.

While *Sins* was a major ratings success, her next mini-series outing, *Monte Carlo*—which Collins produced with her new husband Peter Holm—was a disaster. Apparently so was the marriage: almost immediately after the airing of the mini-series, Collins filed for divorce.

COURTNEY, JACQUELINE

Born September 24, 1946, East Orange, New Jersey.
Alice Matthews, Another World;
Pat Ashley, One Life to Live;
Diane Winston, Loving

One of the few performers on daytime television who really deserve the title "superstar," Jacqueline Courtney practically grew up on television. She attended the Professional Children's School and appeared on several children's shows, including Horn and Hardart's *Children's Hour*. By age nine she was acting in commercials, and by fourteen she was a regular on *The Edge of Night*, playing Viola Smith. The next year she appeared on the *U.S. Steel Hour* with Patty Duke, and soon guested on prime-time shows such as *Route 66*, *Armstrong Circle Theatre*, and *The Jackie Gleason Show*.

On daytime TV, Courtney had parts on *The Doctors*, *The Secret Storm*, and *Love of Life*. In 1962 she was part of the original cast of *Our Five Daughters*, playing Ann Lee, the youngest daughter of Helen Lee, played by silent screen star Esther Ralston. However, it was her poignant performance as Alice Matthews on *Another World* from 1964 to 1975 that endeared her to millions. As the passively sweet Alice, who fell in love with the ambitious Steven Frame and was continually thwarted by the bitchy Rachel, Courtney became daytime's favorite heroine. She won *Daytime TV*'s Best Actress award in 1974. The romantic triangle also propelled *Another World* to the top of the ratings. Yet all was not happy on the set. Reports of back-biting, rewriting, personality clashes, and power struggles soon emanated from the NBC studios.

In February 1975, George Reinholt, who played Steve, and who was also a close friend of the actress, was dismissed. Late in the summer, Paul Rauch, the producer of *Another World*, announced that Courtney would also leave but of her own volition. Courtney said simply, "I was fired." She soon joined George Reinholt on ABC's *One Life to Live* as the independent journalist Pat Ashley. Her character was soon linked to Reinholt's Tony Lord, and a new romantic triangle was spun, to the audience's delight. *One Life to Live*, which aired opposite *Another World*, picked up millions of viewers, and Courtney and Reinholt were instrumental in the show's newfound popularity.

One Life to Live also showcased Courtney's flair for comedy in a short, Tracy-Hepburn–like storyline centering on Pat's relationship with the Gatsby-like Adam Brewster, but the plot soon soured and the writers changed course. However, few will ever forget Courtney's performance as a grieving mother in January 1978 when Pat's son was killed in an automobile accident. Her heartbreaking acting in the week following the accident was deserving of an Emmy, but Courtney is perhaps the only major star in daytime television who has never been nominated for the award. In the fall of 1983, *One Life to Live* unexpectedly passed on renewing her contract, claiming they had no storyline for the actress. Courtney took some time off and returned triumphantly to *Another World* as Alice on May 4, 1984—the twentieth anniversary of the show. Unfortunately, *Another World* used the star ineffectively (ridiculously so) in the following year. The unlucky Courtney, who had played nothing but romantic heroines for over two decades, vowed if she ever returned to daytime, it would be as an all-out, fun-loving, first-class bitch!

In May 1987, Courtney got her wish, cast as Diane Winston, the chic madam of a bordello on *Loving*.

FRANCIS, GENIE

Born May 26, 1962, Englewood, New Jersey.
Laura Webber, General Hospital;
Tyger Hayes, Bare Essence;
Diana Colville, Days of Our Lives

Soap opera's most famous teenage star, Genie Francis is the daughter of character actor and acting teacher Ivor Francis (Professor Mitchell on the Gloria Monty–directed soap *Bright Promise*.) At thirteen she was tapped for a guest shot on ABC's *Family* as an unfriendly classmate of Kristy McNichol's Buddy Lawrence. With this single professional credit under her belt she joined the cast of *General Hospital* the next year as Laura, replacing child actress Stacey Baldwin, who had left the show months before. When Gloria Monty took over as producer of the ailing show and decided that the dramatic focus should be on the younger characters, Douglas Marland wrote a daring story in which the confused, immature Laura took an older man as a lover. When David Hamilton taunted Laura with the fact that it was really her mother that he loved, Laura accidentally killed him, and her mother took the rap for the murder.

Francis's ferocious, highly emotional performance at fifteen amazed her peers and, through word of mouth, brought hordes of teenagers into *General Hospital*'s audience. The melodramatic storyline was beautifully juxtaposed by a sweet, puppy-love romance with Scotty Baldwin. The ratings took off. Then Pat Falken Smith, famous for her rape stories on *Days of Our Lives*, wrote a highly ambiguous, controversial storyline in which Laura would fall in love with her rapist-seducer, Luke Spencer. The chemistry between Francis and Tony Geary, who played Luke, was undeniable, and when "the powers that be" got around to calling the rape a seduction, Francis felt—justifiably—that her highly skilled performance as a rape victim had been negated. Meanwhile, a series of Luke-and-Laura-on-the-run stories brought *General Hospital* unprecedented ratings. By late 1981, with Luke and Laura married before the largest daytime audience recorded, Francis was exhausted. She had been working almost daily for five years, memorizing fifty pages of dialogue every day as well as studying with a high school tutor on the set. Francis had no personal life and felt that she had skipped her adolescence and teenage years. (While she was in the midst of a tumultuous affair onscreen, she had not yet received her first offscreen kiss.) In December, she left *General Hospital*, taping her final episodes in which Laura walked off into a fog while being trailed by a kidnapper.

Armed with a CBS contract that included two big-budget TV movies and a series pilot, Francis made the two-part TV movie *Bare Essence*. Aired in 1982 with high ratings, the drama put an end to the speculation that a former daytime star could not lure a large prime-time audience. When CBS passed on a serial version of *Bare Essence* and did not come up with a series pilot for the star, NBC jumped at the *Bare Essence* project and Francis began filming immediately. Unfortunately, the serial version of *Bare Essence* was so haphazardly and lethargically written that Francis's ingratiating performance as the assertive Tyger Hayes was lost amid the mediocrity.

After *Bare Essence*'s cancellation, Francis left for New York to study and pursue a stage career, but was lured back by *General Hospital* at a huge salary for thirty appearances. On November 14, 1983, she returned, after an absence of almost two years, to finish off soap opera's most famous storyline. During her first week on the show the ratings jumped, adding three million viewers to *General Hospital*'s audience. When Luke and Laura's love story ended happily, Francis stayed true to her theater ambitions and immediately starred in a production of the Pulitzer Prize–winning play *Crimes of the Heart*. She studied acting in New York, then appeared on episodes of *Hotel* and *Murder, She Wrote* before returning for a brief visit to *General Hospital* in November 1984.

In April 1987, Francis popped up as cub reporter Diana Colville on NBC's *Days of Our Lives*.

FREEMAN, AL, JR.

Born Albert Cornelius Freeman, Jr.,
March 21, 1934, San Antonio, Texas.
Ed Hall, One Life to Live

The first black to win a daytime Emmy, Al Freeman fell into acting while studying pre-law at Los Angeles City College, where he won the Outstanding Drama Student award in 1957. After a stint in the Air Force, Freeman began his celebrated career in theater, film, and television with a series of plays on Broadway. In 1962, he starred in *Tiger Tiger Burning Bright* with Ellen Holly, his future co-star on *One Life to Live*. (The rest of the cast in this play reads like a who's who in black drama: Claudia McNeil, Cicely Tyson, Diana Sands, Roscoe Lee Browne, Alvin Ailey, and Billy Dee Williams.) Two years later he was acclaimed for his roles in *Blues for Mr. Charlie* and LeRoi Jones's *Slave*.

However, it was another LeRoi Jones play, the highly controversial *Dutchman*, that made Freeman one of the most sought after black actors in the country. He starred in the film version of *Dutchman* in 1967 and found other movie work in *The Detective, Finian's Rainbow,* and *A Fable,* a film version of *Slave* that Freeman directed and starred in. Television work followed as the actor guested on *The Defenders, The FBI,* and the TV movie *My Sweet Charlie,* in which he earned an Emmy nomination opposite Patty Duke. In 1972 he began to make periodic appearances on *One Life to Live* as Lieutenant Ed Hall, a police officer who eventually wooed and married Carla Gray, played by Ellen Holly.

By the mid '70s Freeman was a regular on the soap, while free-lancing in the theater and in such TV shows as *Maude, Hot L Baltimore,* and *Kojak.* On *One Life to Live* the actor doubled as the show's director on several episodes and was awarded an Emmy for Outstanding Actor in 1979 for his warm, compassionate performance. The same year he was acclaimed for his smashing performance as Malcolm X in the TV mini-series *Roots: The Next Generation.* In 1981 he returned triumphantly to Broadway starring in an all-black version of *Long Day's Journey Into Night.* When Ellen Holly, his leading lady on *One Life to Live,* left on a two-year hiatus, Freeman continued his fine work on the show but on a less demanding schedule. He was nominated for an Emmy as Outstanding Supporting Actor for his soap role in 1983, 1986, and 1987.

FULTON, EILEEN

Born Margaret Elizabeth McLarty,
September 13, 1933, Asheville, North Carolina.
Lisa Miller Hughes Eldridge Shea Colman McColl Mitchell,
As the World Turns *and* Our Private World

Television's most famous villainess and the most popular soap star of the '60s, Eileen Fulton arrived in New York in 1956 with twin desires: to make it as a singer and as an actress. The minister's daughter had just graduated from Greensboro College, where she had received a Best Actress

Award for her performances in *Candide* and Thurber's *Thirteen Clocks*. While Fulton studied her craft, she worked at Macy's selling hats and occasionally modeled for photos used to illustrate stories in *True Confessions*. After a few theater gigs and a co-starring role opposite Anne Francis in the film *Girl of the Night*, in which she coincidentally played a character called Lisa, she fell into the role with which she would forever be identified.

Fulton had auditioned for a soap part on *The Brighter Day* (ironically, as a minister's daughter), but producers thought her better cast as Bob Hughes' social-climbing girlfriend on *As the World Turns* in 1960. Her stint as Lisa Miller was supposed to be temporary, but the writers became intrigued by the charm and energy Fulton brought to the role, and began to develop the character. When the devious Lisa had Bob Hughes (Don Hastings) and his family under her thumb, outraged mail poured into CBS. By the time Lisa had taken up with shoe salesman Bruce Elliott (James Pritchett, who later played Dr. Matt Powers on *The Doctors* from 1963 to 1982), Fulton had to hire a security guard to protect her from the overenthusiastic, sometimes violent fans as she made her way to the studio.

Meanwhile, the actress was making inroads in her theater career, starring in the off-Broadway musical production *The Fantasticks*, the drama *Abe Lincoln in Illinois*, and as Honey in the matinee company of *Who's Afraid of Virginia Woolf?* opposite Henderson Forsythe, her *As the World Turns* co-star. Fulton left the soap to concentrate more fully on her stage career, but was lured back in 1965 to star in a prime-time spin-off of *As the World Turns* entitled *Our Private World*. Fulton played a variation on the Bette Davis character in *Beyond the Forest* ("A twelve o'clock girl in a nine o'clock town"), a girl who pined for fun and freedom in Chicago. Unfortunately, Lisa's stay in Chicago was relegated to a summer's run, and the actress returned to *As the World Turns* for ten weeks to tie up stories begun on *Our Private World*. She then took a year's sabbatical from the show to sing in various nightclubs and returned to the soap on January 16, 1967, as a new, glamorous Lisa.

Although Lisa has been put through some wild situations (three dozen lovers, six marriages, murder trials, rapes, amnesia, a Mexican mudslide, and a phantom fetus), audiences have always been transfixed by Fulton's refreshing originality and enormous vitality, and, in recent years, her flamboyant comedy style. The actress counts among her fans Van Cliburn, Renata Tebaldi, and Bette Davis, the latter calling Fulton "absolutely the most chic, best-looking put-together woman I've ever seen." Since 1974, she has appeared in a series of one-woman shows in the country's most prestigious nightclubs. After twenty years on *As the World Turns* and two offscreen divorces, Fulton in 1983 decided to leave the show to strike out on her own and quickly starred in a series of stage productions. In a burst of publicity, Fulton again returned to Oakdale in the summer of 1984 as Lisa discovered the body of her fifth husband, thus setting off another season of murder, mystery, and melodrama.

GALLAGHER, HELEN

Born July 19, 1926, Brooklyn, New York.
Maeve Ryan, Ryan's Hope

Two-time winner as daytime drama's Outstanding Actress, Helen Gallagher is also one of the most respected actresses of the musical stage. She studied dancing as a child, and as a teenager performed in the chorus of several musicals. Her first big break came with Jerome Robbins' *High Button Shoes*, which was followed by her 1952 Tony award–winning performance as Gladys Bumps in *Pal Joey*. The next year she starred in the ill-fated *Hazel Flagg*, a highly touted Broadway show that proved to be a minor setback for the actress. Gallagher fell into relative obscurity, touring in musicals such as *Finian's Rainbow*, *Guys and Dolls*, and *Pajama Game*.

In 1966, Gallagher staged a comeback with *Sweet Charity*, a musical in which she performed for two years. Three years later she won her second Tony for the long-running, hit Broadway revival, *No, No, Nanette*. After seeing her dramatic performance in the Megan Terry play *Hothouse*, ABC selected her to head up the cast of *Ryan's Hope*. As the warm but outspoken Maeve Ryan, Gallagher soon won back-to-back Emmies for her memorable performances, especially in superbly written scenes between Maeve and her daughters Mary and Siobhan. She was nominated again for Outstanding Actress in 1981 and 1983. While continuing to perform on *Ryan's Hope*, she moonlighted in the 1977 film *Roseland* and in the 1983 Broadway revue *Tallulah*, starring as the outrageous Tallulah Bankhead, who happened to be one of the first famous, ardent fans of TV soap operas.

GEARY, ANTHONY

Born May 29, 1947, Coalville, Utah.
Lucas Lorenzo Spencer, General Hospital

The first media superstar created exclusively by daytime drama, Tony Geary has earned the adulation of millions for his emotionally provocative, often hilarious performance of anti-hero Luke Spencer. Brought up in the small town of Coalville, Utah (population 800), Geary won a scholarship to study theater at the University of Utah. There he was discovered by the Oscar-winning actor Jack Albertson and played Albertson's son on tour in the Pulitzer Prize–winning play *The Subject was Roses*. Geary settled in Hollywood, making the rounds and selling toys in a department store (a highlight was selling trains to Shelley Winters). He worked in odd jobs, as a Vegas chorus boy, and acted in summer stock, eventually racking up credits in over forty stage productions.

For nearly a decade, Geary shuttled back and forth between the stage, film, prime-time television, and soap operas. He made a quickie Western called *Educated Heart* and a horror exploitation film *Blood Sabbath*, which was mercifully never released. Geary's best movie role was a small part in the 1971 anti-war cult film *Johnny Get Your Gun*, adapted from Dalton Trumbo's novel and directed by Trumbo. Geary broke into prime-time TV with guest spots on *Room 222* and *All in the Family* (as a friend of

Mike's whom Archie suspects, incorrectly, of being gay). Usually cast in psychotic/murderer-type roles, Geary appeared in three TV movies and over fifty series, including *Starsky and Hutch, The Mod Squad, Barnaby Jones, Marcus Welby, Six Million Dollar Man*, and *Streets of San Francisco*.

In 1971, the actor had a running role on the serial *Bright Promise* as David Lockhart, a sensitive young man who was unjustly committed to a mental hospital as a child. (Susan Brown, later Dr. Gail Baldwin on *General Hospital*, played a surrogate mother to Geary's David.) In 1973, he joined the cast of the glossy *The Young and the Restless* as George Curtis, the man who eventually raped heroine Chris Brooks. The six-month storyline, shocking in its day, put *The Young and the Restless* in the thick of the ratings race and gave Geary the dubious distinction of perpetrating daytime TV's first (non-marital) rape, a distinction that would later haunt the actor on *General Hospital* when Luke raped—or seduced—Laura on that famous disco floor.

In 1978, Gloria Monty, who had directed Geary in *Bright Promise* and in the TV movie *Sorority Kill*, was in the midst of renovating the ailing *General Hospital*. She remembered Geary's work and he auditioned for the role of Mitch Williams, an ambitious politician who would be paired off romantically with the volatile Tracy Quartermaine. Monty decided his talents would be better used in a different part, and writer Douglas Marland created the pivotal role of Luke Spencer for Geary. At first Luke was seen as a rather sleazy foil for his white-trash sister Bobbie, who played dirty tricks on Laura, the young woman to whom Luke was perversely attracted. But Luke's love for the confused Laura humanized him, and Geary's poignant pantomiming touched a responsive chord among viewers.

Geary's popularity began to skyrocket, especially in a series of Luke-and-Laura-on-the-run stories. The audience found Geary's performance refreshing, especially after a generation of blandly handsome, often passive leading men. Viewers quickly warmed to Luke's street-smart sarcasm, his inventive humor (often improvised), and his outlandish dress—a wardrobe presumably from Mr. Geary's own closet. The actor topped the fan magazine popularity polls, and he and Genie Francis became household names when their faces began to appear on magazine covers everywhere. Recognition from his colleagues came in the form of three straight Emmy nominations for Outstanding Actor, with Geary taking the award in 1982.

In 1983, during a three-month hiatus from *General Hospital*, the actor starred in the TV movie *Intimate Agony* opposite *One Life to Live*'s Judith Light. Geary gave an appealing, low-key performance in the story about a doctor fighting an epidemic of herpes at a popular beach resort. Returning to the soap at a reported salary of $500,000, Geary was back in top form as Luke fought to regain use of his legs after an accident. (The dramatic storyline was a relief after all the spoofy, science fiction adventures the character had been boxed into.) Geary's departure from the show after a year was handled in grand style, with the return of Genie Francis and a happy ending for soap opera's most famous love story.

After a mobbed live appearance with Genie Francis in Atlantic City, Geary began work on a videocassette version of Shakespeare's *Antony and*

Cleopatra, playing Caesar opposite Lynn Redgrave and Timothy Dalton. Then he co-starred with Barbara Carrera and Debby Boone in *Sins of the Past*, a TV-movie murder mystery in which a detective (a straight-haired, mustached Geary) investigated the lives of a group of former call girls who were being knocked off one by one. After appearing in the starring role in a West Coast production of the rock opera *Jesus Christ, Superstar* and filming the TV movie *The Great Pretender*, Geary returned to *General Hospital* in the fall of 1984 in a special, limited appearance.

HAGMAN, LARRY

Born September 21, 1931, Weatherford, Texas.
Ed Gibson, The Edge of Night;
J.R. Ewing, Dallas

"The man you love to hate"—a phrase used to describe the villainous character Erich von Stroheim created in silent films—was immediately reactivated by the press to describe the pop culture phenomenon J.R. Ewing, as portrayed by Larry Hagman on the smash hit *Dallas*. Hagman's smiling, smarmy performance as the amoral oil wheeler-dealer had become so entrenched in the public consciousness that an estimated 90 million people tuned in nationwide (and double that worldwide) to learn who, indeed, had shot J.R. That 1980 episode became the highest-rated program in the history of television, only to be topped a few years later by the final episode of *M*A*S*H*.

The son of Broadway veteran Mary Martin, Hagman was brought up by his father, lawyer Benjamin Hagman, in Texas, and later by his grandmother in Los Angeles. Having trouble dealing with his parents' divorce and his mother's growing fame, Hagman often created discipline problems in a series of private schools he attended. Interested in all aspects of the theater, he worked in various stock companies until 1951, when he joined his mother in London, where she was touring with *South Pacific*. After playing a small part in that show, he stayed in Europe for five years, serving with the U.S. Air Force, directing USO shows. He married Maj Axelsson, a Swedish dress designer, in 1954.

Returning to the States, he worked on and off Broadway and in live TV dramas. In 1961 he joined the cast of *The Edge of Night* as lawyer Ed Gibson, a part he played for two years. Hagman became the second male lead on the serial, his storyline becoming strong when he married Judy Marceau, the mischievous daughter of the police chief. Hagman left the show (as Ed mysteriously disappeared from Monticello) to seek work in Hollywood. In a change-of-pace role, he starred as Major Tony Nelson in NBC's *I Dream of Jeannie*, opposite Barbara Eden. The situation comedy, about an Air Force astronaut who finds a genie in a bottle and is involved in one mishap after another, became a surprise hit and enjoyed a five-year run. (The show still runs in syndication.) After his *Jeannie* stint, he returned to the motion picture career that had begun so promisingly in the mid '60s with *Ensign Pulver*, *Fail Safe*, and *The Group*. He gave one of his best performances in the 1974 film *Harry and Tonto* as Art Carney's son.

Later he surprised audiences with his bizarre performance as an "Ugly American" military officer in the 1977 World War II adventure yarn *The Eagle Has Landed.*

Meanwhile, Hagman had starred in two unsuccessful sitcoms, *The Good Life* in 1971 and *Here We Go Again* in 1973. After playing so many lightweight roles in TV movies and program pilots, Hagman was primed for a meatier role on television. The opportunity came with *Dallas.* Hagman, as the ruthless oil tycoon J.R. Ewing, slipped into the role with such zest and relish, he left audiences alternately amused and horrified. There was nothing J.R. would not do: swindle business partners, sleep with his sister-in-law, commit his wife to a sanatorium. As Hagman's popularity grew, *Dallas*'s ratings zoomed. By the end of the 1980 season, Hagman had the producers over a barrel in a contract dispute. The season ended with J.R. being shot by an unknown assailant. The summer parlor rage became "Who Shot J.R.?" and several magazines ran contests exploiting the cliffhanger. Hagman returned to the show with a contract that paid $75,000 per episode, three times his salary the previous season. He soon began to direct several episodes of *Dallas* and parlayed his fame into appearances in the big-budget features *Superman* and *S.O.B.*

HALL, DEIDRE

Born October 31, 1947, Milwaukee, Wisconsin.
Dr. Marlena Evans Brady, Days of Our Lives

Raised in Lake Worth, Florida, Hall began her career at the age of 12, winning the title of Junior Orange Bowl Queen. She worked her way through Palm Beach College by disc jockeying at an all-women's radio station and modeling. She moved to Hollywood, did commercials and modeling, and studied acting. During this time she wed songwriter-singer Keith Barbour, a marriage that lasted from 1971 to 1978.

From 1973 to 1975, Hall was seen periodically on *The Young and the Restless* as Nurse Barbara Anderson, a sad sack of a character who caused nothing but problems for ex-husband Dr. Brad Eliot. More to the audience's liking, she next landed the role of Dr. Marlena Evans in 1976 on *Days of Our Lives.* Soon she became the central romantic heroine on the show. Hall displayed her versatility opposite such diverse leading men as Jed Allan, Wayne Northrop, and Drake Hogestyn, and was nominated for the Emmy as Outstanding Supporting Actress in the 1979–80 season and as Outstanding Actress in the 1983–84 and 1984–85 seasons. She proved so popular that she appeared on *Daytime TV*'s monthly Best Actress poll over one hundred times.

She has also won *Soap Opera Digest*'s Outstanding Actress (voted by viewers) in 1982, 1983, 1984, and 1985, culminating in an award in 1986 for Outstanding Contribution by a Performer to the Form of Continuing Drama. The year 1986 turned out to be a banner one for Hall, when she began starring in the NBC prime-time series *Our House* and continued to work on *Days*, taping scenes for the daytime show on Saturday. When *Our House* was renewed for the 1987–88 season, Hall's scheduling became so hectic (indeed she was also running two video companies, Customs Last Stand and Tinselvania Video), that the actress left *Days* reluctantly in April, 1987.

HASTINGS, DON

Born Donald Francis Hastings,
April 1, 1934, Brooklyn, New York.
The Video Ranger, Captain Video;
Jack Lane, The Edge of Night;
Dr. Bob Hughes, As the World Turns

Television's first teen idol with *Captain Video*, Don Hastings later enjoyed the distinction, with his long role on *As the World Turns*, of becoming the longest-running romantic male lead on a daytime serial. He began his career at age six on the radio show *Coast to Coast on a Bus*, and appearing with his brother Bob (formerly Captain Burt Ramsey on *General Hospital*) in a number of other radio programs. Later he performed in a series of popular Broadway plays, including *Life with Father*, *I Remember Mama*, *Young Man's Fancy*, and *Summer and Smoke*.

At fifteen he was selected to play the Video Ranger on DuMont's space opera *Captain Video*. For the next six years he became the idol of every youngster across the country—that is, everyone lucky enough to have access to a television set in the early '50s. After stints on the soap opera anthology serials *Date with Life* and *Modern Romances*, Hastings joined the original cast of *The Edge of Night* as Jack Lane, Mike Karr's future brother-in-law, and spoke the opening line on the live premiere episode April 2, 1956. After four years on that show, he switched to the cast of *As the World Turns* (which had premiered the same day as *The Edge of Night*), replacing Ronnie Welch as Bob Hughes. Hastings has played the role of Bob, the perennial loser in love, since 1960. In perhaps the most difficult role in daytime television, that of the sturdy, saintlike matinee idol, the actor has always infused the part with a brisk playing style and refreshing good humor.

In 1971, under the tutelage of Irna Phillips, Hastings began to moonlight as a dialogue writer for the show and later contributed scripts to *The Guiding Light*. (The writer used the pseudonym J.J. Matthew, which combined the names of his children: Julie, Jennifer, and Matthew.) Wanting to stretch his musical talents, abandoned since his radio days (although he had performed on television on *Chevrolet on Broadway* and *The Ed Sullivan Show*), he joined co-star Kathryn Hays in a revue entitled *Hastings and Hays on Love*, which toured in 1977. He has also recorded material for Columbia records. Shortly after a 1978 storyline in which Bob romanced Karen Peters on the show, Hastings married Leslie Denniston, the appealing actress who had played the mysterious Karen. Denniston has been playing Maeve Stoddard on *Guiding Light* since August 1985.

HAYES, SUSAN SEAFORTH

Born July 11, 1943, San Francisco, California.
Julie Olson Williams, Days of Our Lives;
JoAnna Manning, The Young and the Restless

One of daytime's true superstars, and a genuinely superb actress, Susan Seaforth (née Seabold) grew up in Los Angeles, raised by her mother, radio soap opera actress (and later headwriter of *Days of Our Lives*) Elizabeth Harrower. At four years of age she appeared in a local production of *Madame Butterfly* as the orphan child called "Trouble." Amusingly typecast afterwards, she found steady work in television, eventually appearing on over 100 shows. At age eleven she guest-starred on *Lassie* as a brat who fed tainted meat to the champ, and so villainous was her portrayal that she quickly incurred the wrath of America's children. Other TV shots included "the other woman" on several shows, Robbie's girlfriend on *My Three Sons*, and in a series pilot entitled *Kissin' Cousin*, which co-starred Edd "Kookie" Byrnes. In the 1965 film *Billie*, Seaforth played Patty Duke's older sister.

Seaforth grew interested in politics, becoming active in both Barry Goldwater's Presidential campaign in 1964 and George Murphy's Senate campaign. She addressed the platform committee of the Republican National Convention and traveled to Washington, D.C., as part of "Project Prayer," which lobbied for a Constitutional amendment to permit prayer in public schools. But she learned Hollywood does not take kindly to actresses with strong opinions, whether those viewpoints are on the right or the left, and Seaforth found her acting career at a standstill. She found work in daytime television as Dorothy Bradley on *General Hospital* shortly after that show's premiere and later as Carol West on *The Young Marrieds*, a youth-oriented soap also taped in Hollywood. Then she joined the cast of *Days of Our Lives* in 1968 as Julie Olson, replacing a long line of actresses who had failed to make an impact in the role.

As Julie—part Jezebel, part Scarlett O'Hara—Seaforth turned in a fiery performance, alternately alienating and fascinating viewers as the stormy romance on *Days of Our Lives* grew so complex that the line between heroine and villainess blurred. Julie soon met her match in Doug Williams, played by Bill Hayes, and fireworks exploded, both on and off screen. Seaforth and Hayes married in 1974. Afterwards, the actress was billed as Susan Seaforth Hayes.

When Susan Flannery and Denise Alexander left *Days of Our Lives*, Seaforth Hayes was left carrying the show alone, a position she pulled off admirably for several years, especially in a rape story written by Pat Falken Smith. She was nominated for an Emmy as Outstanding Actress in 1975 and 1976, and was instrumental in *Days of Our Lives*' high ratings in the '70s when she was the "front-burner" heroine. (That is, until Julie was given the dubious distinction of becoming soap opera's youngest grandma.) She was also named Most Popular Actress by *Daytime TV* magazine in 1976 and 1977 and Most Popular Daytime Actress by *Photoplay* in 1977. In the spring of 1983, she received a special Emmy for achievement in daytime television, but the next year she and her husband left the show, complaining that storylines for Julie and Doug were few and far between. In November 1984 Seaforth Hayes joined the cast of *The Young and the Restless* as JoAnna Manning, working for Bill Bell, the writer who started it all for her on *Days of Our Lives*.

LASSER, LOUISE

Born April 11, 1939, New York, New York.
Mary Hartman, Mary Hartman, Mary Hartman

Although acclaimed for her work in film and on stage, Louise Lasser's performance as the bewigged, perplexed, comically unflappable Mary Hartman will be forever enshrined in the annals of popular culture. The only child of tax expert S. Jay Lasser, she attended private schools and progressive summer camps before majoring in political theory at Brandeis University. However, before receiving a degree she dropped out of school and returned to New York and studied acting with Sandford Meisner. She understudied Barbra Streisand in the musical *I Can Get It For You Wholesale* in 1962, and later made her Broadway debut replacing Streisand for a week in the play.

After appearing in several nightclubs, Lasser made her move into feature films with roles in *What's New, Pussycat?* and *What's Up, Tiger Lily?*, both written by Woody Allen, whom she had met in 1961. In 1966 she married Allen, and although she divorced him four years later, she continued to appear in his films, delighting audiences with her hilarious work in *Take the Money and Run*, *Bananas*, and *Everything You Always Wanted to Know About Sex But Were Afraid to Ask*. Meanwhile, on television she became a familiar face in a series of popular commercials, a stint on the daytime drama *The Doctors* (as "Jackie"), situation comedies like *The Bob Newhart Show* and *The Mary Tyler Moore Show*, and in the TV drama *The Lie*, written by Swedish director Ingmar Bergman.

However, it was her starring role as Mary Hartman that saw her face decorating the cover of dozens of magazines, made her a household name, and inspired a cultlike following. Wide-eyed and deathly concerned, and costumed in doll-like gingham dresses, Lasser as Mary Hartman pulled on her teeth in confusion, whined and quietly cajoled, and put her distinctive, hesitant comic delivery to full effect in a memorable, appealing characterization. But after an arrest for possession of cocaine and after two seasons with the show—which consisted of a grueling schedule of daily tapings, rumors of temperament on the set, and an alleged dangerous personal overidentification with the character—Lasser left the show. She returned to the stage a few years later with a deliciously comic performance in *A Coupla White Chicks Sitting Around Talking*, directed by soap star Dorothy Lyman (Opal Gardner, *All My Children*). Lasser also later popped up on TV as a regular in the short-lived sitcom *Making a Living* and as Alex's dizzy ex-wife on *Taxi*.

LEMAY, HARDING

Born March 16, 1922, North Bangor, New York.
Headwriter, Another World 1971–79

The controversial writer of *Another World* during the height of its popularity and the creator of two short-lived daytime dramas, Harding Lemay grew up in the farmlands in upper New York near the Canadian border. After a stint with the U.S. Army, he enjoyed a successful career in publishing but left Alfred A. Knopf Inc. to concentrate on a lifelong dream: playwriting. In 1963 *Look at Any Man* was produced, followed two years later by the deeply personal *The Little Birds Fly*, which dramatized the return home of six adults for their father's funeral and their attempt to come to terms with the misery of their childhood, remembering their suicidal father and their insane mother. This was followed in 1971 by an even more revealing autobiography, *Inside, Looking Out*, a beautifully written memoir that described in detail his nightmarish boyhood. Narrated without a trace of self-pity and in unsparing detail, it received excellent reviews, but its sales were not enough to support his wife and two children.

To make ends meet, Lemay taught literature at Hunter College, and, embarrassed, wrote scripts for the final weeks of *Strange Paradise*, a Canadian TV serial modeled on *Dark Shadows*, which featured voodoo and witchcraft. He was commissioned to write a sample script for the CBS soap *Where the Heart Is*, which was turned down with a pungent criticism scrawled across the title page: "This guy will never write for daytime television." Impressed by Lemay's autobiography, which contained material for a dozen soap operas, Procter & Gamble approached the writer about taking over the headwriting chores of *Another World*. Asked what he thought of the show, Lemay, who had watched the show for weeks, replied, "It's shit."

Over a period of eight years, Lemay worked at a feverish pitch to change that assessment. He threw out *Another World*'s crazy melodrama and replaced it with domestic drama, class conflict, and tension created by highly complex characters falling in and out of love. With the addition of some of the finest actors from the New York stage and Paul Rauch's production overhaul, *Another World* soon evolved into a sophisticated drawing-room drama, the closest thing to real theater on television since the days of *Studio One*. In 1975, the serial zoomed to number one in the ratings and Lemay won the Emmy for Outstanding Writing. In the same year, the writer wanted to dispose of two popular actresses, Jacqueline Courtney and Virginia Dwyer, whose acting and timing he thought too "soap operaish," while producer Rauch wanted to unload George Reinholt, the show's troublesome leading man. After the firing of the three performers and the brouhaha that followed, *Another World* was never quite the same.

Lemay's writing was occasionally brilliant, and the introduction of the Frame family—based on the writer's twelve brothers and sisters—provided much of the needed dramatic impetus to the story. But with the creation of Lemay's new soap *Lovers and Friends* in 1977 and the expansion of *Another World* to sixty and then ninety minutes, it was apparent that the writer was spreading himself too thin. Recasting became a problem, and Lemay, who was attempting the herculean task of writing not only the story outlines but also most of the daily scripts, began to depend heavily on soap staples such as murder trials to keep up the ratings. Pressured by P & G executives to develop more plot and cut down on "Chekhovian vignettes" (which made *Another World* a pleasure to watch), Lemay left the show in 1979. He quickly went to work on a book about the show, and in 1981, the fascinating *Eight Years in Another World* was published.

The eyebrow-raising memoir, which skewered some actors, some writers, and especially Procter & Gamble, did not prevent Lemay from returning to daytime television. He became associate writer for headwriter Douglas Marland, who had previously written for Lemay, for the P & G (!) produced *Guiding Light*. After picking up another Emmy for Outstanding Writing, with Marland, Lemay served briefly as headwriter of *Search for Tomorrow* in the summer of 1981. The stint ended with the writers' strike and charges by Lemay that producer Mary-Ellis Bunim urged him to "spice up" the romantic scenes. (She, in turn, merely said that Lemay proved "ineffective.") In 1982, he became headwriter of *The Doctors*, with his son Stephen serving as his associate writer. His stay was short, as *The Doctors* proved to be a revolving door for writers. The show was cancelled shortly after Lemay's departure. He came back to the serial scene in 1985, serving as story consultant to *As the World Turns*.

LIGHT, JUDITH

Born February 9, 1949, Trenton, New Jersey.
Karen Wolek, One Life to Live

The winner of two consecutive Emmys for Outstanding Actress, countless fan magazine awards, and unanimous critical praise for her powerhouse performance as Karen Wolek on *One Life to Live*, Judith Light grew up in New Jersey, the only child of an accountant and his wife. She attended private school, worked in community theater, and earned a drama degree at Carnegie-Mellon University. Then she spent four and a half years in repertory companies in Seattle, Milwaukee, Toronto, and New York, playing a gamut of classic roles, from Thornton Wilder's *Our Town*, to Tennessee Williams' *A Streetcar Named Desire* and *Camino Real*, to Chekhov's *The Seagull*, to Shakespearean characters.

In New York she had a small role in the 1975 Broadway production of *A Doll's House*, which starred Liv Ullmann, and a major guest shot on TV's *Kojak*. In 1977, with her career at a low ebb, Light won a leading role in *Herzl*, a Broadway play about the founding of Zionism. Although the show was short-lived, the actress received high praise for her performance as Julie Herzl, and Light found work in a theater production of *Uncommon Women*. That October, she auditioned for *One Life to Live* to understudy Kathryn Breech, who played the teasing, sexually precocious housewife Karen Wolek. Within a week Light had the part. While Breech had played Karen as a coldly calculating temptress who never delivered, Light tore into the role with a blinding inner rage and guilt-ridden, high-powered sexuality. Light and writer Gordon Russell delved into Karen's promiscuity and self-hatred with such unrelenting passion that Karen's self-destructiveness became almost painful to watch.

In the spring of 1979 all of *One Life to Live*'s complex storylines came to a head with Victoria Lord's trial for murdering Marco Dane. Judith Light's performance—as Karen was forced into confessing her prostitution to save her friend—was a phenomenon, a riveting tour de force that shocked and devastated viewers. The outpouring following Light's magnificent performance was unprecedented. Letters and telephone calls flooded the network and fan magazines. ABC officials and editors said they had never witnessed such a strong, emotional response. Light jumped out of nowhere to the top of *Daytime TV*'s monthly popularity poll.

Light deservedly won the Emmy for Outstanding Actress in 1980, and then took the award again the next year. After the death of Gordon Russell, who had written so many set pieces for the actress, Light never had another equally challenging storyline. She left the show in January 1983 and was successfully teamed with soap superstar Anthony Geary in the TV movie *Intimate Agony*. She then turned up on the prime-time series *St. Elsewhere* in an amusing performance as a pregnant woman who wanted to kill the doctor who had supposedly botched her husband's vasectomy. In the 1983–84 season, Light continued to advance her career, becoming a frequent guest star on prime-time dramatic series. She starred on *Family Ties* as a vamp, on *Mississippi* as a southern novelist accused of libel, and on *Remington Steele* as a sexy jewel thief. She also appeared on the NBC drama special *You Are the Jury* as the passionate defense attorney for a man accused of first-degree murder. In the fall of 1984, Light began a regular starring role, with Tony Danza, in the prime-time situation comedy *Who's the Boss?*.

LUCCI, SUSAN

Born December 23, 1948, Westchester, New York.
Erica Kane, All My Children

Probably the highest paid performer on daytime television, Susan Lucci was brought up on Long Island, then attended Marymount College in Tarrytown, New York. After graduation she filmed a movie which was never released, and then landed the plum role of spoiled teenager Erica Kane on the premiere episode of *All My Children* in 1970. As the impetuous Erica, Lucci was both vivacious and disturbing—an outrageous and self-absorbed young vixen that viewers found hilariously likable. As Erica's emotional pranks multiplied, *All My Children*'s ratings climbed and ABC soon began to promote the character in an unprecedented number of commercial spots.

For her work, Lucci won eight Emmy nominations, the first in 1978. Although the Television Academy may see her as always-a-bridesmaid-never-a-bride, the show is sure to outfit Lucci's Erica in a new wedding gown every few seasons. Erica has been married and divorced four times, as well as being engaged to her half-brother and seeing two of her lovers peek down the wrong end of a gun barrel. Lucci's offscreen life is a bit more peaceful, the actress having married restaurateur Helmut Huber in 1969. Lucci and Huber have two children: Liza, born in 1975, and Andreas, born in 1980. Although *All My Children* has managed a virtual monopoly on the actress, the petite Lucci (5′2″, 95 lbs.) took some time off from the serial to star in the top-rated TV-movie, *Invitation to Hell*. She has also appeared in episodes of *Fantasy Island* and *The Love Boat*, and made a cameo appearance in the comedy film *Young Doctors in Love*.

Lucci also parlayed her daytime success in two other TV movies, *Mafia Princess* and *Secret Passions* and was featured in the mini-series *Anastasia*.

MCKINSEY, BEVERLEE

Born August 9, 1940, McAlester, Oklahoma.
Iris Carrington, Another World and Texas;
Alexandra Spaulding, Guiding Light

Probably the most sophisticated presence to grace daytime drama, McKinsey began her show business career as the hostess of the children's show *The Make Believe Clubhouse* on public television in Boston. She appeared on Broadway in *Who's Afraid of Virginia Woolf?* and *Barefoot in the Park* and was seen in such TV series as *Hawaii Five-O* and *Remington Steele*. Her film credits include *Bronco Billy*, opposite Clint Eastwood.

McKinsey began her daytime drama career as Martha Donnelly (a.k.a Julie Richards) in the 1970–71 season on *Love Is a Many Splendored Thing*, where she played opposite her future husband Berkeley Harris. She did a bit part on *Another World* as Emma Ordway (a farm woman!), then returned triumphantly to the show in 1972 as the snobbish, manipulative Iris Carrington, who was bound and determined to break up any romance between "golddigger" Rachel and Iris's doting father, Mac. For her many exquisite performances she was nominated four times for an Outstanding Actress Emmy. She also was selected in 1978 by the editors of *Afternoon TV* as Best Actress and was voted "Favorite Villainess" by the readers of *Soap Opera Digest* for two years running.

In 1980, her popular character was spun off in a new serial, *Texas*, where she received an unusual billing for a daytime actress: *Texas*—starring Beverlee McKinsey. In February 1984, she joined the cast of *Guiding Light* as the aristocratic Alexandra Spaulding, who has been turning Springfield on its ear ever since.

MARLAND, DOUGLAS

Born May 5, 1935, West Sand Lake, New York.
Creator, A New Day in Eden;
Co-creator, Loving;
Headwriter, General Hospital, Guiding Light,
and As the World Turns

Considered by serial critics and performers alike as the best writer in daytime drama, Douglas Marland began his career not as a writer but as an actor. He appeared in summer stock, on the soap *The Brighter Day*, guest-starred on *The Doctors* (when it was an anthology series in 1963) and had a running role in 1973 on *As the World Turns* as Dr. Eric Lonsberry, Lisa's gynecologist. (The unfortunate Marland was part of the now infamous Irna Phillips' "phantom fetus" story: unstable Lisa ballooned up, had labor pains, Dr. Eric performed a C-section, and, oops, no bambino!) His film credits include *The Great Imposter*, *The Pleasure of His Company*, and *Toward the Light*.

During *Another World*'s golden age, Marland began writing under the tutelage of Harding Lemay and won his first Emmy in 1975. The next year he took over the headwriting chores of *The Doctors* where he developed the fascinating Dancy family, pairing golddigger Nola Dancy with the wealthy Jason Aldrich. Impressed by his work on that show, ABC hired Marland to take over the ailing *General Hospital*, where Marland created wonders: during his two year tenure the show rose from #9 in the ratings to the top spot. He next wrote *As the World Turns* for a thirteen week cycle, then became headwriter of *Guiding Light* in January 1980.

During the next two and a half years, *Guiding Light* saw a critical renaissance (explorations of teenage sexuality and teen alcoholism, the hilarious cinematic fantasies of Nola Reardon), and Marland was rewarded with Emmies in 1981 and 1982. Afterwards, he created the cable soap *A New Day in Eden* in 1982 and co-created (with Agnes Nixon) the ABC serial *Loving* in 1983. Two years later, Marland returned triumphantly to the hour format as headwriter of *As the World Turns*, where his strong storylines and set pieces for characters in all age groups resulted in still another Emmy nomination.

NIXON, AGNES

Born Agnes Eckhardt,
December 10, 1927, Chicago, Illinois.
Creator, All My Children *and* One Life to Live;
Co-creator, Search for Tomorrow, As the World Turns, *and* Loving

The most respected and influential writer in daytime drama, Agnes Eckhardt grew up in a devout Catholic home in Nashville. She has always had a passion for storytelling. As a child she cut out pictures from comic strips such as *Etta Kent* and *Tillie the Toiler*, and played with them as if they were paper dolls, moving them about and creating her own variations of the stories. As she grew older she became enchanted with the novels of Louisa May Alcott, followed the serial *Little Orphan Annie* on the radio, and took drama lessons. She acted in high school and attended Northwestern University, majoring in speech and drama. In her classes were such luminaries as Charlton Heston, Patricia Neal, Martha Hyer, and Cloris Leachman. Feeling she lacked the true singularity that made an exceptional actress, Eckhardt turned to writing. She sold a radio play while still in school, and to avoid working in her father's burial-garment business, went to see soap opera queen Irna Phillips with dreams of becoming a professional writer.

The formidable Phillips took Eckhardt's script and, to the consternation of the young writer, proceeded to read every word of it aloud. After the reading, Phillips turned to the trembling author and asked, "Would you like to work for me?" Under Phillips' tutelage, Eckhardt began her job as a dialogue writer for radio's *Woman in White* at $100 a week. Later, she struck out on her own, free-lancing in New York during television's Golden Age of live drama—a golden age that, she said, "lasted fifteen minutes." She wrote teleplays for *Studio One*, *Playhouse 90*, *The Hallmark Hall of Fame*, and even Hazel Bishop Lipstick's *My True Story*. On April 6, 1951, she married Robert Nixon, an executive with the Chrysler Corporation, and settled in Pennsylvania. Her talent for childbearing proved as prolific as her writing career; she produced four children in five years. (Her eldest daughter, Cathy Chicos, later became a dialogue writer for *All My Children*.)

The same year of her marriage, she created *Search for Tomorrow* with Roy Winsor, writing the first three-month cycle. *Search for Tomorrow*, which became the first successful daytime drama, also was to become one of the longest-running serials in the history of television. A few years later, Nixon was reunited with Irna Phillips, becoming a writer for *The Guiding Light*. After co-creating *As the World Turns* with Phillips in 1956, Nixon became headwriter of *The Guiding Light*. There she began her much-heralded "relevance" campaign, mixing social issues and educational crusades into the story. A storyline about a woman whose life was saved by an early checkup—a pap smear detected uterine cancer—brought an abundance of mail from appreciative women, some of whom said that the story had saved their own lives by prodding them to seek regular checkups.

After a long headwriting stint on *The Guilding Light*, Nixon worked on a new soap, which was to become *All My Children*, but Procter & Gamble, which optioned the show, could not find room for the project. Instead, she was offered in 1965 the headwriting chores for the floundering melodrama *Another World*. Borrowing slightly from her *All My Children* bible, she created the catalyst character of Rachel Davis (a partial reproduction of *All My Children*'s Erica Kane) and positioned her between the sweet blond heroine Alice Matthews and the upwardly mobile Steve Frame. The love story, which was to become daytime's longest romantic triangle, propelled *Another World* to the number-two spot in the daytime ratings.

With her name firmly established in the business, Nixon was given the opportunity to create a new soap, *One Life to Live*, for ABC in 1968. Although *One Life to Live* was built around the serial formula of two families, one rich, one poor, it was unusual in that ethnic types (Polish Catholics, Blacks, Jews), blue-collar workers, and strong male characters were in the forefront of the drama. Even more unusual was the emphasis on social issues. Nixon devised a plot in which a black woman passed as white and became engaged to a white doctor. But Carla later fell in love with a black intern, and when she kissed him on the air, the incident caused an uproar and an ABC affiliate in Texas cancelled the program. Nixon also incorporated actual sessions of addicts, taped at New York's Odyssey House, discussing their problems in a anti-drug storyline.

In 1970 ABC wanted the project that P & G had turned down five years earlier, and the upshot was *All My Children*, a winning mixture of socially-oriented drama, young love, and drawing room comedy. In the decade to follow, the enormously popular show covered such issues as the Vietnam peace movement, ecology, wife and child abuse, prostitution, and abortion. Nixon's love stories—Tara and Phil, Nina and Cliff, and Jenny and Greg—were immensely popular and expertly executed. In 1981, Nixon forged into prime-time television with the mini-series *The Manions of America*, which traced the history of a family from their life in Ireland to their immigration to America.

That same year, Nixon won the Trustees Award from the Academy of Television Arts and Sciences for her thirty years of achievement in TV. It was the first time the special Trustees Emmy was awarded to a woman or to a writer. In the summer of 1983, she created, with Douglas Marland, her fifth daytime drama. *Loving*, which was launched with a two-hour prime-time TV movie on June 26, 1983, broke daytime's last taboo with a story of a father sexually abusing his daughter. The incest storyline was just one of the social issues the entertaining, well-written show tackled in its first year.

PHILLIPS, IRNA

Born July 1, 1901, Chicago, Illinois.
Died December 22, 1973, Chicago, Illinois.
Creator, The Guiding Light, The Brighter Day,
As the World Turns, Another World, Days of Our Lives,
and Love Is a Many Splendored Thing

The single most important force in creating what we now call "soap opera," Irna Phillips was one of ten children born to German-Jewish immigrants William and Betty (Buxbaum) Phillips, who owned a Chicago grocery. Her father died when she was eight. Phillips remembered her early life as quietly dreary, a world in which she sought solace in books and make-believe, a child "with hand-me-down-clothes and no friends." Dreaming of becoming an actress, she received a master's degree in drama at the University of Wisconsin in 1924. But realizing that she was essentially a plain-looking woman, she put aside her show-business aspirations and taught English, public speaking, and drama for five years.

She got a big break acting and working in various capacities for WGN, a radio station in Chicago. While broadcasting a series entitled *Thought for a Day*, Phillips worked from notes and improvised frequently—and apparently successfully, because soon she was offered a job as a writer for the station in 1932. The result was *Painted Dreams*, a ten-minute daily serial centering on an Irish widow struggling to raise a large family. Obviously autobiographical, *Painted Dreams*, which is generally considered radio's first "soap opera," involved an ethnic switch, since Phillips' family was Jewish. Phillips doubled as an actress for the show, playing Mother Monahan, but left the show to create for NBC *Today's Children*, a virtual remake of *Painted Dreams*.

With *Today's Children* established as a smash hit, Phillips then created

The Guiding Light, which followed Dr. Ruthledge, a minister, and his flock. On radio, *The Guiding Light* ran from 1937 to 1956, and, in 1952, was successfully transferred to television. *The Road of Life*, which was also launched in 1937 and featured soap opera's first physician, had a thirty-two-year run on radio. Other Irna Phillips creations included *Woman in White*, a serial about nurses that ran from 1939 to 1942; *The Right to Happiness*, which ran from 1939 to 1960; and *The Brighter Day*, which ran from 1944 to 1956 on radio and from 1954 to 1962 on television. Her most unusual creation was on a segment of *The General Mills Hour*, which had characters from all of Phillips' soaps interacting with one another—a device she would use twenty years later when Mike Bauer was "borrowed" from the TV version of *The Guiding Light* to visit the recently launched *Another World*.

During the '40s, Phillips was writing two million words a year (the equivalent of thirty to forty novels), dictating six to eight hours a day, editing on the spot, and seldom rewriting. She earned $250,000 a year, but her personal life proved uneventful. (She shared her mother's bedroom for thirty-seven years.) She admitted to being in love only once, and told an interviewer that she once had an affair with a man who refused to marry her when he learned she could not have children. At age forty-two, and unmarried, she adopted a son, Thomas Dirk Phillips. A year and a half later, she adopted a daughter, Katherine, who followed her mother's footsteps, later pursuing a writing career.

In January 1949, Phillips created her first serial (and the first on a major network) for television. *These Are My Children* was about a widow and her children, and was obviously patterned on *Painted Dreams* and *Today's Children*. Although the soap ran just a month on NBC, Phillips was not discouraged. She brought *The Guiding Light* to TV in 1952, and this time the soap opera form adapted itself well to the new medium. She also successfully transferred *The Brighter Day* from radio, but not *The Road of Life*, which failed on TV. *As the World Turns* in 1956 became Phillips' biggest triumph. Breaking tradition by running a half hour, the show was a revolutionary visual approach to drama on TV and perfectly suited to the new medium, featuring minimal plot, richer characterizations, and long, serious conversations.

For the next decade the irascible writer ruled her kingdom with an iron hand, frequently terrorizing producers, writers, and directors with long telephone calls that left no doubt how she felt about the execution of her ideas. It was generally agreed that even her bosses, executives with Procter & Gamble, lived in mortal fear of her. (When actress Eileen Fulton accidentally dropped her script, a shocked P & G official retrieved it with the admonition, "An Irna Phillips' script is like the flag; it never touches the floor.") Actors were fired on a whim, or even if Phillips did not like their looks. In person, actors were addressed by their character names, never their real names. Phillips expected everyone to share her all-consuming passion for her stories. Once, while glancing at the TV news in 1964, she pointed at Barry Goldwater and asked, "Who is he?" When it was explained that he was the Republican candidate for President, she stared at him for a moment and murmured, "That's good casting."

Another World, in 1964, was Phillips' first foray into melodrama. When it became clear that the domestically oriented writer was out of her element, the reins were handed over to Agnes Nixon, who made the show a hit. After co-creating *Days of Our Lives* in 1965, Phillips branched out into prime-time, first as a story consultant to *Peyton Place*, and then as the co-creator of *Our Private World*, a spin-off of daytime's *As the World Turns*. In a daring move, Phillips brought to daytime a serial version of the film *Love Is a Many Splendored Thing*. When executives insisted that the interracial romance be dropped, an irate Phillips quit. In 1970, Phillips' daughter created a daytime drama entitled *A World Apart*, about a serial writer and two adopted children. The autobiographical soap, for which Phillips served as story consultant, was a failure, cancelled in little over a year.

In what turned out to be a major mistake, Phillips returned as headwriter to her "baby," *As the World Turns*. While the writer's ideas were still striking, Phillips' day-to-day scripting was not her best and her dialogue was atrocious. Amid grumblings from performers and executives, she retired, citing "health reasons," and began work on her autobiography, entitled *All My Worlds*. On Christmas Day, 1973, Agnes Nixon telephoned to wish her well and was told that Phillips had died in her sleep a few days earlier. The great lady of soap opera had not wanted anyone to be informed of her death.

Throughout her life Irna Phillips was a fascinating paradox. Although she never married, the core of her writing was always the family, the rearing of children, and, ironically, the fulfillment of women through marriage. A career woman, but not a feminist, she deplored the increasing preoccupation with sex and sensationalism in the soaps, although she had created such daring, colorful characters as the free-spirited Edith Hughes in the '50s and, in 1958, had presented perhaps the first illegitimate child on daytime TV (Dan Stewart, *As the World Turns*).

She is credited with pioneering what are now parodied clichés: hospital settings, musical enhancement, amnesia as a plot device, the "tease" ending of an episode, the voice-over thoughts a character shares with the audience, and the involved conversations over the ubiquitous cup of coffee. But she was also the first to insist on total authenticity in her scripts, retaining a lawyer and two doctors for technical advice. Her impact on TV serial drama is inestimable, and her protégés, Agnes Nixon and Bill Bell, have gone on to create their own modern soap operas in the Irna Phillips' tradition.

REINHOLT, GEORGE

Born August 22, 1940, Philadelphia, Pennsylvania.
Steven Frame, Another World;
Tony Lord, One Life to Live

Daytime television's most popular and controversial male star of the '70s, George Reinholt grew up in South Philadelphia, working in local theater. He moved to New York and appeared in a production of *Misalliance* and worked in repertory at Washington, D.C.'s Arena Stage. After touring the West Coast and working at the Pasadena Playhouse with Imogene

Coca, he returned to New York to study with famed acting teacher Milton Katselas. He later appeared on Broadway in *Cabaret* and *The Grand Tour*.

On daytime TV Reinholt played Erik Fulda, a villain, on *The Secret Storm*. In 1968, he joined the cast of *Another World*, then being written by Agnes Nixon, and played his role-of-a-lifetime. As Steve Frame, the ambitious young businessman fascinated with both the sweet Alice and the destructive Rachel, Reinholt was an immediate smash with *Another World*'s growing audience, transfixing them with his brash, complex performances. Steve's fiercely ambivalent scenes with Rachel and his vulnerable, romantic scenes with Alice made stars of Reinholt and of Robin Strasser and Jacqueline Courtney as well. For years he topped the highly competitive poll in *Daytime TV*, and took that magazine's award for Best Actor in 1971 and 1974.

However, all was not well in Bay City and at the NBC studios in Brooklyn. Harding Lemay had become headwriter of *Another World* in 1971, and while he further developed the Alice-Steve-Rachel triangle, Lemay remained privately unenthusiastic about the storyline. On the set Reinholt complained openly about the quality of Lemay's scripts, while the actor's sometimes turbulent behavior put him at odds with producer Paul Rauch. Reinholt's talent was undeniable, and even Lemay conceded that the actor's performances were often "brilliant." However, Reinholt's acting became increasingly mannered, and Paul Rauch considered his onset behavior and his harsh comments to the press not worth the trouble. In February 1975, Reinholt was fired; Steve Frame crashed his helicopter in Australia and was presumed dead. Jacqueline Courtney, whose performances Lemay deemed too "soap operaish," was fired six months later.

Shortly afterwards, Agnes Nixon, who had created the character Steve Frame, offered Reinholt a part on her *One Life to Live*, which aired directly opposite *Another World*. As still another outsider, Tony Lord, the illegitimate son of Victor Lord, Reinholt sustained his popularity, especially when he was reunited with Jacqueline Courtney, who had been signed to play Patricia Kendall. Although the actor's performance was uneven— fresh and engaging one day, mannered the next—the Reinholt-Courtney reunion immediately boosted *One Life to Live*'s sagging ratings. Two years later, Reinholt left the show when his contract expired. But the Pat-Tony romance continued for many years with two other actors attempting, unsuccessfully, to fill Reinholt's formidable boots. The actor soon made his film debut in *Looking Up*, which featured some of his co-stars on *One Life to Live*. Afterwards, Reinholt stayed away from daytime drama, retiring to his native Philadelphia.

SLESAR, HENRY

Born June 12, 1927, Brooklyn, New York.
Headwriter, The Edge of Night 1968–83;
Creator, Executive Suite

The multi-award-winning master of suspense won a wide following with his sarcastically witty dialogue and patently wild denouements. Henry

Slesar grew up in New York and attended the School of Industrial Art. He began to write advertising copy when he was seventeen and continued to churn it out for almost two decades. In 1955, he started to write fiction, selling nearly 200 stories before publishing his first book in 1959, *The Gray Flannel Shroud* (Random House), which won the prestigious Edgar Award for best first mystery novel. This was followed the next year by *Enter Murderers* (Random House) and, in 1961, *Clean Crimes and Neat Murders* (Avon), stories that had been adapted for the television series *Alfred Hitchcock Presents.* Slesar's collection, introduced by Hitchcock, became the first volume in Hitchcock's popular mystery-anthology series. Slesar worked regularly for Hitchcock, eventually writing over sixty scripts for the show.

After the cancellation of *Alfred Hitchcock Presents* in 1960, Slesar published two more books, a second Hitchcock collection *A Crime for Mothers and Others* (Avon, 1962) and *The Bridge of Lions* (Macmillan, 1963). He continued writing teleplays for such popular series as *The Name of the Game*, *Batman*, *Run for Your Life*, and *The Man from U.N.C.L.E.* Slesar also broke into motion pictures, writing screenplays for two films, *Two on a Guillotine* and *Murders in the Rue Morgue*. But writing for Hollywood proved to be a burden for the New York–based writer, who found himself traveling too often to the West Coast for script conferences. His search for regular work in New York came to an end when he was asked to fill in for a vacationing headwriter on *The Edge of Night* for three months.

Eight months later, in March 1968, Slesar took over as headwriter on *The Edge of Night*, a position he was to hold for the next fifteen years, the longest stint for a headwriter in the history of daytime drama. He soon became famous for his sassy characters, intricate plotting, and grand twists of irony, all spiced by a series of amusing "blue herrings." (Ever perverse, Slesar writes that it is his "belief that modern audiences are so accustomed to red herrings that they sniff them out too readily. Therefore, I look for the 'blue herring,' the herring that *looks* red but is really another color.") Slesar techniques proved so popular that Procter & Gamble asked him in 1971 to revive the ailing *Somerset*, a spin-off of *Another World* that was sinking fast. While still writing *The Edge of Night*, he worked simultaneously on *Somerset*, creating the wacky Moore family (who looked as if they had just come down from a bad acid trip) and a splendid suspense story about a clown (one of the Moores) who was terrorizing Somerset's resident ingenue. For two years *Somerset* became a mystery-crime serial, but it was transformed into traditional soap opera fare upon Slesar's departure.

While continuing as *The Edge of Night*'s headwriter, Slesar still found time for outside projects, working on the nighttime series *McMillan and Wife* and *ABC Wide World of Mystery*. He also wrote more short fiction, eventually racking up over 700 story credits. His work has been included in more than 120 anthologies and textbooks. He published two more novels, *The Seventh Mask* (Ace, 1969) and *The Thing at the Door* (Pocket, 1974). In 1976, he created the prime-time serial *Executive Suite*, employing a large Los Angeles conglomerate as the backdrop for romance and intrigue. Although the effort was short-lived, it reinforced Slesar's reputation for wearing two hats with ease. With that in mind, Procter & Gamble appointed him headwriter of *Search for Tomorrow* in 1978. Slesar's stay with *Search* proved brief, like that of most writers on that revolving-door show, but it demonstrated his ability to break out of the crime genre.

Slesar continued to write *The Edge of Night* until the middle of 1983, delighting audiences with his exotically named, spunky heroines (Raven, Brandy, etc.), wisecracking romances, and unforgettable gallery of villainesses, from the insidious Stephanie Martin with her poison chocolates and cryptic quotations from Shakespeare to the tragic Denise Cavanaugh with her soaring monologues on the perfect crime, her own death. For his consistently exhilarating work he was awarded an Emmy for Best Writing in 1974, followed by nominations in 1980 and 1982. (He has also been nominated for six Writers Guild Awards.)

While still writing for daytime television, Slesar branched out to radio with the revival series *CBS Radio Mystery Theater*, and wrote forty scripts for the show. Most of his fiction has been published abroad, and many stories have been adapted for European television. An anthology series based on his stories, entitled *Krimistunde (Crime Hour)* and produced in Munich, has become popular in such countries as West Germany, Switzerland, Italy, Poland, Hungary, and Czechoslovakia. In late 1983, Slesar joined Sam Hall as co-headwriter of *One Life to Live*, and the duo created a few suspenseful, surprising twists and turns for the hapless people of Llanview, before leaving the show in August 1984. He became headwriter of *Capitol* in October of the same year. He left the show in February 1986.

SLEZAK, ERIKA

Born August 5, 1946, Los Angeles, California.
Victoria Lord, One Life to Live

The winner of two Emmies as Outstanding Actress for her role on *One Life to Live*, Erika Slezak is the class act of daytime drama. The daughter of the late stage and film star Walter Slezak (*Lifeboat*, etc), she received her acting training at the Royal Academy of Dramatic Art in London and was a member of the Milwaukee Repertory Company for three seasons and the Alley Theatre in Houston for one season, playing everything from Noel Coward to Chekhov to Shakespeare.

In 1971, Slezak won the pivotal role of Victoria Lord Riley on *One Life to Live* and quickly won a wide following for her appealing performance. Misused for many seasons, but always dependable (indeed, she always brought unerring charm and sophistication to even the simplest of scenes), Slezak took her first Emmy for Outstanding Actress for the 1983–84 season (for the Echo DiSavoy story). When Paul Rauch took over as producer, Slezak's role expanded dramatically in early 1985 when the Viki/Niki split personality storyline was revived after nearly fifteen years. Appearing almost daily, Slezak was magnificent as a woman breaking down and escaping into an alternate, hedonistic personality.

The actress nabbed her second Emmy and the show continued its focus on Viki, reveling in her rich history, and placing the character in a series of melodramatic situations that brought *One Life to Live* its highest ratings in years. Offscreen, Slezak is married to actor Brian Davies and has two children, Michael Lawrence and Amanda Elizabeth.

STRASSER, ROBIN

Born May 7, 1945, New York, New York.
Rachel Davis, Another World;
Dorian Lord, One Life to Live

A sensation as the gutsy Rachel Davis on *Another World* and an Emmy award winner as the sophisticated Dorian Lord on *One Life to Live*, Robin Strasser studied at the Yale Drama School, then apprenticed at both the New York Shakespeare Festival and the Williamstown Summer Theater. In 1963, she made her Broadway debut in *The Irregular Verb to Love*, which was followed by performances in *The Country Girl* and *The Impossible Years*. She got her first break in daytime television when she was selected to play Rachel on Agnes Nixon's *Another World* in 1967. As the girl-from-the-wrong-side-of-the-tracks who became obsessed with the ambitious Steve Frame, Strasser was superb, that rare villainess who stirred primal emotions and provoked audience identification and sympathy. She received considerable attention in the soap opera press and soared in the readers' popularity polls, the first bad-girl characterization to capture such attention since Eileen Fulton's Lisa Hughes on *As the World Turns*.

In 1971, at the height of her popularity, she left the show to pursue a theater career, thus breaking up the team of George Reinholt, Jacqueline Courtney, and Strasser, whose work put *Another World* on the map. When her replacement as Rachel did not pan out, the producers of *Another World* convinced her to return to the show for six months until they could recast. Strasser starred in the 1973 feature horror film *The Bride*, then returned to TV in the daytime drama special *The Child Is Mine*. Directed by soap wizard Gloria Monty, this drama pitted Strasser, as an unhappy actress, against Rosemary Prinz, as an alcoholic housewife, in a child custody case. Strasser then did stage work and, once again, returned to daytime with a regular role as the troubled, haunted Christina Karras on Agnes Nixon's *All My Children*.

In 1979, Strasser jumped from one soap to another, joining the cast of *One Life to Live*, quickly rejuvenating the juicy, pivotal role of Dorian Lord. Strasser's energy and bitchy good humor were perfect for Dorian, and as the role grew more complex, the actress's vulnerability poured out with passionate conviction. The marital squabbles between Dorian and Herb Callison were among the most sophisticated and complex ever on television. The dark-eyed, raven-haired beauty was rewarded for her smashing performance with an Emmy for Outstanding Actress in 1982, sandwiched by nominations in 1981 and 1983.

While acting on *All My Children* and *One Life to Live*, Strasser moonlighted on Broadway with starring roles in *The Shadow Box* and Neil Simon's *Chapter Two*, the latter co-starring her husband Laurence Luckinbill (Frank Carver, *The Secret Storm*; Steve Prescott, *Where the Heart Is*), whom she later divorced. Strasser, a founding member of the American Conservatory Theatre, later staged a new production of *A Coupla White Chicks Sitting Around Talking*, which co-starred Brynn Thayer (Jenny Wolek, *One Life to Live*) and was directed by Dorothy Lyman (Opal Gardner, *All My Children*).

For years Strasser has been hounded by a preposterous, but persistent, rumor that she is comedienne Phyllis Diller's daughter and soap star Susan Lucci's sister. It is one of those silly stories without an ounce of validity that bedevil even the most serious and gifted of actresses.

STUART, MARY

Born Mary Houchins,
July 4, 1926, Miami, Florida.
Jo, Search for Tomorrow

If America's three contributions to world culture are musical comedy, jazz, and soap opera, then it is altogether fitting that the queen of soap opera, the star with the longest continuing role in the history of television, was born on Independence Day. Mary Stuart, who has played Jo on *Search for Tomorrow* since 1951, grew up in Tulsa, Oklahoma, where she launched her career plans early, singing with local bands at age twelve and working with the USO at area military bases during high school. After graduation, she worked briefly in Tulsa as a photojournalist to pay her way to New York so she could pursue an acting career.

She found work as a nightclub photographer and a hat check girl at the Hotel Roosevelt Grill. There she was given the opportunity to sing with the hotel band and was discovered by producer Joe Pasternak, who gave her a screen test and put her under contract with MGM. Before leaving for the coast in 1946, she married a New York–based painter who accompanied her to Hollywood. Their marriage was kept secret for career reasons (the studio preferred their starlets free, to be seen at night spots with famous male celebrities), continued long-distance when he returned to New York, but came to an end two years later. In Hollywood over the next four years, Stuart (she had taken her mother's maiden name) appeared in over twenty movies, mostly in minor parts. She helped in casting (playing Bette Davis's part while producers tested leading men), posed in a bathing suit next to Clark Gable for publicity photographs, and played a patient in a *Dr. Kildare* film.

She finally landed a few leading roles, most notably in *The Girl from Jones Beach* with Ronald Reagan, and *Colt 45* and *The Adventures of Don Juan*, both co-starring Errol Flynn. For *Thunderhoof*, a low-budget Western in which she starred as a sultry Mexican half-breed caught in the center of a romantic triangle, the studio dyed her ash-blond hair black and the wardrobe department, thinking her *derrière* on the skimpy side, padded her jeans. By 1950, Stuart had had enough of Hollywood and returned to New York to pursue a stage career once again.

She enrolled in an acting class taught by the well-known coach David Alexander, and found herself rubbing elbows with fellow students and future luminaries Cliff Robertson and Jack Lemmon. She began dating Time-Life executive Richard Krolik, whom she had met in California. One afternoon, while having lunch with advertising executive Roy Winsor, who was a friend of Krolik, Stuart complained that women on television were not characters with whom women viewers could identify. They were, she argued, too perfect, unrealistic, and mired in fantasy. Unbeknownst to Stuart, Winsor was developing a television serial. He was impressed with the young actress and her arguments, and sent Charles Irving, the director of his new project, to watch Stuart perform in her acting class. Soon Stuart had the lead in his show, tentatively called *Search for Happiness*.

A month before the premiere of *Search for Tomorrow*, she married Krolik, and her life quickly split into two. To millions across the country she was the sensitive widow Joanne, raising a daughter alone and fending off battling in-laws and romantic disasters. Offscreen she was a wife to Krolik and mother to Cynthia and Jeffrey, born fourteen months apart in 1955 and 1956. The first pregnancy was hidden on the show by strategically placed houseplants and careful camera shots; the second was written into the script, even using shots of Stuart and son Jeff in the hospital as Joanne and the infant Duncan Eric. Her dual careers kept her from accepting parts on Broadway, but she finally worked in the theater in 1966, the same year she divorced Krolik, in the play *Marriage Go Round*. She did find time for her singing career, recording an album with Percy Faith in 1956 and collaborating on a few songs with Michel Legrand for another album in 1973.

Stuart had the distinction of starring in television's second longest-running drama, and while other long-running characters had been written out or banished to the sidelines, she remained the pivotal heroine of *Search for Tomorrow* for over thirty years. She survived countless writers who wanted to kill Jo off, several near-cancellation notices of the show, and a network switch. As Jo, she has been married four times, widowed three times, blinded twice, confined to a wheelchair, tried for murder, and held at gunpoint a dozen times. Between endless scenes in which Jo lent a sympathetic ear to all, Stuart can claim that Jill Clayburgh gave birth to the child of her daughter's husband, that Morgan Fairchild shot her sister, and that she adopted Robby Benson, who grew up to be Joel Higgins.

Stuart became the first daytime performer to be nominated for an Emmy, competing against prime-time actresses Shirley Booth and Mary Tyler Moore in 1962. She was nominated for Outstanding Actress in a Daytime Drama Series in 1974, 1976, and 1977, before finally being honored with a Lifetime Achievement Award in 1983. In 1980, she published *Both of Me* (Doubleday), a revealing, incisive autobiography that doubled as a comprehensive history of *Search for Tomorrow*. She has also written countless songs, some of which she has performed on the show, and had a screenplay produced for Canadian television. Shortly before the show's cancellation in December 1986, Stuart married Wolfgang Neumann.

WAGNER, HELEN

Born September 3, 1918, Lubbock, Texas.
Nancy Hughes, As the World Turns

Now holding the record as the longest-running current performer on daytime drama, Helen Wagner spoke the opening line on *As the World Turns* in 1956: "Good morning, Chris." From that inauspicious beginning, the show has become a television phenomenon. Part of that success must be credited to Wagner's ingratiatingly warm performance as Nancy, who has grown over the years from overprotective mother to the wise matriarch of the Hughes clan.

Helen Wagner attended Monmouth College in Illinois, earning degrees in drama and music; sang with the St. Louis Municipal Opera; and performed in New York in Oscar Hammerstein's *Sunny River* and *Oklahoma!* Then, after a tour with the Theater Guild Shakespearean Company, it was back to Broadway with Shakespeare, followed by a second tour of duty with *Oklahoma!* and parts in Gilbert and Sullivan revivals. Wagner's TV debut was as a queen in a fairy tale produced by General Electric on its experimental station in Schenectady. After a short stint as Trudy Bauer on *Guiding Light* in 1952, Wagner played Charlie Ruggles's daughter in *The World of Mr. Sweeney*, a comic serial which had the distinction of running in both daytime and prime-time TV in the 1954–55 season.

Although her thirty-two-year run on *As the World Turns* has kept Wagner busy, the actress has found time to appear on the stage throughout the years as Blanche in *A Streetcar Named Desire* opposite Lee Marvin; as Eleanor of Aquitaine in *The Lion in Winter* opposite Donald May (ex–Adam Drake, *The Edge of Night*); and as two of the four female characters in *Lovers and Other Strangers*. She has been married to producer Robert Willey since 1954.

WARRICK, RUTH

Born June 29, 1916, St. Joseph, Missouri.
Edith Hughes, As the World Turns;
Hannah Cord, Peyton Place;
Phoebe Tyler, All My Children

A colorful star of stage, screen, and television, Ruth Warrick began her career playing in stock at the University of Missouri at Kansas, then won the "Miss Jubilesta" contest and traveled extensively. During the 1938–39 season she appeared in a series of radio programs based in New York, including the soap opera *Joyce Jordan, Girl Interne*. (In the 1954 revised version of the radio serial, she played the lead.) Selected by Orson Welles to play his first wife in *Citizen Kane*—which became the most acclaimed American picture ever made—her performance as the classy, proper Emily Norton Kane both assured Warrick a place in film history and launched her Hollywood career.

From 1940 to 1952, she co-starred in thirty major motion pictures, including *The Corsican Brothers* with Douglas Fairbanks, Jr., *Perilous Holiday* with Pat O'Brien, *China Sky* with Randolph Scott, *Let's Dance* with Fred Astaire and Betty Hutton, *Guest in the House* with Ralph Bellamy, *Daisy Kenyon* with Joan Crawford, and *Three Husbands* with Eve Arden and playwright Emlyn Williams. Afterwards, Warrick returned to New York, causing people to speculate that she had retired from the business. In reality, Warrick had not fallen into obscurity but was constantly busy in television, radio, and the theater. "If being on Broadway was obscure," Warrick bristled at such reports years later, "then I was obscure. I was never unemployed, as I supported and educated my two children single-handedly."

After the actress made TV appearances on *Studio One* and *Robert Montgomery Presents*, Ted Corday offered her a six-month stint on *The Guiding Light* as Janet Johnson, a seductive nurse. Impressed by Warrick's performance, Irna Phillips created a wonderfully innovative leading role for the actress on her new soap *As the World Turns* in 1956. For the next three years Warrick played Chris Hughes' liberated sister Edith, a sympathetic "other woman." The free-spirited Edith turned out to be the most unusual long-running female character in daytime TV during the '50s, becoming such a favorite with audiences that even after Warrick left the show she made guest appearances in Oakdale from time to time for several years.

Warrick began to concentrate on her theater career, appearing on Broadway in *Miss Lonelyhearts* and touring in *The King and I*. After starring as Ellie Banks on the prime-time sitcom *Father of the Bride* in the 1961–62 season, she began tackling tough dramatic roles in theater productions of *Who's Afraid of Virginia Woolf?* and *Long Day's Journey into Night*. She returned triumphantly to the soap opera scene in 1965 with the prime-time TV phenomenon *Peyton Place*. For the next two years her performance as the iron-willed Hannah Cord brought her new-found popularity and an Emmy nomination as Outstanding Actress.

After *Peyton Place*, she toured in a one-woman show and co-starred with Zero Mostel and Kim Novak in the movie *The Great Bank Robbery*. In 1970, she moved back again to New York to join the premiere cast of *All My Children* in the pivotal role of Phoebe Tyler, a grasping, manipulative matriarch. In many ways, her performance became the most exciting and popular of her career as an entire new generation marvelled at her dramatic mettle and comic inventiveness. After seeing radio through its Golden Age, Hollywood through its heyday, and prime-time television through its infancy, Warrick had now become an integral part of the soap opera explosion in the '70s. For her sharp, drawing-room-styled characterization and her larger-than-life energy, she was nominated for an Emmy as Outstanding Actress in 1975 and again in 1977.

Since then, Phoebe English Tyler Wallingford has gone through many changes, mellowed by Warrick, who injects warmth and compassion into the role. No fan of *All My Children* could ever forget her hilarious submissions to the sexual advances of Langley Wallingford, nor, in a poignant sequence, her admission to Benny that as a young society girl she fell in love with a stableboy, a romance doomed from the start. As boldly outspoken onscreen as she is off, Warrick shocked and amused viewers on a live Washington, D.C., talk show, commenting on the problem of today's youth: "S.S.I. is the problem," she explained, "shitty self-image."

In 1980, she published a characteristically frank autobiography, *The Confessions of Phoebe Tyler* (Prentice Hall). It not only reviewed the history of *All My Children* but examined Warrick's personal life, discussing her five stormy marriages, a nervous breakdown, a fling with Orson Welles, and her sultry affair with Anthony Quinn. In 1984, while continuing work on *All My Children*, she returned to motion pictures in *Unknown*, co-starring Farley Granger, who had played Dr. Will Vernon on *One Life to Live* in the mid '70s. The next year, Warrick filmed a mystery feature, released her first record album, and reprised her role as Hannah Cord in the TV movie *Peyton Place: The Next Generation*.

WATSON, DOUGLASS

*Born Larkin Douglass Watson III,
February 24, 1921, Jackson, Georgia.*
Mackenzie Cory, Another World

Before winning two consecutive Emmies for Outstanding Actor in 1980 and 1981 for his appealingly theatrical performance as Mac Cory on *Another World*, Douglass Watson was well known as one of the most accomplished actors of the American stage. He was born in Georgia, where his ancestors were granted land for having fought in the American Revolution. (One of these relatives was Douglass Watson, a famous Indian scout, who discovered Indian Springs, site of the current Georgia State Park.) After graduating from the University of North Carolina in 1942, he studied acting in Hollywood with the legendary Maria Ouspenskaya, then served with the Air Force in World War II and was awarded two Purple Hearts and a Distinguished Flying Cross. Back in the states, he toured as Fenton in *The Merry Wives of Windsor* and made his New York debut in 1947, personally selected by Eugene O'Neill to play Don Parrit in *The Iceman Cometh*.

His theater career quickly took off with a Theatre World Award for his performance the next year as Eros in *Antony and Cleopatra*. In 1949, Watson won the Clarence Derwent Award for *That Lady* opposite Katharine Cornell, and the next year he topped *Variety*'s New York Drama Critics Poll for *The Wisteria Trees* opposite Helen Hayes. A number of critically acclaimed roles followed in the '50s, including Romeo opposite Olivia de Havilland's Juliet, Eben Cabot in *Desire Under the Elms*, Christian de Neuvilette in *Cyrano de Bergerac*, the title role in *Henry V*, Mr. Harcourt in *The Country Wife* opposite Julie Harris, Ralph Touchett in *Portrait of a Lady* opposite Jennifer Jones, Brian O'Bannion in *Auntie Mame* opposite Constance Bennett, and the title role in T. S. Eliot's *The Confidential Clerk*.

Celebrated for his outstanding performances in a series of Shakespearean productions, Watson broke into motion pictures in 1953 as Octavius in *Julius Caesar* opposite Marlon Brando's Mark Antony. Four years later, he was reunited with Brando in the film version of *Sayonara*. During the

'60s he continued his Shakespearean award-winning theater streak, appearing in *A Midsummer Night's Dream*, *The Merchant of Venice*, *King Lear*, and *Othello*. Watson also appeared in a number of non-Shakespearean roles, including King Henry VIII in *A Man For All Seasons*, Herald in *Marat/Sade*, Teddy Lloyd in *The Prime of Miss Jean Brodie* opposite Zoe Caldwell, and the Major General in *The Pirates of Penzance*.

After two decades of busy stage work, Watson starred in his own daytime serial, *Moment of Truth*, in 1965. He played Dr. Bob Wallace, a psychiatrist, in this ill-fated, Canadian produced entry. Then he was seen as Walter Haskins on *Search for Tomorrow* for a while, followed by a stint in 1972 as Dr. Lloyd Phillips on *Love of Life*. (Nancy Marchand played his nasty wife Vinnie.) In 1974, he joined the cast of *Another World*, replacing Robert Emhardt as Mac Cory. As the doting father of the spoiled Iris, who found his match in the fiery Rachel, Watson quickly garnered notice inside the industry for his alternately charming and volatile performances, resulting in two Emmy awards for Outstanding Actor.

Although Mac has been busy enough for a dozen men (three marriages to Rachel, a poisoning administered by wife Janice, a hostage kidnapped for weeks, a plane crash survivor who wandered for days on frozen tundra), Watson has found time for other projects besides the soaps during the last decade. He appeared in the film *Ulzana's Raid* with Burt Lancaster and repeated his stage performance in *The Trial of the Catonsville Nine* in the film version. In 1973, after starring as Don Pedro in the highly praised Joe Papp production of *Much Ado About Nothing*, he repeated the role in a television production. He also appeared on Broadway in the musical *Over Here* with the Andrews Sisters and in the revival of *The Philadelphia Story*.

As if acting with Dame Judith Anderson in *Medea*, dancing with Martha Graham in several of her premier works, and singing with The New York City Opera were not enough, Watson has also managed an equally impressive home life. Since November 28, 1942, he has been married to Harriet Eugenia (Genie) Clark. The Watsons have three children: Larkin Douglass Watson, a construction engineer; Celia Strome, a national award-winning poet; and Randall Forsberg, an internationally recognized expert on world armaments and the originator of the Nuclear Freeze Movement.

WINSOR, ROY

Born April 13, 1912, Chicago, Illinois.
Died May 31, 1987, Pelham Manor, New York.
Creator-producer, Search for Tomorrow, Love of Life,
and The Secret Storm

If Irna Phillips is to be called mother of soap opera, then Roy Winsor must be called father of the television serial. After graduating magna cum laude from Harvard, he began his career in radio, working in various capacities and then directing *Vic and Sade* in its 1938–39 season. During the '40s he was the supervisor of eight Procter & Gamble radio programs, including *The Goldbergs*, *Kitty Keene*, and *Ma Perkins*, serving as director on that program. From 1944 to 1949 Winsor also wrote and directed *Sky King*. After pursuing a free-lance writing career, he joined the Biow Company as vice president of television-radio in 1950. There he served as executive producer to such shows as *I Love Lucy*, *My Little Margie*, and *Project Sound*. Later, at Roy Winsor Productions, he supervised *Have Gun Will Travel*.

Although there had been a few experiments in bringing soap operas to television—the DuMont network's *Faraway Hill* in 1946 and *A Woman to Remember* in 1949 and NBC's *These Are My Children* in 1949—they had all been short-lived failures. NBC tried again in June of 1950 with a serial version of *Hawkins Falls*, an expensively produced series about life in a small town, which Winsor and Doug Johnson created as a nighttime hour program. After airing it over the summer on prime-time, NBC transferred the show to daytime as a full-fledged serial the next year, where it became the first continuing story with staying power, running for four years.

Winsor then turned his attention to producing more serials for daytime television. For the Biow Company, Winsor created the theme, story, and characters for a new soap tentatively titled *Search for Happiness*. The project was sold to Procter & Gamble and the upshot was *Search for Tomorrow*, premiering Labor Day, 1951, with Mary Stuart as Joanne Barron, a kind of young Ma Perkins who attempted to deal with personal problems in an honest and dignified manner. *Search for Tomorrow* was an immediate hit, proving Winsor's contention that while radio soaps depended mostly on plot, TV serials must concentrate on character.

Three weeks later, on September 24, 1951, Winsor launched *Love of Life*, the story of two sisters, one good, one bad, with the emphasis, Winsor wrote years later, on the good Vanessa Dale's "search for honesty in a hypocritical world." In 1954, Winsor's greatest creation, *The Secret Storm*, premiered. The story of widower Peter Ames and his troubled family, their secret passions and private sorrows, captured a vast audience. With three daytime blockbusters under his belt, Winsor formed his own production company in 1955. While still involved with his ongoing successes, *Love of Life* and *The Secret Storm*, he created in 1957 *Hotel Cosmopolitan*, about the comings and goings in a New York hotel. Anthology serials, with the exception of *Modern Romances*, never caught on in daytime, and *Hotel Cosmopolitan* was no different; it was cancelled after seven months. Winsor tried again with *Ben Jerrod*, the story of two small-town attorneys, in 1963. It was cancelled after only three months.

After his production company disbanded in 1969, Winsor's ties with *The Secret Storm* were also broken, marking the beginning of the end for the show. CBS's mismanagement of the soap afterwards caused an untimely cancellation notice, and *The Secret Storm* left the air in 1974 after a run of twenty years. (*Love of Life*, Winsor's second smash hit, was a bit luckier, running thirty years before its cancellation in 1980.) For the next four years Winsor served as a free-lance consultant for various CBS and P & G projects. In 1974, he became the headwriter of *Somerset*, where he turned the show back into a traditional soap opera, with an emphasis on romance and domestic drama, after the show had been transformed into a crime-mystery serial by former writer Henry Slesar.

After his stint with *Somerset*, Winsor taught serial writing at The New School for Social Research for two years. He then settled down to write detective novels, the first of which, *The Corpse That Walked*, won the Edgar Award from the Mystery Writers of America in 1974. Two other novels followed, *Three Motives for Murder* and *Always Lock Your Bedroom*, both of which were published by Fawcett in 1976. Winsor returned to the soap opera scene in 1981 with *Another Life*, a religious serial produced by the Christian Broadcasting Network. The latter, Winsor reported, was a "bizarre experience." He found that he was an outsider, "hoisted into limbo by a petard labelled 'Not a born-again Christian.' " Winsor's character-motivated resolutions to stories were replaced by miraculous, *deus ex machina* denouements.

WYMAN, JANE

Born Sarah Jane Fulks,
January 4, 1914, St. Joseph, Missouri.
Angela Channing, Falcon Crest

The daughter of her hometown's mayor, Jane Wyman traveled to Hollywood as a child with her mother to attempt to break into show business. Failing to impress film producers with her singing and dancing skills, Wyman shuttled back and forth between Hollywood and Missouri during her teens, keeping alive her performing aspirations. In 1935, she registered at the University of Missouri, but dropped out to pursue a career as a radio vocalist, using the professional name Jane Durrell while touring the country.

In 1936, the singer-actress signed a contract with Warner Brothers, who changed her name to Jane Wyman and featured her in a number of light comedies for the next decade. Her big break came with the Oscar-winning drama *The Lost Weekend*, in which she played the long-suffering girlfriend of an alcoholic, played by Ray Milland. Two years later, Wyman was nominated for an Academy Award for her affecting performance opposite Gregory Peck in the family film, *The Yearling*. With her reputation as a serious actress assured, Wyman tackled her most demanding role, *Johnny Belinda*. For the role of a deaf-mute, the actress studied for six months at a school for the deaf and even performed the role with her ears plugged with wax. Wyman's careful preparation paid off with an Oscar for Best Actress, and a string of films that displayed her versatility in melodrama as well as comedy.

While filming *Brother Rat* in 1938, Wyman met Ronald Wilson Reagan, a contract player who was later to become the fortieth President of the United States. Although in the previous year Wyman had married and divorced Myron Futterman, a New Orleans dress manufacturer, the actress had not soured on marriage and became engaged to Reagan during a national vaudeville tour of young Hollywood stars. On January 26, 1940, Wyman and Reagan were married at the Wee Kirk o' the Heather wedding chapel in Hollywood and held their reception at gossip columnist Louella Parsons' plush estate. On her birthday the next year, Wyman gave birth to a daughter, Maureen Elizabeth, and a few years later, the Reagans adopted a son, Michael Edward.

As Wyman's movie career soared during the '40s, Reagan's acting fortunes dwindled. Testifying at her divorce proceedings in 1948, Wyman blamed the failure of her marriage on Reagan's insistence that she share his increasing interest in politics and in his position as President of the Screen Actors Guild. The Reagans were divorced July 19, 1949. Wyman married orchestra leader Freddie Karger in 1952, divorced him in 1954, remarried him in 1961, and divorced him again in 1965. Reagan also remarried in 1952, to actress Nancy Davis, who later became the country's First Lady.

During the early '50s, Wyman received two Oscar nominations for her performances in *The Blue Veil*, opposite Charles Laughton, and *Magnificent Obession*, opposite Rock Hudson. With *All That Heaven Allows* in 1956, also with Hudson, Wyman had become enormously popular as the star of classy movie soap operas. But instead of continuing in movies, she chose to host the television anthology series *Fireside Theatre*. After she starred in several episodes, the show was renamed *The Jane Wyman Show* and enjoyed a three-year run and many more years in syndication. The actress starred in few pictures afterwards, popping up in light comedies such as *Holiday for Lovers* and *How to Commit Marriage*.

In 1981, she came back to television in *Falcon Crest* as the no-nonsense matriarch and tough businesswoman Angela Channing. At first, critics complained that Wyman was turning in a lackluster performance, worried about her image and not really getting into the spirit of Angela's scheming and manipulation. But Wyman's acting warmed up, and she won a Golden Globe for her performance in 1984. Today, of course, Wyman's all-out, nasty merriment is one of the seven wonders of the prime-time world— her Angela the empress of grapes and wrath.

The National Academy of Television Arts and Sciences (NATAS) recognizes excellence in television with its annual Emmy awards. The Academy was formed in 1946 and now claims thousands of members across the country with chapters in over 15 major TV markets. In January 1949 the Academy conferred its first awards and *Pantomine Quiz Time* was proclaimed "The Most Popular Television Program" while Louis McManus won a special Emmy for designing the statuette.

The award itself—a female figure holding a globe over her head—has been described as a "golden portrait of a woman trying to put a hatbox on a top shelf" but a more accurate description might be "an angel shooting baskets." At first it was thought that Harry Lubcke, the then President of the Academy, had called the award "Emmy" after an acquaintance, but he later revealed that the name came from the word "Immy"—TV jargon for an image orthicon camera tube.

Emmy winners are chosen from nominations made by Academy members who vote in their own discipline; that is, performers vote for performers, directors for directors, and so forth. Nominees submit a tape of their best work and a blue ribbon panel, made up of industry professionals, decide the winners. Prime-time shows and performers were recognized throughout the '50s and '60s, but daytime programming was not recognized until 1966. An exception was Mary Stuart of *Search for Tomorrow* who was nominated with prime-time performers for Outstanding Continued Performance by an Actress in a Series in 1962.

From 1966 to 1971 two new categories were added to the Emmy awards: Outstanding Achievement in Daytime Programming, for individuals and for series. Although performers Joan Bennett of *Dark Shadows*, Macdonald Carey of *Days of Our Lives*, and some technical personnel were nominated during the period, no daytime serial or serial performer won either award.

By the 1971–72 season daytime serials were finally recognized. In the next few years more categories were added, and by the 1976–77 season the daytime Emmies had become a separate branch, based in New York, with their own nomination procedure, blue ribbon panels, and award ceremony. In their first few years the daytime Emmies were criticized for nominating only the most celebrated performers, for their anti-CBS bias, and later for their bias against Hollywood-based shows and performers. Although in recent years the nominations, if not the awards, have been more discerning, in 1983 NBC refused to carry the ceremony, claiming the show was a ratings loser. (The audience for the show was much larger than NBC's average rating in recent years; insiders speculated that the network was embarrassed by ABC's nominations sweep.) The following year, NBC refused to participate at all in the Emmy process, complaining of sloppy balloting and midstream rule changes. Amid continual controversy, the Emmy ceremony was again not telecast.

In 1985, the daytime Emmies began to be televised again on a rotating basis among the three networks. However, the Academy was embarrassed by two major gaffs: the year before, the winners had been prematurely published in the New York *Post*, so the stars on the way to the ceremony already knew who had won. In 1986, it was announced that *The Young and the Restless* had won the award for Outstanding Writing, but a few days later it was revealed that someone had written the wrong show on the envelope and the team from *Guiding Light* had actually won. Squabbles continued between the New York and Los Angeles chapters of the Academy, and new rules were promised in the future.

In the following list of nominations and awards, winners are designated by *.

1971–72

OUTSTANDING ACHIEVEMENT IN DAYTIME DRAMA—PROGRAMS

* *The Doctors*. Allen Potter, producer; NBC
  General Hospital. Jim Young, producer; ABC

1972–73

OUTSTANDING PROGRAM ACHIEVEMENT IN DAYTIME DRAMA

Days of Our Lives. Betty Corday, executive producer; H. Wesley Kenney, producer; NBC
The Doctors. Allen Potter, producer; NBC
* *The Edge of Night*. Erwin Nicholson, producer; CBS
One Life to Live. Doris Quinlan and Agnes Nixon, producers; ABC

OUTSTANDING ACHIEVEMENT BY AN INDIVIDUAL IN DAYTIME DRAMA

Macdonald Carey (Dr. Tom Horton, *Days of Our Lives*, NBC)
* Mary Fickett (Ruth Brent, *All My Children*, ABC)
Norman Hall (director, *The Doctors*, NBC)
H. Wesley Kenney (director, *Days of Our Lives*, NBC)
Peter Levin (director, *Love Is a Many Splendored Thing*, CBS)
David Pressman (director, *One Life to Live*, ABC)
Victor Paganuzzi (scenic designer, *Love Is a Many Splendored Thing*, CBS)
John A. Wendell (set decorator, *Love Is a Many Splendored Thing*, CBS)

1973–74

OUTSTANDING DAYTIME DRAMA SERIES

Days of Our Lives. Betty Corday, executive producer; H. Wesley Kenney, producer; NBC
* *The Doctors*. Joseph Stuart, producer; NBC
General Hospital. Jim Young, producer; ABC

BEST ACTOR IN A DAYTIME DRAMA SERIES

John Beradino (Dr. Steve Hardy, *General Hospital*, ABC)
* Macdonald Carey (Dr. Tom Horton, *Days of Our Lives*, NBC)
Peter Hansen (Lee Baldwin, *General Hospital*, ABC)

BEST ACTRESS IN A DAYTIME DRAMA SERIES

Rachel Ames (Audrey Baldwin, R.N., *General Hospital*, ABC)
Mary Fickett (Ruth Martin, R.N., *All My Children*, ABC)
* Elizabeth Hubbard (Dr. Althea Davis, *The Doctors*, NBC)
Mary Stuart (Joanne Vincente, *Search for Tomorrow*, CBS)

BEST INDIVIDUAL DIRECTOR FOR A DAYTIME DRAMA SERIES

Norman Hall, *The Doctors*; NBC
* H. Wesley Kenney, *Days of Our Lives*; NBC
Hugh McPhillips, *The Doctors*; NBC

BEST WRITING FOR A DAYTIME DRAMA SERIES

The Doctors. Eileen and Robert Mason Pollock, James Lipton; NBC
* *The Edge of Night*. Henry Slesar; CBS
General Hospital. Frank and Doris Hursley, Bridget Dobson, Deborah Hardy; ABC

1974–75

OUTSTANDING DAYTIME DRAMA SERIES

Another World. Paul Rauch, executive producer; Mary S. Bonner, Joe Rothenberger, producers; NBC
Days of Our Lives. Betty Corday, executive producer; Jack Herzberg, producer; NBC
* *The Young and the Restless*. John J. Conboy, producer; CBS

OUTSTANDING ACTOR IN A DAYTIME DRAMA SERIES

John Beradino (Dr. Steve Hardy, *General Hospital*, ABC)
* Macdonald Carey (Dr. Tom Horton, *Days of Our Lives*, NBC)
Bill Hayes (Doug Williams, *Days of Our Lives*, NBC)

OUTSTANDING ACTRESS IN A DAYTIME DRAMA SERIES

Rachel Ames (Audrey Hobart, *General Hospital*, ABC)
* Susan Flannery (Dr. Laura Horton, *Days of Our Lives*, NBC)
Susan Seaforth (Julie Banning, *Days of Our Lives*, NBC)
Ruth Warrick (Phoebe Tyler, *All My Children*, ABC)

OUTSTANDING INDIVIDUAL DIRECTOR FOR A DAYTIME DRAMA SERIES

Ira Cirker, *Another World*, May 3, 1974; NBC
Joseph Behar, *Days of Our Lives*, November 20, 1974; NBC
* Richard Dunlap, *The Young and the Restless*, November 25, 1974; CBS

OUTSTANDING WRITING FOR A DAYTIME DRAMA SERIES

* *Another World*. Harding Lemay, Tom King, Charles Kozloff, Jan
   Merlin, Douglas Marland; series; NBC
Days of Our Lives. William J. Bell, Pat Falken Smith, Bill Rega; No-
   vember 21, 1974; NBC
The Young and the Restless. William J. Bell, October 21, 1974; CBS

1975–76

OUTSTANDING DAYTIME DRAMA SERIES

All My Children. Bud Kloss, producer; ABC
* *Another World*. Paul Rauch, executive producer; Mary S. Bonner, Joe
   Rothenberger, producers; NBC
Days of Our Lives. Betty Corday, executive producer; Jack Herzberg,
   Al Rabin, producers; NBC
The Young and the Restless. John J. Conboy, executive producer; Patri-
   cia Wenig, producer; CBS

OUTSTANDING ACTOR IN A DAYTIME DRAMA SERIES

John Beradino (Dr. Steve Hardy, *General Hospital*, ABC)
Macdonald Carey (Dr. Tom Horton, *Days of Our Lives*, NBC)
* Larry Haines (Stu Bergman, *Search for Tomorrow*, CBS)
Bill Hayes (Doug Williams, *Days of Our Lives*, NBC)
Michael Nouri (Steve Kaslow, *Search for Tomorrow*, CBS)
Shepperd Strudwick (Victor Lord, *One Life to Live*, ABC)

OUTSTANDING ACTRESS IN A DAYTIME DRAMA SERIES

Denise Alexander (Dr. Lesley Williams, *General Hospital*, ABC)
* Helen Gallagher (Maeve Ryan, *Ryan's Hope*, ABC)
Frances Heflin (Mona Kane, *All My Children*, ABC)
Susan Seaforth Hayes (Julie Anderson, *Days of Our Lives*, NBC)
Mary Stuart (Joanne Vincente, *Search for Tomorrow*, CBS)

OUTSTANDING INDIVIDUAL DIRECTOR OF A DAYTIME DRAMA SERIES

Richard Dunlap, *The Young and the Restless*, August 22, 1975; CBS
Hugh McPhillips, *The Doctors*, July 15, 1975; NBC
* David Pressman, *One Life to Live*, January 26, 1976; ABC

OUTSTANDING WRITING FOR A DAYTIME DRAMA SERIES

All My Children. Agnes Nixon; series; ABC

* *Days of Our Lives*. William J. Bell, Pat Falken Smith, Kay Lenard, Bill Rega, Margaret Stewart, Sheri Anderson, Wanda Coleman; series; NBC

The Edge of Night. Henry Slesar; series; ABC

The Guiding Light. Jerome and Bridget Dobson, Jean Rouverol; February 3, 1976; CBS

The Young and the Restless. William J. Bell, Kay Alden; September 5, 1975; CBS

1976–77

OUTSTANDING DAYTIME DRAMA SERIES

All My Children. Bud Kloss, Agnes Nixon, producers; ABC

Another World. Paul Rauch, executive producer; Mary S. Bonner, Joe Rothenberger, producers; NBC

Days of Our Lives. Betty Corday, executive producer; H. Wesley Kenney, Jack Herzberg, producers; NBC

The Edge of Night. Erwin Nicholson, producer; ABC

* *Ryan's Hope*. Paul Avila Mayer, Claire Labine, executive producers; Robert Costello, producer; ABC

OUTSTANDING ACTOR IN A DAYTIME DRAMA SERIES

* Val Dufour (John Wyatt, *Search for Tomorrow*, CBS)
  Farley Granger (Dr. Will Vernon, *One Life to Live*, ABC)
  Larry Haines (Stu Bergman, *Search for Tomorrow*, CBS)
  Lawrence Keith (Nick Davis, *All My Children*, ABC)
  James Pritchett (Dr. Matt Powers, *The Doctors*, NBC)

OUTSTANDING ACTRESS IN A DAYTIME DRAMA SERIES

Nancy Addison (Jillian Coleridge, *Ryan's Hope*, ABC)
* Helen Gallagher (Maeve Ryan, *Ryan's Hope*, ABC)
Beverlee McKinsey (Iris Carrington, *Another World*, NBC)
Mary Stuart (Joanne Vincente, *Search for Tomorrow*, CBS)
Ruth Warrick (Phoebe Tyler, *All My Children*, ABC)

OUTSTANDING INDIVIDUAL DIRECTOR FOR A DAYTIME DRAMA SERIES

Joseph Behar, *Days of Our Lives*, March 8, 1977; NBC
Ira Cirker, *Another World*, November 10, 1976; NBC
Paul E. Davis, Leonard Valenta, *As the World Turns*, January 14, 1977; CBS
Al Rabin, *Days of Our Lives*, October 1, 1976 (Julie and Doug's wedding); NBC

John Sedwick, *The Edge of Night*, August 6, 1976; ABC
* Lela Swift, *Ryan's Hope*, February 8, 1977; ABC

OUTSTANDING WRITING FOR A DAYTIME DRAMA SERIES

All My Children. Agnes Nixon, Wisner Washam, Kathyrn McCabe,
    Mary K. Wells, Jack Wood; series; ABC
Another World. Harding Lemay, Tom King, Peter Swet, Barry Berg,
    Jan Merlin, Arthur Giron, Kathy Callaway; series; NBC
As the World Turns. Robert Soderberg, Edith Sommer, Ralph Ellis,
    Theodore Apstein, Eugenie Hunt, Gillian Spencer; October 27,
    1976; CBS
Days of Our Lives. William J. Bell, Pat Falken Smith, William Rega,
    Kay Lenard, Margaret Stewart; series; NBC
* *Ryan's Hope*. Claire Labine, Paul Avila Mayer, Mary Munisteri; se-
    ries; ABC

1977–78

OUTSTANDING DAYTIME DRAMA SERIES

All My Children. Bud Kloss, Agnes Nixon, producers; ABC
* *Days of Our Lives*. Betty Corday, H. Wesley Kenney, executive pro-
    ducers; Jack Herzberg, producer; NBC
Ryan's Hope. Claire Labine, Paul Avila Mayer, executive producers;
    Robert Costello, producer; ABC
The Young and the Restless. John J. Conboy, executive producer; Patri-
    cia Wenig, producer; CBS

OUTSTANDING ACTOR IN A DAYTIME DRAMA SERIES

Matthew Cowles (Billy Clyde Tuggle, *All My Children*, ABC)
Lawrence Keith (Nick Davis, *All My Children*, ABC)
Michael Levin (Jack Fenelli, *Ryan's Hope*, ABC)
* James Pritchett (Dr. Matt Powers, *The Doctors*, NBC)
Andrew Robinson (Frank Ryan, *Ryan's Hope*, ABC)
Michael Storm (Dr. Larry Wolek, *One Life to Live*, ABC)

OUTSTANDING ACTRESS IN A DAYTIME DRAMA SERIES

Mary Fickett (Ruth Martin, *All My Children*, ABC)
Jennifer Harmon (Cathy Craig, *One Life to Live*, ABC)
* Laurie Heineman (Sharlene Frame, *Another World*, NBC)
Susan Lucci (Erica Kane, *All My Children*, ABC)
Beverlee McKinsey (Iris Bancroft, *Another World*, NBC)
Susan Seaforth Hayes (Julie Williams, *Days of Our Lives*, NBC)
Victoria Wyndham (Rachel Cory, *Another World*, NBC)

OUTSTANDING INDIVIDUAL DIRECTOR FOR A DAYTIME DRAMA SERIES

Ira Cirker, *Another World*, December 20, 1977; NBC
* Richard Dunlap, *The Young and the Restless*, March 3, 1978; CBS
Richard T. McCue, *As the World Turns*, April 29, 1977; CBS
Robert Myhrum, *Love of Life*, August 31, 1977; CBS
Al Rabin, *Days of Our Lives*, February 21, 1978 (Julie's rape); NBC
Lela Swift, *Ryan's Hope*, November 3, 1977; ABC

OUTSTANDING WRITING FOR A DAYTIME DRAMA SERIES

All My Children. Agnes Nixon, Wisner Washam, Cathy Chicos, Doris Frankel, Ken Harvey, Mary K. Wells, Kathryn McCabe, Jack Wood; series; ABC
Days of Our Lives. William J. Bell, Pat Falken Smith, Kay Lenard, Bill Rega, Margaret Stewart; April 18, 1977; NBC
The Guiding Light. Jerome and Bridget Dobson, Nancy Ford, Jean Rouverol, Robert White, Phyllis White; series; CBS
* *Ryan's Hope.* Claire Labine, Paul Avila Mayer, Mary Munisteri, Allen Leicht, Judith Pinsker; series; ABC

1978–79

OUTSTANDING DAYTIME DRAMA SERIES

All My Children. Agnes Nixon, Bud Kloss, producers; ABC
Days of Our Lives. Betty Corday, H. Wesley Kenney, executive producers; Jack Herzberg, producer; NBC
* *Ryan's Hope.* Claire Labine, Paul Avila Mayer, executive producers; Ellen Barrett, Robert Costello, producers; ABC
The Young and the Restless. John Conboy, executive producer; Edward Scott, producer; CBS

OUTSTANDING ACTOR IN A DAYTIME DRAMA SERIES

Jed Allan (Don Craig, *Days of Our Lives*, NBC)
Nicholas Benedict (Phillip Brent, *All My Children*, ABC)
John Clarke (Mickey Horton, *Days of Our Lives*, NBC)
Joel Crothers (Dr. Miles Cavanaugh, *The Edge of Night*, ABC)
* Al Freeman, Jr. (Captain Ed Hall, *One Life to Live*, ABC)
Michael Levin (Jack Fenelli, *Ryan's Hope*, ABC)

OUTSTANDING ACTRESS IN A DAYTIME DRAMA SERIES

Nancy Addison (Jillian Coleridge, *Ryan's Hope*, ABC)
* Irene Dailey (Liz Matthews, *Another World*, NBC)
Helen Gallagher (Maeve Ryan, *Ryan's Hope*, ABC)
Beverlee McKinsey (Iris Bancroft, *Another World*, NBC)

Susan Seaforth Hayes (Julie Williams, *Days of Our Lives*, NBC)
Victoria Wyndham (Rachel Cory, *Another World*, NBC)

OUTSTANDING SUPPORTING ACTOR IN A DAYTIME DRAMA SERIES

Lewis Arlt (David Sutton, *Search for Tomorrow*, CBS)
Bernard Barrow (Johnny Ryan, *Ryan's Hope*, ABC)
Joseph Gallison (Dr. Neil Curtis, *Days of Our Lives*, NBC)
Ron Hale (Dr. Roger Coleridge, *Ryan's Hope*, ABC)
* Peter Hansen (Lee Baldwin, *General Hospital*, ABC)
Mandel Kramer (Chief Bill Marceau, *The Edge of Night*, ABC)

OUTSTANDING SUPPORTING ACTRESS IN A DAYTIME DRAMA SERIES

Rachel Ames (Audrey Hardy, R.N., *General Hospital*, ABC)
Susan Brown (Dr. Gail Adamson, *General Hospital*, ABC)
Lois Kibbee (Geraldine Whitney Saxon, *The Edge of Night*, ABC)
Frances Reid (Alice Horton, *Days of Our Lives*, NBC)
* Suzanne Rogers (Maggie Horton, *Days of Our Lives*, NBC)

OUTSTANDING DIRECTION FOR A DAYTIME DRAMA SERIES

All My Children. Jack Coffey, Del Hughes, Henry Kaplan; ABC
Another World. Ira Cirker, Melvin Bernhardt, Paul Lammers, Robert
  Calhoun; NBC
Days of Our Lives. Al Rabin, Joe Behar, Frank Pacelli; NBC
The Edge of Night. John Sedwick, Richard Pepperman; ABC
* *Ryan's Hope.* Lela Swift, Jerry Evans; ABC
The Young and the Restless. Richard Dunlap, Bill Glenn; CBS

OUTSTANDING WRITING FOR A DAYTIME DRAMA SERIES

All My Children. Agnes Nixon, Wisner Washam, Jack Wood, Mary
  K. Wells, Ken Harvey, Cathy Chicos, Caroline Franz, Doris Fran-
  kel, William Delligan; ABC
Days of Our Lives. Ann Marcus, Elizabeth Harrower, Michael Robert
  David, Raymond E. Goldstone, Joyce Perry, Rocci Chatfield,
  Laura Olsher; NBC
* *Ryan's Hope.* Claire Labine, Paul Avila Mayer, Mary Munisteri, Ju-
  dith Pinsker, Jeffrey Lane; ABC
The Young and the Restless. William J. Bell, Kay Alden, Elizabeth Har-
  rower; CBS

1979–80

OUTSTANDING DAYTIME DRAMA SERIES

All My Children. Agnes Nixon, executive producer; Jorn Winther,
  producer; ABC

Another World. Paul Rauch, executive producer; Mary S. Bonner, Robert Costello, producers; NBC
* *The Guiding Light.* Allen Potter, executive producer; Leslie Kwartin, Joe Willmore, producers; ABC

OUTSTANDING ACTOR IN A DAYTIME DRAMA SERIES

John Gabriel (Dr. Seneca Beaulac, *Ryan's Hope*, ABC)
Michael Levin (Jack Fenelli, *Ryan's Hope*, ABC)
Franc Luz (Dr. John Bennett, *The Doctors*, NBC)
James Mitchell (Palmer Cortlandt, *All My Children*, ABC)
William Mooney (Paul Martin, *All My Children*, ABC)
* Douglass Watson (Mac Cory, *Another World*, NBC)

OUTSTANDING ACTRESS IN A DAYTIME DRAMA SERIES

Julia Barr (Brooke English, *All My Children*, ABC)
Leslie Charleson (Dr. Monica Quartermaine, *General Hospital*, ABC)
Kim Hunter (Nola Madison, *The Edge of Night*, ABC)
* Judith Light (Karen Wolek, *One Life to Live*, ABC)
Beverlee McKinsey (Iris Bancroft, *Another World*, NBC)
Kathleen Noone (Ellen Shepherd, *All My Children*, ABC)

OUTSTANDING SUPPORTING ACTOR IN A DAYTIME DRAMA SERIES

* Warren Burton (Eddie Dorrance, *All My Children*, ABC)
Vasili Bogazianos (Mickey Dials, *The Edge of Night*, ABC)
Larry Haines (Stu Bergman, *Search for Tomorrow*, CBS)
Ron Hale (Dr. Roger Coleridge, *Ryan's Hope*, ABC)
Julius La Rosa (Renaldo, *Another World*, NBC)
Shepperd Strudwick (Prof. Timothy McCauley, *Love of Life*, CBS)

OUTSTANDING SUPPORTING ACTRESS IN A DAYTIME DRAMA SERIES

Deidre Hall (Dr. Marlena Craig, *Days of Our Lives*, NBC)
* Francesca James (Kelly Cole, *All My Children*, ABC)
Lois Kibbee (Geraldine Whitney Saxon, *The Edge of Night*, ABC)
Elaine Lee (Mildred Trumble, *The Doctors*, NBC)
Valerie Mahaffey (Ashley Bennett, *The Doctors*, NBC)

OUTSTANDING DIRECTION FOR A DAYTIME DRAMA SERIES

All My Children. Henry Kaplan, Jack Coffey, Sherrell Hoffman, Jorn Winther; ABC
Another World. Ira Cirker, Melvin Berhardt, Robert Calhoun, Barnet Kellman, Jack Hofsiss, Andrew Weyman; NBC
The Edge of Night. John Sedwick, Richard Pepperman; ABC
General Hospital. Marlena Laird, Alan Pultz, Phil Sogard; ABC

Love of Life. Larry Auerbach, Robert Scinto; CBS
* *Ryan's Hope*. Lela Swift, Jerry Evans; ABC

OUTSTANDING WRITING FOR A DAYTIME DRAMA SERIES

All My Children. Agnes Nixon, Wisner Washam, Jack Wood, Caroline Franz, Mary K. Wells, Cathy Chicos, Clarice Blackburn, Anita Jaffe, Ken Harvey; ABC
The Edge of Night. Henry Slesar, Steve Lehram; ABC
One Life to Live. Gordon Russell, Sam Hall, Peggy O'Shea, Don Wallace, Lanie Bertram, Cynthia Benjamin, Marisa Gioffre; ABC
* *Ryan's Hope*. Claire Labine, Paul Avila Mayer, Mary Munisteri, Judith Pinsker, Jeffrey Lane; ABC

OUTSTANDING CAMEO APPEARANCE IN A DAYTIME SERIES

Sammy Davis, Jr. (Chip Warren, *One Life to Live*, ABC)
Joan Fontaine (Page Williams, *Ryan's Hope*, ABC)
Kathryn Harrow (Pat Reyerson, *The Doctors*, NBC)
* Hugh McPhillips (Hugh Pearson, *Days of Our Lives*, NBC)
Eli Mintz (The Locksmith, *All My Children*, ABC)

1980–81

OUTSTANDING DAYTIME DRAMA SERIES

All My Children. Agnes Nixon, executive producer; Jorn Winther, producer; ABC
* *General Hospital*. Gloria Monty, producer; ABC
Ryan's Hope. Paul Avila Mayer, Claire Labine, executive producers; Ellen Barrett, producer; ABC

OUTSTANDING ACTOR IN A DAYTIME DRAMA SERIES

Larry Bryggman (Dr. John Dixon, *As the World Turns*, CBS)
Henderson Forsythe (Dr. David Stewart, *As the World Turns*, CBS)
Anthony Geary (Lucas Lorenzo Spencer, *General Hospital*, ABC)
James Mitchell (Palmer Cortlandt, *All My Children*, ABC)
* Douglass Watson (Mac Cory, *Another World*, NBC)

OUTSTANDING ACTRESS IN A DAYTIME DRAMA SERIES

Julia Barr (Brooke Cudahy, *All My Children*, ABC)
Helen Gallagher (Maeve Ryan, *Ryan's Hope*, ABC)
* Judith Light (Karen Wolek, *One Life to Live*, ABC)
Susan Lucci (Erica Kane *All My Children*, ABC)
Robin Strasser (Dorian Lord Callison, *One Life to Live*, ABC)

OUTSTANDING SUPPORTING ACTOR IN A DAYTIME DRAMA SERIES

Richard Backus (Barry Ryan, *Ryan's Hope*, ABC)
Matthew Cowles (Billy Clyde Tuggle, *All My Children*, ABC)
Justin Deas (Tom Hughes, *As the World Turns*, CBS)
* Larry Haines (Stu Bergman, *Search for Tomorrow*, CBS)
William Mooney (Paul Martin, *All My Children*, ABC)

OUTSTANDING SUPPORTING ACTRESS IN A DAYTIME DRAMA SERIES

Randall Edwards (Delia Reid Ryan Ryan Coleridge, *Ryan's Hope*, ABC)
* Jane Elliot (Tracy Quartermaine Williams, *General Hospital*, ABC)
Lois Kibbee (Geraldine Whitney Saxon, *The Edge of Night*, ABC)
Elizabeth Lawrence (Myra Murdoch, *All My Children*, ABC)
Jacklyn Zeman (Barbara Jean Spencer, *General Hospital*, ABC)

OUTSTANDING DIRECTION FOR A DAYTIME DRAMA SERIES

All My Children. Larry Auerbach, Jack Coffey, Sherrell Hoffman, Jorn Winther; ABC
* *General Hospital*. Marlena Laird, Alan Pultz, Phil Sogard; ABC
One Life to Live. David Pressman, Peter Miner, Norman Hall; ABC

OUTSTANDING WRITING FOR A DAYTIME DRAMA SERIES

All My Children. Agnes Nixon, Wisner Washam, Clarice Blackburn, Jack Woods, Mary K. Wells, Caroline Franz, Cathy Chicos, Cynthia Benjamin; ABC
General Hospital. Pat Falken Smith, Margaret DePriest, Sheri Anderson, Frank Salisbury, Margaret Stewart; ABC
* *The Guiding Light*. Douglas Marland, Harding Lemay, Robert Dwyer, Nancy Franklin; CBS
One Life to Live. Sam Hall, Gordon Russell, Don Wallace, Peggy O'Shea, Lanie Bertram, Fred Corke; ABC

TRUSTEES AWARD FOR SPECIAL ACHIEVEMENT IN TELEVISION

* Agnes Nixon, creator of *All My Children*, *One Life to Live*; co-creator of *As the World Turns*, *Search for Tomorrow*.

1981–82

OUTSTANDING DAYTIME DRAMA SERIES

All My Children. Jorn Winther, producer; ABC
General Hospital. Gloria Monty, producer; ABC

* *The Guiding Light*. Allen Potter, executive producer; Leslie Kwartin, Joe Willmore, producers; CBS
Ryan's Hope. Ellen Barrett, producer; ABC

OUTSTANDING ACTOR IN A DAYTIME DRAMA SERIES

Larry Bryggman (Dr. John Dixon, *As the World Turns*, CBS)
Stuart Damon (Dr. Alan Quartermaine, *General Hospital*, ABC)
* Anthony Geary (Lucas Lorenzo Spencer, *General Hospital*, ABC)
James Mitchell (Palmer Cortlandt, *All My Children*, ABC)
Richard Shoberg (Tom Cudahy, *All My Children*, ABC)

OUTSTANDING ACTRESS IN A DAYTIME DRAMA SERIES

Leslie Charleson (Dr. Monica Quartermaine, *General Hospital*, ABC)
Ann Flood (Nancy Karr, *The Edge of Night*, ABC)
Sharon Gabet (Raven Whitney, *The Edge of Night*, ABC)
Susan Lucci (Erica Kane, *All My Children*, ABC)
* Robin Strasser (Dorian Lord Callison, *One Life to Live*, ABC)

OUTSTANDING SUPPORTING ACTOR IN A DAYTIME DRAMA SERIES

Gerald Anthony (Marco Dane, *One Life to Live*, ABC)
* David Lewis (Edward Quartermaine, *All My Children*, ABC)
Douglas Sheehan (Joe Kelly, *General Hospital*, ABC)
Darnell Williams (Jesse Hubbard, *All My Children*, ABC)

OUTSTANDING SUPPORTING ACTRESS IN A DAYTIME DRAMA SERIES

Elizabeth Lawrence (Myra Murdoch, *All My Children*, ABC)
* Dorothy Lyman (Opal Gardner, *All My Children*, ABC)
Meg Mundy (Mona Aldrich Croft, *The Doctors*, NBC)
Louise Shaffer (Rae Woodard, *Ryan's Hope*, ABC)

OUTSTANDING DIRECTION FOR A DAYTIME DRAMA SERIES

All My Children. Larry Auerbach, Jack Coffey, Sherrell Hoffman, Jorn Winther; ABC
The Edge of Night. John Sedwick, Richard Pepperman; ABC
* *General Hospital*. Marlena Laird, Alan Pultz, Phil Sogard; ABC
One Life to Live. Norman Hall, Peter Miner, David Pressman; ABC

OUTSTANDING WRITING FOR A DAYTIME DRAMA SERIES

All My Children. Agnes Nixon, Wisner Washam, Jack Wood, Mary K. Wells, Clarice Blackburn, Caroline Franz, Lorraine Broderick, Cynthia Benjamin, John Saffron, Elizabeth Wallace; ABC
The Edge of Night. Henry Slesar, Lois Kibbee; ABC
* *The Guiding Light*. Douglas Marland, Frank Salisbury, Nancy Franklin, Gene Palumbo, Patrick Mulcahey; CBS

One Life to Live. Sam Hall, Peggy O'Shea, Don Wallace, Lanie Bertram, Fred Corke, S. Michael Schnessel; ABC

1982–83

OUTSTANDING DAYTIME DRAMA SERIES

All My Children. Jacqueline Babbin, producer; ABC
Days of Our Lives. Mrs. Ted Corday, executive producer; Al Rabin, supervising executive producer; Ken Corday, producer; NBC
General Hospital. Gloria Monty, producer; ABC
One Life to Live. Joseph Stuart, producer; ABC
* *The Young and the Restless.* William J. Bell, H. Wesley Kenney, executive producers; Edward Scott, producer; CBS

OUTSTANDING ACTOR IN A DAYTIME DRAMA SERIES

Peter Bergman (Dr. Cliff Warner, *All My Children*, ABC)
Stuart Damon (Dr. Alan Quartermaine, *General Hospital*, ABC)
Anthony Geary (Lucas Lorenzo Spencer, *General Hospital*, ABC)
James Mitchell (Palmer Cortlandt, *All My Children*, ABC)
* Robert S. Woods (Bo Buchanan, *One Life to Live*, ABC)

OUTSTANDING ACTRESS IN A DAYTIME DRAMA SERIES

Leslie Charleson (Dr. Monica Quartermaine, *General Hospital*, ABC)
Susan Lucci (Erica Kane, *All My Children*, ABC)
* Dorothy Lyman (Opal Gardner, *All My Children*, ABC)
Erika Slezak (Victoria Lord Buchanan, *One Life to Live*, ABC)
Robin Strasser (Dorian Lord Callison, *One Life to Live*, ABC)

OUTSTANDING SUPPORTING ACTOR IN A DAYTIME DRAMA SERIES

Anthony Call (Herb Callison, *One Life to Live*, ABC)
Al Freeman, Jr. (Ed Hall, *One Life to Live*, ABC)
David Lewis (Edward Quartermaine, *General Hospital*, ABC)
Howard E. Rollins, Jr. (Ed Harding, *Another World*, NBC)
John Stamos (Blackie Parrish, *General Hospital*, ABC)
* Darnell Williams (Jesse Hubbard, *All My Children*, ABC)

OUTSTANDING SUPPORTING ACTRESS IN A DAYTIME DRAMA SERIES

Kim Delaney (Jenny Gardner, *All My Children*, ABC)
Eileen Herlie (Myrtle Fargate, *All My Children*, ABC)
Robin Mattson (Heather Webber, *General Hospital*, ABC)
* Louise Shaffer (Rae Woodard, *Ryan's Hope*, ABC)
Brynn Thayer (Jenny Janssen, *One Life to Live*, ABC)
Marcy Walker (Liza Colby, *All My Children*, ABC)

OUTSTANDING DIRECTION FOR A DAYTIME DRAMA SERIES

All My Children. Larry Auerbach, Jack Coffey, Sherrell Hoffman, Francesca James; ABC

General Hospital. Marlena Laird, Alan Pultz, Phil Sogard; ABC

* *One Life to Live*. Allen Fristoe, Norman Hall, Peter Miner, David Pressman; ABC

OUTSTANDING WRITING FOR A DAYTIME DRAMA SERIES

All My Children. Agnes Nixon, Wisner Washam, Lorraine Broderick, Jack Wood, Mary K. Wells, Clarice Blackburn, Caroline Franz, Elizabeth Wallace, John Saffron; ABC

General Hospital. Anne Howard Bailey, A.J. Russell, Leah Laiman, Thom Racina, Jack Turley, Jeanne Glynn, Robert Guza Jr., Charles Pratt Jr., Robert Shaw; ABC

* *Ryan's Hope*. Claire Labine, Paul Avila Mayer, Mary Munisteri, Eugene Price, Judith Pinsker, Nancy Ford, B. K. Perlman, Rory Metcalf, Trent Jones; ABC

TRUSTEES AWARD FOR CONTINUED DISTINGUISHED SERVICE IN TELEVISION

* Robert E. Short, Procter & Gamble production executive

1983–84

OUTSTANDING DAYTIME DRAMA SERIES

All My Children. Jacqueline Babbin, producer; ABC

Days of Our Lives. Mrs. Ted Corday, executive producer; Al Rabin, supervising executive producer; Ken Corday, Shelley Curtis, producers; NBC

* *General Hospital*. Gloria Monty, producer; ABC

OUTSTANDING ACTOR IN A DAYTIME DRAMA SERIES

* Larry Bryggman (Dr. John Dixon, *As the World Turns*, CBS)

Joel Crothers (Dr. Miles Cavanaugh, *The Edge of Night*, ABC)

Stuart Damon (Dr. Alan Quartermaine, *General Hospital*, ABC)

Terry Lester (Jack Abbott, *The Young and the Restless*, CBS)

Larkin Malloy (Sky Whitney, *The Edge of Night*, ABC)

James Mitchell (Palmer Cortlandt, *All My Children*, ABC)

OUTSTANDING ACTRESS IN A DAYTIME DRAMA SERIES

Ann Flood (Nancy Karr, *The Edge of Night*, ABC)

Sharon Gabet (Raven Alexander Whitney, *The Edge of Night*, ABC)

Deidre Hall (Dr. Marlena Evans Brady, *Days of Our Lives*, NBC)

Susan Lucci (Erica Kane Chandler, *All My Children*, ABC)
* Erika Slezak (Victoria Lord Buchanan, *One Life to Live*, ABC)

OUTSTANDING SUPPORTING ACTOR IN A DAYTIME DRAMA SERIES

Anthony Call (Herb Callison, *One Life to Live*, ABC)
* Justin Deas (Tom Hughes, *As the World Turns*, CBS)
Louis Edmonds (Langley Wallingford, *All My Children*, ABC)
David Lewis (Edward Quartermaine, *General Hospital*, ABC)
Paul Stevens (Brian Bancroft, *Another World*, NBC)

OUTSTANDING SUPPORTING ACTRESS IN A DAYTIME DRAMA SERIES

Loanne Bishop (Rose Kelly, *General Hospital*, ABC)
Christine Ebersole (Maxie McDermott, *One Life to Live*, ABC)
* Judi Evans (Beth Raines, *The Guiding Light*, CBS)
Eileen Herlie (Myrtle Fargate, *All My Children*, ABC)
Lois Kibbee (Geraldine Saxon, *The Edge of Night*; ABC)
Marcy Walker (Liza Colby, *All My Children*, ABC)

OUTSTANDING DIRECTION FOR A DAYTIME DRAMA SERIES

All My Children. Jack Coffey, Sherrell Hoffman, Henry Kaplan, Francesca James; ABC
* *One Life to Live*. Larry Auerbach, George Keathley, Peter Miner, David Pressman; ABC

OUTSTANDING WRITING FOR A DAYTIME DRAMA SERIES

All My Children. Agnes Nixon, Wisner Washam, Lorraine Broderick, Dani Morris, Jack Wood, Mary K. Wells, Clarice Blackburn, Elizabeth Wallace, Roni Dengel, Susan Kirshenbaum, Carolina Della Pietra; ABC
* *Ryan's Hope*. Claire Labine, Paul Avila Mayer, Mary Ryan Munisteri, Judith Pinsker, Nancy Ford, B. K. Perlman; ABC
Days of Our Lives. Margaret DePriest, Sheri Anderson, Maralyn Thoma, Michael Robert David, Susan Goldberg, Bob Hansen, Leah Markus, Dana Soloff; NBC
General Hospital. Anne Howard Bailey, A. J. Russell, Leah Laiman, Norma Monty, Thom Racina, Doris Silverton, Robert Guza, Jr., Charles Pratt, Jr., Peggy Schibi, Robert Shaw; ABC

1984–85

OUTSTANDING DAYTIME DRAMA SERIES

All My Children. Jacqueline Babbin, producer; ABC
Days of Our Lives. Mrs. Ted Corday, Al Rabin, executive producers; Ken Corday, Shelley Curtis, producers; NBC

General Hospital. Gloria Monty, executive producer; ABC
Guiding Light. Gail Kobe, executive producer; John P. Whitesell II,
    Robert D. Kochman, Leslie Kwartin, producers; CBS
* *The Young and The Restless*. William J. Bell, H. Wesley Kenney; execu-
    tive producers; Edward Scott, producer; CBS

OUTSTANDING LEAD ACTOR IN A DAYTIME DRAMA SERIES

Larry Bryggman (Dr. John Dixon, *As the World Turns*, CBS)
David Canary (Adam/Stuart Chandler, *All My Children*, ABC)
Terry Lester (Jack Abbott, *The Young and the Restless*, CBS)
James Mitchell (Palmer Cortlandt, *All My Children*, ABC)
* Darnell Williams (Jesse Hubbard, *All My Children*, ABC)

OUTSTANDING LEAD ACTRESS IN A DAYTIME DRAMA SERIES

Deidre Hall (Dr. Marlena Evans Brady, *Days of Our Lives*, NBC)
Susan Lucci (Eric Kane, *All My Children*, ABC)
Gillian Spencer (Daisy Cortlandt, *All My Children*, ABC)
Robin Strasser, (Dorian Lord, *One Life to Live*, ABC)
* Kim Zimmer (Reva Shayne Lewis, *Guiding Light*, CBS)

OUTSTANDING SUPPORTING ACTOR IN A DAYTIME DRAMA SERIES

Anthony Call (Herb Callison, *One Life to Live*, ABC)
Louis Edmonds (Langley Wallingford, *All My Children*, ABC)
* Larry Gates (H. B. Lewis, *Guiding Light*, CBS)
David Lewis (Edward Quartermaine, *General Hospital*, ABC)
Robert LuPone (Zach Grayson, *All My Children*, ABC)

OUTSTANDING SUPPORTING ACTRESS IN A DAYTIME DRAMA SERIES

Norma Connolly (Ruby Anderson, *General Hospital*, ABC)
Eileen Herlie (Myrtle Fargate, *All My Children*, ABC)
Maeve Kinkead (Vanessa Chamberlain Lewis, *Guiding Light*, CBS)
Elizabeth Lawrence (Myra Murdoch Sloane, *All My Children*, ABC)
* Beth Maitland (Traci Abbott Romalotti, *The Young and the Restless*,
    CBS)

OUTSTANDING JUVENILE/YOUNG MAN IN A DAYTIME DRAMA SERIES

* Brian Bloom (Dustin Donovan, *As the World Turns*, CBS)
Steve Caffrey (Andrew Preston Cortlandt, *All My Children*, ABC)
Michael Knight (Tad Gardner Martin, *All My Children*, ABC)

Michael O'Leary (Rick Bauer, *Guiding Light*, CBS)
Jack P. Wagner (Frisco Jones, *General Hospital*, ABC)

OUTSTANDING INGENUE IN A DAYTIME DRAMA SERIES

Kristian Alfonso (Hope Williams Brady, *Days of Our Lives*, NBC)
* Tracey E. Bregman (Lauren Fenmore Williams, *The Young and the Restless*, CBS)
Melissa Leo (Linda Warner, *All My Children*, ABC)
Lisa Trusel (Melissa Anderson, *Days of Our Lives*, NBC)
Tasia Valenza (Dottie Thorton Martin, *All My Children*, ABC)

OUTSTANDING DIRECTION FOR A DAYTIME DRAMA SERIES

All My Children. Jack Coffey, Sherrell Hoffman, Henry Kaplan, Francesca James, Jean Dadario Burke, Barbara Martin Simmons; ABC
As the World Turns. Robert Schwarz, Maria Wagner, Richard Dunlap, Paul Lammers, Richard Pepperman, Portman Paget, Joel Arnowitz; CBS
Days of Our Lives. Susan Orlikoff Simon, Al Rabin, Joseph Behar, Stephen Wyman, Herb Stein, Gay Linvill, Sheryl Harmon, Becky Greenlaw; NBC
* *Guiding Light*. John P. Whitesell II, Irene M. Pace, Bruce Barry, Matthew Diamond, Robert D. Kochman, Jo Ann Rivituso, Jo Anne Sedwick; CBS
One Life to Live. Larry Auerbach, Peter Miner, David Pressman, Melvin Bernhardt, Ron Lagomarsino, Susan Pomerantz, Stuart Silver; ABC

OUTSTANDING WRITING FOR A DAYTIME DRAMA SERIES

* *All My Children*. Agnes Nixon, Wisner Washam, Lorraine Broderick, Victor Miller, Mary K. Wells, Clarice Blackburn, Art Wallace, Susan Kirshenbaum, Carolina Della Pietra, Elizabeth Page, Jack Wood; ABC
Another World. Gary Tomlin, Samuel D. Ratcliffe, Richard Culliton, Carolyn Culliton, Judith Donato, David Cherrill, Judith Pinsker, Frances Myers, Roger Newman, Lloyd Gold, Cynthia Saltzman; NBC
Days of Our Lives. Sheri Anderson, Thom Racina, Maralyn Thoma, Leah Laiman, Michael Robert David, Leah Markus, Anne M. Schoettle, Dana Soloff, Margaret DePriest; NBC
Guiding Light. Pamela K. Long, Jeff Ryder, John Kuntz, Christopher Whitesell, Addie Walsh, Samuel D. Ratcliffe, Robin Amos, Stephanie Braxton, Stephen Demorest, Trent Jones, N. Gail Lawrence, Megan McTavish, Michele Poteet-Lisanti, Elaine Potwardoski, Emily Squires, Pete T. Rich; CBS

TRUSTEES AWARD FOR DISTINGUISHED SERVICE TO DAYTIME TELEVISION

* Charita Bauer (Bert Bauer, *Guiding Light*, CBS)
* Larry Haines (Stu Bergman, *Search for Tomorrow*, NBC)
* Mary Stuart (Jo, *Search for Tomorrow*, NBC)

1985–86

OUTSTANDING DAYTIME DRAMA SERIES

All My Children. Jacqueline Babbin, producer; ABC
As the World Turns. Robert Calhoun, executive producer; Michael Laibson, Bonnie Bogard, Christine Banas, producers; CBS
General Hospital. Gloria Monty, executive producer; Joe Willmore, Jerry Balme, coordinating producers; ABC
* *The Young and the Restless*. William J. Bell, H. Wesley Kenney, executive producers; Edward Scott, Tom Langan, producers; CBS

OUTSTANDING LEAD ACTOR IN A DAYTIME DRAMA SERIES

Scott Bryce (Craig Montgomery, *As the World Turns*, CBS)
Larry Bryggman (Dr. John Dixon, *As the World Turns*, CBS)
* David Canary (Adam/Stuart Chandler, *All My Children*, ABC)
Nicolas Coster (Lionel Lockridge, *Santa Barbara*, NBC)
Terry Lester (Jack Abbott, *The Young and the Restless*, CBS)
Robert S. Woods (Bo Buchanan, *One Life to Live*), ABC)

OUTSTANDING LEAD ACTRESS IN A DAYTIME DRAMA SERIES

Susan Lucci (Erica Kane, *All My Children*, ABC)
Elizabeth Hubbard (Lucinda Walsh, *As the World Turns*, CBS)
Peggy McCay (Caroline Brady, *Days of Our Lives*, NBC)
* Erika Slezak (Victoria Lord Buchanan, *One Life to Live*, ABC)
Kim Zimmer (Reva Shayne, *Guiding Light*, CBS)

OUTSTANDING SUPPORTING ACTOR IN A DAYTIME DRAMA SERIES

Louis Edmonds (Langley Wallingford, *All My Children*, ABC)
Al Freeman, Jr. (Captain Ed Hall, *One Life to Live*, ABC)
Larry Gates (H.B. Lewis, *Guiding Light*, CBS)
Gregg Marx (Tom Hughes, *As the World Turns*, CBS)
* John Wesley Shipp (Douglas Cummings, *As the World Turns*, CBS)

OUTSTANDING SUPPORTING ACTRESS IN A DAYTIME DRAMA SERIES

Dame Judith Anderson (Minx Lockridge, *Santa Barbara*, NBC)
Uta Hagen (Hortense, *One Life to Live*, ABC)
Eileen Herlie (Myrtle Fargate, *All My Children*, ABC)
* Leann Hunley (Anna DiMera, *Days of Our Lives*, NBC)
Kathleen Widdoes (Emma Snyder, *As the World Turns*, CBS)

OUTSTANDING YOUNGER LEADING MAN IN A DAYTIME DRAMA SERIES

Brian Bloom (Dustin Donovan, *As the World Turns*, CBS)
Jon Hensley (Holden Snyder, *As the World Turns*, CBS)
Vincent Irizarry (Lujack, *Guiding Light*, CBS)
* Michael Knight (Tad Gardner Martin, *All My Children*, ABC)
Don Scardino (Dr. Chris Chapin, *Another World*, NBC)

OUTSTANDING INGENUE IN A DAYTIME DRAMA SERIES

Martha Byrne (Lily Walsh, *As the World Turns*, CBS)
Debbi Morgan (Angie Hubbard, *All My Children*, ABC)
Jane Krakowski (T.R. Kendall, *Search for Tomorrow*, NBC)
* Ellen Wheeler (Marley/Victoria Love, *Another World*, NBC)
Robin Wright (Kelly Capwell, *Santa Barbara*, NBC)

OUTSTANDING DIRECTION FOR A DAYTIME DRAMA SERIES

As the World Turns. Paul Lammers, Robert Schwarz, Richard Pepperman, Maria Wagner, Joel Arnowitz, Michael Kerner; CBS
Days of Our Lives. Susan Orlikoff Simon, Joseph Behar, Herb Stein, Stephen Wyman, Gay Linvill, Sheryl Harmon, Becky Greenlaw; NBC
Guiding Light. Bruce Barry, Irene Pace, Matthew Diamond, Jo Ann Rivituso, Jo Anne Sedwick; CBS
One Life to Live. Larry Auerbach, Peter Miner, David Pressman, Susan Pomerantz, Stuart Silverman; ABC
* *The Young and the Restless*. Dennis Steinmetz, Rudy Vejar, Frank Pacelli, Randy Robbins, Betty Rothenberg; CBS

OUTSTANDING WRITING FOR A DAYTIME DRAMA SERIES

As the World Turns. Douglas Marland, Susan Bedsow Horgan, Jeanne Glynn, Garin Wolf, Patti Dizenzo, M.B. Hatch, Chris Auer, Caroline Franz, Meredith Post, Jane Willis; CBS
General Hospital. Pat Falken Smith, Norma Monty, A.J. Russell, James Reilly, Patrick Smith, Robert Guza, Doris Silverton, Robert Soderberg, Maralyn Thoma; ABC

* *Guiding Light.* Pamela K. Long, Jeff Ryder, Addie Walsh, John Kuntz, Christopher Whitesell, Megan McTavish, Stephen Demorest, Victor Gialanella, Mary Pat Gleason, Trent Jones, Nancy Curlee, N. Gail Lawrence, Pete T. Rich; CBS

  The Young and the Restless. William J. Bell, Kay Alden, John F. Smith, Sally Sussman, Eric Freiwald, John Randall Holland, Meg Bennett, Enid Powell; CBS

1986–87

OUTSTANDING DAYTIME DRAMA SERIES

All My Children. Jacqueline Babbin, Jorn Winther, producers; Randi Subarsky, coordinating producer; ABC

* *As the World Turns.* Robert Calhoun, executive producer; Ken Fitts, supervising producer; Christine Banas, Michael Laibson, Lisa Wilson, producers; CBS

Santa Barbara. Jerome and Bridget Dobson, executive producers; Mary-Ellis Bunim, co-executive producer; Steven Kent, Jill Farren Phelps, Leonard Friedlander, producers; NBC

The Young and the Restless. William J. Bell, H. Wesley Kenney, executive producers; Edward Scott, supervising producer; Tom Langan, producer; CBS

OUTSTANDING LEAD ACTOR IN A DAYTIME DRAMA SERIES

Eric Braeden (Victor Newman, *The Young and the Restless*, CBS)
Scott Bryce (Craig Montgomery, *As the World Turns*, CBS)
* Larry Bryggman (Dr. John Dixon, *As the World Turns*, CBS)
Terry Lester (Jack Abbott, *The Young and the Restless*, CBS)
A Martinez (Cruz Castillo, *Santa Barbara*, NBC)

OUTSTANDING LEAD ACTRESS IN A DAYTIME DRAMA SERIES

Elizabeth Hubbard (Lucinda Walsh Dixon, *As the World Turns*, CBS)
Susan Lucci (Erica Kane, *All My Children*, ABC)
Frances Reid (Alice Horton, *Days of Our Lives*, NBC)
Marcy Walker (Eden Capwell, *Santa Barbara*, NBC)
* Kim Zimmer (Reva Shayne, *Guiding Light*, CBS)

OUTSTANDING SUPPORTING ACTOR IN A DAYTIME DRAMA SERIES

Anthony Call (Herb Callison, *One Life to Live*, ABC)
Justin Deas (Keith Timmons, *Santa Barbara*, NBC)
Richard Eden (Brick Wallace, *Santa Barbara*, NBC)

Al Freeman, Jr. (Captain Ed Hall, *One Life to Live*, ABC)
* Gregg Marx (Tom Hughes, *As the World Turns*, CBS)

OUTSTANDING SUPPORTING ACTRESS IN A DAYTIME DRAMA SERIES

Lisa Brown (Iva Snyder, *As the World Turns*, CBS)
Peggy McCay (Caroline Brady, *Days of Our Lives*, NBC)
Robin Mattson (Gina Capwell, *Santa Barbara*, NBC)
* Kathleen Noone (Ellen Chandler, *All My Children*, ABC)
Kathleen Widdoes (Emma Snyder, *As the World Turns*, CBS)

OUTSTANDING YOUNGER LEADING MAN IN A DAYTIME DRAMA SERIES

Brian Bloom (Dustin Donovan, *As the World Turns*, CBS)
Jon Hensley (Holden Snyder, *As the World Turns*, CBS)
* Michael Knight (Tad Martin, *All My Children*, ABC)
Grant Show (Rick Hyde, *Ryan's Hope*, ABC)
Billy Warlock (Frankie Brady, *Days of Our Lives*, NBC)

OUTSTANDING INGENUE IN A DAYTIME DRAMA SERIES

Tracey E. Bregman (Lauren Fenmore, *The Young and the Restless*, CBS)
* Martha Byrne (Lily Walsh, *As the World Turns*, CBS)
Jane Krakowski (T.R. Kendall, *Search for Tomorrow*, NBC)
Krista Tesreau (Mindy Lewis, *Guiding Light*, CBS)
Robin Wright (Kelly Capwell, *Santa Barbara*, NBC)

OUTSTANDING GUEST PERFORMER IN A DAYTIME DRAMA SERIES

Pamela Blair (Ronda, *All My Children*, ABC)
Eileen Heckart (Ruth Perkins, *One Life to Live*, ABC)
Celeste Holm (Clara/Lydia Woodhouse, *Loving*, ABC)
Terrance Mann (Jester, *As the World Turns*, CBS)
* John Wesley Shipp (Martin Ellis, *Santa Barbara*, NBC)

OUTSTANDING DIRECTION FOR A DAYTIME DRAMA SERIES

All My Children. Jack Coffey, Sherrell Hoffman, Francesca James, Henry Kaplan, Jean Dadario Burke, Barbara Martin Simmons, Shirley Simmons; ABC
As the World Turns. Paul Lammers, Robert Schwarz, Maria Wagner, Joel Arnowitz, Michael Kerner; CBS
Days of Our Lives. Joseph Behar, Susan Orlikoff Simon, Herb Stein, Stephen Wyman, Becky Greenlaw, Gay Linvill, Sheryl Harmon; NBC
* *The Young and the Restless*. Frank Pacelli, Rudy Vejar, Randy Robbins, Betty Rothenberg; CBS

OUTSTANDING WRITING FOR A DAYTIME DRAMA SERIES

Days of Our Lives. Leah Laiman, Sheri Anderson, Thom Racina,
   Anne M. Schoettle, Dena Breshears, Richard J. Allen, M.M.
   Shelly Moore, Penina Spiegel; NBC
* *One Life to Live.* Peggy O'Shea, S. Michael Schnessel, Craig Carlson,
   Lanie Bertram, Ethel M. Brez, Mel Brez; ABC
The Young and the Restless. William J. Bell, Kay Alden, John F. Smith,
   Sally Sussman, Eric Freiwald, Enid Powell; CBS

The following are listings of the top-rated daytime dramas during each TV season beginning in September and ranked by audience size.

The Nielsen rating is the percentage of all TV-equipped homes viewing a show during an average day. Since the ratings currently reflect 87.4 million households across the nation equipped with at least one television set, a single rating point represents 874,000 viewing homes. A share refers to the show's portion of the audience actually watching TV at a given time period. Thus a 10.0 rating and 33 share for, say, *General Hospital* means (1) 10 percent of all TV-equipped households were watching *General Hospital* on an average day; (2) that 10 percent translates into about 8.7 million households; and (3) *General Hospital* garnered 33 percent of the total households watching television during that particular show's time period.

The A. C. Nielsen Company changed its method of computing ratings in 1960, so ratings prior to that time are not comparable to those after that date. (Shares are included from that date below.) In addition, as the number of households with television sets grew (from 3.8 million in 1950), a single rating point represented more and more TV households. Therefore, ratings from year to year are also not precisely comparable.

1952–53

Serial	Network	Rating
1. Search for Tomorrow	CBS	16.1
2. Love of Life	CBS	15.1
3. Hawkins Falls	NBC	13.7
4. The Guiding Light	CBS	11.3

1953–54

Serial	Network	Rating
1. Search for Tomorrow	CBS	15.8
2. The Guiding Light	CBS	14.4
3. Love of Life	CBS	14.0
4. Valiant Lady	CBS	10.2

1954–55

Serial	Network	Rating
1. Search for Tomorrow	CBS	15.2
2. The Guiding Light	CBS	14.6
3. Love of Life	CBS	13.1
4. Valiant Lady	CBS	10.5
5. The Secret Storm	CBS	8.5
6. Modern Romances	NBC	8.5
7. The Brighter Day	CBS	8.4

1955–56

Serial	Network	Rating
1. Search for Tomorrow	CBS	13.1
2. The Guiding Light	CBS	13.0
3. Love of Life	CBS	10.9
4. The Brighter Day	CBS	10.6
5. The Secret Storm	CBS	10.2
6. Valiant Lady	CBS	9.2

1956–57

Serial	Network	Rating
1. The Guiding Light	CBS	11.4
2. Search for Tomorrow	CBS	11.0
3. The Secret Storm	CBS	10.0
4. The Edge of Night	CBS	9.7
5. The Brighter Day	CBS	9.2
6. Love of Life	CBS	9.1
7. Modern Romances	NBC	9.0
8. As the World Turns	CBS	8.4

1957–58

Serial	Network	Rating
1. The Guiding Light	CBS	10.1
2. As the World Turns	CBS	9.9
3. The Verdict Is Yours	CBS	9.9
4. Search for Tomorrow	CBS	9.8
5. The Secret Storm	CBS	9.7
6. The Brighter Day	CBS	9.3

1958–59

Serial	Network	Rating
1. As the World Turns	CBS	9.8
2. Search for Tomorrow	CBS	9.8
3. The Guiding Light	CBS	9.7
4. The Verdict Is Yours	CBS	8.7
5. The Secret Storm	CBS	8.6
6. The Edge of Night	CBS	8.6
7. The Brighter Day	CBS	8.2

1959–60

Serial	Network	Rating
1. As the World Turns	CBS	9.9
2. The Guiding Light	CBS	9.6

Serial	Network	Rating
3. Search for Tomorrow	CBS	9.5
4. The Edge of Night	CBS	9.5
5. The Secret Storm	CBS	8.9
6. The Verdict Is Yours	CBS	8.6
7. The Brighter Day	CBS	8.2

1960–61

Serial	Network	Rating	Share
1. As the World Turns	CBS	10.4	44.0
2. The Guiding Light	CBS	9.9	40.4
3. Search for Tomorrow	CBS	9.4	39.3
4. The Edge of Night	CBS	9.4	34.7
5. The Secret Storm	CBS	9.1	36.6
6. The Verdict Is Yours	CBS	8.0	37.2
7. The Brighter Day	CBS	7.9	34.3
8. Love of Life	CBS	7.5	33.0
9. Young Dr. Malone	NBC	6.6	30.3
10. From These Roots	NBC	5.9	27.3
11. The Clear Horizon	CBS	4.8	23.0
12. Road to Reality	ABC	2.4	11.3

1961–62

Serial	Network	Rating	Share
1. As the World Turns	CBS	11.9	47.7
2. The Guiding Light	CBS	10.1	40.9
3. Search for Tomorrow	CBS	9.5	39.6
4. The Edge of Night	CBS	8.2	30.6
5. The Secret Storm	CBS	7.6	30.2
6. The Verdict Is Yours	CBS	7.5	34.0
7. Love of Life	CBS	7.4	31.8
8. The Brighter Day	CBS	6.9	29.4
9. Young Dr. Malone	NBC	6.1	27.0
10. Our Five Daughters	NBC	5.9	25.5
11. From These Roots	NBC	5.6	26.7
12. The Clear Horizon	CBS	3.2	15.5

1962–63

Serial	Network	Rating	Share
1. As the World Turns	CBS	13.7	53.7
2. The Guiding Light	CBS	11.7	51.2
3. Search for Tomorrow	CBS	10.6	43.4
4. The Edge of Night	CBS	9.5	33.7
5. The Secret Storm	CBS	9.0	34.5

Serial	*Network*	*Rating*	*Share*
6. Love of Life	CBS	8.6	37.5
7. Our Five Daughters	NBC	5.5	26.9
8. Young Dr. Malone	NBC	5.5	22.8
9. General Hospital	ABC	3.9	16.7
10. The Brighter Day	CBS	3.7	23.4
11. The Doctors	NBC	3.4	17.0
12. The Verdict Is Yours	CBS	3.2	22.4
13. Ben Jerrod	NBC	2.4	11.6

1963–64

Serial	*Network*	*Rating*	*Share*
1. As the World Turns	CBS	15.4	57.0
2. The Guiding Light	CBS	14.2	57.2
3. Search for Tomorrow	CBS	11.0	44.4
4. The Edge of Night	CBS	10.5	41.4
5. Love of Life	CBS	10.3	43.6
6. The Secret Storm	CBS	9.2	33.8
7. General Hospital	ABC	5.4	22.1
8. The Doctors	NBC	4.7	19.7

1964–65

Serial	*Network*	*Rating*	*Share*
1. As the World Turns	CBS	14.5	51.7
2. Search for Tomorrow	CBS	12.2	46.4
3. The Guiding Light	CBS	12.2	45.7
4. The Secret Storm	CBS	11.5	37.2
5. Love of Life	CBS	10.6	41.8
6. The Edge of Night	CBS	10.4	37.2
7. General Hospital	ABC	8.0	28.5
8. The Doctors	NBC	7.5	28.4
9. Another World	NBC	6.8	24.6
10. Moment of Truth	NBC	5.0	18.9
11. The Young Marrieds	ABC	4.4	15.7
12. Flame in the Wind	ABC	2.8	10.6

1965–66

Serial	*Network*	*Rating*	*Share*
1. As the World Turns	CBS	13.9	49.4
2. The Guiding Light	CBS	11.2	44.4
3. Search for Tomorrow	CBS	11.0	44.2
4. The Secret Storm	CBS	10.9	36.3
5. The Edge of Night	CBS	9.9	39.6

Serial	Network	Rating	Share
6. General Hospital	ABC	7.3	26.3
7. Another World	NBC	6.9	25.1
8. The Doctors	NBC	6.6	25.1
9. Days of Our Lives	NBC	5.3	20.2
10. The Young Marrieds	ABC	4.7	16.7
11. Moment of Truth	NBC	4.3	18.7
12. Morning Star	NBC	4.1	21.6
13. Paradise Bay	NBC	4.1	20.1
14. A Time for Us	ABC	4.0	15.1
15. The Nurses	ABC	3.9	15.2
16. Never Too Young	ABC	3.9	12.8
17. Confidential for Women	ABC	3.4	13.5

1966–67

Serial	Network	Rating	Share
1. As the World Turns	CBS	12.7	45.6
2. The Edge of Night	CBS	10.9	38.6
3. The Guiding Light	CBS	10.8	41.7
4. Search for Tomorrow	CBS	10.7	41.9
5. The Secret Storm	CBS	10.7	35.6
6. Love of Life	CBS	9.5	37.7
7. Another World	NBC	9.0	31.6
8. The Doctors	NBC	7.6	27.9
9. General Hospital	ABC	7.0	24.7
10. Days of Our Lives	NBC	6.9	25.7
11. The Nurses	ABC	4.6	16.2
12. Dark Shadows	ABC	4.3	14.3
13. A Time for Us	ABC	4.0	15.9

1967–68

Serial	Network	Rating	Share
1. As the World Turns	CBS	13.6	45.3
2. Another World	NBC	10.2	34.4
3. The Guiding Light	CBS	10.0	38.3
4. Search for Tomorrow	CBS	9.9	38.7
5. The Doctors	NBC	9.7	33.8
6. The Edge of Night	CBS	9.4	31.6
7. The Secret Storm	CBS	9.4	30.1
8. Love of Life	CBS	9.2	36.3
9. General Hospital	ABC	8.8	29.0
10. Days of Our Lives	NBC	8.7	30.6
11. Love Is a Many Splendored Thing	CBS	7.9	27.5
12. Dark Shadows	ABC	7.3	23.9

1968–69

Serial	Network	Rating	Share
1. As the World Turns	CBS	13.8	46
2. Search for Tomorrow	CBS	10.7	41
3. Another World	NBC	10.5	37
4. The Edge of Night	CBS	9.5	33
5. Love of Life	CBS	9.3	37
6. The Doctors	NBC	9.3	32
7. Days of Our Lives	NBC	9.3	31
8. Love Is a Many Splendored Thing	CBS	9.0	30
9. The Guiding Light	CBS	8.9	31
10. General Hospital	ABC	8.8	30
11. Dark Shadows	ABC	8.4	27
12. The Secret Storm	CBS	7.8	27
13. One Life to Live	ABC	5.4	19
14. Hidden Faces	NBC	3.3	11

1969–70

Serial	Network	Rating	Share
1. As the World Turns	CBS	13.6	46
2. The Edge of Night	CBS	10.8	38
3. Search for Tomorrow	CBS	10.0	39
4. The Guiding Light	CBS	9.8	39
5. Another World—Bay City	NBC	9.6	32
6. Love Is a Many Splendored Thing	CBS	9.5	32
7. Days of Our Lives	NBC	8.8	30
8. The Doctors	NBC	8.6	30
8. (Tie) The Secret Storm	CBS	8.6	30
10. General Hospital	ABC	8.5	29
11. Love of Life	CBS	8.0	36
12. Dark Shadows	ABC	7.3	23
13. Where the Heart Is	CBS	7.0	28
14. One Life to Live	ABC	6.7	23
15. Another World—Somerset	NBC	5.7	20
16. Bright Promise	ABC	5.2	28
17. All My Children	ABC	4.4	16
18. A World Apart	ABC	2.8	11
19. Best of Everything	ABC	1.8	10

1970–71

Serial	Network	Rating	Share
1. As the World Turns	CBS	12.4	42
2. The Edge of Night	CBS	10.1	34

Serial	Network	Rating	Share
3. The Guiding Light	CBS	9.7	33
4. Another World–Bay City	NBC	9.5	32
4. (Tie)Days of Our Lives	NBC	9.5	32
6. General Hospital	ABC	9.5	31
7. The Doctors	NBC	9.4	32
8. Search for Tomorrow	CBS	9.3	36
9. Love Is a Many Splendored Thing	CBS	9.2	31
10. The Secret Storm	CBS	8.0	27
11. Love of Life	CBS	7.9	34
12. Where the Heart Is	CBS	7.0	27
13. Another World—Somerset	NBC	7.0	22
14. Bright Promise	NBC	6.8	23
15. One Life to Live	ABC	6.5	22
16. Dark Shadows	ABC	5.3	16
17. All My Children	ABC	4.8	18
18. A World Apart	ABC	3.4	13

1971–72

Serial	Network	Rating	Share
1. As the World Turns	CBS	11.1	37
2. General Hospital	ABC	10.4	34
3. Days of Our Lives	NBC	9.9	34
4. The Edge of Night	CBS	9.5	32
5. The Doctors	NBC	9.3	32
6. Another World	NBC	9.1	31
7. Search for Tomorrow	CBS	8.8	32
8. The Guiding Light	CBS	8.6	30
9. Love Is a Many Splendored Thing	CBS	8.0	27
10. Love of Life	CBS	7.4	30
11. Return to Peyton Place	NBC	7.4	26
12. The Secret Storm	CBS	7.4	25
13. One Life to Live	ABC	7.3	24
14. Somerset	NBC	6.5	21
15. Where the Heart Is	CBS	6.3	24
16. Bright Promise	NBC	6.1	21
17. All My Children	ABC	5.7	21

1972–73

Serial	Network	Rating	Share
1. As the World Turns	CBS	10.6	34
2. Days of Our Lives	NBC	9.9	32
3. Another World	NBC	9.7	33

Serial	Network	Rating	Share
4. General Hospital	ABC	9.7	31
5. The Doctors	NBC	9.3	32
6. Search for Tomorrow	CBS	8.6	30
7. One Life to Live	ABC	8.3	27
8. All My Children	ABC	8.2	28
9. The Guiding Light	CBS	8.2	27
10. The Edge of Night	CBS	7.9	28
11. The Secret Storm	CBS	7.3	24
12. Love of Life	CBS	7.2	29
13. Return to Peyton Place	NBC	7.2	24
14. Love Is a Many Splendored Thing	CBS	7.1	24
15. Somerset	NBC	6.8	21
16. Where the Heart Is	CBS	6.4	23
17. The Young and the Restless	CBS	5.0	20

1973–74

Serial	Network	Rating	Share
1. As the World Turns	CBS	9.7	33
2. Another World	NBC	9.7	32
2. (Tie) Days of Our Lives	NBC	9.7	32
4. The Doctors	NBC	9.5	33
5. General Hospital	ABC	9.2	30
6. All My Children	ABC	9.1	32
7. The Guiding Light	CBS	8.1	27
8. One Life to Live	ABC	7.8	25
9. Search for Tomorrow	CBS	7.7	29
10. The Edge of Night	CBS	7.4	26
11. Return to Peyton Place	NBC	7.0	23
12. How to Survive a Marriage	NBC	6.4	21
13. The Young and the Restless	CBS	6.2	24
14. Somerset	NBC	6.1	19
15. Love of Life	CBS	6.0	26
16. The Secret Storm	CBS	5.8	18

1974–75

Serial	Network	Rating	Share
1. As the World Turns	CBS	10.8	37
2. Another World	NBC	9.7	31
3. Days of Our Lives	NBC	9.6	33
4. Search for Tomorrow	CBS	9.4	35
5. All My Children	ABC	9.3	32

Serial	Network	Rating	Share
6. The Doctors	NBC	9.0	32
7. The Guiding Light	CBS	8.5	29
8. General Hospital	ABC	8.5	27
9. The Young and the Restless	CBS	8.4	32
10. The Edge of Night	CBS	7.6	27
11. One Life to Live	ABC	7.4	23
12. Love of Life	CBS	7.0	30
13. Somerset	NBC	6.0	18
14. How to Survive a Marriage	NBC	5.7	19

1975–76

Serial	Network	Rating	Share
1. As the World Turns	CBS	9.4	34
2. Another World	NBC	8.9	30
3. The Young and the Restless	CBS	8.6	35
4. Search for Tomorrow	CBS	8.3	33
5. Days of Our Lives	NBC	8.3	30
6. All My Children	ABC	8.1	31
7. The Guiding Light	CBS	8.1	30
8. The Doctors	NBC	7.3	28
9. Love of Life	CBS	7.2	32
10. General Hospital	ABC	7.1	24
11. One Life to Live	ABC	6.8	21
12. The Edge of Night	CBS, ABC	6.7	24
13. Somerset	NBC	5.9	18
14. Ryan's Hope	ABC	5.7	21

1976–77

Serial	Network	Rating	Share
1. As the World Turns	CBS	9.9	34
2. Another World	NBC	9.0	29
3. The Guiding Light	CBS	8.9	32
4. The Young and the Restless	CBS	8.7	36
5. Search for Tomorrow	CBS	8.6	34
6. All My Children	ABC	8.2	30
7. Days of Our Lives	NBC	7.8	27
8. Ryan's Hope	ABC	7.3	27
9. One Life to Live	ABC	7.3	26
10. General Hospital	ABC	7.0	22
11. The Doctors	NBC	6.9	25
12. Love of Life	CBS	6.3	28
13. The Edge of Night	ABC	6.2	19

Serial	Network	Rating	Share
14. Somerset	NBC	5.2	16
15. Lovers and Friends	NBC	2.9	11

1977–78

Serial	Network	Rating	Share
1. As the World Turns	CBS	8.6	31
2. Another World	NBC	8.6	28
3. All My Children	ABC	8.4	31
4. The Guiding Light	CBS	8.0	28
5. The Young and the Restless	CBS	7.8	32
6. Search for Tomorrow	CBS	7.5	30
7. One Life to Live	ABC	7.2	26
8. Ryan's Hope	ABC	7.0	28
9. General Hospital	ABC	7.0	23
10. Days of Our Lives	NBC	6.9	25
11. The Doctors	NBC	6.5	23
12. Love of Life	CBS	6.0	27
13. The Edge of Night	ABC	5.2	16
14. For Richer, For Poorer	NBC	3.9	15

1978–79

Serial	Network	Rating	Share
1. All My Children	ABC	9.0	33
2. General Hospital	ABC	8.7	28
3. The Young and the Restless	CBS	8.6	34
4. As the World Turns	CBS	8.2	29
5. The Guiding Light	CBS	8.1	28
6. One Life to Live	ABC	8.0	28
7. Search for Tomorrow	CBS	7.6	29
8. Another World	NBC	7.5	25
9. Ryan's Hope	ABC	7.2	28
10. Days of Our Lives	NBC	6.8	24
11. The Doctors	NBC	6.3	22
12. Love of Life	CBS	5.8	25
13. The Edge of Night	ABC	5.8	18
14. For Richer, For Poorer	NBC	2.1	9

1979–80

Serial	Network	Rating	Share
1. General Hospital	ABC	9.9	32
2. All My Children	ABC	9.2	32

Serial	Network	Rating	Share
3. The Young and the Restless	CBS	8.8	32
4. One Life to Live	ABC	8.7	30
5. The Guiding Light	CBS	8.3	27
6. As the World Turns	CBS	7.9	28
7. Search for Tomorrow	CBS	7.6	30
8. Another World	NBC	7.1	23
9. Ryan's Hope	ABC	7.0	26
10. Days of Our Lives	NBC	6.6	23
11. The Doctors	NBC	6.1	21
12. The Edge of Night	ABC	5.3	16
13. Love of Life	CBS	3.5	11

1980–81

Serial	Network	Rating	Share
1. General Hospital	ABC	11.4	37
2. All My Children	ABC	9.1	33
3. One Life to Live	ABC	9.1	32
4. The Guiding Light	CBS	8.2	26
5. As the World Turns	CBS	7.9	28
6. The Young and the Restless	CBS	7.8	29
7. Ryan's Hope	ABC	6.7	26
8. Search for Tomorrow	CBS	6.3	25
9. Days of Our Lives	NBC	5.6	20
10. Another World	NBC	5.1	18
11. The Edge of Night	ABC	5.0	16
12. Texas	NBC	4.7	15
13. The Doctors	NBC	3.8	15

1981–82

Serial	Network	Rating	Share
1. General Hospital	ABC	11.2	35
2. All My Children	ABC	9.4	32
3. One Life to Live	ABC	9.3	32
4. The Guiding Light	CBS	8.0	25
5. The Young and the Restless	CBS	7.4	28
6. As the World Turns	CBS	7.4	25
7. Ryan's Hope	ABC	6.9	26
8. Search for Tomorrow	CBS	6.8	23
9. Capitol	CBS	5.8	22
10. Days of Our Lives	NBC	5.5	19
11. The Edge of Night	ABC	5.0	15
12. Another World	NBC	4.7	16

Serial	Network	Rating	Share
13. Texas	NBC	3.6	12
14. Search for Tomorrow	NBC	3.4	13
15. The Doctors	NBC	3.3	13

1982–83

Serial	Network	Rating	Share
1. General Hospital	ABC	9.8	32
2. All My Children	ABC	9.4	32
3. One Life to Live	ABC	8.1	29
4. The Young and the Restless	CBS	8.0	30
5. As the World Turns	CBS	7.6	26
6. The Guiding Light	CBS	7.4	25
7. Capitol	CBS	6.0	22
8. Days of Our Lives	NBC	5.7	19
9. Ryan's Hope	ABC	5.6	21
10. Another World	NBC	4.8	17
11. The Edge of Night	ABC	3.8	12
12. Texas	NBC	2.7	12
13. Search for Tomorrow	NBC	2.7	10
14. The Doctors	NBC	1.6	7

1983–84

Serial	Network	Rating	Share
1. General Hospital	ABC	10.0	32
2. All My Children	ABC	9.1	28
3. The Young and the Restless	CBS	8.8	31
4. One Life to Live	ABC	8.2	27
5. The Guiding Light	CBS	8.1	24
6. As the World Turns	CBS	7.9	26
7. Days of Our Lives	NBC	7.1	22
8. Capitol	CBS	6.4	22
9. Another World	NBC	5.6	19
10. Ryan's Hope	ABC	5.0	17
11. Loving	ABC	3.9	15
12. The Edge of Night	ABC	3.5	10
13. Search for Tomorrow	NBC	3.2	12

1984–85

Serial	Network	Rating	Share
1. General Hospital	ABC	9.1	28
2. All My Children	ABC	8.2	26

Serial	Network	Rating	Share
3. The Young and the Restless	CBS	8.1	29
4. Guiding Light	CBS	7.5	24
5. One Life to Live	ABC	7.3	25
6. (Tie) As the World Turns	CBS	7.1	23
6. Days of Our Lives	NBC	7.1	23
8. Capitol	CBS	5.8	20
9. Another World	NBC	5.5	19
10. Loving	ABC	4.1	15
11. Ryan's Hope	ABC	3.4	12
12. Santa Barbara	NBC	3.4	11
13. Search for Tomorrow	NBC	3.3	12
14. The Edge of Night	ABC	2.6	8

1985–86

Serial	Network	Rating	Share
1. General Hospital	ABC	9.2	29
2. The Young and the Restless	CBS	8.3	29
3. All My Children	ABC	8.0	26
4. One Life to Live	ABC	7.8	26
5. Days of Our Lives	NBC	7.2	23
6. Guiding Light	CBS	6.8	21
7. As the World Turns	CBS	6.7	22
8. Capitol	CBS	5.1	18
9. Another World	NBC	5.1	17
10. Loving	ABC	4.2	15
11. Santa Barbara	NBC	4.2	13
12. Ryan's Hope	ABC	3.2	11
13. Search for Tomorrow	NBC	2.9	10

1986–87

Serial	Network	Rating	Share
1. General Hospital	ABC	8.3	27
2. The Young and the Restless	CBS	8.0	29
3. One Life to Live	ABC	7.2	25
4. (Tie) As the World Turns	CBS	7.0	23
4. Days of Our Lives	NBC	7.0	23
4. All My Children	ABC	7.0	23
7. Guiding Light	CBS	6.3	21
8. The Bold and the Beautiful	CBS	5.6	19
9. Capitol	CBS	5.2	18
10. Another World	NBC	5.1	17
11. Santa Barbara	NBC	4.3	14
12. Loving	ABC	3.9	14
13. Ryan's Hope	ABC	2.7	10
14. Search for Tomorrow	NBC	2.5	9

APPENDIX 3—Famous Graduates of Daytime Drama

Before making names in other media, many of today's stars acted on daytime TV soap operas. Listed below are the soaps' most famous alumni.

Alan Alda	Gilbert Parker, *The House on High Street*
Ana Alicia	Alicia Nieves, *Ryan's Hope*
Susan Anspach	Angela Carter, *The Doctors*
Armand Assante	Johnny McGhee, *How to Survive a Marriage*; Mike Powers, *The Doctors*
Kevin Bacon	Tod Adamson, *Search for Tomorrow*; Tim Werner, *Guiding Light*
Martin Balsam	*Love of Life*
Warren Beatty	*Love of Life*
Bonnie Bedelia	Sandy Porter, *Love of Life*
Robby Benson	Bruce Carson, *Search for Tomorrow*
Tom Berenger	Tim Siegel, *One Life to Live*
Ellen Burstyn	Dr. Kate Bartok, *The Doctors*
Dyan Cannon	Lisa Crowder, *Full Circle*
Kate Capshaw	Jinx Avery, *The Edge of Night*
Nell Carter	Ethel Green, *Ryan's Hope*
Jill Clayburgh	Grace Bolton, *Search for Tomorrow*
James Coco	*Search for Tomorrow*
Gary Coleman	hit & run victim, *The Edge of Night*
Ted Danson	Tom Conway, Dr. Jerry Kane, *Somerset*
Brad Davis	Alexander Kronos, *How to Survive A Marriage*
Ruby Dee	Martha Frazier, *Guiding Light*
Sandy Dennis	Alice Holden, *Guiding Light*
Robert De Niro	*Search for Tomorrow*
Patty Duke	Ellen Dennis, *The Brighter Day*
Charles Durning	Gil McGowan, *Another World*
Peter Falk	*Love of Life*
Morgan Fairchild	Jennifer Pace, *Search for Tomorrow*
Mike Farrell	Scott Banning, *Days of Our Lives*
Genie Francis	Laura Spencer, *General Hospital*
Anthony Geary	Luke Spencer, *General Hospital*
Paul Michael Glaser	Dr. Joe Corelli, *Love of Life*
Scott Glenn	Calvin Brenner, *The Edge of Night*
Lee Grant	Rose Peabody, *Search for Tomorrow*
Joan Hackett	Gail Prentiss, *Young Dr. Malone*
Larry Hagman	Ed Gibson, *The Edge of Night*
Mark Hamill	Kent Murray, *General Hospital*
Kathryn Harrold	Nola Dancy, *The Doctors*
David Hasselhoff	Dr. Snapper Foster, *The Young and the Restless*
Richard Hatch	Phillip Brent, *All My Children*
Joel Higgins	Bruce Carson, *Search for Tomorrow*
Dustin Hoffman	*Search for Tomorrow*
Hal Holbrook	Grayling Dennis, *The Brighter Day*
Alexandra Isles	Victoria Winters, *Dark Shadows*
Anne Jackson	*Love of Life*

Kate Jackson	Daphne Harridge, *Dark Shadows*
James Earl Jones	Dr. Jerry Turner, *As the World Turns*; Dr. Jim Frazier, *Guiding Light*
Tommy Lee Jones	Mark Toland, *One Life to Live*
Raul Julia	Miguel Garcia, *Love of Life*
Ken Kercheval	Larry Kirby, *How to Survive a Marriage*; Archie Borman, *The Secret Storm*
Kevin Kline	Woody Reed, *Search for Tomorrow*
Don Knotts	Wilbur Peabody, *Search for Tomorrow*
Diane Ladd	Kitty Styles, *The Secret Storm*
Audrey Landers	Heather Kane, *Somerset*; Joanna Morrison, *The Secret Storm*
Louise Lasser	Jackie, *The Doctors*
Jack Lemmon	*The Brighter Day, The Road of Life*
Judith Light	Karen Wolek, *One Life to Live*
Hal Linden	Larry Carter, *Search for Tomorrow*
Audra Lindley	Liz Matthews, *Another World*
Tony LoBianco	Dr. Joe Corelli, *Love of Life*
Andrea McArdle	Wendy Wilkins, *Search for Tomorrow*
Rue McClanahan	Caroline Johnson, *Another World*
Nancy Marchand	Therese Lamonte, *Another World*; Vinnie Phillips, *Love of Life*
Marsha Mason	Judith Cole, *Love of Life*; Laura Blackburn, *Where the Heart Is*; the vampire girl, *Dark Shadows*
George Maharis	Bud Gardner, *Search for Tomorrow*
Bette Midler	*The Edge of Night*
Donna Mills	Rocket, *The Secret Storm*, Laura Elliott, *Love Is a Many Splendored Thing*
Kate Mulgrew	Mary Ryan, *Ryan's Hope*
Michael Nader	Kevin Thompson, *As the World Turns*
Patricia Neal	*The Secret Storm*
Barry Newman	John Barnes, *The Edge of Night*
Lois Nettleton	Patsy Hamilton, *The Brighter Day*
Michael Nouri	Steve Kaslo, *Search for Tomorrow*
Jameson Parker	Brad Vernon, *One Life to Live*; Dale Robinson, *Somerset*
Christopher Reeve	Ben Harper, *Love of Life*
Eric Roberts	Ted Bancroft, *Another World*
Gena Rowlands	Paula Graves, *The Way of the World*
Mark Rydell	Jeff Baker, *As the World Turns*
Eva Marie Saint	*The Edge of Night*
Gary Sandy	Randy Buchanan, *Somerset*; Stacey Reddin, *The Secret Storm*
Susan Sarandon	Patrice Kahlman, *A World Apart*; Sarah Fairbanks, *Search for Tomorrow*
Roy Scheider	Bob Hill, *The Secret Storm*; Jonas Falk, *Love of Life*; Dr. Wheeler, *Search for Tomorrow*
David Selby	Quentin Collins, *Dark Shadows*

Tom Selleck	Jed Andrews, *The Young and the Restless*
Ted Shackelford	Ray Gordon, *Another World*
Martin Sheen	Roy Sanders, *The Edge of Night*
Richard Simmons	Richard Simmons, *General Hospital*
Rick Springfield	Dr. Noah Drake, *General Hospital*
Beatrice Straight	Vinnie Phillips, *Love of Life*
Dolph Sweet	Gil McGowan, *Another World*
Susan Sullivan	Lenore Curtin, *Another World*
Richard Thomas	Tom Hughes, *As the World Turns*; Chris Austen, *A Time for Us*
Ernest Thompson	Tony Cooper, *Somerset*
Daniel J. Travanti	Spence Andrews, *General Hospital*
John Travolta	*The Edge of Night*
Kathleen Turner	Nola Dancy, *The Doctors*
Cicely Tyson	Martha Frazier, *Guiding Light*
Joan Van Ark	Janene Whitney, *Days of Our Lives*
Trish Van Devere	Meredith Lord, *One Life to Live*; Patti Barron, *Search for Tomorrow*
Abe Vigoda	Ezra Braithwaite, *Dark Shadows*
Jessica Walter	Julie Murano, *Love of Life*
Sigourney Weaver	Avis Ryan, *Somerset*
Billy Dee Williams	Assistant D.A., *Another World*; Dr. Jim Frazier, *Guiding Light*
JoBeth Williams	Carrie Wheeler, *Somerset*; Brandy Shellooe, *Guiding Light*
Efrem Zimbalist, Jr.	Jim Gavin, *Concerning Miss Marlowe*

APPENDIX 4—Longest-Running Performers in TV Soap Opera

The following is a ranking of the top twenty longest-running serial performances.

1. Mary Stuart   Joanne Barron, *Search for Tomorrow* 1951–86
2. Larry Haines   Stu Bergman, *Search for Tomorrow* 1951–86
3. Charita Bauer   Bert Bauer, *The Guiding Light* 1952–84*
4. Helen Wagner   Nancy Hughes, *As the World Turns* 1956–
5. Don MacLaughlin   Chris Hughes, *As the World Turns* 1956–86
6. Eileen Fulton   Lisa Miller, *As the World Turns* 1960–
7. Don Hastings   Bob Hughes, *As the World Turns* 1960–
8. Patricia Bruder   Ellen Stewart, *As the World Turns* 1960–
9. Henderson Forsythe   David Stewart, *As the World Turns* 1960–
10. John Beradino   Steve Hardy, *General Hospital* 1963–
11. Emily McLaughlin   Jessie Brewer, *General Hospital* 1963–
12. Rachel Ames   Audrey Hardy, *General Hospital* 1964–
13. Ann Flood   Nancy Karr, *The Edge of Night* 1962–84
14. William Johnstone   Judge Lowell, *As the World Turns* 1956–78
15. Theo Goetz   Papa Bauer, *The Guiding Light* 1952–73**
16. Ron Tomme   Bruce Sterling, *Love of Life* 1959–80
17. Audrey Peters   Vanessa Sterling, *Love of Life* 1959–80
18. Macdonald Carey   Tom Horton, *Days of Our Lives* 1965–
19. Frances Reid   Alice Horton, *Days of Our Lives* 1965–
20. John Clarke   Mickey Horton, *Days of Our Lives* 1965–

* Charita Bauer played Bert Bauer on radio beginning in 1950.
** Theo Goetz played Papa Bauer on radio beginning in 1949.

APPENDIX 5—*Chronology of Television Serial Drama*

The following is a listing, by date of premiere, of all the network serials, plus a selection of foreign, cable, and syndicated TV soaps featured in this book.

Faraway Hill. DuMont 1946
These Are My Children. NBC 1949
A Woman to Remember. DuMont 1949
The O'Neills. DuMont 1949–50
One Man's Family. NBC 1949–55
Hawkins Falls. NBC 1950–55
The First Hundred Years. CBS 1950–52
Miss Susan. NBC 1951
Search for Tomorrow. CBS, NBC 1951–86
Love of Life. CBS 1951–80
The Egg and I. CBS 1951–52
Fairmeadows, USA. NBC 1951–52
The Guiding Light. CBS 1952–
The Bennetts. NBC 1953–54
Three Steps to Heaven. NBC 1953–54
Follow Your Heart. NBC 1953–54
Valiant Lady. CBS 1953–57
The Brighter Day. CBS 1954–62
Woman with a Past. CBS 1954
The Secret Storm. CBS 1954–74
The World of Mr. Sweeney. NBC 1954–55
Portia Faces Life. CBS 1954–55
The Seeking Heart. CBS 1954–55
First Love. NBC 1954–55
A Time to Live. NBC 1954
Concerning Miss Marlowe. NBC 1954–55
Golden Windows. NBC 1954–55
The Greatest Gift. NBC 1954–55
Modern Romances. NBC 1954–58
Road of Life. CBS 1954–55
Way of the World. NBC 1955
A Date with Life. NBC 1955–56
As the World Turns. CBS 1956–
The Edge of Night. CBS, ABC 1956–84
Hotel Cosmopolitan. CBS 1957–58
The Verdict Is Yours. CBS 1957–62
Kitty Foyle. NBC 1958
Today is Ours. NBC 1958
From These Roots. NBC 1958–61
Young Dr. Malone. NBC 1958–63
For Better or Worse. CBS 1959–60
The House on High Street. NBC 1959–60
Full Circle. CBS 1960–61

The Clear Horizon. CBS 1960–62
Road to Reality. ABC 1960–61
Our Five Daughters. NBC 1962
Ben Jerrod. NBC 1963
The Doctors. NBC 1963–82
General Hospital. ABC 1963–
Another World. NBC 1964–
Peyton Place. ABC 1964–69
The Young Marrieds. ABC 1964–66
A Time for Us. ABC 1964–66
Moment of Truth. NBC 1965
Our Private World. CBS 1965
Morning Star. NBC 1965–66
Paradise Bay. NBC 1965–66
Scarlett Hill. Syndicated 1965–66
Never Too Young. ABC 1965–66
The Nurses. ABC 1965–67
Days of Our Lives. NBC 1965–
Confidential for Women. ABC 1966
Dark Shadows. ABC 1966–71
Love Is a Many Splendored Thing. CBS 1967–73
One Life to Live. ABC 1968–
Hidden Faces. NBC 1968–69
Where the Heart Is. CBS 1969–73
The Survivors. ABC 1969–70
Bright Promise. NBC 1969–72
The Forsyte Saga. NET 1969–70
Strange Paradise. Syndicated 1969
All My Children. ABC 1970–
Best of Everything. ABC 1970
A World Apart. ABC 1970–71
Somerset. NBC 1970–76
Return to Peyton Place. NBC 1972–74
The Young and the Restless. CBS 1973–
Upstairs, Downstairs. PBS 1974–77
How to Survive a Marriage. NBC 1974–75
Ryan's Hope. ABC 1975–
Beacon Hill. CBS 1975
Executive Suite. CBS 1976–77
Mary Hartman, Mary Hartman. Syndicated 1976–78
Lovers and Friends. NBC 1977
Soap. ABC 1977–81
For Richer, For Poorer. NBC 1977–78
High Hopes. Syndicated 1978
Dallas. CBS 1978–
Knots Landing. CBS 1979–
Texas. NBC 1980–82
Secrets of Midland Heights. CBS 1980–81
Flamingo Road. NBC 1981–82

Dynasty. ABC 1981–
Another Life. CBN 1981–84
Behind the Screen. CBS 1981–82
Falcon Crest. CBS 1981–
Capitol. CBS 1982–87
King's Crossing. ABC 1982
Romance Theatre. Syndicated 1982–83
A New Day in Eden. Showtime 1982–83
The Catlins. TBS 1983–85
Loving. ABC 1983–
Emerald Point, N.A.S. CBS 1983–84
Santa Barbara. NBC 1984–
Rituals. Syndicated 1984–85
Paper Dolls. ABC 1984
Berrenger's. NBC 1985
The Colbys. ABC 1985–87
The Bold and the Beautiful. CBS 1987–

APPENDIX 6—Longest-Running Daytime Dramas

The following is a listing of the top-twenty daytime dramas, ranked by longevity.

1. *The Guiding Light.*   June 30, 1952–*
2. *Search for Tomorrow.*   September 3, 1951–December 26, 1986
3. *As the World Turns.*   April 2, 1956–
4. *The Edge of Night.*   April 2, 1956–December 28, 1984
5. *Love of Life.*   September 24, 1951–February 1, 1980
6. *General Hospital.*   April 1, 1963–
7. *Another World.*   May 4, 1964–
8. *Days of Our Lives.*   November 8, 1965–
9. *The Secret Storm.*   February 1, 1954–February 8, 1974
10. *The Doctors.*   April 1, 1963–December 31, 1982
11. *One Life to Live.*   July 15, 1968–
12. *All My Children.*   January 5, 1970–
13. *The Young and the*   March 26, 1973–
    Restless.
14. *Ryan's Hope.*   July 7, 1975–
15. *The Brighter Day.*   January 4, 1954–September 28, 1962
16. *Love Is a Many*   September 18, 1967–March 23, 1973
    Splendored Thing.
17. *Somerset.*   March 30, 1970–December 31, 1976
18. *Capitol.*   March 26, 1982–March 20, 1987
19. *Dark Shadows.*   June 27, 1966–April 2, 1971
20. *Young Dr. Malone.*   December 29, 1958–March 29, 1963

* *The Guiding Light* is also the longest-running drama in broadcasting history, having begun its radio run January 25, 1937.

APPENDIX 7—Current and Long-Running Serials: Broadcast History, Production Credits, Addresses

In the following appendix, air times are Eastern Standard Time (E.S.T.). Credits for producers and writers are listed in order of when individuals held position. Fan mail for shows and performers will be accepted at addresses below.

ALL MY CHILDREN

Broadcast History: Jan 1970–Jul 1975, ABC Mon–Fri 1:00–1:30
July 1975–Dec 1976, ABC Mon–Fri 12:30–1:00
Jan 1977–Apr 1977, ABC Mon–Fri 1:00–1:30
Apr 1977–   , ABC Mon–Fri 1:00–2:00
Creator: Agnes Nixon
Producers: Agnes Nixon, Bud Kloss, Jorn Winther, Jacqueline Babbin, Jorn Winther (again), Stephen D. Schenkel
Headwriters: Agnes Nixon, Wisner Washam
Directors: Del Hughes, Jack Wood, Henry Kaplan, Jack Coffey, Robert Myhrum, Bruce Minnix, Peter Andrews, Sherrell Hoffman, Jorn Winther, Robert Scinto, Larry Auerbach, Francesca James, Jean Dadario Burke, Conal O'Brien, Tony Morina, Barbara Martin Simmons, Shirley Simmons
Production Companies: Creative Horizons, ABC Productions
Address: All My Children
% ABC-TV
1330 Avenue of the Americas
New York, NY 10019

ANOTHER WORLD

Broadcast History: May 1964–Jan 1975, NBC Mon–Fri 3:00–3:30
Jan 1975–Mar 1979, NBC Mon–Fri 3:00–4:00
Mar 1979–Aug 1980, NBC Mon–Fri 2:30–4:00
Aug 1980–   , NBC Mon–Fri 2:00–3:00
Creator: Irna Phillips with William J. Bell
Executive Producers: Lyle B. Hill, Paul Rauch, Allen Potter, Stephen D. Schenkel, John P. Whitesell II
Producers: Allen Potter, Paul Roberts, Doris Quinlan, Mary Harris, Lyle B. Hill, Sid Sirulnick, Joe Rothenberger, Mary S. Bonner, Joseph D. Manetta, Gail Kobe, Joe Willmore, Robert Costello, Robert Calhoun, James A. Baffico, Kathlyn Chambers, Rina Bellamy, Karen Stevens, Linda Barker Laundra
Headwriters: Irna Phillips and William J. Bell; James Lipton; Agnes Nixon; Robert Cenedélla; Harding Lemay; Tom King and Robert Soderberg; L. Virginia Browne; Corinne Jacker; Robert Soderberg and Dorothy Ann Purser; Dorothy Ann Purser; Rich-

ard Culliton; Gary Tomlin with Samuel D. Ratcliffe and
Gillian Spencer; Sam Hall; Margaret DePriest
Directors: Leonard Valenta, Tom Donovan, David Pressman, Ira Cirker,
Melvin Bernhardt, Paul Lammers, Robert Calhoun, Barnet
Kellman, Jack Hofsiss, Andrew Weyman, Christopher Gout-
man, Ron Lagomarsino, William Ludel, Don Scardino, Michael
Eilbaum, A.C. Weary
Production Company: Benton and Bowles, Inc., for Procter & Gamble
Address: Another World
% NBC-TV
30 Rockefeller Plaza
New York, NY 10112

AS THE WORLD TURNS

Broadcast History: Apr 1956–Nov 1975, CBS Mon–Fri 1:30–2:00
Dec 1975–Feb 1980, CBS Mon–Fri 1:30–2:30
Feb 1980–Jun 1981, CBS Mon–Fri 2:00–3:00
Jun 1981–Mar 1987, CBS Mon–Fri 1:30–2:30
Mar 1987–   , CBS Mon–Fri 2:00–3:00
Creator: Irna Phillips
Executive Producers: Ted Corday, Joe Willmore, Joe Rothenberger, Fred
Bartholemew, Mary-Ellis Bunim, Robert Calhoun
Producers: Charles Fisher, Allen Potter, Lyle B. Hill, Mary Harris, Rob-
ert Driscoll, Arthur Richards, Susan Bedsow Horgan, Robert
Rigamonti, Michael Laibson, Brenda Greenberg, Bonnie Bo-
gard, Christine Banas, Ken Fitts, Lisa Wilson
Headwriters: Irna Phillips with Agnes Nixon; Irna Phillips with William
J. Bell; Irna Phillips; Joe Kane and Winifred Wolfe; Katherine
L. Phillips; Warren Swanson, Elizabeth Tillman, and John
Boruff; Irna Phillips with David Lesan; Robert Soderberg
and Edith Sommer; Ralph Ellis and Eugenie Hunt; Douglas
Marland; Bridget and Jerome Dobson; Paul Roberts; K.C.
Collier and Tom King; Bridget and Jerome Dobson (again);
Caroline Franz and John Saffron; John Saffron; Tom King
and Millee Taggart; Cynthia Benjamin and Susan Bedsow
Horgan; Douglas Marland (again)
Directors: Ted Corday, Bill Howell, Walter Gorman, James MacAllen,
Cort Steen, Leonard Valenta, Paul Lammers, Robert Myhrum,
Allen Fristoe, Heather H. Hill, Bruce Barry, Richard Dunlap,
Robert Schwarz, Peter Brickerhoff, Maria Wagner, Bruce Min-
nix, Richard Pepperman, Joel Arnowitz, Michael Kerner, Jill
Mitwell
Production Company: Compton Advertising for Procter & Gamble
Address: As the World Turns
% CBS-TV
51 West 52nd Street
New York, NY 10019

THE BOLD AND THE BEAUTIFUL

Broadcast History: Mar 1987–   , CBS Mon–Fri 1:30–2:00
Creators: William J. Bell and Lee Phillip
Executive Producer: William J. Bell
Producer: Gail Kobe
Headwriter: William J. Bell
Directors: Michael Stich, Bill Glenn
Production Company: Bell-Phillip Productions
Address: The Bold and the Beautiful
          % CBS-TV
          7800 Beverly Blvd
          Hollywood, CA 90036

DALLAS

Broadcast History: Apr 1978, CBS Sun 10:00–11:00
                     Sep 1978–Oct 1978, CBS Sat 10:00–11:00
                     Oct 1978–Jan 1979, CBS Sun 10:00–11:00
                     Jan 1979–Dec 1981, CBS Fri 10:00–11:00
                     Dec 1981–   , CBS Fri 9:00–10:00
Creator: David Jacobs
Executive Producers: Lee Rich, Philip Capice, Leonard Katzman
Producer: Leonard Katzman, Arthur Bernard Lewis, David Paulsen
Writers: David Jacobs, Camille Marchetta, Arthur Bernard Lewis, David
          Paulsen, Leah Markus, Michael Wayne Katzman
Directors: Irving J. Moore, Robert Day, Alexander Singer, Leonard Katz-
          man, Michael Preece, Larry Hagman, Patrick Duffy, Linda
          Gray
Production Company: Lorimar
Address: Dallas
          % Lorimar
          3970 Overland Avenue
          Culver City, CA 90230

DAYS OF OUR LIVES

Broadcast History: Nov 1965–Apr 1975, NBC Mon–Fri 2:00–2:30
                     Apr 1975–Mar 1979, NBC Mon–Fri 1:30–2:30
                     Mar 1979–   , NBC Mon–Fri 1:00–2:00
Creators: Irna Phillips, Allan Chase, and Ted Corday
Executive Producers: Ted Corday, Betty Corday, H. Wesley Kenney, Jack
                       Herzberg, Al Rabin
Producers: Ken Corday, Gene Banks, Lynne Osborne, Patricia Wenig,
          Shelley Curtis
Headwriters: Peggy Phillips and Kenneth M. Rosen; William J. Bell; Pat
          Falken Smith; Ann Marcus; Elizabeth Harrower; Ruth Brooks
          Flippen; Nina Laemmle; Gary Tomlin and Michele Poteet-

> Lisanti; Pat Falken Smith (again); Margaret DePriest; Sheri Anderson; Thom Racina; Leah Laiman

Directors: Joseph Behar, Ira Cirker, Herbert Kenwith, Livia Granito, H. Wesley Kenney, Frank Pacelli, Alan Pultz, Al Rabin, Ken Herman, Jr., Edward Mallory, Richard Dunlap, Herb Stein, Arlene Sanford, Susan Orlikoff Simon, Gay Linvill, Becky Greenlaw, Stephen Wyman, Sheryl Harmon

Production Company: Corday Productions for Screen Gems and Columbia Pictures Television

Address: Days of Our Lives
% NBC-TV
3000 West Alameda Avenue
Burbank, CA 91523

THE DOCTORS

Broadcast History: Apr 1963–Mar 1979, NBC Mon–Fri 2:30–3:00
Mar 1979–Aug 1980, NBC Mon–Fri 2:00–2:30
Aug 1980–Mar 1982, NBC Mon–Fri 12:30–1:00
Mar 1982–Dec 1982, NBC Mon–Fri 12:00–12:30

Creator: Orvin Tovrov

Executive Producers: James A. Baffico, Robert Costello, Gerald T. Straub

Producers: Jerry Layton, Bertram Berman, Allen Potter, Joseph Stuart, Jeff Young, Doris Quinlan, Joe Rothenberger, George Barimo

Headwriters: Orvin Tovrov, Ian Martin, James Lipton, Lillian Andrews, John Kubec, Rita Lakin, Rick Edelstein, Ira Avery, Eileen and Robert Mason Pollock, Robert Cenedella, Margaret DePriest, Linda Grover, Elizabeth Levin with David Cherrill, Ralph Ellis and Eugenie Hunt, Lawrence and Ronnie Wencker-Konner, Harding Lemay, Barbara Morgenroth and Leonard Kantor

Directors: H. Wesley Kenney, Paul Lammers, Hugh McPhillips, Norman Hall, Robert Myhrum, Herbert Kenwith, Jeff Young, Gordon Rigsby, Dino Narizzano, Stephen Wyman, Robert Scinto, Henry Kaplan

Production Companies: Colgate-Palmolive; NBC-TV

DYNASTY

Broadcast History: Jan 1981–Apr 1981, ABC Mon 9:00–10:00
Jul 1981–Sep 1983, ABC Wed 10:00–11:00
Sep 1983–   , ABC Wed 9:00–10:00

Creators: Richard and Esther Shapiro

Executive Producers: Richard and Esther Shapiro, Douglas Cramer, and Aaron Spelling

Producers: E. Duke Vincent and Philip Parslow; Elaine Rich and E. Duke Vincent; Camille Marchetta and Edward DeBlasio; Diana Gould and Edward DeBlasio; Lawrence Heath and Edward DeBlasio; Rita Lakin and Edward DeBlasio

Headwriters: Richard and Esther Shapiro; Eileen and Robert Mason Pollock; Camille Marchetta and Edward DeBlasio; Diana Gould and Edward DeBlasio; Diana Gould and Scott M. Hamner; Lawrence Heath and Rita Lakin
Directors: Gabrielle Beaumont, Philip Leacock, Don Medford, Ralph Senensky, Irving J. Moore, Jerome Courtland, Curtis Harrington, Nancy Malone
Production Company: Richard & Esther Shapiro Productions and Aaron Spelling Productions
Address: Dynasty
          % Aaron Spelling Productions
          1041 North Formosa Avenue
          Los Angeles, CA 90046

EDGE OF NIGHT

Broadcast History: Apr 1956–Jun 1963, CBS Mon–Fri 4:30–5:00
                     Jul 1963–Sep 1972, CBS Mon–Fri 3:30–4:00
                     Sep 1972–Nov 1975, CBS Mon–Fri 2:30–3:00
                     Dec 1975–Dec 1984, ABC Mon–Fri 4:00–4:30
Creator: Irving Vendig
Executive Producers: Lawrence White, Don Wallace, Erwin Nicholson
Producers: Werner Michel, Charles Pollacheck, Charles Fisher, Erwin Nicholson, Rick Edelstein, Robert Driscoll, Jacqueline Haber
Headwriters: Irving Vendig, Lou Scofield, James Lipton, Henry Slesar, Lee Sheldon
Directors: Don Wallace, Fred Bartholemew, Allen Fristoe, Leonard Valenta, John Sedwick, Andrew D. Weyman, Richard Pepperman, Joanne Goodhart
Production Company: Benton and Bowles, Inc., for Procter & Gamble

FALCON CREST

Broadcast History: Dec 1981–   , CBS Fri 10:00–11:00
Creator: Earl Hamner
Executive Producers: Earl Hamner and Michael Filerman; Joanne Brough, Jeff Freilich, Michael Filerman
Producers: Robert L. McCullough, Barry Steinberg, John F. Perry, Ann Marcus, Rod Peterson, E. F. Wallengren
Writers: Earl Hamner, Robert L. McCullough, E.F. Wallengren, Ann and Ellis Marcus, Claire Whitaker, William R. Schmidt, Howard Lakin
Directors: Jeffrey Hayden, Joseph Manduke, Harry Harris, Fernando Lamas, Larry Elikann, Roy Campanella, Jr.
Production Company: Lorimar
Address: Falcon Crest
          % Lorimar
          3970 Overland Avenue
          Culver City, CA 90230

GENERAL HOSPITAL

Broadcast History: Apr 1963–Dec 1963, ABC Mon–Fri 1:00–1:30
      Dec 1963–Dec 1964, ABC Mon–Fri 3:00–3:30
      Dec 1964–Apr 1965, ABC Mon–Fri 2:00–2:30
      Apr 1965–Jul 1976, ABC Mon–Fri 3:00–3:30
      Jul 1976–Jan 1978, ABC Mon–Fri 3:15–4:00
      Jan 1978–   , ABC Mon–Fri 3:00–4:00
Creators: Frank and Doris Hursley
Executive Producers: Selig Seligman, Gloria Monty, H. Wesley Kenney
Producers: Gene Banks, James Young, Tom Donovan, Gloria Monty, Jerry
  Balme, Joe Willmore
Headwriters: Theodore and Mathilde Ferro; Frank and Doris Hursley;
  Bridget and Jerome Dobson; Richard and Suzanne Holland;
  Eileen and Robert Mason Pollock; Irving and Tex Elman;
  Richard and Suzanne Holland; Douglas Marland; Pat Falken
  Smith; Robert J. Shaw; Joyce and John William Corrington;
  Anne Howard Bailey; Pat Falken Smith with Norma Monty;
  Ann Marcus with Norma Monty
Directors: James Young, Ken Herman Jr., Lamar Caselli, Ross Bowman,
  Peter Levin, Alan Pultz, Phil Sogard, Marlena Laird, Hal Alex-
  ander, Heather H. Hill
Production Company: ABC Entertainment
Address: General Hospital
  % ABC-TV
  4151 Prospect Avenue
  Los Angeles, CA 90027

THE GUIDING LIGHT

Broadcast History: Jun 1952–Dec 1952, CBS Mon–Fri 2:30–2:45
      Dec 1952–Sep 1968, CBS Mon–Fri 12:45–1:00
      Sep 1968–Sep 1972, CBS Mon–Fri 2:30–3:00
      Sep 1972–Nov 1975, CBS Mon–Fri 2:00–2:30
      Dec 1975–Nov 1977, CBS Mon–Fri 2:30–3:00
      Nov 1977–Feb 1980, CBS Mon–Fri 2:30–3:30
      Feb 1980–   , CBS Mon–Fri 3:00–4:00
Creator: Irna Phillips
Executive Producers: Lucy Ferri Rittenberg, Allen Potter, Gail Kobe, Joe
  Willmore
Producers: David Lesan, Richard Dunn, Peter Andrews, Harry Eggart,
  Charlotte Savitz, Leslie Kwartin, Joe Willmore, Robert Cal-
  houn, John P. Whitesell II, Robert D. Kochman, Kathlyn
  Chambers
Headwriters: Irna Phillips; Agnes Nixon; David Lesan and Julian Funt;
  Theodore and Mathilde Ferro; John Boruff; James Lipton;
  Gabrielle Upton; Jane and Ira Avery; Robert Soderberg and
  Edith Sommer; James Gentile; Robert Cenedella; Bridget and
  Jerome Dobson; Douglas Marland; Pat Falken Smith; L. Vir-

ginia Browne; Richard Culliton; Pamela K. Long; Jeff Ryder;
Mary Ryan Munisteri; Joseph D. Manetta; Sheri Anderson;
Pamela K. Long (again)

Directors: Ted Corday, Walter Gorman, Jack Wood, Leonard Valenta,
Nick Havinga, John Ritvack, Jeff Bleckner, Peter Miner, John
Sedwick, Allen Fristoe, Harry Eggart, Lynwood King, John
Pasquin, Michael Gliona, Bruce Barry, Jill Mitwell, John P.
Whitesell II, Irene M. Pace, Dan Smith, Matthew Diamond,
Scott McKinsey, M. J. McDonnell, Jo Ann Rivituso, Jo Anne
Sedwick

Production Company: Compton Advertising for Procter & Gamble

Address: Guiding Light
% CBS-TV
51 West 52nd Street
New York, NY 10019

KNOTS LANDING

Broadcast History: Dec 1979–   , CBS Thurs 10:00–11:00

Creator: David Jacobs

Executive Producers: Lee Rich and Michael Filerman; David Jacobs and
Michael Filerman

Producers: Joseph B. Wallenstein; Peter Dunne; Lawrence Kasha

Writers: David Jacobs, Joseph B. Wallenstein, John Pleshette, Ellis Marcus, Diana Gould, Mann Rubin, Richard Gollance; Lynn Latham

Directors: Peter Levin, James Sheldon, Roger Young, Jeff Bleckner, Alexander Singer, Bill Duke, Larry Elikann, Joseph L. Scanlan

Production Company: Lorimar

Address: Knots Landing
% Lorimar
3970 Overland Avenue
Culver City, CA 90230

LOVE OF LIFE

Broadcast History: Sep 1951–Apr 1958, CBS Mon–Fri 12:15–12:30
Apr 1958–Oct 1962, CBS Mon–Fri 12:00–12:30
Oct 1962–Sep 1969, CBS Mon–Fri 12:00–12:25
Sep 1969–Mar 1973, CBS Mon–Fri 11:30–12:00
Mar 1973–Apr 1979, CBS Mon–Fri 11:30–11:55
Apr 1979–Feb 1980, CBS Mon–Fri 4:00–4:30

Creator: Roy Winsor

Executive Producers: Roy Winsor, Bertram Berman, Darryl Hickman

Producers: Charles Schenck, Richard Dunn, Ernest Ricca, Al Morrison,
John Green, Robert Driscoll, Joseph Hardy, Tony Converse,
Freyda Rothstein, Tom Donovan, Jean Arley, Cathy Abbi

Headwriters: John Hess; Harry Junkin; Don Ettlinger; John Pickard and
Frank Provo; Lillian and Martin Andrews; Loring Mandel;
Robert Soderberg; Robert J. Shaw; Roy Winsor; Eileen and

Robert Mason Pollock; Ray Goldstone; Paul Roberts and Don Wallace; Esther and Richard Shapiro; Claire Labine and Paul Avila Mayer; Margaret DePriest; Paul and Margaret Schneider; Gabrielle Upton; Jean Holloway; Ann Marcus

Directors: Larry Auerbach (the entire run), Burt Brinckerhoff, Art Wolff, Jerry Evans, Gordon Rigsby, Robert Myhrum, Dino Narizzano, Heather H. Hill, Lynwood King, Robert Nigro, Robert Scinto, John Pasquin

Production Companies: Biow Company; Roy Winsor Productions; CBS-TV

LOVING

Broadcast History: Jun 1983–Oct 1984, ABC Mon–Fri 11:30–12:00
Oct 1984–   , ABC Mon–Fri 12:30–1:00
Creators: Agnes Nixon and Douglas Marland
Producer: Joseph Stuart
Directors: Andrew Weyman, Robert Scinto, Peter Brinckerhoff, Joseph Stuart
Headwriters: Douglas Marland; Agnes Nixon; Ralph Ellis
Production Company: Dramatic Creations, Inc.
Address: Loving
% ABC-TV
1330 Avenue of the Americas
New York, NY 10019

ONE LIFE TO LIVE

Broadcast History: Jul 1968–Jul 1976, ABC Mon–Fri 3:30–4:00
Jul 1976–Jan 1978, ABC Mon–Fri 2:30–3:15
Jan 1978–   , ABC Mon–Fri 2:00–3:00
Creator: Agnes Nixon
Producers: Doris Quinlan, Joseph Stuart, Jean Arley, Paul Rauch
Headwriters: Agnes Nixon, Paul Roberts, Don Wallace; Gordon Russell; Sam Hall and Peggy O'Shea; Sam Hall and Henry Slesar; Joyce and John William Corrington; Sam Hall and Peggy O'Shea (again); Peggy O'Shea; S. Michael Schnessel
Directors: Don Wallace, Jack Wood, Walter Gorman, Del Hughes, David Pressman, Peter Miner, Gordon Rigsby, Al Freeman, Jr., Norman Hall, George Keathley, Lynwood King, Joseph Stuart, Allen Fristoe, Larry Auerbach, John Sedwick, Ron Lagomarsino, Melvin Bernhardt, Barnet Kellman; Susan Pomerantz, Stuart Silverman
Production Company: ABC-TV
Address: One Life to Live
% ABC-TV
1330 Avenue of the Americas
New York, NY 10019

RYAN'S HOPE

Broadcast History: Jul 1975–Dec 1976, ABC Mon–Fri 1:00–1:30
                    Jan 1977–Oct 1984, ABC Mon–Fri 12:30–1:00
                    Oct 1984–   , ABC Mon–Fri 12:00–12:30
Creators: Claire Labine and Paul Avila Mayer
Executive Producers: Claire Labine and Paul Avila Mayer, Joseph Hardy
Producers: George Lefferts, Robert Costello, Ellen Barrett, Felicia Minei
            Behr
Headwriters: Claire Labine and Paul Avila Mayer; Mary Ryan Munisteri;
              Labine and Mayer; Pat Falken Smith; Tom King, Millee
              Taggart, and Dorothy Ann Purser; Claire Labine and Eleanor
              Mancusi
Directors: Lela Swift, Jerry Evans, Robert Myhrum, Bruce Minnix, Lyn-
            wood King, Stephen Wyman, Tom Donovan, John Desmond
Production Company: Labine-Mayer Productions; ABC Productions
Address: Ryan's Hope
          % ABC-TV
          1330 Avenue of the Americas
          New York, NY 10019

SANTA BARBARA

Broadcast History: Jul 1984–   , NBC Mon–Fri 3:00–4:00
Creators: Jerome and Bridget Dobson
Executive Producers: Jerome and Bridget Dobson and Jeffrey Hayden; Charles
                      Pratt, Sr.; Mary-Ellis Bunim; Jerome and Bridget Dob-
                      son
Producers: Steven Kent, Jill Farren Phelps, Leonard Friedlander
Headwriters: Jerome and Bridget Dobson; Anne Howard Bailey
Directors: Gordon Rigsby, Norman Hall, Rick Bennewitz, John Sedwick,
            Gary Bowen, Andrew Weyman, Dennis Steinmetz
Production Company: Dobson Productions
Address: Santa Barbara
          % NBC-TV
          3000 West Alameda Avenue
          Burbank, CA 91523

SEARCH FOR TOMORROW

Broadcast History: Sep 1951–Sep 1968, CBS Mon–Fri 12:30–12:45
                    Sept 1968–Jun 1981, CBS Mon–Fri 12:30–1:00
                    Jun 1981–Mar 1982, CBS Mon–Fri 2:30–3:00
                    Mar 1982–Dec 1986, NBC Mon–Fri 12:30–1:00
Creators: Roy Winsor with Agnes Nixon
Executive Producers: Roy Winsor, Woody Klose, Mary-Ellis Bunim, Fred
                      Bartholemew, Joanna Lee, Ellen Barrett, Erwin Ni-
                      cholson; John P. Whitesell II, David Lawrence
Producers: Charles Irving, Myron Golden, Everett Gammon, Frank Dodge,

               Robert Driscoll, John Edwards, Bernie Solfronski, Mary-Ellis Bunim, Robert Getz, Gail Starkey, Jean Arley; John Valente

Headwriters: Agnes Nixon; Irving Vendig; Charles Gussman; Frank and Doris Hursley; Julian Funt and David Lesan; Leonard Kantor and Doris Frankel; Lou Scofield; Robert Soderberg and Edith Sommer; Ralph Ellis and Eugenie Hunt; Theodore Apstein; Gabrielle Upton; Ann Marcus; Peggy O'Shea; Irving and Tex Elman; Robert J. Shaw; Henry Slesar; Joyce and John William Corrington; Linda Grover; Harding Lemay; Don Chastain; Ralph Ellis and Eugenie Hunt (again); C. David Colson; Gary Tomlin; Jeanne Glynn and Madeline David; Caroline Franz and Jeanne Glynn; Paul Avila Mayer and Stephanie Braxton; Gary Tomlin (again); Pamela K. Long and Addie Walsh

Directors: Charles Irving, Hal Cooper, Ira Cirker, Dan Levin, John Frankenheimer, Bruce Minnix, Ned Stark, Joseph Stuart, Robert Schwarz, Richard T. McCue, Don Wallace, Paul Lammers, Robert Nigro, Henry Kaplan, Andrew D. Weyman, Richard Dunlap, Robert Rigamonti, Charles Dyer, Jim Kramer, Harry Eggart, Gregory Lehane, Ned Stark

Production Company: Compton Advertising for Procter & Gamble

THE SECRET STORM

Broadcast History: Feb 1954–Jun 1962, CBS Mon–Fri 4:15–4:30
                 Jun 1962–Sep 1968, CBS Mon–Fri 4:00–4:30
                 Sep 1968–Sep 1972, CBS Mon–Fri 3:00–3:30
                 Sep 1972–Mar 1973, CBS Mon–Fri 3:30–4:00
                 Mar 1973–Feb 1974, CBS Mon–Fri 4:00–4:30

Creator: Roy Winsor

Executive Producers: Roy Winsor, Charles Weiss

Producers: Richard Dunn, Ernest Ricca, Tony Converse, Robert Driscoll, Robert Costello, Joseph D. Manetta

Headwriters: William Kendall Clarke; Henry Selinger and Harrison Bingham; Stanley H. Silverman; Lou Scofield; Will Lorin; Max Wylie; Orvin Tovrov; Carl Bixby; Jane and Ira Avery; John Hess and Don Ettlinger; Don Ettlinger; Gabrielle Upton; Gerry Day and Bethel Leslie; Robert Cenedella; Frances Rickett with Sheldon Stark; Gabrielle Upton (again)

Directors: Gloria Monty, Portman Paget, David Roth, Robert Myhrum, Joe Scanlan

Production Companies: Roy Winsor Productions; CBS-TV

THE YOUNG AND THE RESTLESS

Broadcast History: Mar 1973–Feb 1980, CBS Mon–Fri 12:00–12:30
                     Feb 1980–Jun 1981, CBS Mon–Fri 1:00–2:00
                     Jun 1981–   , CBS Mon–Fri 12:30–1:30
Creators: William J. Bell and Lee Phillip
Executive Producers: John Conboy; H. Wesley Kenney and William J. Bell;
         William J. Bell
Producers: Patricia Wenig, Edward Scott, Tom Langan
Headwriter: William J. Bell
Directors: Richard Dunlap, Bill Glenn, Herbert Kenwith, Frank Pacelli,
         Rudy Vejar, Dennis Steinmetz; Betty Rothenberg, Randy Robbins, Edward Mallory, John Zak, Heather H. Hill
Production Company: Columbia Pictures Television
Address: The Young and the Restless
         % CBS-TV
         7800 Beverly Blvd
         Los Angeles, CA 90036

BIBLIOGRAPHY

Allen, Robert C. *Speaking of Soap Operas*. Chapel Hill, NC: University of North Carolina Press, 1985.

Angel, Velma. *Those Sensational Soaps: How Soap Operas Affect You Emotionally, Physically, Spiritually*. Brea, CA: Uplift Books, 1983.

Bennett, Joan and Lois Kibbee. *The Bennett Playbill*. New York: Holt, Rinehart & Winston, 1970.

Blumenthal, John. *Anthony Geary*. New York: Wallaby, 1982.

Bonderoff, Jason. *Daytime TV 1977*. New York: Manor, 1976.

——— *Soap Opera Babylon*. New York: Putnam, 1987.

Brooks, Tim and Earle Marsh. *The Complete Directory to Prime Time Network Television Shows 1946 to Present*. New York: Ballantine, 1979. Revised and Enlarged 1981, 1985.

Brown, Les. *Les Brown's Encyclopedia of Television*. New York: New York Zoetrope, 1982. (Revised version of *The New York Times Encyclopedia of Television*. New York: Times Books, 1977.)

Buckman, Peter. *All For Love: A Study in Soap Opera*. Salem, N.H.: Salem House, 1985.

Cantor, Muriel and Suzanne Pingree. *The Soap Opera*. Beverly Hills, CA: Sage, 1983.

Cassata, Mary and Thomas Skill. *Life on Daytime Television: Tuning-In American Serial Drama*. Norwood, NJ: Ablex, 1983.

Collins, Joan. *Past Imperfect*. New York: Simon and Schuster, 1984.

Cooke, Alistair. *A Decade of Masterpiece Theatre Masterpieces*. New York: Knopf, 1981.

Crawford, Christina. *Mommie Dearest*. New York: Morrow, 1978.

Denis, Paul and the staff of Daytime TV Magazine. *Daytime TV's Star Directory*. New York: Sterling, 1976.

Denis, Paul. *Inside the Soaps*. Secaucus, NJ: Citadel Press, 1985.

Dyer, Richard et al. *Coronation Street*. London: BFI, 1981.

Edmondson, Madeleine and David Rounds. *From Mary Noble to Mary Hartman: The Complete Soap Opera Book*. Briarcliff Manor, NY: Stein & Day, 1976. (Revised edition of *The Soaps: Daytime Serials of Radio and TV*. Briarcliff Manor, NY: Stein & Day, 1973.)

Fulton, Eileen with Brett Bolton. *How My World Turns*. New York: Warner Books, 1970.

Genovese, John Kelly with the editors of Soap Opera Digest. *Soap Opera Digest Scrapbook*. Chicago: Contemporary Books, 1984.

Gilbert, Annie. *All My Afternoons*. New York: A & W, 1979.

Groves, Seli and the Associated Press. *Soaps: A Pictorial History of America's Daytime Dramas*. Chicago: Contemporary Books, 1983.

Hardwick, Mollie. *The World of Upstairs, Downstairs*. New York: Holt, Rinehart & Winston, 1976.

Hawkesworth, John. *Upstairs, Downstairs*. New York: Dell, 1971.

Intintoli, Michael James. *Taking Soaps Seriously: The World of Guiding Light*. New York: Praeger, 1984.

Kalter, Suzy. *The Complete Book of Dallas*. New York: Abrams, 1986.

Kutler, Jane and Patricia Kearney. *Super Soaps*. New York, Grosset and Dunlap, 1977.

Lackmann, Ron. *TV Soap Opera Almanac*. New York: Berkley, 1976.

LaGuardia, Robert. *From Ma Perkins to Mary Hartman*. New York: Ballantine, 1977.

————— *Soap World*. New York: Arbor House, 1983.

————— *The Wonderful World of TV Soap Operas*. New York: Ballantine, 1974. Revised, 1977.

Laub, Bryna. *The Official Soap Opera Annual*. New York: Ballantine, 1977.

Lemay, Harding. *Eight Years in Another World*. New York: Atheneum, 1981.

McNeil, Alex. *Total Television: A Comprehensive Guide to Programming from 1948 to 1980*. New York: Penguin, 1980. Revised, 1984.

Mann, Patrick. *Falcon Crest*. New York: Dell, 1984.

Meyer, Richard. *The Illustrated Soap Opera Companion.*New York: Drake, 1977.

Modleski, Tania. *Loving with a Vengeance: Mass Produced Fantasies for Women*. Hamden, CT: Shoe String Press, 1982.

Raintree, Lee. *Dallas*. New York: Dell, 1980.

Rogers, Lynne. *The Loves of their Lives*. New York: Dell, 1979.

Rouverol, Jean. *Writing for the Soaps*. Cincinnati, OH: Writer's Digest Books, 1984.

Schemering, Christopher. *Guiding Light: A 50th Anniversary Celebration*. New York: Ballantine, 1987.

Scott, Kathyrn Leigh. *My Scrapbook Memories of Dark Shadows*. Temple City, CA: Pomegrante Press, 1987.

Shapiro, Esther. *Dynasty: The Authorized Biography of the Carringtons*. Garden City, NY: Doubleday, 1984.

Soares, Manuella. *The Soap Opera Book*. New York: Latham, 1978.

Stedman, Raymond William. *The Serials: Suspense and Drama by the Installment*. Norman, OK: University of Oklahoma Press,1971. Revised, 1977.

Stuart, Mary. *Both of Me*. New York: Doubleday, 1980.

Terrace, Vincent. *The Complete Encyclopedia of Television Programs 1947–1976*. Cranbury,NJ: A.S. Barnes, 1976.

————— *Television 1970–1980*. LaJolla, CA: A.S. Barnes, 1981.

Thomas, Mona Bruns. *By Emily Possessed*. Jericho, NY: Exposition Press, 1973.

Townley, Rod. *The Year in Soaps*. New York: Crown, 1984.

Van Wormer, Laura. *Dallas: The Complete Ewing Saga*. Garden City, NY: Doubleday, 1985.

Wakefield, Dan. *All Her Children*. Garden City, NY: Doubleday, 1976.

Walter, Norman and Rita Walter with Pam Proctor. *No Shadow of Turning*. Garden City, NY: Doubleday, 1980.

Warrick, Ruth. *The Confessions of Phoebe Tyler*. Englewood Cliffs, NJ: Prentice Hall, 1980.

Whitley, Dianna and Ray Manzella. *Soap Stars*. Garden City, NY: Doubleday, 1985.

INDEX